Over One Thousand Copies Sold!!!

"Jon Sasaki has written a necessary guide for anyone considering taking the customs broker exam. The business section answers many common questions new brokers face. All in all, a great resource for the new broker"

-Jennifer Henning, LCB, CCS
National Account Manager
SmartBorder

2017 Customs Broker Exam Study Guide & How to Start Your Own CHB Business®
Thru Oct. 2016 Exam Edition

Jon K Sasaki, LCB

ATTACHÉ BOOKS PUBLISHING

Published 2010, 2011, 2012, 2013, 2014, 2015, 2016, 2017 by CHB Solutions, A division of Attaché Books Publishing, Vancouver, Washington, U.S.A.

 CHB Solutions

Manufactured in the United States of America

10   9   8   7   6   5   4   3   2   1

Library of Congress Cataloging-in-Publication Data

Sasaki, Jon K.
    2017 Customs Broker Exam Study Guide & How to Start Your Own CHB Business:
       Thru Oct. 2016 Exam Edition / Jon K Sasaki, LCB.

Business & Economics, Exports & Imports

ISBN-13: 978-1542712026
ISBN-10: 1542712025

© 2017 Jon K Sasaki.
All rights reserved.

The internet web addresses in this book were confirmed to be valid and correct at the time of the book's publication but may be subject to change.

Disclaimer:

This book is designed to provide expert guidance regarding the subject matter covered. This information is given with the understanding that neither the author nor the publisher is engaged in rendering legal, accounting, or other professional advice. Since the details of your situation are fact dependent, you should also seek the advice of a competent professional.

Pass the Exam & Right us a Review! Get a Free $20 Starbucks Gift Card on Us!!!

To receive your $20 Starbucks Gift Card, just email the following 4 items to us!

1) Copy of proof of book* purchase from Amazon.com (e.g. copy of order confirmation from Amazon)

2) Copy of Amazon.com book* customer review (e.g. screen print of posted review)

3) Copy of letter from CBP confirming attainment of passing score on customs broker exam

4) Mailing address for us to send you your gift card!!!**

We want you to pass the Exam! Let us provide you with the Motivation and Tools to do so!

CHB Solutions Email addresses

jonsasaki3939@gmail.com

*Customs Broker Exam Study Guide & How to Start Your Own CBH Business (will accept proof of purchase for any edition).

**Please allow for 1-2 weeks for delivery of your gift card

Starbucks is a registered trademark of Starbucks U.S. Brands, LLC. Starbucks is not a participating partner or sponsor of this offer.

Contents at a Glance

Book 1
Customs Broker Exam Study Guide

Part		Pg.
1.	Book 1 Introduction	1
2.	Getting Started	3
3.	Nature of the Exam	4
	Exam ref. material frequency by source & year	6
	Exam ref. materials list	7
4.	How to Use this Book	8
5.	HTS Classification Tips	10
	Sub-part 1: The HTSUS	**10**
	4 major components of the HTSUS	11
	HTSUS exam frequency: by Chapters	15
	HTSUS exam frequency: by General Notes	16
	HTSUS contents at a glance	18
	Sub-part 2: The HTS Number	**25**
	HTSUS number structure breakdown	25
	Basic classification procedure	28
	Basic exam classification strategy	29
	Sub-part 3: General Rules of Interpretation	**30**
	"HUM SELMA" acronym	31
	Breakdown of each GRI	32
	GRI snapshot from the HTSUS	40
	Sub-part 4: GRI's explained in exam examples	**42**
6.	Free Trade Agreements	65
	Special programs quick reference and guide	66
	Countries and their eligibility table	67
	Beneficiary countries sorted by special program	68
	Rules to determine special program eligibility	69
7.	Most Commonly Tested 19 CFR Sections and Paragraphs	71
8.	All 19 CFR Sections Appearing on Exams	101
	List of 19 CFR parts that appear on exam	102
	All sections appearing on exams table	103
9.	Exam with Broker Commentary (Oct. 2016)	117
10.	Exam with Broker Commentary (Apr. 2016)	214
11.	Exam with Broker Commentary (Oct. 2015)	307

Contents at a Glance

Book 2
How to Start Your Own CHB Business

Part		Pg.
1.	Book 2 Introduction	410
2.	Necessary Links	411
3.	Start with Customs	412
	Customs broker license	412
	To operate under a trade name	412
	District permit request	414
	Filer code request	416
4.	Type of Organization	418
	Legal designation	418
	Taxes	419
5.	Marketing your CHB Business	420
6	ABI Vendor	421
	Selecting an ABI vendor	421
	Reproducing customs forms	422
	Letter of intent	422
	VPN ISA	424
7.	Selecting a Surety Company	425
9.	Running Your CHB Business	426
	Power of attorney	426
	ACH payment	429

Book 1 Part 1

Book 1 Introduction
Customs Broker Exam Study Guide

In This Part
Apply "sabermetrics" to the customs broker exam!

"Sabermetrics" -- it is in an analogy of this obscure term that I feel best communicates the spirit of this book.

So, what is "sabermetrics"? It is the empirical (i.e. verifiable) analysis of baseball and baseball statistics. For example, a baseball team utilizing the relatively new concept of sabermetrics will measure a baseball player's effectiveness and potential based on the player's slugging percentage and on-base percentage. While in contrast, in the past, baseball teams have dogmatically gauged a baseball player's worth based on traditionally followed statistics such as batting average and stolen bases.

The concept of sabermetrics truly revolutionized the world of major league baseball. They even made a movie on the subject featuring one of its major advocates, portrayed by Brad Pitt, and was based on Michael Lewis' book "Moneyball". Sabermetrics is now widely recognized as a much more objective and proven system for locating overlooked talent baseball, and at a deep discount. For nearly half a century it lingered in obscurity. Now, it is most likely adopted, in at least some shape or form, by all MLB teams.

…why not apply the sabermetrics-like principles to the game of basketball, or to football? Why not apply it to the customs broker exam?

What's the correlation between the sabermetrics phenomenon and the passing of the customs broker exam? Well, why not apply the sabermetrics-like principles to the game of basketball, or to football? Why not apply it to the customs broker exam?

This study guide does its best to dissuade the examinee from studying, in-depth, ALL of the exam reference material, as traditionally may have been the practice for customs brokers past. Instead, this study guide helps the student target his or her finite study time by isolating the most frequent and trending aspects of the exam, working large to small, and based on empirical data (i.e. observations from previous exams).

Now, visualize yourself and your studies as a laser guided missile amongst a sea of aimless shotguns.

• • • • • • • • •

Instead, this study guide helps the student target his or her finite study time by isolating the most frequent and trending aspects of the exam, working large to small, and based on empirical data (i.e. observations from previous exams).

• • • • • • • • •

$ Money Saving Tip $ The 19 CFR and HTS publications are quite significant investments (approx. $200/ea.). You may save money on these items by buying used or older versions of each. The difference in content from issue to issue and year to year isn't really that significant.

Book 1 Part 2

Getting Started

In This Part
Current web addresses for obtaining essential exam reference material

FOR...
- *past customs broker exams and exam keys*
- *notice of examinations*
- *application for customs broker license examination (CBP Form 3124E)*
    - *GO TO...*

US Customs' (CBP) website:
http://www.cbp.gov/document/publications/past-customs-broker-license-examinations-answer-keys

http://www.cbp.gov/trade/broker/exam/announcement

http://www.cbp.gov/document/forms/form-3124-application-customs-broker-license

FOR...
- *Code of Federal Regulations (CFR) "online version"*
    - *GO TO...*

US Government Printing Office (GPO) website:
www.eCFR.gov

FOR...
- *Harmonized Tariff Schedule of the United States (HTSUS) "online version"*
    - *GO TO...*

United States International Trade Commission (ITC) website:
https://hts.usitc.gov/current

FOR...
- *"hardcopies" of HTS and CFR Title 19 for sale*
    - *GO TO...*

Boskage Commerce Publications **and/or** U.S. Government Bookstore websites:
https://tax.thomsonreuters.com/checkpoint/boskage/trade-publications

http://bookstore.gpo.gov
(and search "Code of Federal Regulations Title 19" **and** "Harmonized Tariff Schedule of the United States")

Book 1 Part 3

Nature of the Exam

In This Part
Requirements for becoming a licensed customs broker
What types of questions appear on the exam?
Exam reference material breakdown by source and by year
Next exam may be written using what reference materials?

In order to become a customs broker there are a few requirements. Anyone is eligible to apply to become a customs broker as long as they're at least 21 years of age, a US citizen, and not a federal employee. Second, and the aim of this book, is the requirement of passing the customs broker exam—a 4.5 hour open-book test consisting of 80 multiple choice questions and requiring a 75% to pass. As you may already be aware, the exam is administered twice a year, once on the first Wednesday of each April, and once on the first Wednesday of each October. Applications for the exam are to be submitted your nearest service port (or the location where you would like to sit for the exam) within at least about a month prior to the test. A list of customs service ports, sorted by state can be found on Customs' website at http://www.cbp.gov/contact/ports. The exam application and further instructions are found at Customs' website as well (see also previous page). And, ultimately, upon passing the exam, the applicant is to submit their official application to become a customs broker to US Customs.

It is said that the average passing rate for the exam, which, by the way varies remarkably from year-to-year, can be as low as 5 to 10%, though most years it is much higher. Regardless of these statistics, your experience will be entirely unique, based mainly on your preparation and mindset.

… … I realized a remarkable pattern. A majority of the questions were simply being drawn directly from the 19 CFR (as opposed to the HTSUS, other material, etc.)

Nature of the Exam — Study Guide

What about my (the author's) experience with the exam? When I made my mind up to start studying for my first attempt at the exam, I began by just reviewing a few of the previous exams. And, in the process I realized a remarkable pattern. A MAJORITY of the questions were simply being drawn directly from the 19 CFR (as opposed to the HTSUS, other material, etc.), AND, many of the same subjects and questions were being repeated from one exam to the next. So, I made note of which 19 CFR Parts, Sections, and Paragraphs were a part of this pattern. I then removed the "unnecessary" parts and pages from my newly purchased 19 CFR, and did my best to focus on the items that would most likely appear on the exam (as I will further outline for you in this book). With this newly conceived strategy of mine, and a commitment to study at least a little each day all the way up to the date of the next exam, the goal was in sight and I felt a surge of confidence. And what was the result? On my first attempt at the exam, I surprised myself by scoring a passing grade!

Notated immediately below this paragraph is a quick snapshot of each of the major sources of exam reference materials, and the approximate number of occurrences and percentages of each over the last 10 exams.

Nature of the Exam • Study Guide

Exam Reference Material Frequency by Source & Year

of Occurrences per Exam

Exam Date	19 CFR	HTSUS	Form 7501 Inst.	Directives	CATAIR
2016 Oct.	56	22	4	1	1
2016 Apr.	62	11	5	0	2
2015 Oct.	53	20	7	0	0
2015 Apr.	58	18	2	0	1
2014 Oct.	55	21	6	1	0
2014 Apr.	44	28	9	1	0
2013 Oct.	44	34	1	1	0
2013 Apr.	35	34	5	4	2
2012 Oct.	40	27	6	3	3
2012 Apr.	44	33	2	3	0
AVERAGE	**49**	**25**	**5**	**1**	**1**

% of Exam

Exam Date	19 CFR	HTSUS	Form 7501 Inst.	Directives	CATAIR
2016 Oct.	70%	28%	5%	1%	1%
2016 Apr.	78%	14%	6%	0%	3%
2015 Oct.	67%	25%	9%	0%	0%
2015 Apr.	70%	22%	2%	0%	1%
2014 Oct.	67%	26%	7%	1%	0%
2014 Apr.	55%	35%	11%	1%	0%
2013 Oct.	55%	43%	1%	1%	0%
2013 Apr.	44%	43%	6%	5%	3%
2012 Oct.	49%	33%	7%	4%	4%
2012 Apr.	52%	39%	2%	4%	0%
AVERAGE	**61%**	**31%**	**6%**	**2%**	**1%**

Nature of the Exam — Study Guide

It has been announced that the April 2017 examination will be written using the following references:

- Harmonized Tariff Schedule of the United States (2016 Basic Edition)

- Title 19, Code of Federal Regulations (2016, Parts 1 to 199)

- Customs and Trade Automated Interface Requirements (CATAIR/ACE)
  - Appendix B - Valid Codes
  - Appendix G - ACE ABI Condition Codes & Narrative Test
  - Appendix H – Census Warning Messages and Override Codes

- Instructions for Preparation of CBP Form 7501 (July 24, 2012)

- Right to Make Entry Directive 3530-002A

· · · · · · · · ·

As the personal finance icon and pragmatist, Dave Ramsey says, "Get gazelle intense!" Act as if you didn't want to take the test more than once.

· · · · · · · · ·

Note: See below for CBP's notice in regards to exam reference material.

Applicants must provide their own reference materials.

Examinees may use any written reference material; however, use of any electronic device during the exam (e.g., laptop, iPad / Nook / Kindle, smart phone, personal digital assistant, etc.) is strictly prohibited.

Cell phones, laptops, pagers, and other communication devices may not be used inside the examination room.

Book 1 Part 4

How to Use This Book

In This Part
Step-by-step instructions for preparing for your studies
How to most effectively study for the exam

This book, by itself, will not guarantee your success on the customs broker exam. It is, however, one of several tools that will best prepare you for the big day. "Preparation" is the key word and preparedness in context of the customs broker exam means studying as efficiently as possible and on a daily basis. As the personal finance icon and pragmatist, Dave Ramsey says, "get gazelle intense!" Act as if you didn't want to take the test more than once. Listed below is a sort of checklist of things we suggest you should do in about the same order before wandering too far into your studies.

√ First, go to the following link to Customs' website.

http://www.cbp.gov/trade/broker/exam/announcement

Here, you will find a list of all the reference materials (HTSUS, 19 CFR, 7501 Instructions etc.) that Customs says it may draw from for the exam. You are not just allowed, but actually encouraged to bring all of these reference materials to the actual exam.

√ Print out all of the reference materials except for the Title 19 Code of Federal Regulations (19 CFR) and the Harmonized Tariff Schedule (HTS). These two items contain too many pages to print on your own. Instead, ask to borrow these items from work or a friend, or purchase from one of the resources listed in the section of this book marked "Getting Started".

The CATAIR, for example, consists of over 70 pages, yet has only historically appeared on only 1% of the exam.

√ Make yourself familiar with the reference material you have just printed (except for the HTS and 19 CFR, which require more involved study and I will further explain here in a bit). Just be aware and prepared to look something up in these printouts during the actual exam, and I wouldn't recommend trying to memorize too much here. The CATAIR, for example, consists of over 70 pages, yet has only historically appeared on only 1% of the exam.

√ Next, begin printing out a few of the old exams and exam keys, starting with the most recent exams. Take time to just peruse through these exams and try to get a feeling of what kinds of questions are being asked, and how they are presented, etc. Once you get a little more familiar with everything, you will want to take mock exams utilizing these old exams to improve on your skills and gauge your progress.

√ Once you have a Title 19 CFR available to use, go to the section of this study guide marked "All Sections Appearing on Exams". In this section of the study guide is a table, which lists in order by CFR Part, Section, Paragraph, then Subparagraph, all of the 19 CFR-related materials tested over the last 10 exams. With a highlighter, begin highlighting or otherwise notate directly into your 19 CFR, these Parts, Sections, and Paragraphs that most frequently appear on exams as indicated on this table. Not only will this process improve your familiarity with the 19 CFR and these various entries, but it will also make these items more easily stand out when you are searching for answers during your mock exams and during the actual exam.

√ Once you have an HTS at your disposal, you will want to affix sticky tabs for all chapters (on the side) and for all sections (on top) for the purpose of simplified navigation through the HTSUS text. Undoubtedly, the best training method for strengthening your HTS classification skills is to simply go through the old exams and try to classify all the different sorts of merchandise described throughout the previous exams. This process will expose you to a wide variety of products and materials. It will also help to get you used to the kinds of HTS-based questions appearing on exams that require you to check chapter notes, section notes, general notes, and consider the general rules of interpretation (GRI) before deciding on the most appropriate classification and answer. This book also includes an "HTS Classification Tips" section, which explains the fundamentals of classification, and dissects a few classification questions derived directly from previous exams.

√ Next to last, this study guide includes a section called "Most Commonly Tested". This part of the book isolates and quotes the specific "Sections" and "Paragraphs" of the 19 CFR that have most often appeared within exam questions during the last ten customs broker exams. It is, for the sake of prioritizing study time and for ease of navigation, arranged by frequency of appearances in the past ten exams and then numerically by CFR Part, Section, and then by Paragraph. Attempt to memorize as much as you can of this section. The reason for this is that the more you are able to answer exam questions from memory and on the fly, then the more time you will have to focus on the more time-consuming parts, namely HTS classification.

√ Finally, this study guide also includes the most recent exams with commentary and answers. The commentary will provide you with explanations, detailed in proportion to the complexity of each particular exam question. Direct excerpts from the HTSUS, 19 CFR, etc. are also included as supporting points of reference for each answer.

Book 1 Part 5

HTS Classification Tips

Sub-part 1
The HTSUS

In This Sub-part
What is the "HTS"?
The 4 Major Components of the HTSUS
HTSUS Chapters Frequency for last 10 exams
HTSUS General Notes (GN) Frequency for last 10 exams
HTSUS Contents (including Sections Titles & Chapter Titles) at a Glance

The Harmonized Tariff Schedule (HTS) of the United States (HTSUS) is available via both ...

A. hardcopy version:

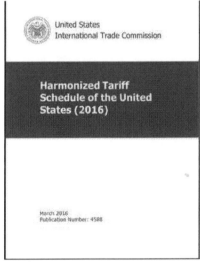

And

B. online version:

https://hts.usitc.gov/current

The HTSUS consists of 4 major components ...

1) The General Rules of Interpretation (GRI), which are U.S. Customs' instructions for HTS classification (see excerpt below):

GENERAL RULES OF INTERPRETATION

Classification of goods in the tariff schedule shall be governed by the following principles:

1. The table of contents, alphabetical index, and titles of sections, chapters and sub-chapters are provided for ease of reference only; for legal purposes, classification shall be determined according to the terms of the headings and any relative section or chapter notes and, provided such headings or notes do not otherwise require, according to the following provisions:

2. (a) Any reference in a heading to an article shall be taken to include a reference to that article incomplete or unfinished, provided that, as entered, the incomplete or unfinished article has the essential character of the complete or finished article. It shall also include a reference to that article complete or finished (or falling to be classified as complete or finished by virtue of this rule), entered unassembled or disassembled.

   (b) Any reference in a heading to a material or substance shall be taken to include a reference to mixtures or combinations of that material or substance with other materials or substances. Any reference to goods of a given material or substance shall be taken to include a reference to goods consisting wholly or partly of such material or substance. The classification of goods consisting of more than one material or substance shall be according to the principles of rule 3.

3. When, by application of rule 2(b) or for any other reason, goods are, prima facie, classifiable under two or more headings, classification shall be effected as follows:

   (a) The heading which provides the most specific description shall be preferred to headings providing a more general description. However, when two or more headings each refer to part only of the materials or substances contained in mixed or composite goods or to part only of the items in a set put up for retail sale, those headings are to be regarded as equally specific in relation to those goods, even if one of them gives a more complete or precise description of the goods.

   (b) Mixtures, composite goods consisting of different materials or made up of different components, and goods put up in sets for retail sale, which cannot be classified by reference to 3(a), shall be classified as if they consisted of the material or component which gives them their essential character, insofar as this criterion is applicable.

   (c) When goods cannot be classified by reference to 3(a) or 3(b), they shall be classified under the heading which occurs last in numerical order among those which equally merit consideration.

4. Goods which cannot be classified in accordance with the above rules shall be classified under the heading appropriate to the goods to which they are most akin.

5. In addition to the foregoing provisions, the following rules shall apply in respect of the goods referred to therein:

   (a) Camera cases, musical instrument cases, gun cases, drawing instrument cases, necklace cases and similar containers, specially shaped or fitted to contain a specific article or set of articles, suitable for long-term use and entered with the articles for which they are intended, shall be classified with such articles when of a kind normally sold therewith. This rule does not, however, apply to containers which give the whole its essential character;

   (b) Subject to the provisions of rule 5(a) above, packing materials and packing containers entered with the goods therein shall be classified with the goods if they are of a kind normally used for packing such goods. However, this provision is not binding when such packing materials or packing containers are clearly suitable for repetitive use.

6. For legal purposes, the classification of goods in the subheadings of a heading shall be determined according to the terms of those subheadings and any related subheading notes and, mutatis mutandis, to the above rules, on the understanding that only subheadings at the same level are comparable. For the purposes of this rule, the relative section, chapter and subchapter notes also apply, unless the context otherwise requires.

2) The General Notes (GN), which include important interpretive notes for using the HTSUS, such as defining what is the "Customs Territory of the United States", outlining the rules of NAFTA and other Free Trade Agreements (FTA), etc. (Excerpt of HTSUS General Notes 1, 2, and partial of 3 below):

General Notes

1. <u>Tariff Treatment of Imported Goods and of Vessel Equipments, Parts and Repairs</u>. All goods provided for in this schedule and imported into the customs territory of the United States from outside thereof, and all vessel equipments, parts, materials and repairs covered by the provisions of subchapter XVIII to chapter 98 of this schedule, are subject to duty or exempt therefrom as prescribed in general notes 3 through 29, inclusive.

2. <u>Customs Territory of the United States</u>. The term "<u>customs territory of the United States</u>", as used in the tariff schedule, includes only the States, the District of Columbia and Puerto Rico.

3. <u>Rates of Duty</u>. The rates of duty in the "Rates of Duty" columns designated 1 ("General" and "Special") and 2 of the tariff schedule apply to goods imported into the customs territory of the United States as hereinafter provided in this note:

    (a) <u>Rate of Duty Column 1</u>.

... ...

3) Section Notes (HTSUS Section I Notes below):

Harmonized Tariff Schedule of the United States (2016)
Annotated for Statistical Reporting Purposes

SECTION I

LIVE ANIMALS; ANIMAL PRODUCTS

Notes

1. Any reference in this section to a particular genus or species of an animal, except where the context otherwise requires, includes a reference to the young of that genus or species.

2. Except where the context otherwise requires, throughout the tariff schedule any reference to "dried" products also covers products which have been dehydrated, evaporated or freeze-dried.

& Chapter Notes. (HTSUS Chapter 1 Notes below):

Harmonized Tariff Schedule of the United States (2016)
Annotated for Statistical Reporting Purposes

CHAPTER 1

LIVE ANIMALS

Note

1. This chapter covers all live animals except:

    (a) Fish and crustaceans, molluscs and other aquatic invertebrates, of heading 0301, 0306, 0307 or 0308;

    (b) Cultures of microorganisms and other products of heading 3002; and

    (c) Animals of heading 9508.

Additional U.S. Notes

1. The expression "purebred breeding animals" covers only animals certified to the U.S. Customs Service by the Department of Agriculture as being purebred of a recognized breed and duly registered in a book of record recognized by the Secretary of Agriculture for that breed, imported specially for breeding purposes, whether intended to be used by the importer himself or for sale for such purposes. 1/

2. Certain special provisions applying to live animals are in chapter 98.

HTS Classification Tips   Study Guide

4) Classifications and their corresponding descriptions, reportable unit of measure, duty rate, and special program indicator (SPI) availability for anything and everything under the sun. (Excerpt from HTSUS Chapter 1 below):

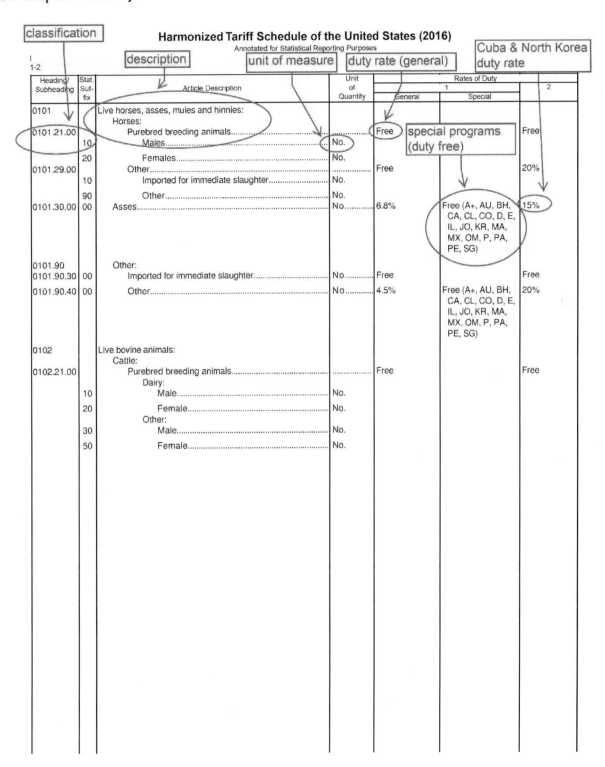

HTSUS Chapters Frequency for last 10 exams (thru. October 2016 exam):

HTS Chapter	Occurrences	HTS Chapter	Occurrences
General Notes	55	54	2
1	1	55	1
2	3	58	3
3	1	59	2
4	2	60	1
5	1	61	17
7	4	62	12
8	5	63	7
9	1	64	4
12	2	66	1
13	1	67	2
16	5	68	3
17	5	69	9
18	1	70	5
19	1	71	5
20	13	72	3
21	6	73	8
22	2	74	2
25	1	76	1
26	2	82	6
27	1	83	2
28	1	84	18
29	6	85	8
30	2	86	1
31	4	87	3
33	3	88	4
38	5	90	4
39	7	92	2
40	3	94	4
42	11	95	6
44	4	96	1
46	2	97	3
48	3	98	19
50	1	99	2
51	2	ANNEX A	1
52	2	ANNEX B	4
53	1	ANNEX C	7

HTS Classification Tips — Study Guide

HTSUS General Notes (GN) Frequency over last 10 exams (thru. Oct. 2016 exam):

Exam		General Note Number (Name)	Paragraph
2013 October	GN	2 (Customs Territory of the U.S.)	
2015 October	GN	3 (Rates of Duty)	(a)
2012 April	GN	3 (Rates of Duty)	(a)
2012 April	GN	3 (Rates of Duty)	(a)
2016 April	GN	3 (Rates of Duty)	(c)
2015 April	GN	3 (Rates of Duty)	(c)
2015 April	GN	3 (Rates of Duty)	(c)
2014 October	GN	3 (Rates of Duty)	(c)
2013 October	GN	3 (Rates of Duty)	(c)
2014 April	GN	3 (Rates of Duty)	
2014 October	GN	4 (Generalized System of Preferences)	(a)
2014 April	GN	4 (Generalized System of Preferences)	(b)
2016 October	GN	4 (Generalized System of Preferences)	(c)
2014 October	GN	4 (Generalized System of Preferences)	(c)
2014 April	GN	4 (Generalized System of Preferences)	(d)
2013 October	GN	4 (Generalized System of Preferences)	(d)
2016 April	GN	4 (Generalized System of Preferences)	
2015 October	GN	4 (Generalized System of Preferences)	
2014 October	GN	4 (Generalized System of Preferences)	
2014 April	GN	4 (Generalized System of Preferences)	
2016 October	GN	5 (Automotive Products and Motor Vehicles Eligible ...)	(b)
2012 October	GN	6 (Agreement on Trade in Civil Aircraft)	(b)
2013 October	GN	8 (Israel FTA)	(b)
2014 April	GN	11 (Andean Trade Preference Act)	(a)
2013 April	GN	12 (NAFTA)	(a)
2013 April	GN	12 (NAFTA)	(b)
2013 April	GN	12 (NAFTA)	(c)
2012 April	GN	12 (NAFTA)	(d)
2016 October	GN	12 (NAFTA)	(n)
2012 October	GN	12 (NAFTA)	(n)
2016 October	GN	12 (NAFTA)	(q)
2015 October	GN	12 (NAFTA)	(t)
2013 October	GN	12 (NAFTA)	(t)
2012 April	GN	12 (NAFTA)	(t)
2013 April	GN	12 (NAFTA)	
2012 April	GN	12 (NAFTA)	
2012 April	GN	12 (NAFTA)	
2014 October	GN	13 (Pharmaceutical Products)	
2014 October	GN	14 (Intermediate Chemicals for Dyes)	
2015 October	GN	15 (Exclusions)	
TABLE CONTINUED BELOW			

HTSUS General Notes (GN) Frequency over last 10 exams (thru. Oct. 2016 exam):

Exam		General Note Number (Name)	Paragraph
2016 October	GN	16 (African Growth and Opportunity Act)	(a)
2014 October	GN	16 (African Growth and Opportunity Act)	
2012 April	GN	17 (Caribbean Basin Trade Partnership Act)	(e)
2014 April	GN	25 (Singapore FTA)	(m)
2015 October	GN	27 (Morocco FTA)	
2015 April	GN	28 (Australia FTA)	(k)
2014 April	GN	28 (Australia FTA)	(k)
2014 October	GN	29 (Dominican Republic FTA)	(a)
2013 October	GN	29 (Dominican Republic FTA)	(a)
2014 October	GN	29 (Dominican Republic FTA)	(d)
2014 October	GN	29 (Dominican Republic FTA)	
2014 April	GN	33 (Korea FTA)	(c)
2013 October	GN	33 (Korea FTA)	(c)
2014 April	GN	33 (Korea FTA)	(o)
2014 October	GN	34 (Colombia Trade Promotion Agreement)	(o)

HTSUS Contents at a Glance:
(please note: Section titles and Chapter titles are for reference purposes only—use the General Rules of Interpretation to classify).

Cover

Change Record
(The record of legal and statistical changes in this edition of the Harmonized Tariff Schedule)

Preface

General Notes; General Rules of Interpretation; General Statistical Notes

Notice to Exporters

Section I: Live Animals; Animal Products
Chapter 1	Live animals
Chapter 2	Meat and edible meat offal
Chapter 3	Fish and crustaceans, molluscs and other aquatic invertebrates
Chapter 4	Dairy produce; birds eggs; natural honey; edible products of animal origin, not elsewhere specified or included
Chapter 5	Products of animal origin, not elsewhere specified or included

Section II: Vegetable Products
Chapter 6	Live trees and other plants; bulbs, roots and the like; cut flowers and ornamental foliage
Chapter 7	Edible vegetables and certain roots and tubers
Chapter 8	Edible fruit and nuts; peel of citrus fruit or melons
Chapter 9	Coffee, tea, maté and spices
Chapter 10	Cereals
Chapter 11	Products of the milling industry; malt; starches; inulin; wheat gluten
Chapter 12	Oil seeds and oleaginous fruits; miscellaneous grains, seeds and fruits; industrial or medicinal plants; straw and fodder
Chapter 13	Lac; gums, resins and other vegetable saps and extracts
Chapter 14	Vegetable plaiting materials; vegetable products not elsewhere specified or included

HTSUS Contents at a Glance:

Section III: Animal or Vegetable Fats and Oils and Their Cleavage Products; Prepared Edible Fats; Animal or Vegetable Waxes

Chapter 15	Animal or vegetable fats and oils and their cleavage products prepared edible fats; animal or vegetable waxes

Section IV: Prepared Foodstuffs; Beverages, Spirits, and Vinegar; Tobacco and Manufactured Tobacco Substitutes

Chapter 16	Preparations of meat, of fish or of crustaceans, mollusks or other aquatic invertebrates
Chapter 17	Sugars and sugar confectionery
Chapter 18	Cocoa and cocoa preparations
Chapter 19	Preparations of cereals, flour, starch or milk; bakers' wares
Chapter 20	Preparations of vegetables, fruit, nuts or other parts of plants
Chapter 21	Miscellaneous edible preparations
Chapter 22	Beverages, spirits and vinegar
Chapter 23	Residues and waste from the food industries; prepared animal feed
Chapter 24	Tobacco and manufactured tobacco substitutes

Section V: Mineral Products

Chapter 25	Salt; sulfur; earths and stone; plastering materials, lime and cement
Chapter 26	Ores, slag and ash
Chapter 27	Mineral fuels, mineral oils and products of their distillation; bituminous substances; mineral waxes

Section VI: Products of Chemical or Allied Industries

Chapter 28	Inorganic chemicals; organic or inorganic c compounds of precious metals, of rare-earth metals, of radioactive elements or of isotopes
Chapter 29	Organic chemicals
Chapter 30	Pharmaceutical products
Chapter 31	Fertilizers
Chapter 32	Tanning or dyeing extracts; dyes, pigments, paints, varnishes, putty and mastics
Chapter 33	Essential oils and resinoids; perfumery, cosmetic or toilet preparations
Chapter 34	Soap, organic surface-active agents, washing preparations, lubricating preparations, artificial waxes, prepared waxes, polishing or scouring preparations, candles and similar articles, modeling pastes, "dental waxes" and dental preparations with a basis of plaster
Chapter 35	Albuminoidal substances; modified starches; glues; enzymes
Chapter 36	Explosives; pyrotechnic products; matches; pyrophoric alloys; certain combustible preparations
Chapter 37	Photographic or cinematographic goods
Chapter 38	Miscellaneous chemical products

HTSUS Contents at a Glance:

Section VII: Plastics and Articles Thereof Rubber and Articles Thereof

Chapter 39	Plastics and articles thereof
Chapter 40	Rubber and articles thereof

Section VIII: Raw Hides and Skins, Leather, Fur skins and Articles Thereof; Saddlery and Harness; Travel Goods, Handbags and Similar Containers; Articles of Animal Gut (Other Than Silkworm Gut)

Chapter 41	Raw hides and skins (other than fur skins) and leather
Chapter 42	Articles of leather; saddlery and harness; travel goods, handbags and similar containers; articles of animal gut (other than silkworm gut)
Chapter 43	Furskins and artificial fur; manufactures thereof

Section IX: Wood and Articles of Wood; Wood Charcoal; Cork and Articles of Cork; Manufacturers of Straw, of Esparto or of Other Plaiting Materials; Basketware and Wickerwork

Chapter 44	Wood and articles of wood; wood charcoal
Chapter 45	Cork and articles of cork
Chapter 46	Manufactures of straw, of esparto or of other plaiting materials; basketware and wickerwork

Section X: Pulp of Wood or of Other Fibrous Cellulosic Material; Waste and Scrap of Paper or Paperboard; Paper and Paperboard and Articles Thereof

Chapter 47	Pulp of wood or of other fibrous cellulosic material; waste and scrap of paper or paperboard
Chapter 48	Paper and paperboard; articles of paper pulp, of paper or of paperboard
Chapter 49	Printed books, newspapers, pictures and other products of the printing industry; manuscripts, typescripts and plans

HTSUS Contents at a Glance:

Section XI: Textile and Textile Articles

Chapter 50	Silk
Chapter 51	Wool, fine or coarse animal hair; horsehair yarn and woven fabric
Chapter 52	Cotton
Chapter 53	Other vegetable textile fibers; paper yarn and woven fabric of paper yarn
Chapter 54	Man-made filaments
Chapter 55	Man-made staple fibers
Chapter 56	Wadding, felt and nonwovens; special yarns, twine, cordage, ropes and cables and articles thereof
Chapter 57	Carpets and other textile floor coverings
Chapter 58	Special woven fabrics; tufted textile fabrics; lace, tapestries; trimmings; embroidery
Chapter 59	Impregnated, coated, covered or laminated textile fabrics; textile articles of a kind suitable for industrial use
Chapter 60	Knitted or crocheted fabrics
Chapter 61	Articles of apparel and clothing accessories, knitted or crocheted
Chapter 62	Articles of apparel and clothing accessories, not knitted or crocheted
Chapter 63	Other made up textile articles; sets; worn clothing and worn textile articles; rags

Section XII: Footwear, Headgear, Umbrellas, Sun Umbrellas, Walking Sticks, Seatsticks, Whips, Riding-Crops and Parts Thereof; Prepared Feathers and Articles Made Therewith; Artificial Flowers; Articles of Human

Chapter 64	Footwear, gaiters and the like; parts of such articles
Chapter 65	Headgear and parts thereof
Chapter 66	Umbrellas, sun umbrellas, walking sticks, seatsticks, whips, riding-crops and parts thereof
Chapter 67	Prepared feathers and down and articles made of feathers or of down; artificial flowers; articles of human hair

Section XIII: Articles of Stone, Plaster, Cement, Asbestos, Mica or Similar Materials; Ceramic Products; Glass and Glassware

Chapter 68	Articles of stone, plaster, cement, asbestos, mica or similar materials
Chapter 69	Ceramic products
Chapter 70	Glass and glassware

Section XIV: Natural or Cultured Pearls, Precious or Semiprecious Stones, Precious Metals, Metals Clad With Precious Metal, and Articles Thereof; Imitation Jewelry; Coin

Chapter 71	Natural or cultured pearls, precious or semi-precious stones, precious metals, metals clad with precious metal and articles thereof; imitation jewelry; coin

HTSUS Contents at a Glance:

Section XV: Base Metals and Articles of Base Metal

Chapter 72	Iron and steel
Chapter 73	Articles of iron or steel
Chapter 74	Copper and articles thereof
Chapter 75	Nickel and articles thereof
Chapter 76	Aluminum and articles thereof
Chapter 77	(Reserved for possible future use)
Chapter 78	Lead and articles thereof
Chapter 79	Zinc and articles thereof
Chapter 80	Tin and articles thereof
Chapter 81	Other base metals; cermets; articles thereof
Chapter 82	Tools, implements, cutlery, spoons and forks, of base metal; parts thereof of base metal
Chapter 83	Miscellaneous articles of base metal

Section XVI: Machinery and Mechanical Appliances; Electrical Equipment; Parts Thereof; Sound Recorders and Reproducers, Television Image and Sound Recorders and Reproducers, and Parts and Accessories of Such Articles

Chapter 84	Nuclear reactors, boilers, machinery and mechanical appliances; parts thereof
Chapter 85	Electrical machinery and equipment and parts thereof; sound recorders and reproducers, television image and sound recorders and reproducers, and parts and accessories of such articles

Section XVII: Vehicles, Aircraft, Vessels and Associated Transport Equipment

Chapter 86	Railway or tramway locomotives, rolling-stock and parts thereof; railway or tramway track fixtures and fittings and parts thereof; mechanical (including electro-mechanical) traffic signaling equipment of all kinds
Chapter 87	Vehicles other than railway or tramway rolling stock, and parts and accessories thereof
Chapter 88	Aircraft, spacecraft, and parts thereof
Chapter 89	Ships, boats and floating structures

Section XVIII: Optical, Photographic, Cinematographic, Measuring, Checking, Precision, Medical or Surgical Instruments and Apparatus; Clocks and Watches; Musical Instruments; Parts and Accessories Thereof

Chapter 90	Optical, photographic, cinematographic, measuring, checking, precision, medical or surgical instruments and apparatus; parts and accessories thereof
Chapter 91	Clocks and watches and parts thereof
Chapter 92	Musical instruments; parts and accessories of such articles

HTSUS Contents at a Glance:

Section XIX: Arms and Ammunition; Parts & Accessories Thereof
Chapter 93 — Arms and ammunition; parts and accessories thereof

Section XX: Miscellaneous Manufactured Articles
Chapter 94 — Furniture; bedding, mattresses, mattress supports, cushions and similar stuffed furnishings; lamps and lighting fittings, not elsewhere specified or included; illuminated sign illuminated nameplates and the like; prefabricated buildings
Chapter 95 — Toys, games and sports requisites; parts and accessories thereof
Chapter 96 — Miscellaneous manufactured articles

Section XXI: Works of Art, Collectors' Pieces and Antiques
Chapter 97 — Works of art, collectors' pieces and antiques

Section XXII: Special Classification Provisions; Temporary Legislation; Temporary Modifications Proclaimed pursuant to Trade Agreements Legislation; Additional Import Restrictions Proclaimed Pursuant to Section 22 of the Agricultural Adjustment Act, As Amended
Chapter 98 — Special classification provisions
Chapter 99 — Temporary legislation; temporary modifications proclaimed pursuant to trade agreements legislation; additional import restrictions proclaimed pursuant to section 22 of the Agricultural Adjustment Act, as amended

Chemical Appendix to the Tariff Schedule

Pharmaceutical Appendix to the Tariff Schedule

Intermediate Chemicals for Dyes Appendix to the Tariff Schedule

Statistical Annexes

Annex A - Schedule C, Classification of Country and Territory Designations for U.S. Import Statistics
Annex B - International Standard Country Codes
Annex C - Schedule D, Customs District and Port Codes

Alphabetical Index

(This Page Intentionally Left Blank)

Book 1 Part 5

HTS Classification Tips

Sub-part 2
The HTS Number

In This Sub-part
What is an "HTS Number"?
HTSUS Number Structure & Breakdown
Basic Classification Procedure
Basic Exam Classification Strategy

An HTS number ("HTS" is the abbreviation for "Harmonized Tariff Schedule") is a 10-digit number (in the case of the United States) and it determines the admissibility of and duty rate for goods imported into the United States. There are over 17,000 HTS numbers within the Harmonized Tariff Schedule of the United States (also known as HTSUS). Let's break it down here!

Here's a breakdown (of the components of) of the HTS classification number:

(Example: HTSUS classification for a male purebred horse)

LIVE ANIMALS	Live horses, asses, mules and hinnies:	Horses: Purebred breeding animals	Males
01	01.	21.00	10
Chapter			
	Heading		
	Subheading		Statistical

Here's what the classification looks like in the HTSUS:

Heading/ Subheading	Stat. Suffix	Article Description	Unit of Quantity	General
0101		Live horses, asses, mules and hinnies: ↳ Horses:		
0101.21.00		↳ Purebred breeding animals................................	....	Free
	10	↳ Males...	No.	
	20	Females..	No.	

Chapter

The first two digits of the HTS number represent the "Chapter" number. There are 99 chapters (which are further logically sub-divided into 22 sections). Think of these chapters and sections as the A to Z alphabetic lookup system of a city's phone book. For example, if you don't know the spelling of a person's last name you're looking for, the alphabetic lookup will assist, though it is for reference purposes only.

Heading

The first four digits of the HTS number represent the "Heading". The chapter number combined with the subsequent two digits make up what Customs refers to as the classification "Heading". You may think of the "Heading" in the HTSUS as last names (a.k.a. surnames) in a phone book. Meaning, if you're looking for a person in the phone book, first you locate for the person's last name, not the first name first.

Subheading & Statistical

Practically speaking, after the chapter and heading, it is only important to note that the last six digits of the HTS further break down the classifications into increasingly more specific descriptions. This is the person's first and middle name in the above-mentioned phone book analogy.

Here's another example of HTSUS number breakdown:

(Example: HTSUS classification for cross-country skis)

TOYS, GAMES AND SPORTS EQUIPMENT; PARTS AND ACCESSORIES THEREOF	Articles and equipment for general physical exercise, gymnastics, athletics, other sports (including table-tennis) or outdoor games, not specified or included elsewhere in this chapter; swimming pools and wading pools; parts and accessories thereof:	Snow-skis and other snow-ski equipment; parts and accessories thereof:	Cross-country skis	(N/A for this item)
95	**06.**	**11.20**		**00**
Chapter				
	Heading			
		Subheading		Statistical

Chapter
Using the HTS number for cross-country skis, for example, Chapter 95 is the chapter for "Toys, Games, and Sports Equipment".

Heading
For example, heading 9506 provides for "equipment for … … outdoor games … …"

Subheading & Statistical
The complete classification number for "cross-country skis" is 9506.11.2000.

✓ **Note:** HTSUS article descriptions are separated by either a "," (comma) or by a ";" (semi-colon). The commas are used to continue a description. The semi-colons are used to start a new description

Basic Classification Procedure:

- The structure of the HTS is hierarchical in nature. Start at the appropriate heading (first 4 digits).
- Then work from left-to-right, choosing among the descriptions available at the same indentations.
- Repeat until you arrive at your 10-digit classification.

(The example below shows how we arrive at the HTS classification for cross-country skis.)

Heading/ Subheading	Stat. Suffix	Article Description	Unit of Quantity	Rates of Duty General	Rates of Duty Special
9505		Festive, carnival or other entertainment articles, including magic tricks and practical joke articles; parts and accessories thereof:			
9505.10		Articles for Christmas festivities and parts and accessories thereof:			
		Christmas ornaments:			
9505.10.10	00	Of glass.............	X........	Free	
		Other:			
9505.10.15	00	Of wood.............	X........	Free	
9505.10.25	00	Other.............	X........	Free	
9505.10.30	00	Nativity scenes and figures thereof.............	X........	Free	
		Other:			
9505.10.40		Of plastics.............	....	Free	
	10	Artificial Christmas trees.............	No.		
	20	Other.............	X		
9505.10.50		Other.............	....	Free	
	10	Artificial Christmas trees.............	No.		
	20	Other.............	X		
9505.90		Other:			
9505.90.20	00	Magic tricks and practical joke articles; parts and accessories thereof.............	X........	Free	
9505.90.40	00	Confetti, paper spirals or streamers, party favors and noisemakers; parts and accessories thereof.............	X........	Free	
9505.90.60	00	Other.............	X........	Free	
9506		Articles and equipment for general physical exercise, gymnastics, athletics, other sports (including table-tennis) or outdoor games, not specified or included elsewhere in this chapter; swimming pools and wading pools; parts and accessories thereof:			
		↪ Snow-skis and other snow-ski equipment; parts and accessories thereof:			
9506.11		↪ Skis and parts and accessories thereof, except ski poles:			
9506.11.20	00	↪ Cross-country skis.............	prs........	Free	
9506.11.40		Other skis.............	....	2.6%	Free (A, AU, BH, CA, CL, CO, E, IL, JO, KR, MA, MX, OM, P, PA, PE, SG)

For HTS classification, there's just one more thing to consider, the General Rules of Interpretation (discussed in detail later in this part of the study guide), but essentially that's it. Depending on the item, the process of selecting the correct HTSUS can be either a trek up Mount Everest or a leisurely trip down the bunny hill.

Basic Exam Classification Strategy:

Which chapters do I study?

The exam may produce HTS classification-based questions pulled anywhere from Chapter 1 thru Chapter 99 of the HTS. One could say that for the last ten exams, Customs has pretty evenly spread out the use of the various chapters throughout. However, there are definitely some outliers. Several chapters have, historically speaking, never appeared, and yet others are almost sure to appear on each exam. For example, chapter 61 (knitted apparel) has appeared nearly 20 times over the last 10 exams, whereas chapter 65 ("headgear") hasn't appeared even once.

Do the classifications last?

The HTS classification portion of the exam can easily end up taking up the lion's share of the examinee's time. Therefore, my first recommendation for those taking the exam, and especially for those whose strong point isn't in classification, is to budget sufficient time for, and tackle the classification part of the test last. It is imperative to have a plan before you enter the test room. Then implement that plan accordingly.

What are your options?

When you take on the classification portion of the exam try this. After you read through the question and have made mental notes on what you guess to be the key points, quickly scan over the five multiple choice answers and take stock of which chapters of the HTS are give to you as an options. You may ask yourself the following types of questions. Which chapters are overrepresented? Are there any seemingly dead giveaways or tells? Which classifications can be disregarded right of the back? Should I skip the question for now and revisit it later?

• • • • • • • • •

Several chapters have, historically speaking, never appeared, and yet others are almost sure to appear on each exam.

• • • • • • • • •

Book 1 Part 5

HTS Classification Tips

Sub-part 3
The General Rules of Interpretation (GRI)
"HUM SELMA"

In This Sub-part
An easy way to remember the GRI's
Breakdown of each GRI
GRI snapshot from the HTSUS

The complete procedural how-to for correctly classifying imported products and materials is included in the GRI's (General Rules of Interpretation). Basically, there are six GRI's. As is true with any other disciplines, as a person gains more experience in HTS classification, these "rules" eventually almost become second nature, and the act of classification becomes a mostly automatic endeavor.

HTS Classification Tips   Study Guide

Let's Get to Know the GRI's

To remember the GRI's, try remembering the following acronym **"HUM SELMA"**

H Headings and any relative Section & Chapter Notes determine the HTS number. **GRI 1**

U Unfinished items are classified as if finished (if unfinished has essential character of finished). **GRI 2(a)**

M Mixtures may be implied (unless prohibited in headings or notes). Go to GRI 3. **GRI 2(b)**

S Specific HTS heading/description preferred (over less descriptive),
for prima facie items. **GRI 3(a)**

E Essential character of item determines HTS number (if item cannot be classified by 3(a)),
for prima facie items. **GRI 3(b)**

L Last in order HTS# shall be used (if item cannot be classified by 3(a) or by 3(b)),
for prima facie items. **GRI 3(c)**

M Most akin item's HTS# is to be used (if not classifiable by the preceding rules). **GRI 4**

A Article-specific cases & packaging are classified with item (unless they are "the item"). **GRI 5(a) & (b)**

BREAKDOWN OF EACH GRI:

GRI 1: Headings and any relative Section & Chapter Notes determine the HTS number.

Most items are classifiable based on GRI 1. The titles of sections & chapters, the HTSUS alphabetical index, etc. are for reference purposes ONLY. To classify, use the Heading Article Description and Section & Chapter Notes. An example of the application of this rule would be the classification of chocolate-covered peanuts. Although Chapter 20 is named "PREPARATIONS OF VEGETABLES, FRUIT, NUTS OR OTHER PARTS OF PLANTS", Chapter 20 Note 2 states that heading 2008 does not apply to "chocolate confectionery (heading 1806)". Instead, the chocolate-covered peanuts would be classified in Chapter 18 (cocoa and cocoa preparations).

Directly quoting GRI 1 from the HTSUS General Rules of Interpretation...

1. The table of contents, alphabetical index, and titles of sections, chapters and sub-chapters are provided for ease of reference only; for legal purposes, classification shall be determined according to the terms of the headings and any relative section or chapter notes and, provided such headings or notes do not otherwise require, according to the following provisions:

BREAKDOWN OF EACH GRI:

GRI 2(a): Unfinished items are classified as if finished (if unfinished item has essential character of finished).

Any reference in an HTS Heading Article Description to an article shall apply to the same article even if the said article is incomplete or unfinished. An example of this would be a pair of basketball shoes imported without its laces. Though not completely functional or ready for use in their imported state, the item is still essentially basketball shoes, even without laces.

 Quoting GRI 2(a) directly from the HTSUS General Rules of Interpretation...

2. (a) Any reference in a heading to an article shall be taken to include a reference to that article incomplete or unfinished, provided that, as entered, the incomplete or unfinished article has the essential character of the complete or finished article. It shall also include a reference to that article complete or finished (or falling to be classified as complete or finished by virtue of this rule), entered unassembled or disassembled.

GRI 2(b): Mixtures may be implied (unless otherwise prohibited in the headings or notes). Go to GRI 3.

This rule is, in a way, the flipside of GRI 2(a). GRI 2(b) says that an item may be classified under a specific classification even if the item is combined with other substances. In other words, mixtures may be implied (unless otherwise prohibited in the section notes, chapter notes, or headings). An example of this could be a chrome-plated steel wire garment hanger (clothes hanger). "Garment hangers" are specifically provided for in the HTSUS and classified under 7326.20.0020 following the sub-heading of "Articles of iron or steel wire". Since no Section Note, no Chapter Note, and no Classification Heading advise otherwise, the inconsequential presence of the "chrome plating" in this instance does not affect the classification of the item as a "steel" wire garment hanger. Just to be sure, we proceed to GRI 3.

 Quoting GRI 2(b) directly from the HTSUS General Rules of Interpretation...

2. (b) Any reference in a heading to a material or substance shall be taken to include a reference to mixtures or combinations of that material or substance with other materials or substances. Any reference to goods of a given material or substance shall be taken to include a reference to goods consisting wholly or partly of such material or substance. The classification of goods consisting of more than one material or substance shall be according to the principles of rule 3.

BREAKDOWN OF EACH GRI:

GRI 3(a): **S**pecific HTS heading/description preferred (over less descriptive), for prima facie items.

This rule says that, for prima facie items, the HTS heading that most specifically describes the product should be used. "Prima Facie" (often pronounced "preemuh face-she"), in the context of customs, simply means an item is potentially classifiable under more than one classification in the HTS. For example, which of the two following classifications more specifically describes a keyboard for a desktop computer?

A) 8471.60.2000   Automatic data processing machines and units thereof…>>Input or output units…>>Other>>**Keyboards**

Or

B) 8537.10.9070   Boards, panels, consoles…equipped with two or more apparatus of heading 8535 or 8536, for electric control…>>For a voltage not exceeding 1,000V>>Other>>Other>>Other

"A" is a more specific description than "B". The word "keyboards" is explicitly part of the description (note: Customs' word for "computer" is "Automatic Data Processing Machines"). "B" is a commonly used classification for control units in general.

 Quoting GRI 3(a) directly from the HTSUS General Rules of Interpretation…

3. When, by application of rule 2(b) or for any other reason, goods are, prima facie, classifiable under two or more headings, classification shall be effected as follows:

(a) The heading which provides the most specific description shall be preferred to headings providing a more general description. However, when two or more headings each refer to part only of the materials or substances contained in mixed or composite goods or to part only of the items in a set put up for retail sale, those headings are to be regarded as equally specific in relation to those goods, even if one of them gives a more complete or precise description of the goods.

BREAKDOWN OF EACH GRI:

GRI 3(b): **E**ssential character of item determines HTS# (if unclassifiable by 3(a)), for prima facie items.

If GRI 3(a) does not work, this rule says that products consisting of multiple materials or components, or sets shall be classified under the material which gives the product its essential character. For example, a nice leather baseball glove for an adult, which has been packaged with a gratuitous baseball and small bottle of glove oil, would still just be classified as a baseball glove (4203.21.4000), as this main component of the set clearly gives the set its essential character.

 Quoting GRI 3(b) directly from the HTSUS General Rules of Interpretation…

3. When, by application of rule 2(b) or for any other reason, goods are, prima facie, classifiable under two or more headings, classification shall be effected as follows:

(b) Mixtures, composite goods consisting of different materials or made up of different components, and goods put up in sets for retail sale, which cannot be classified by reference to 3(a), shall be classified as if they consisted of the material or component which gives them their essential character, insofar as this criterion is applicable.

GRI 3(c): **L**ast in order HTS# shall be used (if unclassifiable by 3(a) or by 3(b)), for prima facie items.

If neither GRI 3(a) nor GRI 3(b) works, this rule says that the largest (numerically speaking) classification prevails. For example, if an item is classifiable in both chapter 84 AND chapter 85, then choose the classification in chapter 85, as this classification numerically occurs later in the HTSUS than does the chapter 84 item.

 Quoting GRI 3(c) directly from the HTSUS General Rules of Interpretation…

3. When, by application of rule 2(b) or for any other reason, goods are, prima facie, classifiable under two or more headings, classification shall be effected as follows:

(c) When goods cannot be classified by reference to 3(a) or 3(b), they shall be classified under the heading which occurs last in numerical order among those which equally merit consideration.

BREAKDOWN OF EACH GRI:

GRI 4: **M**ost akin item's HTS# is to be used (if not classifiable by the preceding rules).

This rule concedes that goods still unclassifiable per the previously mentioned rules (GRI 1 thru. GRI 3) shall be classified under the heading for goods that are most similar in character. For example, a "computer monitor magnifier" (accessory attached to front of monitor to magnify items on screen) is classifiable as 9013.80.2000. This classification's description is "Hand magnifiers, magnifying glasses, loupes, thread counters and similar apparatus", which certainly could be considered most akin to the computer monitor magnifier.

 Quoting GRI 4 directly from the HTSUS General Rules of Interpretation...

4. Goods which cannot be classified in accordance with the above rules shall be classified under the heading appropriate to the goods to which they are most akin.

BREAKDOWN OF EACH GRI:

GRI 5(a) & (b): Article-specific cases & packaging are classified with item (unless *they are* "the item").

These rules deal with (a) cases and (b) packaging, and are fairly self-explanatory.

Example of 5(a): A (real) gold-plated case for reading glasses would not be classified with the relatively insignificant reading glasses for which it contains. The valuable case, itself, would be given its own classification. On the other hand, a basic plastic protective case for and imported with reading glasses would not be separately classified—it would be classified with the glasses.

Example of 5(b): A shipment of bulk-packaged styrofoam packaging peanuts, and nothing else, for a packaging supplies importer, would be classified and entered as styrofoam packaging peanuts. On the other hand, styrofoam peanuts used as protective packaging for delicate electronic goods would not be classified separately—it would be classified with the electronics.

 Quoting GRI 5(a) & (b) directly from the HTSUS General Rules of Interpretation...

5. In addition to the foregoing provisions, the following rules shall apply in respect of the goods referred to therein:

(a) Camera cases, musical instrument cases, gun cases, drawing instrument cases, necklace cases and similar containers, specially shaped or fitted to contain a specific article or set of articles, suitable for long-term use and entered with the articles for which they are intended, shall be classified with such articles when of a kind normally sold therewith. This rule does not, however, apply to containers which give the whole its essential character;

(b) Subject to the provisions of rule 5(a) above, packing materials and packing containers entered with the goods therein shall be classified with the goods if they are of a kind normally used for packing such goods. However, this provision is not binding when such packing materials or packing containers are clearly suitable for repetitive use.

BREAKDOWN OF EACH GRI:

GRI 6: Apply the GRI's to the headings, then the sub-headings, then ...

This means the logic and application of the GRI's are to be applied and repeated from one level (e.g. heading) to the next lower level (e.g. sub-heading), and so on. In our humble opinion, this rule is self-evident, and so we have thus omitted this GRI from the acronym H.U.M. S.E.L.M.A. to keep things as simple as possible.

 Quoting GRI 6 directly from the HTSUS General Rules of Interpretation...

6. For legal purposes, the classification of goods in the subheadings of a heading shall be determined according to the terms of those subheadings and any related subheading notes and, mutatis mutandis, to the above rules, on the understanding that only subheadings at the same level are comparable. For the purposes of this rule, the relative section, chapter and subchapter notes also apply, unless the context otherwise requires.

BREAKDOWN OF EACH GRI:

Additional U.S. Rules of Interpretation:

Also worth noting, but omitted from the acronym are the "Additional U.S. Rules of Interpretation". Notably, Additional Rule 1(c), which says that (in general) "parts and accessories" may be classified as "parts", UNLESS the part in question happens to be specifically provided for in the HTSUS. A good example of this is the question of where to classify a "glass fuse" manufactured for an automobile. Many might just classify as "a part" for an automobile in Chapter 87. However, since a "glass fuse" is specifically provided for in Chapter 85 with other electronics, the fuse if classifiable accordingly in Chapter 85. This rule, however, is just in general. Wherever applicable, Section Notes and Chapter Notes, include instructions for classifying parts for those Sections and Chapters.

 Quoting Additional U.S. Rules of Interpretation from the HTSUS General Rules of Interpretation...

ADDITIONAL U.S. RULES OF INTERPRETATION

1. In the absence of special language or context which otherwise requires--

(a) a tariff classification controlled by use (other than actual use) is to be determined in accordance with the use in the United States at, or immediately prior to, the date of importation, of goods of that class or kind to which the imported goods belong, and the controlling use is the principal use;

(b) a tariff classification controlled by the actual use to which the imported goods are put in the United States is satisfied only if such use is intended at the time of importation, the goods are so used and proof thereof is furnished within 3 years after the date the goods are entered;

(c) a provision for parts of an article covers products solely or principally used as a part of such articles but a provision for "parts" or "parts and accessories" shall not prevail over a specific provision for such part or accessory; and

(d) the principles of section XI regarding mixtures of two or more textile materials shall apply to the classification of goods in any provision in which a textile material is named.

GRI snapshot from the HTSUS:

In their entirety, the General Rules of Interpretation as presented on pages 1 & 2 of the HTSUS:

GENERAL RULES OF INTERPRETATION

Classification of goods in the tariff schedule shall be governed by the following principles:

1. The table of contents, alphabetical index, and titles of sections, chapters and sub-chapters are provided for ease of reference only; for legal purposes, classification shall be determined according to the terms of the headings and any relative section or chapter notes and, provided such headings or notes do not otherwise require, according to the following provisions:

2. (a) Any reference in a heading to an article shall be taken to include a reference to that article incomplete or unfinished, provided that, as entered, the incomplete or unfinished article has the essential character of the complete or finished article. It shall also include a reference to that article complete or finished (or falling to be classified as complete or finished by virtue of this rule), entered unassembled or disassembled.

   (b) Any reference in a heading to a material or substance shall be taken to include a reference to mixtures or combinations of that material or substance with other materials or substances. Any reference to goods of a given material or substance shall be taken to include a reference to goods consisting wholly or partly of such material or substance. The classification of goods consisting of more than one material or substance shall be according to the principles of rule 3.

3. When, by application of rule 2(b) or for any other reason, goods are, prima facie, classifiable under two or more headings, classification shall be effected as follows:

   (a) The heading which provides the most specific description shall be preferred to headings providing a more general description. However, when two or more headings each refer to part only of the materials or substances contained in mixed or composite goods or to part only of the items in a set put up for retail sale, those headings are to be regarded as equally specific in relation to those goods, even if one of them gives a more complete or precise description of the goods.

   (b) Mixtures, composite goods consisting of different materials or made up of different components, and goods put up in sets for retail sale, which cannot be classified by reference to 3(a), shall be classified as if they consisted of the material or component which gives them their essential character, insofar as this criterion is applicable.

   (c) When goods cannot be classified by reference to 3(a) or 3(b), they shall be classified under the heading which occurs last in numerical order among those which equally merit consideration.

4. Goods which cannot be classified in accordance with the above rules shall be classified under the heading appropriate to the goods to which they are most akin.

5. In addition to the foregoing provisions, the following rules shall apply in respect of the goods referred to therein:

   (a) Camera cases, musical instrument cases, gun cases, drawing instrument cases, necklace cases and similar containers, specially shaped or fitted to contain a specific article or set of articles, suitable for long-term use and entered with the articles for which they are intended, shall be classified with such articles when of a kind normally sold therewith. This rule does not, however, apply to containers which give the whole its essential character;

   (b) Subject to the provisions of rule 5(a) above, packing materials and packing containers entered with the goods therein shall be classified with the goods if they are of a kind normally used for packing such goods. However, this provision is not binding when such packing materials or packing containers are clearly suitable for repetitive use.

6. For legal purposes, the classification of goods in the subheadings of a heading shall be determined according to the terms of those subheadings and any related subheading notes and, mutatis mutandis, to the above rules, on the understanding that only subheadings at the same level are comparable. For the purposes of this rule, the relative section, chapter and subchapter notes also apply, unless the context otherwise requires.

GRI snapshot from the HTSUS:

ADDITIONAL U.S. RULES OF INTERPRETATION

1. In the absence of special language or context which otherwise requires--

    (a) a tariff classification controlled by use (other than actual use) is to be determined in accordance with the use in the United States at, or immediately prior to, the date of importation, of goods of that class or kind to which the imported goods belong, and the controlling use is the principal use;

    (b) a tariff classification controlled by the actual use to which the imported goods are put in the United States is satisfied only if such use is intended at the time of importation, the goods are so used and proof thereof is furnished within 3 years after the date the goods are entered;

    (c) a provision for parts of an article covers products solely or principally used as a part of such articles but a provision for "parts" or "parts and accessories" shall not prevail over a specific provision for such part or accessory; and

    (d) the principles of section XI regarding mixtures of two or more textile materials shall apply to the classification of goods in any provision in which a textile material is named.

Book 1 Part 5

HTS Classification Tips

Subpart 4
GRI's Explained in Exam Examples

In This Sub-part
Each GRI applied to solve actual previous exam questions
Further GRI 1 through GRI 6 analysis

This subpart puts to use the General Rules of Interpretation by solving actual past exam problems.

Please note that classification descriptions notated to the right of exam question HTSUS number have been added by the author of this book for ease of reference. These classification descriptions are not annotated or provided on the actual exams. Also, some HTSUS numbers and excerpts may not be up-to-date, and some HTSUS numbers have been slightly updated or modified for the sake of these exercises.

Exam Example of GRI 1

"Headings and any relative Section & Chapter Notes determine the HTS#."

(Exam Question) What is the correct classification for fresh sweet corn?

A) 0709.99.4500   Other vegetables, fresh or chilled>>Other>>Other>>Sweet corn

B) 0710.40.0000   Vegetables (uncooked or cooked by steaming or boiling in water), frozen>>Sweet corn

C) 0712.90.8550   Dried vegetables, whole, cut, sliced, broken or in powder, but not further prepared>>Other vegetables; mixtures of vegetables>>Other>>Sweet corn seeds of a kind used for sowing

D) 1005.10.0010   Corn (maize)>>Seed>>Yellow corn

E) 1005.90.4060   Corn (maize)>>Other>>Other>>Other

 Here's a perfect exam example to demonstrate the application of GRI 1. The item in question is fresh sweet corn.

First off, as per GRI 1, Chapter titles have no bearing on classification and are for reference purposes only. So, as just a side note, Chapter 7's title is "EDIBLE VEGETABLES AND CERTAIN ROOTS AND TUBERS" and Chapter 10's title is "CEREALS".

GRI 1 dictates that we must classify based on Chapter Notes, Section Notes, and Headings.

Note that Chapter 10, Note 2 says:

CHAPTER 10
CEREALS

II
10-1

Notes

1. (a) The products specified in the headings of this chapter are to be classified in those headings only if grains are present, whether or not in the ear or on the stalk.

   (b) This chapter does not cover grains which have been hulled or otherwise worked. However, rice, husked, milled, polished, glazed, parboiled or broken remains classified in heading 1006.

2. Heading 1005 does not cover sweet corn (chapter 7).

The item in question is fresh sweet corn. Per the note, we may eliminate Heading 1005 multiple choice options "D" and "E".

The heading for multiple choice "B" is for "frozen" vegetables, so we eliminate this one. The heading for multiple choice "C" is for "dried" vegetables, so we may eliminate this one as well.

"A" is the classification for fresh sweet corn, and is the correct answer.

✓ **Just a side note:** "Maize" is a type of corn grown by Native Americans.

HTS Classification Tips — Study Guide

Heading/ Subheading	Stat. Suf- fix	Article Description	Unit of Quantity	Rates of Duty 1 General	Rates of Duty 1 Special	Rates of Duty 2
0709 (con.)		Other vegetables, fresh or chilled: (con.) Other:				
0709.91.00	00	Globe artichokes....................................	kg............	11.3%	Free (A, AU, BH, CA, CL, CO, E, IL, JO, KR, MA, MX, OM, P, PA, PE, SG)	50%
0709.92.00	00	Olives..	kg............	8.8¢/kg	Free (A+, AU, BH, CA, CL, CO, D, E, IL, JO, KR, MA, MX, OM, P, PA, PE, SG)	11¢/kg
0709.93		Pumpkins, squash and gourds (*Curcubita* spp.):				
0709.93.10	00	Pumpkins..	kg............	11.3%	Free (A, AU, BH, CA, CL, CO, E, IL, JO, KR, MA, MX, OM, P, PA, PE, SG)	50%
0709.93.20	00	Squash..	kg............	1.5¢/kg	Free (A, AU, BH, CA, CL, CO, E, IL, JO, KR, MA, MX, OM, P, PA, PE, SG)	4.4¢/kg
0709.93.30	00	Gourds (*Curcubita* spp.).................	kg............	20%	Free (A+, BH, CA, CL, CO, D, E, IL, JO, KR, MA, MX, OM, P, PA, PE, SG) 6.5% (AU)	50%
0709.99		Other:				
0709.99.05	00	Jicamas, and breadfruit...................	kg............	11.3%	Free (A, AU, BH, CA, CL, CO, E, IL, JO, KR, MA, MX, OM, P, PA, PE, SG)	50%
0709.99.10	00	Chayote (*Sechium edule*)...............	kg............	5.6%	Free (A, AU, BH, CA, CL, CO, E, IL, JO, KR, MA, MX, OM, P, PA, PE, SG)	50%
0709.99.14	00	Okra..	kg............	20%	Free (A, AU, BH, CA, CL, CO, E, IL, JO, KR, MA, MX, OM, P, PA, PE, SG)	50%
0709.99.30	00	Fiddlehead greens..........................	kg............	8%	Free (A+, AU, BH, CA, CL, CO, D, E, IL, JO, KR, MA, MX, OM, P, PA, PE, SG)	20%
0709.99.45	00	Sweet corn......................................	kg............	21.3%	Free (AU, BH, CA, CL, CO, D, E, IL, JO, KR, MA, MX, P, PA, PE, SG) 4.2% (OM)	50%
0709.99.90	00	Other...	kg............	20%	Free (A+, BH, CA, CL, CO, D, E, IL, JO, KR, MA, MX, OM, P, PA, PE, SG) 6.5% (AU)	50%

(Another) Exam Example of GRI 1 (classifying "parts" of machines)

(Exam Question) What is the CLASSIFICATION for a submersible pump o-ring? The o-ring is made of vulcanized rubber and for use within a saltwater submersible pump.

A.	4016.93.1010	Other articles of vulcanized rubber other than hard rubber>>Other>>Gaskets, washers, and other seals>>Of a kind used in the automotive goods of chapter 87>>O-rings
B.	4016.93.5010	Other articles of vulcanized rubber other than hard rubber>>Other>>Gaskets, washers, and other seals>>Other>>O-rings
C.	4016.93.5050	Other articles of vulcanized rubber other than hard rubber>>Other>>Gaskets, washers, and other seals>>Other>>Other
D.	8413.70.2004	Pumps for liquids, whether or not fitted with a measuring device; liquid elevators; part thereof>>Other centrifugal pumps>>Other>>Submersible pumps
E.	8413.91.9080	Pumps for liquids, whether or not fitted with a measuring device; liquid elevators; part thereof>>Parts>>Of pumps>>Other>>Other

Note that for classifying "parts of" machinery or electronics; refer to the rules for doing so in the Section Notes and/or Chapter Notes (i.e. classify via GRI 1). **The following note is quite relevant as both Chapters 84 & 85 quite often appear on the exams.**

As per Section XVI (Chapters 84 & 85), Note 2:

2. Subject to note 1 to this section, note 1 to chapter 84 and to note 1 to chapter 85, **parts of machines** (not being parts of the articles of heading 8484, 8544, 8545, 8546 or 8547) **are to be classified according to the following rules:**

(a) Parts which are goods included in any of the headings of chapter 84 or 85 (other than headings 8409, 8431, 8448, 8466, 8473, 8487, 8503, 8522, 8529, 8538 and 8548) **are in all cases to be classified in their respective headings**

... ...

The above note means that, except for the headings listed in the parentheses of both paragraphs (e.g. 8484, 8409, etc.), if the part is described in another chapter or heading in the HTS, then classify using that ("respective") heading, and do not classify as a "part of" the machine, electronic device, etc.

The item in question is a simple rubber o-ring for use with a submersible pump. Per the above-mentioned Section Note, if o-rings are provided for in another Chapter/Heading, then we'll use that classification, instead of classifying the o-ring as a part of a pump.

The HTSUS does indeed describe "O-rings", in multiple choices "A" and "B". So, we'll disregard the parts of pump classification "E". "A", however, is for O-rings for use in automobiles, and may be disregarded. "B" is the correct answer.

✓ **Just a side note:** An "O-ring" is simply a circular gasket (for creating a water-tight seal, for example) with a round cross-section.

HTS Classification Tips — Study Guide

Heading/ Subheading	Stat Suf- fix	Article Description	Unit of Quantity	Rates of Duty General	Rates of Duty Special	2
4016		Other articles of vulcanized rubber other than hard rubber:				
4016.10.00	00	Of cellular rubber...	X	Free		25%
		Other:				
4016.91.00	00	Floor coverings and mats...	X	2.7% 1/	Free (A,AU,BH,B, CA,CL,CO,E,IL, JO,KR,MA, MX,OM,P, PA,PE,SG)	40%
4016.92.00	00	Erasers...	X	4.2% 2/	Free (A,AU,BH, CA,CL,CO,E,IL, JO,KR,MA, MX,OM,P, PA,PE,SG)	35%
4016.93		Gaskets, washers and other seals:				
4016.93.10		Of a kind used in the automotive goods of chapter 87...		2.5%	Free (A,AU,BH,B, CA,CL,CO,E,IL, JO,KR,MA, MX,OM,P, PA,PE,SG)	25%
	10	O-Rings...	kg			
	20	Oil seals...	No. kg			
	50	Other...	kg			
4016.93.50		Other...		2.5%	Free (A,AU,BH,C, CA,CL,CO,E,IL, JO,KR,MA, MX,OM,P, PA,PE,SG)	25%
	10	O-Rings...	kg			
	20	Oil seals...	No. kg			
	50	Other...	kg			
4016.94.00	00	Boat or dock fenders, whether or not inflatable...	X	4.2%	Free (A,AU,BH, CA,CL,CO,E,IL, JO,KR,MA, MX,OM,P, PA,PE,SG)	80%
4016.95.00	00	Other inflatable articles...	X	4.2%	Free (A,AU,BH, CA,CL,CO,E,IL, JO,KR,MA, MX,OM,P, PA,PE,SG)	25%

HTS Classification Tips   Study Guide

Exam Example of GRI 2(a)
"Unfinished items are classified as if finished (if unfinished has essential character of finished)."

(Exam Question)

A shipment arrives at the port of Champlain, New York, destined for your client, Ice Jewels, located in Burlington, Vermont. The exporter is located in Ottawa, Canada. The merchandise is invoiced as unfinished jewelry boxes. Examination of the load reveals 1,000 boxes (without lids) that are lined with red velvet fabric, 2,000 small steel hinges (2 per box), 1,000 carved wooden lids. You contact your client, who states that he ordered jewelry boxes from the Ottawa company, but had them shipped down unassembled, because of a rush order he received. The correct classification for this merchandise is:

A) Wooden box bottoms-4420.90.80, carved lids-4421.90.94, hinges-8302.10.90.

B) Wooden box bottoms-4420.90.65, carved lids-4421.90.98, hinges-8302.10.90

C) Wooden bottoms and lids-4421.90.98, hinges-8302.10.90

D) 4420.90.65   Wood marquetry and inlaid wood; caskets and cases for jewelry or cutlery and similar articles, of wood; statuettes and other ornaments, of wood; wooden articles of furniture not falling within chapter 94>>Other>>Jewelry boxes, silverware chests, cigar and cigarette boxes, microscope cases, tool or utensil cases and similar boxes, cases and chests, all the foregoing of wood>>Other>>Lined with textile fabrics

E) 4202.39.20   Trunks, suitcases, vanity cases, attache cases, briefcases, school satchels, spectacle cases, binocular cases, camera cases, musical instrument cases, gun cases, holsters and similar containers; … …>>Articles of a kind normally carried in the pocket or in the handbag>>Other>>Of material (other than leather, composition leather, sheeting of plastics, textile materials, vulcanized fiber or paperboard) wholly or mainly covered with paper>>Of wood

 Here's an easy one! Should the shipment be classified as jewelry boxes, or should each separate component of the boxes be classified separately? Remember that as per GRI 2(a):

"Any reference in a heading to an article shall be taken to include a reference to that article incomplete or unfinished, provided that, as entered, the incomplete or unfinished article has the essential character of the complete or finished article. It shall also include a reference to that article complete or finished (or failing to be classified as complete or finished by virtue of this rule) entered unassembled or disassembled".

In other words, if an unfinished, unassembled, or incomplete item still manages to maintain the essential character (in name and in general) of the item as if it were finished, then the unfinished item should be classified just as the finished item would. So, in terms of the jewelry box in question, although the box is unassembled, it is still considered, for all intents and purposes, to be a jewelry box. Therefore, by application of GRI 2(a), and noting that "jewelry boxes" are provided for in the classification description, we may deduce that the correct answer is "D".

✓ **Note:** The HTS numbers used in this exam question are shortened to 8 digits (instead of the complete 10 digits). The customs broker exam classification questions are occasionally abbreviated this way, possibly in an attempt to simplify things.

Heading/ Subheading	Stat. Suffix	Article Description	Unit of Quantity	Rates of Duty General	Rates of Duty 1 Special	Rates of Duty 2
4419.00		Tableware and kitchenware, of wood:				
4419.00.40	00	Forks and spoons.............	X.......	5.3%	Free (A, AU, BH, CA, CL, CO, E, IL, JO, KR, MA, MX, OM, P, PA, PE, SG)	33 1/3%
4419.00.80	00	Other.............	X.......	3.2%	Free (A, AU, BH, CA, CL, CO, E, IL, JO, KR, MA, MX, OM, P, PA, PE, SG)	33 1/3%
4420		Wood marquetry and inlaid wood; caskets and cases for jewelry or cutlery and similar articles, of wood; statuettes and other ornaments, of wood; wooden articles of furniture not falling within chapter 94:				
4420.10.00	00	Statuettes and other ornaments, of wood.............	X.......	3.2%	Free (A, AU, BH, CA, CL, CO, E, IL, JO, KR, MA, MX, OM, P, PA, PE, SG)	33 1/3%
4420.90		Other: Jewelry boxes, silverware chests, cigar and cigarette boxes, microscope cases, tool or utensil cases and similar boxes, cases and chests, all the foregoing of wood:				
4420.90.20	00	Cigar and cigarette boxes.............	No.......	Free		60%
		Other:				
4420.90.45	00	Not lined with textile fabrics.............	No.......	4.3%	Free (A, AU, BH, CA, CL, CO, E, IL, JO, KR, MA, MX, OM, P, PA, PE, SG)	33 1/3%
4420.90.65	00	Lined with textile fabrics.............	kg....... No.	Free		11¢/kg + 20%
4420.90.80	00	Other.............	X.......	3.2%	Free (A, AU, BH, CA, CL, CO, E, IL, JO, KR, MA, MX, OM, P, PA, PE, SG)	33 1/3%

HTS Classification Tips   Study Guide

Exam Example of GRI 2(b)

"Mixtures may be implied (unless otherwise prohibited in the headings or notes). Go to GRI 3."

(Exam Question)

What is the CLASSIFICATION for dried and prepared seaweed from Korea? The edible food is made from raw kelp-type seaweed that is filtered for impurities, pressed, formed into square sheets, dried, and finally roasted and seasoned with sesame oil, salt, MSG, and soy sauce.

A.	1212.21.0000	Locust beans, seaweeds and other algae … of a kind used primarily for human consumption, not elsewhere specified or included>>Seaweeds and other algae>>Fit for human consumption
B.	1212.29.0000	Locust beans, seaweeds and other algae … of a kind used primarily for human consumption, not elsewhere specified or included>>Seaweeds and other algae>>Other
C.	2008.99.6100	Fruit, nuts and other edible parts of plants, otherwise prepared or preserved, whether or not containing added sugar or other sweetening matter or spirit, not elsewhere specified or included>>Other>>Other>>Soybeans
D.	2008.99.9090	Fruit, nuts and other edible parts of plants, otherwise prepared or preserved, whether or not containing added sugar or other sweetening matter or spirit, not elsewhere specified or included>>Other>>Other>>Other>>Other
E.	2103.10.0000	Sauces and preparations therefore: mixed condiments and mixed seasonings; mustard flour and meal and prepared mustard>>Soy sauce

 Simply stated, GRI 2(b) says that an item may be classifiable under a single heading/classification even if the item is combined with other substances.

In other words, mixtures may be implied (unless otherwise prohibited in the section notes, chapter notes, and headings). For the sake of demonstrating this rule, we'll go ahead and disclose that multiple choice "D" is the correct classification for "prepared" edible seaweed.

The dried seaweed snack in question contains, in addition to seaweed, a multitude of other substances (i.e. sesame oil, salt, MSG, and soy sauce). So, can it still be classified as seaweed? Yes, and that is the main point of this exam problem. As per GRI 2(b), these additional ingredients are inconsequential to the nature of the item. This should be further confirmed by going to GRI 3, though for the purpose of explaining the GRI 2(b), we can digress at this point.

✓ **Note:** The other multiple choices may be addressed as per the following. Multiple choices "C" and "E" are the classifications for prepared soybeans and soy sauce, respectively. Both "A" and "B" are located within the heading 1212, which does include items such as seaweed, though ONLY IF the item to be classified is "not elsewhere specified or included" in the HTSUS. However, the item in question IS INDEED (though somewhat vaguely) described under heading 2008, which includes "prepared" plant food items. Prepared "Seaweed" is not specifically provided for in heading 2008, so it is thus classified, as customs brokers commonly say, "other, other". Once again, "D" is the correct answer.

Heading/ Subheading	Stat Suffix	Article Description	Unit of Quantity	Rates of Duty		
				1		2
				General	Special	
2008 (con.)		Fruit, nuts and other edible parts of plants, otherwise prepared or preserved, whether or not containing added sugar or other sweetening matter or spirit, not elsewhere specified or included (con.):				
		Other, including mixtures other than those of subheading 2008.19 (con.):				
2008.99 (con.)		Other (con.):				
2008.99.40	00	Mangoes.............................	kg......	1.5¢/kg	Free (A,AU,BH,CA, CL,CO,E,IL,JO, KR,MA,MX,OM,P, PA,PE,SG)	33¢/kg
		Papayas:				
2008.99.45	00	Pulp.............................	kg......	14%	Free (A,AU,BH,CA, CL,CO,E,IL,JO, MA,MX,OM,P,PA, PE,SG) 5.6% (KR)	35%
2008.99.50	00	Other.............................	kg......	1.8%	Free (A,AU,BH,CA, CL,CO,E,IL,JO, KR,MA,MX,OM,P, PA,PE,SG)	35%
2008.99.60	00	Plums (including prune plums and sloes)............................	kg......	11.2%	Free (A+,AU,BH, CA,CL,CO,D,E, IL,JO,KR,MX, OM,P,PA,PE,SG) 1.1% (MA)	35%
2008.99.61	00	Soybeans........................	kg......	3.8%	Free (A,AU,BH,CA, CL,CO,E,IL,JO, KR,MA,MX,OM,P, PA,PE,SG)	35%
2008.99.63	00	Sweet ginger.....................	kg......	4.4%	Free (A,AU,BH,CA, CL,CO,E,IL,JO, KR,MA,MX,OM,P, PA,PE,SG)	35%
2008.99.65	00	Cassava (manioc)................	kg......	7.9%	Free (A,AU,BH,CA, CL,CO,E,IL,JO, MA,MX,OM,P,PA, PE,SG) 3.1% (KR)	35%
		Chinese water chestnuts:				
2008.99.70	00	Frozen........................	kg......	11.2%	Free (A+,AU,BH, CA,CL,CO,D,E, IL,JO,MX,OM,P, PA,PE,SG) 1.1% (MA) 6.4% (KR)	35%
2008.99.71		Other.........................		Free		35%
	10	Sliced......................	kg			
	20	Whole......................	kg			
		Other:				
2008.99.80	00	Pulp............................	kg......	9.6%	Free (A*,AU,BH, CA,CL,CO,E,IL, JO,KR,MA,MX, OM,P,PA,PE,SG)	35%
2008.99.90		Other.........................		6%	Free (A,AU,BH,CA, CL,CO,E,IL,JO, KR,MA,MX,OM,P, PA,PE,SG)	35%
	10	Bean cake, bean stick, miso and similar products......................	kg			
	90	Other.........................	kg			

HTS Classification Tips — Study Guide

Exam Example of GRI 3(a)

"Specific HTS heading/description preferred (over less descriptive), for prima facie items."

(Exam Question) What is the classification for a diffusing apparatus used for the commercial extraction of sugar juice?

A.	8419.40.0040	Machinery, plant or laboratory equipment, whether or not electrically heated ... ..., for the treatment of materials by a process involving a change of temperature such as heating, cooking, roasting, distilling, rectifying, sterilizing, pasteurizing, steaming, drying, evaporating, vaporizing, condensing or cooling, other than machinery or plant of a kind used for domestic purposes; instantaneous or storage water heaters, nonelectric; parts thereof>>Distilling or rectifying plant>>For food and beverages
B.	8421.22.0000	Centrifuges, including centrifugal dryers; filtering or purifying machinery and apparatus, for liquids or gases; parts thereof>>Filtering or purifying machinery and apparatus for liquids>>For filtering or purifying beverages other than water
C.	8435.10.0000	Presses, crushers and similar machinery, used in the manufacture of wine, cider, fruit juices or similar beverages; parts thereof>>Machinery
D.	8438.30.0000	Machinery, not specified or included elsewhere in this chapter, for the industrial preparation or manufacture of food or drink, other than machinery for the extraction or preparation of animal or fixed vegetable fats or oils; parts thereof>>Machinery for sugar manufacture
E.	8509.40.0030	Electromechanical domestic appliances, with self-contained electric motor, other than vacuum cleaners of heading 8508; parts thereof>>Food grinders, processors and mixes; fruit or vegetable juice extractors>>Juice extractors

The item in question is a commercial sugar juice extractor. To begin with, by application of GRI 1, let's disregard multiple choices "A" and "E", as both headings 8419 and 8509 state in their article descriptions that the machines classified therein are for "domestic" purposes/appliances (i.e. not commercial).

Now, since the item in question is a prima facie item (i.e. classifiable under more than one heading), we first try to apply GRI 3(a), which says to select the most specific description. "D", which is the classification for machinery for "sugar manufacture" is relatively the most descriptive. "B" and "C", which are the classifications for machines for filtering juices, and for juice presses, respectively, are relatively less descriptive, AND each just potentially refers to part of the process of sugar manufacturing. Furthermore, Chapter 84, Note 2 (see below) makes reference that heading 8438 is for "sugar juice extraction". The correct answer is "D".

Heading 8419 does not, however, cover:

... ...

(c) Diffusing apparatus for sugar juice extraction (heading 8438);

✓ **Just a Side Note:** The sugar (cane) manufacturing process (among others steps) washing, crushing, extracting, filtering, evaporating, centrifuging, and drying.

Heading/ Subheading	Stat. Suffix	Article Description	Unit of Quantity	Rates of Duty General	Rates of Duty 1 Special	Rates of Duty 2
8438		Machinery, not specified or included elsewhere in this chapter, for the industrial preparation or manufacture of food or drink, other than machinery for the extraction or preparation of animal or fixed vegetable fats or oils; parts thereof:				
8438.10.00		Bakery machinery and machinery for the manufacture of macaroni, spaghetti or similar products............	....	Free		35%
	10	Bakery machinery...	No.			
	90	Other...	No.			
8438.20.00	00	Machinery for the manufacture of confectionery, cocoa or chocolate..	No............	Free		35%
8438.30.00	00	Machinery for sugar manufacture...............................	No............	Free		Free
8438.40.00	00	Brewery machinery..	No............	2.3%	Free (A, AU, BH, CA, CL, CO, E, IL, JO, KR, MA, MX, OM, P, PA, PE, SG)	35%
8438.50.00		Machinery for the preparation of meat or poultry...............	....	2.8%	Free (A, AU, BH, CA, CL, CO, E, IL, JO, KR, MA, MX, OM, P, PA, PE, SG)	35%
	10	Meat- and poultry-packing plant machinery...............	No.			
	90	Other...	No.			
8438.60.00	00	Machinery for the preparation of fruits, nuts or vegetables..	No............	Free		35%
8438.80.00	00	Other machinery..	No............	Free		40%
8438.90		Parts:				
8438.90.10	00	Of machinery for sugar manufacture............................	X............	Free		Free
8438.90.90		Other...	....	2.8%	Free (A, AU, BH, CA, CL, CO, E, IL, JO, KR, MA, MX, OM, P, PA, PE, SG)	35%
	15	Of bakery machinery and machinery for the manufacture of macaroni, spaghetti or similar products...	X			
	30	Of machinery for the manufacture of confectionery, cocoa or chocolate...	X			
	60	Of machinery for the preparation of meat or poultry..	X			
	90	Other...	X			

Exam Example of GRI 3(b)

Essential character of item determines HTS# (if unclassifiable by 3(a)), for prima facie items.

(Question) What is the CLASSIFICATION for a woven cotton baseball cap with detachable sunglasses attached under the bill of the cap?

A. 6505.90.2590   Hats and other headgear, knitted or crocheted, or made up from lace, felt or other textile fabric, in the piece (but not in strips), whether or not lined or trimmed; ... ... >>Other>>Of cotton, flax or both>>Not knitted>>Other>>Other

B. 9004.10.0000   Spectacles, goggles and the like, corrective, protective or other>>Sunglasses

C. 6505.90.0800   Hats and other headgear, knitted or crocheted, or made up from lace, felt or other textile fabric, in the piece (but not in strips), whether or not lined or trimmed; ... ... >>Other>>Felt hats and other felt headgear ... ... >>Other

D. 9004.90.0000   Spectacles, goggles and the like, corrective, protective or other>>Other

E. 9003.19.0000   Frames and mountings for spectacles, goggles or the like, and parts thereof>>Frames and mountings>>Of other materials

Here's a great example of a prima facie item (i.e. an item classifiable under more than one heading). The item is a cotton woven (i.e. not knitted) baseball cap with detachable sunglasses. First off, we're unable to classify via GRI 3(a), which says to choose the most descriptive heading, as all the headings presented here only refer to parts (i.e. either cap or sunglasses) of the item. So, next we have to try to classify by using GRI 3(b).

Accordingly, as per GRI 3(b), we try to classify based on the "essential character" of the item. It would be reasonable to say that the baseball cap ("A") gives the item its essential character, and that the detachable sunglasses ("B") do not give the item its essential character. Therefore, the correct answer and classification is "A".

Heading/ Subheading	Stat. Suffix	Article Description	Unit of Quantity	Rates of Duty		
				1		2
				General	Special	
6505		Hats and other headgear, knitted or crocheted, or made up from lace, felt or other textile fabric, in the piece (but not in strips), whether or not lined or trimmed; hair-nets of any material, whether or not lined or trimmed:				
6505.10.00	00	Hair-nets	kg	9.4%	Free (A,AU,BH,CA, CL,E,IL,J,JO, MX, SG) 7.3% (MA) 7.5% (P)	90%
6505.90		Other: Felt hats and other felt headgear, made from the hat bodies, hoods or plateaux of heading 6501, whether or not lined or trimmed:				
6505.90.04		Of fur felt		Free		$16/doz. + 25%
	10	For men or boys	doz. kg			
	50	Other	doz. kg			
6505.90.08	00	Other	No. kg	13.5¢/kg + 6.3% + 1.9¢/article	Free (AU,BH,CA, IL,JO,MX, P,SG) 10.5¢/kg + 4.8% + 1.4¢/article (MA)	88.2¢/kg + 55% + 12.5¢/ article
		Other: Of cotton, flax or both:				
6505.90.15		Knitted		7.9%	Free (AU,BH,CA, CL,E*,IL,JO, MX,P,SG) 6.2% (MA)	45%
		Of cotton:				
	15	For babies (239)	doz. kg			
	25	Other: Visors, and other headgear which provides no covering for the crown of the head (359)	doz. kg			
	40	Other (359)	doz. kg			
	60	Other (859)	doz. kg			
6505.90.20		Not knitted: Certified hand-loomed and folklore products; and headwear of cotton		7.5%	Free (AU,BH,CA, E*,IL,J*,JO, MX,P,SG) 5.9% (MA)	37.5%
	30	For babies (239)	doz. kg			
	60	Other (359)	doz. kg			
6505.90.25		Other		7.5%	Free (AU,BH,CA, CL,E*,IL,JO, MX,P,SG) 5.9% (MA)	37.5%
	45	Visors, and other headgear of cotton which provides no covering for the crown of the head (359)	doz. kg			
	90	Other (859)	doz. kg			

Exam Example of GRI 3(c)

"Last in order HTS# shall be used (if item cannot be classified by 3(a) or by 3(b)), for prima facie items."

(Question)

Which of the following HTS headings should be used in classifying the following hairdressing set?

Towel classified in HTS heading 6302
Shampoo classified in HTS heading 3305
Hair gel classified in HTS heading 3305
Brush classified in HTS heading 9603
Comb classified in HTS heading 9615
Hair dryer classified in HTS heading 8516
Leather case to hold the above items classified in HTS heading 4202

A. 6302
B. 3305
C. 9615
D. 8516
E. 4202

The format of this particular previous exam question provides an easy-to-understand example of applying GRI 3(c).

First, note that the item, a hairdressing set, is prima facie (i.e. classifiable under more than one heading) as it contains 7 different components. No single classification specifically provides for a "hairdressing set" so we cannot classify by GRI 3(a). Further, no single classification clearly imparts the essential character of the set, so we cannot classify by GRI 3(b). Therefore, we classify based on last option GRI 3(c), which says to classify the prima facie item by selecting the heading/classification that occurs numerically last. 9615 is highest number here, so we conclude that the correct answer is "C".

Heading/ Subheading	Stat. Suf- fix	Article Description	Unit of Quantity	Rates of Duty General	Rates of Duty Special	Rates of Duty 2
9615		Combs, hair-slides and the like; hairpins, curling pins, curling grips, hair-curlers and the like, other than those of heading 8516, and parts thereof:				
		Combs, hair-slides and the like:				
9615.11		Of hard rubber or plastics:				
		Combs:				
9615.11.10	00	Valued not over $4.50 per gross..................	gross.......	14.4¢/gross + 2%	Free (A, AU, BH, CA, CL, CO, E, IL, JO, KR, MA, MX, OM, P, PA, PE, SG)	$1.44/gross + 25%
		Valued over $4.50 per gross:				
9615.11.20	00	Of hard rubber........................	gross.......	5.2%	Free (A, AU, BH, CA, CL, CO, E, IL, JO, KR, MA, MX, OM, P, PA, PE, SG)	36%
9615.11.30	00	Other..........................	gross.......	28.8¢/gross + 4.6%	Free (A, AU, BH, CA, CL, CO, E, IL, JO, KR, MA, MX, OM, P, PA, PE, SG)	$2.88/gross + 35%
		Other:				
9615.11.40	00	Not set with imitation pearls or imitation gemstones.................	X.............	5.3%	Free (A, AU, BH, CA, CL, CO, E, IL, JO, KR, MA, MX, OM, P, PA, PE, SG)	80%
9615.11.50	00	Other..........................	X.............	Free		110%
9615.19		Other:				
		Combs:				
9615.19.20	00	Valued not over $4.50 per gross..................	gross.......	9.7¢/gross + 1.3%	Free (A, AU, BH, CA, CL, CO, E, IL, JO, KR, MA, MX, OM, P, PA, PE, SG)	$1.44/gross + 25%
9615.19.40	00	Valued over $4.50 per gross...................	gross.......	28.8¢/gross + 4.6%	Free (A, AU, BH, CA, CL, CO, E, IL, JO, KR, MA, MX, OM, P, PA, PE, SG)	$2.88/gross + 35%
9615.19.60	00	Other..........................	X.............	11%	Free (A, AU, BH, CA, CL, CO, E, IL, JO, MA, MX, OM, P, PA, PE, SG) 5.5% (KR)	110%

HTS Classification Tips   Study Guide

(ANOTHER) Exam Example of GRI 3(c)

"Last in order HTS# shall be used (if item cannot be classified by 3(a) or by 3(b)) for prima facie items."

(Question)

What is the CLASSIFICATION for a high-end youth fishing combo set composed of 1 fishing rod, 1 fishing reel, and 1 snelled fish hook? All three articles are packaged together, though they are not attached within the clear plastic packaging, and are all made in Japan. The fishing set is intended for freshwater use and is marketed as a "set" by the manufacturer. The value of the rod is $50 USD. The value of the reel is $50 USD. The value of the hook is $1 USD.

A.	9507.10.0040	Fishing rods, fish hooks and other line fishing tackle; ...; parts and accessories thereof>>Fishing rods and parts and accessories thereof>>Fishing rods
B.	9507.10.0080	Fishing rods, fish hooks and other line fishing tackle; ...; parts and accessories thereof>>Fishing rods and parts and accessories thereof>>Parts and accessories
C.	9507.20.4000	Fishing rods, fish hooks and other line fishing tackle; ...; parts and accessories thereof>>Fish hooks, whether or not snelled>>Snelled hooks
D.	9507.30.6000	Fishing rods, fish hooks and other line fishing tackle; ...; parts and accessories thereof>>Fishing reels and parts and accessories thereof>>Fishing reels>>Valued over $8.45 each
E.	9507.90.8000	Fishing rods, fish hooks and other line fishing tackle; ...; parts and accessories thereof>>Other>>Other, including parts and accessories>>Other, including parts and accessories

 The item in question is "Prima Facie" (i.e. classifiable under two or more different headings). There are three distinct items (rod, reel, & hook) within the fishing combo set, and they are represented by multiple choices "A", "D", and "C", respectively.

Each item is specifically provided for within the HTSUS, though all refer to only part of the item. Thus, the set cannot be classified under GRI 3(a). Next, GRI 3(b) says to classify based on the component that gives the set its essential character. The fishing hook definitely does not do this, so we may disregard "C". However, in the case of the fishing rod compared to the fishing reel, neither value nor functionality of either definitively imparts the essential character of the set over the other.

Subsequently we proceed to GRI 3(c), which says to classify based on the classification that (numerically) occurs last. Accordingly, 9507.30.6000 (the reel) occurs in order after 9507.10.0040 (the rod). "D", the reel classification, is the correct answer.

Heading/ Subheading	Stat. Suf- fix	Article Description	Unit of Quantity	Rates of Duty General	Rates of Duty Special	2
9507		Fishing rods, fish hooks and other line fishing tackle; fish landing nets, butterfly nets and similar nets; decoy "birds" (other than those of heading 9208 or 9705) and similar hunting or shooting equipment; parts and accessories thereof:				
9507.10.00		Fishing rods and parts and accessories thereof....		6%	Free (A+,AU,BH, CA,CL,CO,D,E,IL, JO,KR,MA,MX, OM,P,PA,PE,SG)	55%
	40	Fishing rods....	No.			
	80	Parts and accessories....	X			
9507.20		Fish hooks, whether or not snelled:				
9507.20.40	00	Snelled hooks....	X	4%	Free (A,AU,BH,CA, CL,CO,E,IL,JO, KR,MA,MX,OM, P,PA,PE,SG)	55%
9507.20.80	00	Other....	X	4.8%	Free (A,AU,BH,CA, CL,CO,E,IL,JO, KR,MA,MX,OM, P,PA,PE,SG)	45%
9507.30		Fishing reels and parts and accessories thereof: Fishing reels:				
9507.30.20	00	Valued not over $2.70 each....	No.	9.2%	Free (A+,AU,BH, CA,CL,CO,D,E,IL, JO,KR,MA,MX, OM,P,PA,PE,SG)	55%
9507.30.40	00	Valued over $2.70 but not over $8.45 each....	No.	24¢ each	Free (A+,AU,BH, CA,CL,CO,D,E,IL, JO,KR,MA,MX, OM,P,PA,PE,SG)	55%
9507.30.60	00	Valued over $8.45 each....	No.	3.9%	Free (A,AU,BH,CA, CL,CO,E,IL,JO, KR,MA,MX,OM, P,PA,PE,SG)	55%
9507.30.80	00	Parts and accessories....	X	5.4%	Free (A,AU,BH,CA, CL,CO,E,IL,JO, KR,MA,MX,OM, P,PA,PE,SG)	55%
9507.90		Other:				
9507.90.20	00	Fishing line put up and packaged for retail sale....	X	3.7%	Free (A,AU,BH,CA, CL,CO,E,IL,JO, KR,MA,MX,OM, P,PA,PE,SG)	65%
9507.90.40	00	Fishing casts or leaders....	doz.	5.6%	Free (A,AU,BH,CA, CL,CO,E,,IL, JO,KR,MA,MX, OM,P,PA,PE,SG)	55%
9507.90.60	00	Fish landing nets, butterfly nets and similar nets....	No.	5%	Free (A,AU,BH,CA, CL,CO,E,IL,JO, KR,MA,MX,OM, P,PA,PE,SG)	40%
		Other, including parts and accessories:				
9507.90.70	00	Artificial baits and flies....	doz.	9%	Free (A+,AU,BH, CA,CL,CO,D,E,IL, JO,KR,MA,MX, OM,P,PA,PE,SG)	55%
9507.90.80	00	Other, including parts and accessories....	X	9%	Free (A,AU,BH,CA, CL,CO,E,IL,JO, KR,MA,MX,OM, P,PA,PE,SG)	55%
9508		Merry-go-rounds, boat-swings, shooting galleries and other fairground amusements; traveling circuses and traveling menageries; traveling theaters; parts and accessories thereof:				
9508.10.00	00	Traveling circuses and traveling menageries; parts and accessories....	X	Free		35%
9508.90.00	00	Other....	X	Free		35%

Exam Example of GRI 4

"Most akin item's HTS# is to be used (if not classifiable by the preceding rules)."

(Question)

What is the CLASSIFICATION for a "dummy launcher"? The dummy launcher is a stationary device that uses a .22 caliber blank to launch a bird dummy (not included with item) in the air from the ground for the purpose of training hunting dogs.

A. 9303.90.4000		Other firearms and similar devices which operate by the firing of an explosive charge (for example, sporting shot- guns and rifles, muzzle-loading firearms, Very pistols and other devices designed to project only signal flares, pistols and revolvers for firing blank ammunition, captive-bolt humane killers, line-throwing guns)>>Other>>Pistols and revolvers designed to fire only blank cartridges or blank ammunition
B. 9303.90.8000		Other firearms and similar devices which operate by the firing of an explosive charge (for example, sporting shot- guns and rifles, muzzle-loading firearms, Very pistols and other devices designed to project only signal flares, pistols and revolvers for firing blank ammunition, captive-bolt humane killers, line-throwing guns)>>Other>>Other
C. 9304.00.4000		Other arms (for example, spring, air or gas guns and pistols, truncheons), excluding those of heading 9307>>Pistols, rifles and other guns which eject missiles by release of compressed air or gas, or by the release of a spring mechanism or rubber held under tension>>Other
D. 9503.00.0090		Tricycles, scooters, pedal cars and similar wheeled toys; dolls' carriages; dolls, other toys; reduced-scale ("scale") models and similar recreational models, working or not; puzzles of all kinds; parts and accessories thereof>>Other
E. 9506.99.6080		Articles and equipment for general physical exercise, gymnastics, athletics, other sports (including table-tennis) or outdoor games, not specified or included elsewhere in this chapter, swimming pools and wading pools; parts and accessories thereof>>Other>>Other>>Other>>Other

 The item in question, a dummy launcher, does not appear to be specifically provided for or otherwise described in any of the classification options, nor do the Section or Chapter Notes instruct how they are to be classified (no GRI 1).

Furthermore, the dummy launcher does not appear to be a prima facie (i.e. classifiable under more than one heading) item (no GRI 2(b) & no GRI 3).

Therefore, and as a last resort, we use the classification of the item that is most akin to the item to be classified by applying GRI 4. One could make a reasonable case that "line-throwing guns" are most akin to our dummy launcher. Line-throwing guns are described under multiple choice "B".

Just a Side Note: A "line-throwing gun", as the name suggests, launches a lifeline to a boat or person in distress.

Heading/ Subheading	Stat. Suffix	Article Description	Unit of Quantity	Rates of Duty General	Rates of Duty Special	2
9303		Other firearms and similar devices which operate by the firing of an explosive charge (for example, sporting shot-guns and rifles, muzzle-loading firearms, Very pistols and other devices designed to project only signal flares, pistols and revolvers for firing blank ammunition, captive-bolt humane killers, line-throwing guns):				
9303.10.00	00	Muzzle-loading firearms............	No............	Free		Free
9303.20.00		Other sporting, hunting or target-shooting shotguns, including combination shotgun-rifles..........	....	2.6%	Free (A, AU, BH, CA, CL, CO, E, IL, JO, KR, MA, MX, OM, P, PA, PE, SG)	65%
		Shotguns:				
	20	Autoloading............	No.			
	30	Pump action............	No.			
	40	Over and under............	No.			
	65	Other............	No.			
	80	Combination shotgun-rifles............	No.			
9303.30		Other sporting, hunting or target-shooting rifles:				
9303.30.40		Valued over $25 but not over $50 each............	....	3.8% on the value of the rifle + 10% on the value of the telescopic sight, if any	Free (A, AU, BH, CA, CL, CO, E, IL, JO, KR, MA, MX, OM, P, PA, PE, SG)	65%
	10	Telescopic sights imported with rifles............	No. 1/			
		Rifles:				
	20	Centerfire............	No. 1/			
	30	Rimfire............	No. 1/			
9303.30.80		Other............	....	3.1% on the value of the rifle + 13% on the value of the telescopic sight, if any	Free (A, AU, BH, CA, CL, CO, E, IL, JO, KR, MA, MX, OM, P, PA, PE, SG)	65%
	05	Telescopic sights imported with rifles............	No. 1/			
		Rifles: Centerfire:				
	10	Autoloading............	No. 1/			
		Bolt action:				
	12	Single shot............	No. 1/			
	17	Other............	No. 1/			
	25	Other............	No. 1/			
	30	Rimfire............	No. 1/			
9303.90		Other:				
9303.90.40	00	Pistols and revolvers designed to fire only blank cartridges or blank ammunition............	No............	4.2%	Free (A, AU, BH, CA, CL, CO, E, IL, JO, KR, MA, MX, OM, P, PA, PE, SG)	105%
9303.90.80	00	Other............	No............	Free		27.5%

Exam Example of GRI 5 (a)
"Article-specific cases are classified with item (unless they are 'the item')"

(Question)

What is (are) the classification(s) of a clarinet and its fitted case, with an outer surface of plastic sheeting, imported together from China?

A.	9205.90.4020	Wind musical instruments (for example, keyboard pipe organs, accordions, clarinets, trumpets, bagpipes), other than fairground organs and mechanical street organs>>Other>>Woodwind instruments>>Other>>Clarinets
	AND 9209.99.4040	Parts (for example, mechanisms for music boxes) and accessories (for example, cards, discs and rolls for mechanical instruments) of musical instruments; metronomes, tuning forks and pitch pipes of all kinds>>Other>>Other>>Other>>For other woodwind and brass wind musical instruments>>For woodwind musical instruments
B.	9205.90.4020	Wind musical instruments (for example, keyboard pipe organs, accordions, clarinets, trumpets, bagpipes), other than fairground organs and mechanical street organs>>Other>>Woodwind instruments>>Other>>Clarinets
	AND 9209.99.4080	Parts (for example, mechanisms for music boxes) and accessories (for example, cards, discs and rolls for mechanical instruments) of musical instruments; metronomes, tuning forks and pitch pipes of all kinds>>Other>>Other>>Other>>For other woodwind and brass wind musical instruments>>Other

C. 9205.90.4020 ONLY

D.	9205.90.4020	Wind musical instruments (for example, keyboard pipe organs, accordions, clarinets, trumpets, bagpipes), other than fairground organs and mechanical street organs>>Other>>Woodwind instruments>>Other>>Clarinets
	AND 4202.92.5000	Trunks, suitcases, vanity cases, attaché cases, …, musical instrument cases, …, and similar containers, of leather or of composition leather, of sheeting of plastics, of textile materials, of vulcanized fiber or of paperboard, or wholly or mainly covered with such materials or with paper>>Other>>With outer surface of sheeting of plastic or textile materials>>Musical instrument cases

E. 4202.92.5000 ONLY

 GRI 5(a) states that cases (including musical instrument cases) fitted to contain a specific article shall be classified with such articles, except when such cases give the whole its essential character.

The correct classification for the "clarinet" is 9205.90.4020. The "clarinet case" will definitely NOT BE CLASSIFED SEPARATELY since it is only of any use as a protective container for the clarinet. . "C" is the correct answer.

HTS Classification Tips — Study Guide

Heading/ Subheading	Stat. Suf- fix	Article Description	Unit of Quantity	Rates of Duty General	Rates of Duty Special	2
9205		Wind musical instruments (for example, keyboard pipe organs, accordions, clarinets, trumpets, bagpipes), other than fairground organs and mechanical street organs:				
9205.10.00		Brass-wind instruments............................		2.9%	Free (A,AU,BH,CA, CL,CO,E,IL,JO, KR,MA,MX,OM, P,PA,PE,SG)	40%
	40	Valued not over $10 each....................	No.			
	80	Valued over $10 each........................	No.			
9205.90		Other: Keyboard pipe organs; harmoniums and similar keyboard instruments with free metal reeds:				
9205.90.12	00	Keyboard pipe organs.....................	No.	Free		35%
9205.90.14	00	Other....................................	No.	2.7%	Free (A,AU,BH,CA, CL,CO,E,IL,JO, KR,MA,MX,OM,P, PA,PE,SG)	40%
		Accordions and similar instruments; mouth organs: Accordions and similar instruments:				
9205.90.15	00	Piano accordions.....................	No.	Free		40%
9205.90.18	00	Other..................................	No.	2.6%	Free (A,AU,BH,CA, CL,CO,E,IL,JO, KR,MA,MX,OM, P,PA,PE,SG)	40%
9205.90.19	00	Mouth organs...........................	doz.	Free		40%
		Woodwind instruments:				
9205.90.20	00	Bagpipes.............................	No.	Free		40%
9205.90.40		Other................................		4.9%	Free (A,AU,BH,CA, CL,CO,E,IL,JO, KR,MA,MX,OM, P,PA,PE,SG)	40%
	20	Clarinets............................	No.			
	40	Saxophones.........................	No.			
	60	Flutes and piccolos (except bamboo)...	No.			
	80	Other................................	No.			
9205.90.60	00	Other...................................	No.	Free		40%
9206.00		Percussion musical instruments (for example, drums, xylophones, cymbals, castanets, maracas):				
9206.00.20	00	Drums...................................	No.	4.8%	Free (A,AU,BH,CA, CL,CO,E,IL,JO, KR,MA,MX,OM, P,PA,PE,SG)	40%
9206.00.40	00	Cymbals.................................	No.	Free		40%
9206.00.60	00	Sets of tuned bells known as chimes, peals or carillons...............................	No.	Free		50%
9206.00.80	00	Other....................................	No.	5.3%	Free (A,AU,BH,CA, CL,CO,E,IL,JO, KR,MA,MX,OM, P,PA,PE,SG)	40%

Exam Example of GRI 5 (b)
"Packaging is classified with item (unless it is 'the item')"

(Question)

An importer in the U.S. receives 500 single action economy stopwatches shipped by air from Munich, Germany. The stopwatches are individually packaged in plastic blister packaging for retail sale. Which statement regarding the plastic blister packaging is TRUE?

    A.   The packaging is classified with the stopwatches
    B.   The packaging is classified separately as articles of plastic
    C.   The packaging costs are deducted from the entered value
    D.   The importer's name must be on the packaging
    E.   The manufacturer's name must be on the packaging

Paraphrasing GRI 5(b), packaging used as packaging is to be classified with the goods packaged therein. "A" is the correct answer.

Just a Side Note: Occasionally, the Classification Section of the exam will include a GRI-focused narrative-type question such as this one. These are by far easier and much less time consuming than the traditional Classification Section questions with HTS number lookups.

(This Page Intentionally Left Blank)

Book 1 Part 6

Free Trade Agreements
(FTA's)

In This Part
What kinds of FTA questions & topics appear on the exam?
Table of Special Programs Quick Reference & Guide
Table of Countries and Their Eligible Special Programs
Rules to determine special program eligibility (in general)

The "Free Trade Agreements" portion of the exam is one of the more time-consuming sections of the exam. Free Trade Agreements are unique in that they are explained in length in both the HTSUS (General Notes) AND in the 19 CFR (Part 10). **Bookmark the three quick reference tables on the next three pages as they include important and time-saving information such as each special program's symbol, HTSUS General Note number, starting page number in the HTSUS, MPF & HMF exemption status, corresponding 19 CFR Parts, Tariff Change Rules starting page number in the HTSUS, all countries eligible for which special programs, and each special program countries list.**

What are the Free Trade Agreements and Preferential Trade Programs?

Free Trade Agreements and Preferential Trade Programs are "special programs" in place for the purpose of allowing qualifying products the benefit of duty free (or at least reduced duty) entry into the United States.

What kinds of FTA questions & topics appear on the exam?

- Is this (described) shipment eligible for GSP (or other special program)?
- Is the special program-eligible shipment exempt from the Merchandise Processing Fee?
- Is the percentage of value from beneficiary inputs sufficient to make the item eligible for the special program?
- The certificate of origin must be kept on file / maintained for five years.
- Which of the following countries designated as beneficiaries (a.k.a. signatories or parties to the agreement) of the (named) special program?
- Distinguish between the special program-eligible inputs and ineligible inputs.
- What is the Special Program Indicator (SPI) symbol for the (named) FTA?
- Does the (described) HTSUS tariff number change make the transformed item eligible for the special program?

Just a Side Note: FTA tool at http://export.gov/fta/ftatarifftool/TariffSearch.aspx

SPECIAL PROGRAMS QUICK REFERENCE & GUIDE (Version: 2016 HTSA Basic Edition)

	SPECIAL PROGRAM	ABBREV.	SPI	GN	PG#	PARTIES	Imported	%	MPF	HMF	SEE ALSO	TCR PG#
1	African Growth and Opportunity Act	AGOA	D	16	194	38	Directly	35 ≤			19 CFR 10.211-217	n/a
2	Australia FTA	UAFTA	AU	28	407	1		10 >	EXEMPT	EXEMPT	19 CFR 10.721-741	417
3	Automotive Products	APTA	B	5	16	1		n/a			19 CFR 10.84	n/a
4	Bahrain FTA	UBFTA	BH	30	568	1	Directly	35 ≤	EXEMPT	EXEMPT	19 CFR 10.801-10.827	573
5	Caribbean Basin Economic Recovery Act	CBERA	E, E*	7	17	18	Directly	35 ≤	EXEMPT	EXEMPT	19 CFR 10.191-199	n/a
6	Caribbean Basin Trade Partnership Act	CBTPA	R	17	196	8	Directly	7 >			19 CFR 10.221-237	309
7	Chile FTA	UCFTA	CL	26	301	1		10 >	EXEMPT	EXEMPT	19 CFR 10.401-10.490	n/a
8	Civil Aircraft Agreement on Trade	n/a	C	6	17	all**		n/a	EXEMPT	EXEMPT	19 CFR 10.183	n/a
9	Colombia TPA	COTPA	CO	34	750	1		10 >	EXEMPT	EXEMPT	19 CFR 10.3001-3034	762
10	Dominican Republic-Central America	DR-CAFTA	P, P+	29	480	6		10 >	EXEMPT	EXEMPT	19 CFR 10.581-625	493
11	Generalized System of Preferences	GSP	A, A*, A+	4	10	122		35 ≤	EXEMPT*	EXEMPT*	19 CFR 10.171-178	15
12	Intermediate Chemicals for Dyes (Uruguay round)	n/a	L	n/a	897	all**		n/a	EXEMPT	EXEMPT	n/a	n/a
13	Israel FTA ACT	ILFTA	IL	8	20	3	Directly	35 ≤	EXEMPT	EXEMPT	19 CFR 10.701-712	n/a
14	Jordan FTA ACT	JOFTA	JO	18	198	1	Directly	35 ≥			19 CFR 10.701-712	n/a
15	Korea FTA	UKFTA	KR	33	679	1		10 >	EXEMPT	EXEMPT	19 CFR 10.1001-1034	669
16	Morocco FTA	UMFTA	MA	27	386	1	Directly	35 ≤			19 CFR 10.761-787	391
17	North American Free Trade Agreement	NAFTA	CA, MX	12	22	2		7 >	EXEMPT	EXEMPT	19 CFR 181	32
18	Oman FTA	UOFTA	OM	31	587	1	Directly	35 ≤	EXEMPT	EXEMPT	19 CFR 10.861-890	592
19	Panama TPA	PATPA	PA	35	823	1		10 >	EXEMPT	EXEMPT	19 CFR 10.2001-2034	836
20	Peru TPA	PTPA	PE	32	605	1		10 >	EXEMPT	EXEMPT	19 CFR 10.901-934	618
21	Pharmaceutical Products (Agreement on Trade in)	ATP	K	13	193	all**		n/a	EXEMPT	EXEMPT	HTSUS Pharma Appendix	n/a
22	Singapore FTA	SFTA	SG	25	201	1		10 >	EXEMPT	EXEMPT	19 CFR 10.501-570	220

LEGEND:
GN = HTSUS General Note
PG# = general note for the special program starts on this page number in version of the HTSUS
PARTIES = number of beneficiary countries (not including the U.S.)
IMPORTED: must be imported directly from a beneficiary country to the U.S. to qualify for the special program
% = allowable percentage of originating or non-originating inputs that qualifies or disqualifies the product for the special program
MPF = Merchandise Processing Fee
HMF = Harbor Maintenance Fee
TCR PG# = Tariff Change Requirements starts on this page (also known as product specific rules)

* exemption applies to GSP "least-developed beneficiary countries" (i.e. SPI symbol "A+")
** generally applies to all countries with normal trade relations (NTR) with the U.S. (i.e. other than "Column 2 Countries" Cuba or North Korea)
≤ originating inputs value must be greater than or equal to this percentage
> non-originating inputs value must be less than this percentage

COUNTRIES AND ELIGIBLE SPECIAL PROGRAMS QUICK REFERENCE & GUIDE

Country	Special Program	Country	Special Program	Country	Special Program
Anguilla	GSP	Falkland Islands		Oman	UOFTA
Antigua and Barbuda	CBERA	Fiji	GSP	Pakistan	GSP
Armenia	GSP	Gabon	GSP, AGOA	Panama	PATPA
Aruba	CBERA	Gambia, The	GSP	Papua New Guinea	GSP
Australia	UAFTA	Georgia	GSP	Paraguay	GSP
Azerbaijan	GSP	Ghana	GSP, AGOA	Peru	PTPA
Bahamas	CBERA	Grenada	GSP, CBERA	Philippines	GSP
Bahrain	UBFTA	Guatemala	DR-CAFTA	Pitcairn Islands	GSP
Barbados	CBERA, CBTPA	Guinea	GSP	Republic of Yemen	GSP
Belize	GSP, CBERA, CBTPA	Guinea-Bissau	GSP, AGOA	Rwanda	GSP, AGOA
Benin	GSP, AGOA	Guyana	GSP, CBERA, CBTPA	Saint Helena	GSP
Bhutan	GSP	Haiti	GSP, CBERA, CBTPA	Saint Lucia	GSP, CBERA, CBTPA
Bolivia	GSP	Heard and McDonald Islands	GSP	Saint Vincent/ Grenadines	GSP, CBERA
Bosnia and Herzegovina	GSP	Honduras	DR-CAFTA	Samoa	GSP
Botswana	GSP, AGOA	India	GSP	Sao Tomé and Príncipe	GSP, AGOA
Brazil	GSP	Indonesia	GSP	Senegal	GSP, AGOA
British Indian Ocean Territory	GSP	Iraq	GSP	Serbia	GSP
Burkina Faso	GSP, AGOA	Jamaica	GSP, CBERA, CBTPA	Seychelles	GSP, AGOA
Burundi	GSP	Jordan	GSP, JOFTA	Sierra Leone	GSP, AGOA
Cambodia	GSP	Kazakhstan	GSP	Singapore	SFTA
Cameroon	GSP, AGOA	Kenya	GSP, AGOA	Solomon Islands	GSP
Canada	NAFTA, APTA	Kiribati	GSP	Somalia	GSP
Cape Verde	GSP, AGOA	Korea	UKFTA	South Africa	GSP, AGOA
Central African Republic	GSP	Kosovo	GSP	South Sudan	GSP
Chad	GSP	Kyrgyzstan	GSP	Sri Lanka	GSP
Chile	UCFTA	Lebanon	GSP	St. Kitts and Nevis	CBERA
Christmas Island (Australia)	GSP	Lesotho	GSP, AGOA	Suriname	GSP
Cocos (Keeling) Islands	GSP	Liberia	GSP, AGOA	Swaziland	GSP, AGOA
Colombia	COTPA	Macedonia	GSP	Tanzania	GSP, AGOA
Comoros	GSP, AGOA	Madagascar	GSP, AGOA	Thailand	GSP
Congo (Brazzaville)	GSP, AGOA	Malawi	GSP, AGOA	Timor-Leste	GSP
Congo (Kinshasa)	GSP, AGOA	Maldives	GSP	Togo	GSP, AGOA
Cook Islands	GSP	Mali	GSP, AGOA	Tokelau	GSP
Costa Rica	DR-CAFTA	Mauritania	GSP, AGOA	Tonga	GSP
Côte d'Ivoire	GSP, AGOA	Mauritius	GSP, AGOA	Trinidad and Tobago	CBERA, CBTPA
Curacao	CBERA, CBTPA	Mexico	NAFTA	Tunisia	GSP
Djibouti	GSP, AGOA	Moldova	GSP	Turkey	GSP
Dominica	GSP, CBERA	Mongolia	GSP	Tuvalu	GSP
Dominican Republic	DR-CAFTA	Montenegro	GSP	Uganda	GSP, AGOA
Ecuador	GSP	Montserrat	GSP, CBERA	Ukraine	GSP
Egypt	GSP	Morocco	UMFTA	Uruguay	GSP
El Salvador	DR-CAFTA	Mozambique	GSP, AGOA	Uzbekistan	GSP
Eritrea	GSP	Namibia	GSP, AGOA	Vanuatu	GSP
Ethiopia	GSP, AGOA	Nepal	GSP	Venezuela	GSP
Anguilla	GSP	Netherlands Antilles	CBERA	Virgin Islands, British	GSP, CBERA
Antigua and Barbuda	CBERA	Nicaragua	DR-CAFTA	Wallis and Futuna	GSP, ILFTA
Armenia	GSP	Niger	GSP, AGOA	West Bank and Gaza Strip	GSP
Aruba	CBERA	Nigeria	GSP, AGOA	Western Sahara	GSP
Australia	UAFTA	Niue	GSP	Zambia	GSP, AGOA
Azerbaijan	GSP	Norfolk Island	GSP	Zimbabwe	GSP

Free Trade Agreements — Study Guide

Beneficiary Countries Sorted by Special Program (excludes single-country programs)

GSP	AGOA	CBERA	CBTPA	DR-CAFTA	NAFTA	APTA
Afghanistan+	Angola	Antigua and Barbuda	Barbados	Costa Rica	Canada	Canada
Albania	Benin	Aruba	Belize	Dominican Rep.	Mexico	
Algeria	Botswana	Bahamas	Costa Rica*	El Salvador		
Angola+	Burkina Faso	Barbados	Dominican Republic*	Guatemala		
Anguilla	Cameroon	Belize	El Salvador*	Honduras		
Armenia	Cape Verde	Costa Rica*	Guatemala*	Nicaragua		
Azerbaijan	Central African Rep.*	Curacao	Guyana			
Belize	Chad	Dominica	Haiti			
Benin+	Comoros	Dominican Republic*	Honduras*			
Bhutan+	Congo (Brazzaville)	El Salvador*	Jamaica			
Bolivia	Congo (Kinshasa)	Grenada	Nicaragua*			
Bosnia and Hercegovina	Côte d'Ivoire	Guatemala*	Panama*			
Botswana	Djibouti	Guyana	Saint Lucia			
Brazil	Eritrea*	Haiti	Trinidad and Tobago			
British Indian Ocean Territory	Ethiopia	Honduras*				
Burkina Faso+	Gabon	Jamaica				
Burundi	Ghana	Montserrat				
Cambodia+	Guinea-Bissau	Netherlands Antilles				
Cameroon	Kenya	Nicaragua*				
Cape Verde	Lesotho	Panama*				
Central African Republic+	Liberia	Saint Lucia				
Chad+	Madagascar	Saint Vincent/Grenadines				
Christmas Island (Australia)	Malawi	St. Kitts and Nevis				
Cocos (Keeling) Islands	Mali	Trinidad and Tobago				
Comoros+	Mauritania	Virgin Islands, British				
Congo (Brazzaville)	Mauritius					
Congo (Kinshasa)+	Mozambique					
Cook Islands	Namibia					
Côte d'Ivoire	Niger					
Djibouti	Nigeria					
Dominica	Rwanda					
Ecuador	Sao Tomé and Principe					
Egypt	Senegal					
Eritrea	Seychelles					
Ethiopia+	Sierra Leone					
Falkland Islands (is. Malvinas)	South Africa					
Fiji	Tanzania					
Gabon	Togo					
Gambia, The+	Uganda					
Georgia	Zambia					
Ghana						
Grenada						
Guinea+						
Guinea-Bissau+						
Guyana						
Haiti+						
Heard Island/McDonald is.						
India						
Indonesia						
Iraq						
Jamaica						
Jordan						
Kazakhstan						
Kenya						
Kiribati+						
Kosovo						
Kyrgyzstan						
Lebanon						
Lesotho+						
Liberia+						
Macedonia						
Madagascar+						
Malawi+						
Maldives						
Mali+						
Mauritania+						
Mauritius						
Moldova						
Mongolia						
Montenegro						
Montserrat						
Mozambique+						
Namibia						
Nepal+						
Niger+						
Nigeria						
Niue						
Norfolk Island						
Pakistan						
Papua New Guinea						
Paraguay						
Philippines						
Pitcairn Islands						
Republic of Yemen+						
Rwanda+						
Saint Helena						
Saint Lucia						
Saint Vincent/Grenadines						
Samoa+						
Sao Tomé and Principe+						
Senegal+						
Serbia						
Seychelles						
Sierra Leone+						
Solomon Islands+						
Somalia+						
South Africa						
South Sudan+						
Sri Lanka						
Suriname						
Swaziland						
Tanzania+						
Thailand						
Timor-Leste+						
Togo+						
Tokelau						
Tonga						
Tunisia						
Turkey						
Tuvalu+						
Uganda+						
Ukraine						
Uruguay						
Uzbekistan						
Vanuatu+						
Venezuela						
Virgin Islands, British						
Wallis and Futuna						
West Bank and Gaza Strip						
Western Sahara						
Zambia+						
Zimbabwe						

* former beneficiary countries
+ GSP least-developed beneficiary

Rules to determine special program eligibility (in general*):

1) The product must have the special program indicator (SPI) symbol included in the "Special" subcolumn of the HTSUS column 1, AND

(Example of DR-CAFTA SPI symbol "P" available for food processors as per HTSUS Chapter 85)

Heading/ Subheading	Stat. Suffix	Article Description	Unit of Quantity	Rates of Duty General	Rates of Duty Special	2
8509		Electromechanical domestic appliances, with self-contained electric motor, other than vacuum cleaners of heading 8508; parts thereof:				
8509.40.00		Food grinders, processors and mixers; fruit or vegetable juice extractors............	....	4.2% 1/	Free (A, AU, BH, CA, CL, CO, E, IL, JO, MA, MX, OM, ⓟ PA, PE, SG) 2.1% (KR)	40%

2) The country of origin(s) of the product is listed as a designated beneficiary country, AND

(Snapshot of DR-CAFTA beneficiary countries list per HTSUS GN 29)

DR-CAFTA

(iii) except as provided in individual notes or tariff provisions, the terms "party to the Agreement" and "parties to the Agreement" refer to the following countries: Costa Rica, Dominican Republic, El Salvador, Guatemala, Honduras, Nicaragua or the United States.

3) The product officially qualifies as an "originating good" of the beneficiary country(s), meaning ANY of the following:

a) the product wholly originates from the beneficiary country(s) OR

(Partial excerpt from HTSUS GN 29 definition of a good "wholly obtained or produced")

(i) For purposes of subdivision (b)(i) of this note, the expression "good wholly obtained or produced" means any of the following goods:

(A) plants and plant products harvested or gathered in the territory of one or more of the parties to the Agreement;

(B) live animals born and raised in the territory of one or more of the parties to the Agreement;

b) each non-originating material undergoes a specific change in HTS number OR

(Example of an eligible HTSUS DR-CAFTA Tariff Change Requirement [TCR] range that includes a change to the food processor subheading 8509.40 from any other article subheading)

(n) Change in tariff classification rules.

(A) A change to subheadings 8509.10 through 8509.80 from any other heading;

c) the values attributed to the subject country(s), is within the allowable %

(Excerpt from the HTSUS DR-CAFTA de minimis [i.e. maximum % of non-originating inputs allowed] explanation)

(e) De minimis amounts of nonoriginating materials.

(i) Except as provided in subdivisions (d)(i), (e)(ii) and (m) below, a good that does not undergo a change in tariff classification pursuant to subdivision (n) of this note is an originating good if--

(A) the value of all nonoriginating materials that--

(1) are used in the production of the good, and

(2) do not undergo the applicable change in tariff classification set out in subdivision (n) of this note,

does not exceed 10 percent of the adjusted value of the good;

Note: The above rules for determining special program eligibility are broad in scope. To verify eligibility, refer also to the appropriate HTSUS General Note.

So, for example, the following three shipments would qualify for duty-free treatment under the DR-CAFTA free trade agreement.

Example a) An electronic food grinder is assembled in Costa Rica from materials wholly produced in The Dominican Republic. The food grinder is wholly obtained from and produced by parties to the agreement, and is thus eligible for duty free treatment under the DR-CAFTA.

Example b) An electronic food processor is assembled in El Salvador from electronic components, wholly produced in either Guatemala or China. When assembled into a food processor, the electronic components sourced from China all undergo an HTSUS tariff number change to subheading 8509.40. The food processor's non-originating material underwent a qualifying change in HTS number, and is thus eligible for duty-free treatment under the DR-CAFTA.

Example c) An electronic fruit juice extractor wholly originates in Honduras, except for the unit's specially designed printed circuit board assembly, which is produced in Mexico. The printed circuit board's HTSUS tariff number heading is 8509 (i.e. no tariff change occurs), yet represents only 9 % of the juice extractor's total value. The juice extractor's non-originating material does not exceed 10% of the finished good, and is thus eligible for duty-free treatment under the DR-CAFTA.

Book 1 Part 7

Most Commonly Tested
TITLE 19 CFR

In This Part
Overview of the most commonly tested 19 CFR sections and paragraphs
Organized by frequency of occurrence **for maximum study prioritization!!!**

This section singles out parts, sections, and paragraphs of the 19 CFR that have most often appeared as questions over the last ten exams. It is arranged by frequency of appearances from the past ten exams, and then numerically by CFR Part, Section, and then by Paragraph. Attempt to memorize as much as you can of the major points of this part of the study guide. The more you are able to answer exam questions "on the fly" (i.e. without having to refer to your 19 CFR, HTS, directives, etc.), then the more time you will have to focus on the more time-consuming parts of the exam, especially HTS classification questions.

Most Commonly Tested
TITLE 19 CFR

Part 152.103(a)
CLASSIFICATION AND APPRAISEMENT OF MERCHANDISE>>Valuation of Merchandise>>Transaction value>>Price actually paid or payable

Number of times appearing in last 10 exams: 13
Last appeared in exam: April 2016

The gist of it...
 This paragraph explains that the price actually paid or payable is to be used when determining an import's transaction value, which may be derived by means of additions to or deductions from the invoice value (e.g. deducting freight charges from invoice value, etc.). Several helpful examples are provided as a reference.

Excerpt from 19 CFR...

(a) Price actually paid or payable—(1) General. In determining transaction value, the price actually paid or payable will be considered without regard to its method of derivation. It may be the result of discounts, increases, or negotiations, or may be arrived at by the application of a formula, such as the price in effect on the date of export in the London Commodity Market. The word "payable" refers to a situation in which the price has been agreed upon, but actual payment has not been made at the time of importation. Payment may be made by letters of credit or negotiable instruments and may be made directly or indirectly.

Example 1. In a transaction with foreign Company X, a U.S. firm pays Company X $10,000 for a shipment of meat products, packed ready for shipment to the United States. No selling commission, assist, royalty, or license fee is involved. Company X is not related to the U.S. purchaser and imposes no condition or limitation on the buyer.

The customs value of the imported meat products is $10,000—the transaction value of the imported merchandise.

Example 2. A foreign shipper sold merchandise at $100 per unit to a U.S. importer. Subsequently, the foreign shipper increased its price to $110 per unit. The merchandise was exported after the effective date of the price increase. The invoice price of $100 was the price originally agreed upon and the price the U.S. importer actually paid for the merchandise.

How should the merchandise be appraised?

Actual transaction value of $100 per unit based on the price actually paid or payable.

Example 3. A foreign shipper sells to U.S. wholesalers at one price and to U.S. retailers at a higher price. The shipment undergoing appraisement is a shipment to a U.S. retailer. There are continuing shipments of identical and similar merchandise to U.S. wholesalers.

How should the merchandise be appraised?

Actual transaction value based on the price actually paid or payable by the retailer.

Example 4. Company X in the United States pay $2,000 to Y Toy Factory abroad for a shipment of toys. The $2,000 consists of $1,850 for the toys and $150 for ocean freight and insurance. Y Toy Factory would have *charged Company X $2,200 for the toys; however, because Y owed Company X $350, Y charged only $1,850 for the toys. What is the transaction value?*

The transaction value of the imported merchandise is $2,200, that is, the sum of the $1,850 plus the $350 indirect payment. Because the transaction value excludes C.I.F. charges, the $150 ocean freight and insurance charge is excluded.

Example 5. A seller offers merchandise at $100, less a 2% discount for cash. A buyer remits $98 cash, taking advantage of the cash discount.

The transaction value is $98, the price actually paid or payable.

(2) Indirect payment. An indirect payment would include the settlement by the buyer, in whole or in part, of a debt owed by the seller, or where the buyer receives a price reduction on a current importation as a means of settling a debt owed him by the seller. Activities such as advertising, undertaken by the buyer on his own account, other than those for which an adjustment is provided in §152.103(b), will not be considered an indirect payment to the seller though they may benefit the seller. The costs of those activities will not be added to the price actually paid or payable in determining the customs value of the imported merchandise.

(3) Assembled merchandise. The price actually paid or payable may represent an amount for the assembly of imported merchandise in which the seller has no interest other than as the assembler. The price actually paid or payable in that case will be calculated by the addition of the value of the components and required adjustments to form the basis for the transaction value.

Example 1. The importer previously has supplied an unrelated foreign assembler with fabricated components ready for assembly having a value or cost at the assembler's plant of $1.00 per unit. The importer pays the assembler 50¢ per unit for the assembly. The transaction value for the assembled unit is $1.50.

Example 2. Same facts as Example 1 above except the U.S. importer furnishes to the foreign assembler a tooling assist consisting of a tool acquired by the importer at $1,000. The transportation expenses to the foreign assembler's plant for the tooling assist equal $100. The transaction value for the assembled unit would be $1.50 per unit plus a pro rata share of the tooling assist valued at $1,100.

(4) Rebate. Any rebate of, or other decrease in, the price actually paid or payable made or otherwise effected between the buyer and seller after the date of importation of the merchandise will be disregarded in determining the transaction value under §152.103(b).

(5) Foreign inland freight and other inland charges incident to the international shipment of merchandise—(i) Ex-factory sales. If the price actually paid or payable by the buyer to the seller for the imported merchandise does not include a charge for foreign inland freight and other charges for services incident to the international shipment of merchandise (an ex-factory price), those charges will not be added to the price.

... ...

Most Commonly Tested
TITLE 19 CFR

Part 24.23(c)
CUSTOMS FINANCIAL AND ACCOUNTING PROCEDURE>>Fees for processing merchandise>>Exemptions and limitations

Number of times appearing in last 10 exams: 8
Last appeared in exam: October 2016

The gist of it...
　　This paragraph lists the transactions that are exempt from the Merchandise Processing Fee (MPF), such as most all of the HTSUS Chapter 98 items (e.g. U.S. Goods Returned), multiple Free Trade Agreements, etc.

Excerpt from 19 CFR...

(c) Exemptions and limitations. (1) The ad valorem fee, surcharge, and specific fees provided for under paragraphs (b)(1) and (b)(2) of this section will not apply to:

(i) Except as provided in paragraph (c)(2) of this section, articles provided for in chapter 98, Harmonized Tariff Schedule of the United States (HTSUS; 19 U.S.C. 1202);

(ii) Products of insular possessions of the U.S. (General Note 3(a)(iv), HTSUS);

(iii) Products of beneficiary countries under the Caribbean Basin Economic Recovery Act (General Note 7, HTSUS);

(iv) Products of least-developed beneficiary developing countries (General Note 4(b)(i), HTSUS); and

(v) Merchandise described in General Note 19, HTSUS, merchandise released under 19 U.S.C. 1321, and merchandise imported by mail.

(2) In the case of any article provided for in subheading 9802.00.60 or 9802.00.80, HTSUS:

(i) The surcharge and specific fees provided for under paragraphs (b)(1)(ii) and (b)(2) of this section will remain applicable; and

(ii) The ad valorem fee provided for under paragraph (b)(1)(i) of this section will be assessed only on that portion of the cost or value of the article upon which duty is assessed under subheadings 9802.00.60 and 9802.00.80.

... ...

Most Commonly Tested
TITLE 19 CFR

Part 111.30(d)
CUSTOMS BROKERS>>Duties and Responsibilities of Customs Brokers>>Notification of change of business address, organization name, or location of business records; status report; termination of brokerage business>>Status Report

Number of times appearing in last 10 exams: 8
Last appeared in exam: April 2016

The gist of it...
  This paragraph provides instructions on the customs broker triennial status report. The next status reports are due Feb. 2018 and Feb. 2021.

Excerpt from 19 CFR...

(d) Status report—(1) General. Each broker must file a written status report with Customs on February 1, 1985, and on February 1 of each third year after that date. The report must be accompanied by the fee prescribed in §111.96(d) and must be addressed to the director of the port through which the license was delivered to the licensee (see §111.15). A report received during the month of February will be considered filed timely. No form or particular format is required.

(2) Individual. Each individual broker must state in the report required under paragraph (d)(1) of this section whether he is actively engaged in transacting business as a broker. If he is so actively engaged, he must also:

(i) State the name under which, and the address at which, his business is conducted if he is a sole proprietor;

(ii) State the name and address of his employer if he is employed by another broker, unless his employer is a partnership, association or corporation broker for which he is a qualifying member or officer for purposes of §111.11(b) or (c)(2); and

(iii) State whether or not he still meets the applicable requirements of §111.11 and §111.19 and has not engaged in any conduct that could constitute grounds for suspension or revocation under §111.53.

(3) Partnership, association or corporation. Each corporation, partnership or association broker must state in the report required under paragraph (d)(1) of this section the name under which its business as a broker is being transacted, its business address, the name and address of each licensed member of the partnership or licensed officer of the association or corporation who qualifies it for a license under §111.11(b) or (c)(2), and whether it is actively engaged in transacting business as a broker, and the report must be signed by a licensed member or officer.

(4) Failure to file timely. If a broker fails to file the report required under paragraph (d)(1) of this section by March 1 of the reporting year, the broker's license is suspended by operation of law on that date. By March 31 of the reporting year, the port director will transmit written notice of the suspension to the broker by certified mail, return receipt requested, at the address reflected in Customs records. If the broker files the required report and pays the required fee within 60 calendar days of the date of the notice of suspension, the license will be reinstated. If the broker does not file the required report within that 60-day period, the broker's license is revoked by operation of law without prejudice to the filing of an application for a new license. Notice of the revocation will be published in the Customs Bulletin.

Most Commonly Tested
TITLE 19 CFR

Part 152.103(d)
CLASSIFICATION AND APPRAISEMENT OF MERCHANDISE>>Valuation of Merchandise>>Transaction Value>>Assist

Number of times appearing in last 10 exams: 8
Last appeared in exam: October 2016

The gist of it...
    This paragraph explains methods for and examples of assessing the value for assists. Particularly, the exam often makes reference to the fact that design work done in the U.S. (as opposed to foreign design work) does not count as an assist.

Excerpt from 19 CFR...

(d) Assist. If the value of an assist is to be added to the price actually paid or payable, or to be used as a component of computed value, the port director shall determine the value of the assist and apportion that value to the price of the imported merchandise in the following manner:

(1) If the assist consist of materials, components, parts, or similar items incorporated in the imported merchandise, or items consumed in the production of the imported merchandise, acquired by the buyer from an unrelated seller, the value of the assist is the cost of its acquisition. If the assist were produced by the buyer or a person related to the buyer, its value would be the cost of its production. In either case, the value of the assist would include transportation costs to the place of production.

(2) If the assist consists of tools, dies, molds, or similar items used in the production of the imported merchandise, acquired by the buyer from an unrelated seller, the value of the assist is the cost of its acquisition. If the assist were produced by the buyer or a person related to the buyer, its value would be cost of its production. If the assist has been used previously by the buyer, regardless of whether it had been acquired or produced by him, the original cost of acquisition or production would be adjusted downward to reflect its use before its value could be determined. ... ...

Example 1. A U.S. importer supplied detailed designs to the foreign producer. These designs were necessary to manufacture the merchandise. The U.S. importer bought the designs from an engineering company in the U.S. for submission to his foreign supplier.

Should the appraised value of the merchandise include the value of the assist?

No, design work undertaken in the U.S. may not be added to the price actually paid or payable.

Example 2. A U.S. importer supplied molds free of charge to the foreign shipper. The molds were necessary to manufacture merchandise for the U.S. importer. The U.S. importer had some of the molds manufactured by a U.S. company and others manufactured in a third country.

Should the appraised value of the merchandise include the value of the molds?

Yes. It is an addition required to be made to transaction value.

Most Commonly Tested
TITLE 19 CFR

Part 111.2(a)
CUSTOMS BROKERS>>General Provisions>>License and district permit required>>License

Number of times appearing in last 10 exams: 7
Last appeared in exam: October 2016

The gist of it...
　　This section explicitly describes which "customs-related activities" do (and do not) necessitate the possession of a license.

Excerpt from 19 CFR...

(a) License—(1) General. Except as otherwise provided in paragraph (a)(2) of this section, a person must obtain the license provided for in this part in order to transact customs business as a broker.

(2) Transactions for which license is not required—(i) For one's own account. An importer or exporter transacting customs business solely on his own account and in no sense on behalf of another is not required to be licensed, nor are his authorized regular employees or officers who act only for him in the transaction of such business.

(ii) As employee of broker—(A) General. An employee of a broker, acting solely for his employer, is not required to be licensed where:

(1) Authorized to sign documents. The broker has authorized the employee to sign documents pertaining to customs business on his behalf, and has executed a power of attorney for that purpose. The broker is not required to file the power of attorney with the port director, but must provide proof of its existence to Customs upon request; or

(2) Authorized to transact other business. The broker has filed with the port director a statement identifying the employee as authorized to transact customs business on his behalf. However, no statement will be necessary when the broker is transacting customs business under an exception to the district permit rule.

(B) Broker supervision; withdrawal of authority. Where an employee has been given authority under paragraph (a)(2)(ii) of this section, the broker must exercise sufficient supervision of the employee to ensure proper conduct on the part of the employee in the transaction of customs business, and the broker will be held strictly responsible for the acts or omissions of the employee within the scope of his employment and for any other acts or omissions of the employee which, through the exercise of reasonable care and diligence, the broker should have foreseen. The broker must promptly notify the port director if authority granted to an employee under paragraph (a)(2)(ii) of this section is withdrawn. The withdrawal of authority will be effective upon receipt by the port director.

... ...

Most Commonly Tested
TITLE 19 CFR

Part 111.23(b)
CUSTOMS BROKERS>>Duties and Responsibilities of Customs Brokers>>Retention of records>>Period of retention

Number of times appearing in last 10 exams: 7
Last appeared in exam: October 2016

The gist of it...
    This paragraph simply describes the length of time (generally 5 years) required, for customs brokers' record keeping.

Excerpt from 19 CFR...

(b) Period of retention. The records described in this section, other than powers of attorney, must be retained for at least 5 years after the date of entry. Powers of attorney must be retained until revoked, and revoked powers of attorney and letters of revocation must be retained for 5 years after the date of revocation or for 5 years after the date the client ceases to be an "active client" as defined in §111.29(b)(2)(ii), whichever period is later. When merchandise is withdrawn from a bonded warehouse, records relating to the withdrawal must be retained for 5 years from the date of withdrawal of the last merchandise withdrawn under the entry.

Most Commonly Tested
TITLE 19 CFR

Part 111.45(a) & (b)
CUSTOMS BROKERS>>Duties and Responsibilities of Customs Brokers>>Revocation by operation of law

Number of times appearing in last 10 exams: 7
Last appeared in exam: April 2016

The gist of it...
Although there is an exception request available for the district permit rule, here, the regulations explain that a customs brokerage operation must maintain at least one license holder to avoid revocation of the business' customs license and permit(s).

Excerpt from 19 CFR...

(a) License. If a broker that is a partnership, association, or corporation fails to have, during any continuous period of 120 days, at least one member of the partnership or at least one officer of the association or corporation who holds a valid individual broker's license, that failure will, in addition to any other sanction that may be imposed under this part, result in the revocation by operation of law of the license and any permits issued to the partnership, association, or corporation. The Assistant Commissioner or his designee will notify the broker in writing of an impending revocation by operation of law under this section 30 calendar days before the revocation is due to occur.

(b) Permit. If a broker who has been granted a permit for an additional district fails, for any continuous period of 180 days, to employ within that district (or region, as defined in §111.1, if an exception has been granted pursuant to §111.19(d)) at least one person who holds a valid individual broker's license, that failure will, in addition to any other sanction that may be imposed under this part, result in the revocation of the permit by operation of law.

(c) Notification. If the license or an additional permit of a partnership, association, or corporation is revoked by operation of law under paragraph (a) or (b) of this section, the Assistant Commissioner or his designee will notify the organization of the revocation. If an additional permit of an individual broker is revoked by operation of law under paragraph (b) of this section, the Assistant Commissioner or his designee will notify the broker. Notice of any revocation under this section will be published in the Customs Bulletin.

(d) Applicability of other sanctions. Notwithstanding the operation of paragraph (a) or (b) of this section, each broker still has a continuing obligation to exercise responsible supervision and control over the conduct of its brokerage business and to otherwise comply with the provisions of this part. Any failure on the part of a broker to meet that continuing obligation during the 120 or 180-day period referred to in paragraph (a) or (b) of this section, or during any shorter period of time, may result in the initiation of suspension or revocation proceedings or the assessment of a monetary penalty under subpart D or subpart E of this part.

Most Commonly Tested
TITLE 19 CFR

Part 152.103(b)
CLASSIFICATION AND APPRAISEMENT OF MERCHANDISE>>Valuation of Merchandise>>Transaction value>>Additions to price actually paid or payable

Number of times appearing in last 10 exams: 7
Last appeared in exam: April 2016

The gist of it...
　　This paragraph states that packing costs, selling commissions, assists, royalties, and proceeds to seller are to be added to the transaction value, in order to arrive at the entered value. You just have to remember the acronym "C.R.A.P.P." (Commissions, Royalties, Assists, Packaging, Proceeds).

Excerpt from 19 CFR...

(b) Additions to price actually paid or payable. (1) The transaction value of imported merchandise is the price actually paid or payable for the merchandise when sold for exportation to the United States, plus amounts equal to:

(i) The packing costs incurred by the buyer with respect to the imported merchandise;

(ii) Any selling commission incurred by the buyer with respect to the imported merchandise;

(iii) The value, apportioned as appropriate, of any assist;

(iv) Any royalty or license fee related to the imported merchandise that the buyer is required to pay, directly or indirectly, as a condition of the sale of the imported merchandise for exportation to the United States; and

(v) The proceeds of any subsequent resale, disposal, or use of the imported merchandise that accrue, directly or indirectly, to the seller.

(2) The price actually paid or payable for imported merchandise will be increased by the amounts attributable to the items (and no others) described in paragraphs (b)(1) (i) through (v) of this section to the extent that each amount is not otherwise included within the price actually paid or payable, and is based on sufficient information. If sufficient information is not available, for any reason, with respect to any amount referred to in this section, the transaction value will be treated as one that cannot be determined.

... ...

Most Commonly Tested
TITLE 19 CFR

Part 111.28(b)
CUSTOMS BROKERS>>Duties and Responsibilities of Customs Brokers>>Responsible supervision>>Employee information

Number of times appearing in last 10 exams: 6
Last appeared in exam: October 2016

The gist of it...
   This paragraph outlines the customs broker's reporting requirements for reporting current, new, and terminated employee information to the affected port director(s).

Excerpt from 19 CFR...

(b) Employee information—(1) Current employees—(i) General. Each broker must submit, in writing, to the director of each port at which the broker intends to transact customs business, a list of the names of persons currently employed by the broker at that port. The list of employees must be submitted upon issuance of a permit for an additional district under §111.19, or upon the opening of an office at a port within a district for which the broker already has a permit, and before the broker begins to transact customs business as a broker at the port. For each employee, the broker also must provide the social security number, date and place of birth, current home address, last prior home address, and, if the employee has been employed by the broker for less than 3 years, the name and address of each former employer and dates of employment for the 3-year period preceding current employment with the broker. After the initial submission, an updated list, setting forth the name, social security number, date and place of birth, and current home address of each current employee, must be submitted with the status report required by §111.30(d).

(ii) New employees. In the case of a new employee, the broker must submit to the port director the written information required under paragraph (b)(1)(i) of this section within 10 calendar days after the new employee has been employed by the broker for 30 consecutive days.

(2) Terminated employees. Within 30 calendar days after the termination of employment of any person employed longer than 30 consecutive days, the broker must submit the name of the terminated employee, in writing, to the director of the port at which the person was employed.

(3) Broker's responsibility. Notwithstanding a broker's responsibility for providing the information required in paragraph (b)(1) of this section, in the absence of culpability by the broker, Customs will not hold him responsible for the accuracy of any information that is provided to the broker by the employee.

Most Commonly Tested
TITLE 19 CFR

Part 152.103(j)
CLASSIFICATION AND APPRAISEMENT OF MERCHANDISE>>Valuation of Merchandise>>Transaction value>>Limitations on use of transaction value

Number of times appearing in last 10 exams: 6
Last appeared in exam: October 2014

The gist of it...
   This paragraph lists the types of import transactions that will preclude the importer or broker from using the preferred method of appraisement—the transaction value.

Excerpt from 19 CFR...

(j) Limitations on use of transaction value—(1) In general. The transaction value of imported merchandise will be the appraised value only if:

(i) There are no restrictions on the disposition or use of the imported merchandise by the buyer, other than restrictions which are imposed or required by law, limit the geographical area in which the merchandise may be resold, or do not affect substantially the value of the merchandise;

(ii) The sale of, or the price actually paid or payable for, the imported merchandise is not subject to any condition or consideration for which a value cannot be determined;

(iii) No part of the proceeds of any subsequent resale, disposal, or use of the imported merchandise by the buyer will accrue directly or indirectly to the seller, unless an appropriate adjustment can be made under paragraph (b)(1)(v) of this section; and

(iv) The buyer and seller are not related, or the buyer and seller are related but the transaction value is acceptable.

(2) Related person transactions. (i) The transaction value between a related buyer and seller is acceptable if an examination of the circumstances of sale indicates that their relationship did not influence the price actually paid or payable, or if the transaction value of the imported merchandise closely approximates:

(A) The transaction value of identical merchandise; or of similar merchandise, in sales to unrelated buyers in the United States; or

(B) The deductive value or computed value of identical merchandise, or of similar merchandise; and

(C) Each value referred to in paragraph (j)(2)(i) (A) and (B) of this section that is used for comparison relates to merchandise that was exported to the United States at or about the same time as the imported merchandise.

... ...

Most Commonly Tested
TITLE 19 CFR

Part 159.32
LIQUIDATION OF DUTIES>>Conversion of Foreign Currency>>Date of exportation

Number of times appearing in last 10 exams: 6
Last appeared in exam: October 2015

The gist of it...
 Customs states that that the currency conversion rate to be used to convert commercial invoice values stated in foreign currency amounts is to be based on the date of exportation. The related section 152.1 defines "date of exportation".

Excerpt from 19 CFR...

159.32 Date of exportation.

The date of exportation for currency conversion shall be fixed in accordance with §152.1(c) of this chapter.

152.1 Definitions.

The following are general definitions for the purposes of part 152:

(a)-(b) [Reserved]

(c) Date of exportation. "Date of exportation," or the "time of exportation" referred to in section 402, Tariff Act of 1930, as amended (19 U.S.C. 1401a), means the actual date the merchandise finally leaves the country of exportation for the United States. If no positive evidence is at hand as to the actual date of exportation, the port director shall ascertain or estimate the date of exportation by all reasonable ways and means in his power, and in so doing may consider dates on bills of lading, invoices, and other information available to him.

Most Commonly Tested
TITLE 19 CFR

Part 191.3(b)
DRAWBACK>>General Provisions>>Duties and fees subject or not subject to drawback>>Duties and fees not subject to drawback

Number of times appearing in last 10 exams: 6
Last appeared in exam: October 2015

The gist of it...
    This paragraph states that (in general) fees and duties paid for HMF, MPF, and ADD/CVD will NOT be refunded with drawback.

Excerpt from 19 CFR...

(b) Duties and fees not subject to drawback include:

(1) Harbor maintenance fee (see §24.24 of this chapter);

(2) Merchandise processing fees (see §24.23 of this chapter), except where unused merchandise drawback pursuant to 19 U.S.C. 1313(j) or drawback for substitution of finished petroleum derivatives pursuant to 19 U.S.C. 1313(p)(2)(A)(iii) or (iv) is claimed; and

(3) Antidumping and countervailing duties on merchandise entered, or withdrawn from warehouse, for consumption on or after August 23, 1988.

Most Commonly Tested
TITLE 19 CFR

Part 111.29(a)
CUSTOMS BROKERS>>Duties and Responsibilities of Customs Brokers>>Diligence in correspondence and paying monies>>Due diligence by broker

Number of times appearing in last 10 exams: 5
Last appeared in exam: October 2016

The gist of it...
    This paragraph states the responsibilities of customs broker in making payments to Customs on behalf of their customers. Payments from clients must be made to Customs by the due date, or within 5 working days if received late from client.

Excerpt from 19 CFR...

(a) Due diligence by broker. Each broker must exercise due diligence in making financial settlements, in answering correspondence, and in preparing or assisting in the preparation and filing of records relating to any customs business matter handled by him as a broker. Payment of duty, tax, or other debt or obligation owing to the Government for which the broker is responsible, or for which the broker has received payment from a client, must be made to the Government on or before the date that payment is due. Payments received by a broker from a client after the due date must be transmitted to the Government within 5 working days from receipt by the broker. Each broker must provide a written statement to a client accounting for funds received for the client from the Government, or received from a client where no payment to the Government has been made, or received from a client in excess of the Governmental or other charges properly payable as part of the client's customs business, within 60 calendar days of receipt. No written statement is required if there is actual payment of the funds by a broker.

Most Commonly Tested
TITLE 19 CFR

Part 132.5
QUOTAS>>General Provisions>>Merchandise imported in excess of quota quantities

Number of times appearing in last 10 exams: 5
Last appeared in exam: April 2016

The gist of it...
　　　This section covers the two different types of quota merchandise—1) Absolute Quota Merchandise & 2) Tariff-Rate Quota Merchandise. It also lists options for disposal of items imported in excess of quota limits. Just remember that absolute quotas are different than tariff-rate quotas in that absolute quotas are "absolute" (i.e. fixed, and "absolutely" cannot be entered in excess of the quote; even at a higher duty rate).

Excerpt from 19 CFR...

(a) Absolute quota merchandise. Absolute quota merchandise imported in excess of the quantity admissible under the applicable quota must be disposed of in accordance with paragraph (c) of this section.

(b) Tariff-rate quota merchandise. Merchandise imported in excess of the quantity admissible at the reduced quota rate under a tariff-rate quota is permitted entry at the higher duty rate. However, it may be disposed of in accordance with paragraph (c) of this section.

(c) Disposition of excess merchandise. Merchandise imported in excess of either an absolute or a tariff-rate quota may be held for the opening of the next quota period by placing it in a foreign-trade zone or by entering it for warehouse, or it may be exported or destroyed under Customs supervision.

Most Commonly Tested
TITLE 19 CFR

Part 134.2
COUNTRY OF ORIGIN MARKINGS>>General Provisions>>Additional duties

Number of times appearing in last 10 exams: 5
Last appeared in exam: October 2016

The gist of it...
  Imports missing proper country of origin markings may either be 1) destroyed, 2) exported, or 3) entered and assessed an additional 10% in duties.

Excerpt from 19 CFR...

134.2 Additional duties.

Articles not marked as required by this part shall be subject to additional duties of 10 percent of the final appraised value unless exported or destroyed under Customs supervision prior to liquidation of the entry, as provided in 19 U.S.C. 1304(f). The 10 percent additional duty is assessable for failure either to mark the article (or container) to indicate the English name of the country of origin of the article or to include words or symbols required to prevent deception or mistake.

Most Commonly Tested
TITLE 19 CFR

Part 141.34
ENTRY OF MERCHANDISE>>Powers of Attorney>> Duration of power of attorney

Number of times appearing in last 10 exams: 5
Last appeared in exam: October 2016

The gist of it...
    Powers of attorney from partnerships are unique from POA's received from other legal entities in that the partnership POA is valid for a maximum of 2 years, at which time a new POA must be issued.

Excerpt from 19 CFR...

141.34 Duration of power of attorney.

Powers of attorney issued by a partnership shall be limited to a period not to exceed 2 years from the date of execution. All other powers of attorney may be granted for an unlimited period.

Most Commonly Tested
TITLE 19 CFR

Part 152.102(a)
CLASSIFICATION AND APPRAISEMENT OF MERCHANDISE>>Valuation of Merchandise>>Definitions>>Assist

Number of times appearing in last 10 exams: 5
Last appeared in exam: October 2016

The gist of it…
Here, an "assist" is defined as an item provided free-of-charge or at a discount from the importer to the foreign manufacturer used in or to make the imported product. Design work undertaken in the U.S., however, is not considered to be an "assist".

Excerpt from 19 CFR…

152.102 Definitions.

As used in this subpart, the following terms will have the meanings indicated:

(a) Assist. (1) "Assist" means any of the following if supplied directly or indirectly, and free of charge or at reduced cost, by the buyer of imported merchandise for use in connection with the production or the sale for export to the United States of the merchandise:

(i) Materials, components, parts, and similar items incorporated in the imported merchandise.

(ii) Tools, dies, molds, and similar items used in the production of the imported merchandise.

(iii) Merchandise consumed in the production of the imported merchandise.

(iv) Engineering, development, artwork, design work, and plans and sketches that are undertaken elsewhere than in the United States and are necessary for the production of the imported merchandise.

(2) No service or work to which paragraph (a)(1)(iv) of this section applies will be treated as an assist if the service or work:

(i) Is performed by an individual domiciled within the United States;

(ii) Is performed by that individual while acting as an employee or agent of the buyer of the imported merchandise; and

(iii) Is incidental to other engineering, development, artwork, design work, or plans or sketches that are undertaken within the United States.

(3) The following apply in determining the value of assists described in paragraph (a)(1)(iv) of this section:
… …

Most Commonly Tested
TITLE 19 CFR

Part 152.102(f)
CLASSIFICATION AND APPRAISEMENT OF MERCHANDISE>>Valuation of Merchandise>>Definitions>>Price Actually paid or payable

Number of times appearing in last 10 exams: 5
Last appeared in exam: April 2015

The gist of it...
    This paragraph defines the customs phrase "price actually paid or payable", otherwise known as the "transaction value". Remember that international freight and insurance charges are excluded from the transaction value.

Excerpt from 19 CFR...

(f) Price actually paid or payable. "Price actually paid or payable" means the total payment (whether direct or indirect, and exclusive of any charges, costs, or expenses incurred for transportation, insurance, and related services incident to the international shipment of the merchandise from the country of exportation to the place of importation in the United States) made, or to be made, for imported merchandise by the buyer to, or for the benefit of, the seller.

Most Commonly Tested
TITLE 19 CFR

Part 351.402(f)
ANTIDUMPING AND COUNTERVAILING DUTIES>>Calculation of export price and constructed export price; reimbursement of antidumping and countervailing duties

Number of times appearing in last 10 exams: 5
Last appeared in exam: April 2016

The gist of it...
  Most notably, this paragraph states that the importer must have an antidumping/countervailing duty non-reimbursement certificate on file for all applicable entries.

Excerpt from 19 CFR...

  ... ...

(2) Certificate. The importer must file prior to liquidation a certificate in the following form with the appropriate District Director of Customs:

I hereby certify that I (have) (have not) entered into any agreement or understanding for the payment or for the refunding to me, by the manufacturer, producer, seller, or exporter, of all or any part of the antidumping duties or countervailing duties assessed upon the following importations of (commodity) from (country): (List entry numbers) which have been purchased on or after (date of publication of antidumping notice suspending liquidation in the Federal Register) or purchased before (same date) but exported on or after (date of final determination of sales at less than fair value).

(3) Presumption. The Secretary may presume from an importer's failure to file the certificate required in paragraph (f)(2) of this section that the exporter or producer paid or reimbursed the antidumping duties or countervailing duties.

Most Commonly Tested
TITLE 19 CFR

Part 101.1
GENERAL PROVISIONS>>Definitions

Number of times appearing in last 10 exams: 4
Last appeared in exam: April 2014

The gist of it...
    Here, regularly used Customs terms are given their definition for the purpose of adding more clarity to the Customs regulations. For example, the term "service port" refers to a Customs location having a full range of cargo processing functions, including inspections, entry, collections, and verification.

Excerpt from 19 CFR...

As used in this chapter, the following terms shall have the meanings indicated unless either the context in which they are used requires a different meaning or a different definition is prescribed for a particular part or portion thereof:

Business day. A "business day" means a weekday (Monday through Friday), excluding national holidays as specified in §101.6(a).

Customs station. A "Customs station" is any place, other than a port of entry, at which Customs officers or employees are stationed, under the authority contained in article IX of the President's Message of March 3, 1913 (T.D. 33249), to enter and clear vessels, accept entries of merchandise, collect duties, and enforce the various provisions of the Customs and navigation laws of the United States.

Customs territory of the United States. "Customs territory of the United States" includes only the States, the District of Columbia, and Puerto Rico.

Date of entry. The "date of entry" or "time of entry" of imported merchandise shall be the effective time of entry of such merchandise, as defined in §141.68 of this chapter.

Date of exportation. "Date of exportation" or "time of exportation" shall be as defined in §152.1(c) of this chapter.

Date of importation. "Date of importation" means, in the case of merchandise imported otherwise than by vessel, the date on which the merchandise arrives within the Customs territory of the United States. In the case of merchandise imported by vessel, "date of importation" means the date on which the vessel arrives within the limits of a port in the United States with intent then and there to unlade such merchandise.

Duties. "Duties" means Customs duties and any internal revenue taxes which attach upon importation.

Entry or withdrawal for consumption. "Entry or withdrawal for consumption" means entry for consumption or withdrawal from warehouse for consumption.

Exportation. "Exportation" means a severance of goods from the mass of things belonging to this country with the intention of uniting them to the mass of things belonging to some foreign country. The shipment of merchandise abroad with the intention of returning it to the United States with a design to circumvent provisions of restriction or limitation in the tariff laws or to secure a benefit accruing to imported merchandise is not an exportation. Merchandise of foreign origin returned from abroad under these circumstances is dutiable according to its nature, weight, and value at the time of its original arrival in this country.

Importer. "Importer" means the person primarily liable for the payment of any duties on the merchandise, or an authorized agent acting on his behalf. The importer may be:

(1) The consignee, or

(2) The importer of record, or

(3) The actual owner of the merchandise, if an actual owner's declaration and superseding bond has been filed in accordance with §141.20 of this chapter, or

(4) The transferee of the merchandise, if the right to withdraw merchandise in a bonded warehouse has been transferred in accordance with subpart C of part 144 of this chapter.

Port and port of entry. The terms "port" and "port of entry" refer to any place designated by Executive Order of the President, by order of the Secretary of the Treasury, or by Act of Congress, at which a Customs officer is authorized to accept entries of merchandise to collect duties, and to enforce the various provisions of the Customs and navigation laws. The terms "port" and "port of entry" incorporate the geographical area under the jurisdiction of a port director. (The Customs ports in the Virgin Islands, although under the jurisdiction of the Secretary of the Treasury, have their own Customs laws (48 U.S.C. 1406(i)). These ports, therefore, are outside the Customs territory of the United States and the ports thereof are not "ports of entry" within the meaning of these regulations).

Principal field officer. A "principal field officer" is an officer in the field service whose immediate supervisor is located at Customs Service Headquarters.

Service port. The term "service port" refers to a Customs location having a full range of cargo processing functions, including inspections, entry, collections, and verification.

Shipment. "Shipment" means the merchandise described on the bill of lading or other document used to file or support entry, or in the oral declaration when applicable.

Most Commonly Tested
TITLE 19 CFR

Part 134.32
COUNTRY OF ORIGIN MARKING>>Exceptions to Marking Requirements>> General exceptions to marking requirements

Number of times appearing in last 10 exams: 4
Last appeared in exam: October 2016

The gist of it...
    This section of the regulations lists, in general, the types of products that are (reasonably) excepted from the country of origin marking requirements. It would be impossible, for example to mark crude oil product.

Excerpt from 19 CFR...

134.32 General exceptions to marking requirements.

The articles described or meeting the specified conditions set forth below are excepted from marking requirements (see subpart C of this part for marking of the containers):

(a) Articles that are incapable of being marked;

(b) Articles that cannot be marked prior to shipment to the United States without injury;

(c) Articles that cannot be marked prior to shipment to the United States except at an expense economically prohibitive of its importation;

(d) Articles for which the marking of the containers will reasonably indicate the origin of the articles;

(e) Articles which are crude substances;

(f) Articles imported for use by the importer and not intended for sale in their imported or any other form;

(g) Articles to be processed in the United States by the importer or for his account otherwise than for the purpose of concealing the origin of such articles and in such manner that any mark contemplated by this part would necessarily be obliterated, destroyed, or permanently concealed;

(h) Articles for which the ultimate purchaser must necessarily know, or in the case of a good of a NAFTA country, must reasonably know, the country of origin by reason of the circumstances of their importation or by reason of the character of the articles even though they are not marked to indicate their origin;

(i) Articles which were produced more than 20 years prior to their importation into the United States;

(j) Articles entered or withdrawn from warehouse for immediate exportation or for transportation and exportation;

... ...

Most Commonly Tested
TITLE 19 CFR

Part 141.89
ENTRY OF MERCHANDISE>>Invoices>>Additional information for certain classes of merchandise

Number of times appearing in last 10 exams: 4
Last appeared in exam: April 2014

The gist of it...
   For some imported items, Customs requires additional information to be provided with the entry. Some chemicals, for example, require a Chemical Abstracts Service (CAS) number to be provided as part of the customs entry.

Excerpt from 19 CFR...

(a) Invoices for the following classes of merchandise, classifiable under the Harmonized Tariff Schedule of the United States (HTSUS), shall set forth the additional information specified: [75-42, 75-239, 78-53, 83-251, 84-149.]

Aluminum and alloys of aluminum classifiable under subheadings 7601.10.60, 7601.20.60, 7601.20.90, or 7602.00.00, HTSUS (T.D. 53092, 55977, 56143)—Statement of the percentages by weight of any metallic element contained in the article.

Articles manufactured of textile materials, Coated or laminated with plastics or rubber, classifiable in Chapter(s) 39, 40, and 42—Include a description indicating whether the fabric is coated or laminated on both sides, on the exterior surface or on the interior surface.

Bags manufactured of plastic sheeting and not of a reinforced or laminated construction, classified in Chapter 39 or in heading 4202—Indicate the gauge of the plastic sheeting.

Ball or roller bearings classifiable under subheading 8482.10.50 through 8482.80.00, HTSUS (T.D. 68-306)—(1) Type of bearing (i.e., whether a ball or roller bearing); (2) If a roller bearing, whether a spherical, tapered, cylindrical, needled or other type; (3) Whether a combination bearing (i.e., a bearing containing both ball and roller bearings, etc.); and (4) If a ball bearing (not including ball bearing with integral shafts or parts of ball bearings), whether or not radial, the following: (a) outside diameter of each bearing; and (b) whether or not a radial bearing (the definition of radial bearing is, for Customs purposes, an antifriction bearing primarily designed to support a load perpendicular to shaft axis).

Beads (T.D. 50088, 55977)—(1) The length of the string, if strung; (2) The size of the beads expressed in millimeters; (3) The material of which the beads are composed, i.e., ivory, glass, imitation pearl, etc.

Bed linen and Bedspreads—Statement as to whether or not the article contains any embroidery, lace, braid, edging, trimming, piping or applique work.

Chemicals—Furnish the use and Chemical Abstracts Service number of chemical compounds classified in Chapters 27, 28 and 29, HTSUS.

... ...

Most Commonly Tested
TITLE 19 CFR

Part 152.1(c)
CLASSIFICATION AND APPRAISEMENT OF MERCHANDISE>>General Provisions>>Definitions>>Date of exportation

Number of times appearing in last 10 exams: 4
Last appeared in exam: October 2014

The gist of it...
　　This paragraph defines the term "date of exportation" as the date the merchandise leaves the actual "country of export". Note that CBP defines the "country of export" as the country from which the merchandise was last part of the commerce (i.e. before "in-bond" status) before being shipped to the U.S. without diversion.

Excerpt from 19 CFR...

(c) Date of exportation. "Date of exportation," or the "time of exportation" referred to in section 402, Tariff Act of 1930, as amended (19 U.S.C. 1401a), means the actual date the merchandise finally leaves the country of exportation for the United States. If no positive evidence is at hand as to the actual date of exportation, the port director shall ascertain or estimate the date of exportation by all reasonable ways and means in his power, and in so doing may consider dates on bills of lading, invoices, and other information available to him.

Most Commonly Tested
TITLE 19 CFR

Part 162.74(b)
INSPECTION, SEARCH, AND SEIZURE>>Special Procedures for Certain Violations>>Prior disclosure>> Disclosure of the circumstances of a violation

Number of times appearing in last 10 exams: 4
Last appeared in exam: October 2016

The gist of it...
　　This paragraph lists the four specific elements (i.e. circumstances) to be provided to CBP when submitting a prior disclosure.

Excerpt from 19 CFR...

(b) Disclosure of the circumstances of a violation. The term "discloses the circumstances of a violation" means the act of providing to Customs a statement orally or in writing that:

(1) Identifies the class or kind of merchandise involved in the violation;

(2) Identifies the importation or drawback claim included in the disclosure by entry number, drawback claim number, or by indicating each concerned Customs port of entry and the approximate dates of entry or dates of drawback claims;

(3) Specifies the material false statements, omissions or acts including an explanation as to how and when they occurred; and

(4) Sets forth, to the best of the disclosing party's knowledge, the true and accurate information or data that should have been provided in the entry or drawback claim documents, and states that the disclosing party will provide any information or data unknown at the time of disclosure within 30 days of the initial disclosure date. Extensions of the 30-day period may be requested by the disclosing party from the concerned Fines, Penalties, and Forfeitures Officer to enable the party to obtain the information or data.

Most Commonly Tested
TITLE 19 CFR

Part 163.5(b)
RECORDKEEPING>>Methods for storage of records>> Alternative method of storage

Number of times appearing in last 10 exams: 4
Last appeared in exam: April 2016

The gist of it...
 This paragraph explains that alternative (to physical paper copies) methods for recordkeeping are available, though advance notification must be sent to the "CBP Regulatory Audit office in Charlotte, NC".

Excerpt from 19 CFR...

(b) Alternative method of storage—(1) General. Any of the persons listed in §163.2 may maintain any records, other than records required to be maintained as original records under laws and regulations administered by other Federal government agencies, in an alternative format, provided that the person gives advance written notification of such alternative storage method to the Regulatory Audit, U.S. Customs and Border Protection, 2001 Cross Beam Dr., Charlotte, North Carolina 28217, and provided further that the Director of Regulatory Audit, Charlotte office does not instruct the person in writing as provided herein that certain described records may not be maintained in an alternative format. The written notice to the Director of Regulatory Audit, Charlotte office must be provided at least 30 calendar days before implementation of the alternative storage method, must identify the type of alternative storage method to be used, and must state that the alternative storage method complies with the standards set forth in paragraph (b)(2) of this section. If an alternative storage method covers records that pertain to goods under CBP seizure or detention or that relate to a matter that is currently the subject of an inquiry or investigation or administrative or court proceeding, the appropriate CBP office may instruct the person in writing that those records must be maintained as original records and therefore may not be converted to an alternative format until specific written authorization is received from that CBP office. A written instruction to a person under this paragraph may be issued during the 30-day advance notice period prescribed in this section or at any time thereafter, must describe the records in question with reasonable specificity but need not identify the underlying basis for the instruction, and shall not preclude application of the planned alternative storage method to other records not described therein.

(2) Standards for alternative storage methods. Methods commonly used in standard business practice for storage of records include, but are not limited to, machine readable data, CD ROM, and microfiche. Methods that are in compliance with generally accepted business standards will generally satisfy CBP requirements, provided that the method used allows for retrieval of records requested within a reasonable time after the request and provided that adequate provisions exist to prevent alteration, destruction, or deterioration of the records. The following standards must be applied by recordkeepers when using alternative storage methods ... ...

Most Commonly Tested
TITLE 19 CFR

Part 163.6(b)
RECORDKEEPING>> Production and examination of entry and other records and witnesses; penalties>> Failure to produce entry records

Number of times appearing in last 10 exams: 4
Last appeared in exam: April 2016

The gist of it...
　　This paragraph explains the penalties for failure to provide Customs with entry documents when requested. It explains the monetary penalties for willful reasons and for negligent reasons for failing to comply.

Excerpt from 19 CFR...

(b) Failure to produce entry records—(1) Monetary penalties applicable. The following penalties may be imposed if a person fails to comply with a lawful demand for the production of an entry record and is not excused from a penalty pursuant to paragraph (b)(3) of this section:

(i) If the failure to comply is a result of the willful failure of the person to maintain, store, or retrieve the demanded record, such person shall be subject to a penalty, for each release of merchandise, not to exceed $100,000, or an amount equal to 75 percent of the appraised value of the merchandise, whichever amount is less; or

(ii) If the failure to comply is a result of negligence of the person in maintaining, storing, or retrieving the demanded record, such person shall be subject to a penalty, for each release of merchandise, not to exceed $10,000, or an amount equal to 40 percent of the appraised value of the merchandise, whichever amount is less.

(2) Additional actions—(i) General. In addition to any penalty imposed under paragraph (b)(1) of this section, and except as otherwise provided in paragraph (b)(2)(ii) of this section, if the demanded entry record relates to the eligibility of merchandise for a column 1 special rate of duty in the Harmonized Tariff Schedule of the United States (HTSUS), the entry of such merchandise:

(A) If unliquidated, shall be liquidated at the applicable HTSUS column 1 general rate of duty; or

... ...

Most Commonly Tested
TITLE 19 CFR

Part 181.31
NORTH AMERICAN FREE TRADE AGREEMENT>>Post-Importation Duty Refund Claims>>Right to make post importation claim and refund duties

Number of times appearing in last 10 exams: 4
Last appeared in exam: October 2016

The gist of it...
 This section provides the importer the right to make an eligible NAFTA claim within one year of the original non-NAFTA importation and entry.

Excerpt from 19 CFR...

181.31 Right to make post-importation claim and refund duties.

Notwithstanding any other available remedy, including the right to amend an entry so long as liquidation of the entry has not become final, where a good would have qualified as an originating good when it was imported into the United States but no claim for preferential tariff treatment on that originating good was made at that time under §181.21(a) of this part, the importer of that good may file a claim for a refund of any excess duties at any time within one year after the date of importation of the good in accordance with the procedures set forth in §181.32 of this part. Subject to the provisions of §181.23 of this part, Customs may refund any excess duties by liquidation or reliquidation of the entry covering the good in accordance with §181.33(c) of this part.

Book 1 Part 8

All Sections Appearing on Exams
TITLE 19 CFR

This section of the study guide lists nearly all instances of Title 19 of the United States Code of Federal Regulations (19 CFR) appearing throughout the last 10 exams.

The contents of all Titles of the Code of Federal Regulations (CFR) are logically organized in hierarchical order. Essentially, the United States regulations publications are broken down first by 1) "Title", then 2) "Part", then 3) "Section", then 4) "Paragraph", and then in some cases additionally by 5) "Subparagraph". So, for example, 19 CFR 134.1(b) (the paragraph of the regulations where Customs defines the term "country of origin") is located within Title 19, Part 134, Section 1, Paragraph (b). You can remember this structure of the regulations by remembering the initials "P.S.P.S" (part, section, paragraph, and sub-paragraph).

Accordingly, the following "All Sections Appearing on Exams Table" is arranged in ascending order by "Part", then by "Section", then by "Paragraph" level, and then further sorted by exam date with the most recent exam instances appearing first for each repeating set of section and paragraph occurrences. Within the table, if reference to a specific "Paragraph" has been left blank, then either there may not be a "Paragraph" breakdown for that particular "Section", or the answer for that particular exam question may refer to multiple "Paragraphs" within that Section. As you can see from the table, we start from "Part" 4, because "Part" 0 (Transferred or Delegated Authority) has not appeared in any of the last 10 exams. It is a safe bet to assume that although you can be aware that this part exists, there is no reason to memorize anything contained therein.

The best way to make use of the "All Sections Appearing on Exams Table" is as follows. First, feel free to remove from your 19 CFR binder the "Parts" that do not appear on the "Parts List" (located on the following page). You can move these extra pages to a different folder or binder that can be label "just in case" if, by chance, these obscure Parts show up in the next exam. By doing so, you reduce the number of pages you must shuffle through to find what you're looking for. This is helpful during both study time and exam time.

Next, go through the remaining part of your newly condensed 19 CFR, and with a highlighter marker, highlight onto your CFR, as many "Sections", and "Paragraphs" as possible that appear in the All Sections Appearing on Exams table. This is a great way to get to know the regulations better, and it will also allow these frequently tested items to jump out at you when you're speedily scanning through the pages during exam time.

$ Money Saving Tip $
Let your employer know that you're interested in taking the exam. Ask if they can help cover some of the expenses. Or, they may do so on the condition that you pass in order to get reimbursed.

19 CFR "Parts List"

Of the 70 Parts that comprise Title 19 CFR, only the following 43 Parts (and even then, some appear only once or twice) have appeared on the last 10 customs broker exams...

Part 4:	VESSELS IN FOREIGN AND DOMESTIC TRADES
Part 7:	CUSTOMS RELATIONS WITH INSULAR POSSESSIONS AND GUANTANAMO BAY
Part 10:	ARTICLES CONDITIONALLY FREE, SUBJECT TO A REDUCED RATE, ETC.
Part 11:	PACKING AND STAMPING; MARKING
Part 12:	SPECIAL CLASSES OF MERCHANDISE
Part 18:	TRANSPORTATION IN BOND AND MERCHANDISE IN TRANSIT
Part 19:	CUSTOMS WAREHOUSES, CONTAINER STATIONS AND CONTROL OF MERCHANDISE
Part 24:	CUSTOMS FINANCIAL AND ACCOUNTING PROCEDURE
Part 101:	GENERAL PROVISIONS
Part 102:	RULES OF ORIGIN
Part 103:	AVAILABILITY OF INFORMATION
Part 111:	CUSTOMS BROKERS
Part 113:	CUSTOMS BONDS
Part 114:	CARNETS
Part 122:	AIR COMMERCE REGULATIONS
Part 123:	CBP RELATIONS WITH CANADA AND MEXICO
Part 127:	GENERAL ORDER, UNCLAIMED, AND ABANDONED MERCHANDISE
Part 132:	QUOTAS
Part 133:	TRADEMARKS, TRADE NAMES, AND COPYRIGHTS
Part 134:	COUNTRY OF ORIGIN MARKING
Part 141:	ENTRY OF MERCHANDISE
Part 142:	ENTRY PROCESS
Part 143:	SPECIAL ENTRY PROCEDURES
Part 144:	WAREHOUSE AND REWAREHOUSE ENTRIES AND WITHDRAWALS
Part 145:	MAIL IMPORTATIONS
Part 146:	FOREIGN TRADE ZONES
Part 148:	PERSONAL DECLARATIONS AND EXEMPTIONS
Part 149:	IMPORTER SECURITY FILING
Part 151:	EXAMINATION, SAMPLING, AND TESTING OF MERCHANDISE
Part 152:	CLASSIFICATION AND APPRAISEMENT OF MERCHANDISE
Part 158:	RELIEF FROM DUTIES ON MERCHANDISE LOST, DAMAGED, ABANDONED, EXPORTED
Part 159:	LIQUIDATION OF DUTIES
Part 162:	INSPECTIONS, SEARCH, AND SEIZURE
Part 163:	RECORDKEEPING
Part 171:	FINES, PENALTIES, AND FORFEITURES
Part 172:	CLAIMS FOR LIQUIDATED DAMAGES; PENALTIES SECURED BY BONDS
Part 173:	ADMINISTRATIVE REVIEW IN GENERAL
Part 174:	PROTESTS
Part 177:	ADMINISTRATIVE RULINGS
Part 181:	NORTH AMERICAN FREE TRADE AGREEMENT (NAFTA)
Part 191:	DRAWBACK
Part 192:	EXPORT CONTROL
Part 351:	ANTIDUMPING AND COUNTERVAILING DUTIES

All Sections Appearing on Exams Table

EXAM DATE	"PART"	"SECTION"	"PARAGRAPH"
Part 4: VESSELS IN FOREIGN AND DOMESTIC TRADES			
2015 April	4	37	(a)
Part 7: CUSTOMS RELATIONS WITH INSULAR POSSESSIONS AND GUANTANAMO BAY			
2013 April	7	2	(c)
2012 April	7	2	(c)
Part 10: ARTICLES CONDITIONALLY FREE, SUBJECT TO A REDUCED RATE, ETC.			
2012 October	10	1	(a)
2016 October	10	1	(h)
2016 October	10	16	(a)
2013 October	10	16	(b)
2013 October	10	16	(c)
2012 April	10	16	
2016 October	10	31	(f)
2015 October	10	31	(h)
2016 April	10	37	
2013 October	10	37	
2016 April	10	39	(e)
2016 April	10	39	(f)
2015 April	10	39	(f)
2012 October	10	41	(a)
2012 April	10	43	
2013 April	10	100	
2012 April	10	100	
2016 October	10	101	(d)
2012 April	10	133	(a)
2016 October	10	151	
2014 October	10	175	(c)
2013 October	10	175	(d)
2014 April	10	176	(a)
2016 April	10	178	
2015 April	10	440	
2012 April	10	453	
2015 October	10	761	
2015 April	10	910	
2014 October	10	910	
2015 October	10	1005	(a)
2015 April	10	1010	
2015 April	10	3010	
Part 11: PACKING AND STAMPING; MARKING			
2012 October	11	6	(c)
2015 October	11	12	(b)
Part 12: SPECIAL CLASSES OF MERCHANDISE			
2012 October	12	1	(a)
2014 April	12	3	(b)
2016 October	12	10	
2016 October	12	26	(a)

All Sections Appearing on Exams Table

EXAM DATE	"PART"	"SECTION"	"PARAGRAPH"
2012 October	12	26	
2016 April	12	39	(b)
2015 October	12	39	(b)
2016 October	12	42	(b)
2016 October	12	42	
2016 October	12	43	(a)
2013 October	12	73	(d)
2016 October	12	73	(e)
2013 April	12	115	
2013 April	12	121	(a)
2012 April	12	124	
2013 October	12	150	(a)
Part 18: TRANSPORTATION IN BOND AND MERCHANDISE IN TRANSIT			
2014 October	18	8	
2016 October	18	10	
2014 April	18	25	(a)
2014 April	18	25	(b)
Part 19: CUSTOMS WAREHOUSES, CONTAINER STATIONS AND CONTROL OF MERCHANDISE THEREIN			
2012 October	19	1	(a)
2014 April	19	4	(b)
2014 October	19	11	(d)
2014 October	19	12	(d)
2013 October	19	12	(d)
2013 April	19	44	(a)
2012 April	19	44	
2015 April	19	48	(a)
Part 24: CUSTOMS FINANCIAL AND ACCOUNTING PROCEDURE			
2012 October	24	3	(a)
2016 April	24	3	(e)
2015 April	24	3	(e)
2016 October	24	3a	(c)
2015 October	24	5	(c)
2013 April	24	5	(e)
2016 October	24	23	(b)
2015 October	24	23	(b)
2015 October	24	23	(b)
2016 October	24	23	(c)
2016 April	24	23	(c)
2014 October	24	23	(c)
2014 October	24	23	(c)
2014 October	24	23	(c)
2014 April	24	23	(c)
2013 October	24	23	(c)
2012 October	24	23	(c)
2016 April	24	23	(d)
2014 October	24	24	(c)
2012 October	24	36	

All Sections Appearing on Exams Table

EXAM DATE	"PART"	"SECTION"	"PARAGRAPH"
	Part 101: GENERAL PROVISIONS		
2014 April	101	1	
2012 October	101	1	
2012 April	101	1	
2012 April	101	1	
2016 October	101	2	(a)
	Part 102: RULES OF ORIGIN		
2016 October	102	13	(c)
2013 April	102	20	(g)
2016 April	102	21	(b)
2012 October	102	21	
	Part 103: AVAILABILITY OF INFORMATION		
2013 October	103	31	(d)
	Part 111: CUSTOMS BROKERS		
2016 April	111	1	
2014 October	111	1	
2014 April	111	1	
2016 October	111	2	(a)
2015 October	111	2	(a)
2015 April	111	2	(a)
2015 April	111	2	(a)
2014 October	111	2	(a)
2014 October	111	2	(a)
2012 October	111	2	(a)
2014 October	111	2	(b)
2013 April	111	2	(b)
2013 April	111	2	(b)
2014 April	111	11	(a)
2012 October	111	11	(a)
2012 October	111	11	(c)
2014 October	111	19	(d)
2013 October	111	21	(a)
2016 October	111	23	(b)
2016 October	111	23	(b)
2015 October	111	23	(b)
2015 April	111	23	(b)
2014 October	111	23	(b)
2013 October	111	23	(b)
2013 October	111	23	(b)
2016 October	111	28	(b)
2014 October	111	28	(b)
2014 October	111	28	(b)
2014 April	111	28	(b)
2012 October	111	28	(b)

All Sections Appearing on Exams Table

EXAM DATE	"PART"	"SECTION"	"PARAGRAPH"
2014 April	111	28	(c)
2016 October	111	29	(a)
2014 October	111	29	(a)
2013 October	111	29	(a)
2013 October	111	29	(a)
2013 April	111	29	(a)
2016 October	111	29	(b)
2014 October	111	29	(b)
2013 October	111	29	(b)
2013 October	111	30	(a)
2016 October	111	30	(c)
2016 October	111	30	(c)
2016 April	111	30	(d)
2014 October	111	30	(d)
2014 October	111	30	(d)
2014 April	111	30	(d)
2014 April	111	30	(d)
2013 October	111	30	(d)
2013 April	111	30	(d)
2013 April	111	30	(d)
2015 April	111	31	(c)
2013 April	111	31	(c)
2012 April	111	31	(c)
2016 April	111	36	(a)
2013 April	111	36	(c)
2013 April	111	37	
2013 April	111	39	(b)
2014 April	111	42	(a)
2016 April	111	45	(a)
2016 April	111	45	(a)
2015 April	111	45	(a)
2016 April	111	45	(b)
2015 October	111	45	(b)
2015 April	111	45	(b)
2013 April	111	45	(b)
2012 April	111	53	(a)
2012 April	111	53	(b)
2013 October	111	53	(e)
2013 April	111	53	(e)
2016 October	111	56	
2014 April	111	79	
2013 April	111	81	
2015 April	111	91	(b)
2013 October	111	91	(b)
2015 April	111	92	(b)
2014 April	111	96	(c)
2013 October	111	96	(d)

All Sections Appearing on Exams Table

EXAM DATE	"PART"	"SECTION"	"PARAGRAPH"
Part 113: CUSTOMS BONDS			
2015 April	113	1	
2014 April	113	1	
2014 October	113	11	
2014 October	113	13	(a)
2012 October	113	13	(a)
2016 October	113	13	(d)
2014 April	113	23	(b)
2014 October	113	26	(a)
2014 April	113	40	(a)
2016 April	113	62	(j)
2014 October	113	62	
2012 April	113	62	
2016 April	113	63	(c)
2016 October	113	66	(b)
2016 April	113	66	(b)
2014 April	113	66	
Part 114: CARNETS			
2016 October	114	1	(c)
2012 April	114	23	(a)
2011 October	114	23	(a)
Part 122: AIR COMMERCE REGULATIONS			
2014 October	122	50	(a)
2012 October	122	119	
Part 123: CBP RELATIONS WITH CANADA AND MEXICO			
2014 October	123	10	(b)
Part 127: GENERAL ORDER, UNCLAIMED, AND ABANDONED MERCHANDISE			
2012 April	127	2	
2012 April	127	12	(a)

All Sections Appearing on Exams Table

EXAM DATE	"PART"	"SECTION"	"PARAGRAPH"
Part 132: QUOTAS			
2015 April	132	3	
2014 April	132	3	
2015 April	132	5	(c)
2016 April	132	5	
2015 October	132	5	
2013 April	132	5	
2012 April	132	5	
2016 April	132	13	(a)
2015 April	132	17	(c)
2016 October	132	22	
2016 October	132	24	
Part 133: TRADEMARKS, TRADE NAMES, AND COPYRIGHTS			
2013 April	133	1	
2015 April	133	2	(e)
2016 April	133	3	(b)
2016 October	133	12	
2016 October	133	21	(a)
2015 April	133	21	(a)
2016 April	133	21	(b)
2015 October	133	21	(b)
2015 April	133	21	(b)
2016 October	133	21	(g)
2016 April	133	21	(g)
2015 October	133	21	(g)
2014 April	133	21	
2013 April	133	21	
2015 April	133	23	(a)
2015 April	133	23	(a)
2013 October	133	23	(a)
2015 October	133	23	(b)
2013 October	133	25	(a)
2015 April	133	25	(b)
2013 October	133	34	(b)
2016 April	133	51	(b)
2016 April	133	52	(c)
2016 April	133	53	
Part 134: COUNTRY OF ORIGIN MARKING			
2015 October	134	1	(b)
2013 April	134	1	(b)
2012 April	134	1	(b)
2016 October	134	2	
2016 October	134	2	
2016 April	134	2	
2014 April	134	2	
2014 April	134	2	
2012 October	134	32	(i)

All Sections Appearing on Exams Table

EXAM DATE	"PART"	"SECTION"	"PARAGRAPH"
2016 October	134	32	
2016 April	134	32	
2015 October	134	32	
2015 April	134	32	
2015 October	134	33	
2015 April	134	33	
2015 April	134	33	
2012 October	134	33	
2015 April	134	41	(a)
2012 April	134	41	(b)
2014 October	134	43	(a)
2012 October	134	43	(a)
2014 October	134	51	(a)
2013 October	134	51	(a)
2016 October	134	54	(a)
	Part 141: ENTRY OF MERCHANDISE		
2016 April	141	2	
2014 October	141	2	
2012 October	141	3	
2016 October	141	4	(c)
2014 October	141	4	(c)
2012 April	141	5	
2012 October	141	13	
2015 October	141	18	
2015 October	141	20	(a)
2014 October	141	20	(a)
2016 October	141	31	(a)
2012 October	141	31	
2016 October	141	32	
2016 April	141	32	
2012 April	141	32	
2016 October	141	34	
2016 April	141	34	
2015 April	141	34	
2014 April	141	34	
2012 October	141	34	
2015 October	141	35	
2012 October	141	36	
2013 October	141	37	
2016 April	141	39	(a)
2015 April	141	39	(a)
2014 April	141	39	(a)
2016 October	141	46	
2016 October	141	46	
2016 April	141	57	(b)
2014 April	141	61	(b)
2015 October	141	68	(c)

All Sections Appearing on Exams Table

EXAM DATE	"PART"	"SECTION"	"PARAGRAPH"
2012 October	141	68	(c)
2015 April	141	69	(b)
2014 April	141	69	(b)
2012 October	141	69	(b)
2013 October	141	86	(a)
2012 April	141	86	
2012 April	141	89	(a)
2014 April	141	89	
2012 April	141	89	
2012 April	141	89	
2013 April	141	92	(a)
2013 April	141	113	(b)
2013 October	141	113	(c)
2012 October	141	113	(c)
2012 October	141	113	(i)
Part 142: ENTRY PROCESS			
2016 April	142	4	(a)
2012 October	142	6	
2012 April	142	6	
2015 April	142	12	(b)
2015 October	142	15	
Part 143: SPECIAL ENTRY PROCEDURES			
2016 April	143	2	
2016 October	143	8	
2015 October	143	28	
2012 April	143	43	(b)
Part 144: WAREHOUSE AND REWAREHOUSE ENTRIES AND WITHDRAWALS			
2015 April	144	1	(a)
2012 October	144	5	
2012 April	144	15	(c)
2015 April	144	41	(a)
Part 145: MAIL IMPORTATIONS			
2012 October	145	35	
Part 146: FOREIGN TRADE ZONES			
2013 October	146	22	(a)
2015 October	146	25	(a)
2015 April	146	25	(a)
2014 April	146	25	(a)
2015 October	146	32	(a)
2014 October	146	32	(a)
2014 April	146	35	(b)
2015 October	146	39	(a)

All Sections Appearing on Exams Table

EXAM DATE	"PART"	"SECTION"	"PARAGRAPH"
2015 April	146	44	(c)
2016 April	146	52	(a)
2014 April	146	53	(b)
2016 October	146	53	(d)
2016 April	146	62	(b)
2016 April	146	63	(c)
2015 April	146	63	(c)
2016 October	146	64	(d)
2015 April	146	66	(a)
2012 April	146	67	(c)
2016 October	146	71	(c)
2012 April	146	71	(c)
Part 149: IMPORTER SECURITY FILING			
2012 April	149	3	(a)
Part 151: EXAMINATION, SAMPLING, AND TESTING OF MERCHANDISE			
2013 October	151	16	(c)
2015 October	151	16	(f)
Part 152: CLASSIFICATION AND APPRAISEMENT OF MERCHANDISE			
2014 October	152	1	(c)
2012 October	152	1	(c)
2012 October	152	1	(c)
2012 April	152	1	(c)
2015 April	152	2	
2013 April	152	13	
2015 April	152	23	
2014 October	152	101	(d)
2014 April	152	101	(d)
2016 October	152	102	(a)
2016 October	152	102	(a)
2016 April	152	102	(a)
2014 October	152	102	(a)
2014 April	152	102	(a)
2016 October	152	102	(c)
2014 April	152	102	(d)
2015 April	152	102	(f)
2014 October	152	102	(f)
2014 October	152	102	(f)
2014 October	152	102	(f)
2012 April	152	102	(f)
2016 April	152	102	(g)
2016 April	152	102	(g)
2014 October	152	102	(g)
2014 April	152	102	(i)
2016 April	152	103	(a)
2015 October	152	103	(a)
2015 April	152	103	(a)
2015 April	152	103	(a)

All Sections Appearing on Exams Table

EXAM DATE	"PART"	"SECTION"	"PARAGRAPH"
2015 April	152	103	(a)
2014 October	152	103	(a)
2014 April	152	103	(a)
2013 October	152	103	(a)
2013 October	152	103	(a)
2013 October	152	103	(a)
2013 April	152	103	(a)
2012 October	152	103	(a)
2012 April	152	103	(a)
2016 April	152	103	(b)
2016 April	152	103	(b)
2015 October	152	103	(b)
2014 October	152	103	(b)
2014 April	152	103	(b)
2013 October	152	103	(b)
2012 October	152	103	(b)
2012 October	152	103	(c)
2016 October	152	103	(d)
2015 October	152	103	(d)
2014 October	152	103	(d)
2014 April	152	103	(d)
2013 October	152	103	(d)
2013 October	152	103	(d)
2012 April	152	103	(d)
2012 April	152	103	(d)
2013 October	152	103	(e)
2012 October	152	103	(f)
2015 October	152	103	(i)
2014 October	152	103	(j)
2013 October	152	103	(j)
2012 October	152	103	(j)
2012 October	152	103	(j)
2012 October	152	103	(j)
2012 October	152	103	(j)
2013 October	152	103	(k)
2012 October	152	103	(k)
2012 October	152	103	(k)
2012 April	152	103	
2015 April	152	104	(d)
2014 April	152	105	(d)
2013 October	152	106	(a)
2013 October	152	106	(b)
2014 April	152	107	(b)
2016 October	152	108	(c)

All Sections Appearing on Exams Table

EXAM DATE	"PART"	"SECTION"	"PARAGRAPH"
Part 158: RELIEF FROM DUTIES ON MERCHANDISE LOST, DAMAGED, ABANDONED, OR EXPORTED			
2012 October	158	43	(a)
Part 159: LIQUIDATION OF DUTIES			
2013 October	159	1	
2014 April	159	9	(c)
2014 October	159	11	(a)
2015 October	159	12	(a)
2015 October	159	12	(a)
2013 April	159	12	(a)
2015 October	159	12	(e)
2013 April	159	12	(e)
2015 October	159	12	(f)
2015 October	159	32	
2014 October	159	32	
2013 October	159	32	
2012 October	159	32	
2012 October	159	32	
2012 April	159	32	
2012 April	159	41	
2015 October	159	51	
2016 April	159	61	(c)
Part 162: INSPECTIONS, SEARCH, AND SEIZURE			
2015 October	162	0	
2016 October	162	23	
2013 October	162	73	(b)
2014 October	162	74	(a)
2016 October	162	74	(b)
2016 April	162	74	(b)
2015 October	162	74	(b)
2014 October	162	74	(b)
2016 April	162	74	(c)
2014 October	162	74	(c)
2015 April	162	74	(h)
2013 April	162	74	
2016 April	162	77	(b)
Part 163: RECORDKEEPING			
2012 October	163	2	(a)
2012 October	163	2	(a)
2012 October	163	2	(c)
2012 April	163	2	(c)
2014 October	163	4	(a)
2016 October	163	4	(b)
2016 October	163	4	(b)
2016 April	163	5	(b)
2015 April	163	5	(b)
2014 October	163	5	(b)
2013 October	163	5	(b)

All Sections Appearing on Exams Table

EXAM DATE	"PART"	"SECTION"	"PARAGRAPH"
2016 April	163	6	(b)
2015 October	163	6	(b)
2015 April	163	6	(b)
2013 October	163	6	(b)
Part 171: FINES, PENALTIES, AND FORFEITURES			
2015 October	171	2	(b)
2015 April	171	2	(b)
2015 April	171	2	(c)
2015 April	171	22	
2013 April	171	23	
2015 October	171	62	(a)
2016 April	171	APPENDIX B	C
2012 April	171	APPENDIX B	C
2013 October	171	APPENDIX B	E
2013 October	171	APPENDIX B	F
2016 October	171	APPENDIX B	
2015 April	171	APPENDIX B	
2015 October	171	APPENDIX C	V.
2012 April	171	APPENDIX C	XI.
2016 October	171	APPENDIX C	
2016 October	171	APPENDIX C	
2015 April	171	APPENDIX C	
Part 172: CLAIMS FOR LIQUIDATED DAMAGES; PENALTIES SECURED BY BONDS			
2012 April	172	1	
2015 October	172	2	(a)
2016 April	172	3	(b)
2012 April	172	11	
2015 October	172	31	
2013 October	172	41	
Part 173: ADMINISTRATIVE REVIEW IN GENERAL			
2016 October	173	2	
2016 April	173	5	
Part 174: PROTESTS			
2014 October	174	12	(a)
2013 October	174	12	(b)
2016 October	174	12	(e)
2015 April	174	12	(e)
2014 October	174	13	(a)
2012 April	174	21	
2014 April	174	22	(d)
2016 April	174	31	
2015 October	174	31	
2012 October	174	31	
Part 177: ADMINISTRATIVE RULINGS			
2016 April	177	23	

All Sections Appearing on Exams Table

EXAM DATE	"PART"	"SECTION"	"PARAGRAPH"
Part 181: NORTH AMERICAN FREE TRADE AGREEMENT (NAFTA)			
2016 October	181	11	(b)
2015 October	181	21	(a)
2014 April	181	21	(b)
2013 April	181	21	
2016 April	181	22	(a)
2014 October	181	22	(b)
2014 October	181	22	(b)
2012 October	181	22	(b)
2012 October	181	22	(d)
2016 October	181	31	
2016 April	181	31	
2014 October	181	31	
2012 October	181	31	
2015 April	181	32	(a)
2012 October	181	45	(b)
2012 April	181	64	(a)
2012 April	181	64	(b)
Part 191: DRAWBACK			
2014 April	191	2	(g)
2014 April	191	2	(i)
2016 October	191	2	(o)
2015 October	191	3	(b)
2015 April	191	3	(b)
2015 April	191	3	(b)
2014 April	191	3	(b)
2014 April	191	3	(b)
2012 October	191	3	(b)
2016 April	191	6	(a)
2016 October	191	11	(a)
2016 April	191	14	(c)
2013 October	191	15	
2015 October	191	21	
2015 April	191	21	
2015 October	191	22	
2015 April	191	22	
2014 April	191	28	
2015 October	191	31	
2015 April	191	31	
2012 October	191	33	(a)
2014 October	191	35	(a)
2015 April	191	41	
2016 April	191	42	(c)
2012 October	191	42	(c)
2015 October	191	51	(a)
2012 October	191	51	(a)
2015 October	191	51	(b)

All Sections Appearing on Exams Table

EXAM DATE	"PART"	"SECTION"	"PARAGRAPH"
2015 April	191	51	(b)
2014 October	191	51	(e)
2014 April	191	51	(e)
2012 October	191	51	(e)
2016 April	191	52	(a)
2012 October	191	53	(b)
2016 October	191	166	(b)
2015 October	191	171	
2015 April	191	171	
2016 April	191	192	(b)
Part 192: EXPORT CONTROL			
2012 April	192	4	
2012 April	192	14	(b)
Part 351: ANTIDUMPING AND COUNTERVAILING DUTIES			
2015 April	351	107	(a)
2015 October	351	107	(b)
2013 April	351	206	(a)
2016 April	351	402	(f)
2015 October	351	402	(f)
2015 April	351	402	(f)
2015 April	351	402	(f)
2014 October	351	402	(f)

Book 1 Part 9

Exam with Broker Commentary
October 2016 Customs Broker License Examination

This section of the study guide analyzes an actual customs broker exam. It presents the actual question and its multiple choices. For HTSUS classification questions, the author of this book has included abbreviated HTSUS Article Descriptions notated directly to the right of each multiple choice classification for the student's convenience and ease of reference purposes. As necessary, and in proportion to the complexity of each particular exam question, an analysis of the question and path to the correct answer has been provided. Direct excerpts from the HTSUS, 19 CFR, etc. are also included as supporting points of reference for each answer, as necessary. This exam (without commentary, etc.) and its answer key, as well as other previous customs exams can be downloaded directly from Customs' website at...

http://www.cbp.gov/document/publications/past-customs-broker-license-examinations-answer-keys

Exam Refs: Harmonized Tariff Schedule of the United States
Title 19, Code of Federal Regulations
Customs and Trade Automated Interface Requirements (CATAIR)
* Appendix B - Valid Codes
* Appendix D - Metric Conversion
* Appendix E - Valid Entry Numbers
* Appendix G - Common Errors
* Glossary of Terms
Instructions for Preparation of CBP Form 7501
Right to Make Entry Directive, 3530-002A

Exam Breakdown by Subject:

Category I –	Marking	Questions 1-3
Category II –	Power of Attorney	Questions 4-9
Category III –	Intellectual Property Rights	Questions 10-13
Category IV –	Practical Exercise	Questions 14-21
Category V –	Broker Compliance	Questions 22-27
Category VI –	Anti-Dumping/Countervailing	Questions 28-30
Category VII –	Bonds	Questions 31-34
Category VIII –	Classification	Questions 35-47
Category IX –	Drawback	Questions 48-51
Category X –	Free Trade Agreements	Questions 52-57
Category XI –	Value	Questions 58-61
Category XII –	Fines and Penalties	Questions 62-65
Category XIII –	Entry	Questions 66-76
Category XIV –	Foreign Trade Zones	Questions 77-80

Exam with Broker Commentary (Oct. 2016) — Study Guide

Category I: Marking

1. A CBP officer examines a shipment of widgets and determines that they are not legally marked. Which of the following statements is FALSE?

A. The importer may export the shipment

B. The importer may mark the shipment within 60 days

C. The importer may destroy the shipment

D. Failure to export, destroy or mark the shipment within the specified timeframe will result in additional duties of 10%

E. Failure to export, destroy or mark the shipment within the specified timeframe will result in liquidated damages equivalent to the value of the merchandise.

 As per 19 CFR 134.2 & 134.54(a):

134.2 Additional duties.
*Articles not marked as required by this part shall be **subject to additional duties of 10 percent of the final appraised value unless exported or destroyed under Customs supervision** prior to liquidation of the entry, as provided in 19 U.S.C. 1304(f). The 10 percent additional duty is assessable for failure either to mark the article (or container) to indicate the English name of the country of origin of the article or to include words or symbols required to prevent deception or mistake.*

134.54 Articles released from Customs custody.
*(a) Demand for liquidated damages. If within 30 days from the date of the notice of redelivery, or such additional period as the port director may allow for good cause shown, the importer does not properly mark or redeliver all merchandise previously released to him, **the port director shall demand payment of liquidated damages incurred under the bond in an amount equal to the entered value of the articles not properly marked or redelivered.***

 The answer is "B".

✓ **JUST A SIDE NOTE:** "Marking" refers to "Country of Origin Marking".

2. What is the amount of additional duties to which articles NOT marked as required under 19 CFR Part 134 may be subject?

A. $5,000 for each violation discovered.

B. 10 percent of the final appraised value of the merchandise.

C. The lesser of the domestic value of the merchandise or four times the loss of duties, taxes and fees; or if no loss of duties, taxes and fees, 40 percent of dutiable value of the merchandise.

D. A maximum of $10,000 for any one incident.

E. The entire bond amount in the case of an entry with single entry bond or in the case of continuous bond, the amount if the merchandise had been released under a single entry bond.

As per 19 CFR 134.2:

134.2 Additional duties.
Articles not marked as required by this part shall be subject to additional duties of 10 percent of the final appraised value unless exported or destroyed under Customs supervision prior to liquidation of the entry, as provided in 19 U.S.C. 1304(f). The 10 percent additional duty is assessable for failure either to mark the article (or container) to indicate the English name of the country of origin of the article or to include words or symbols required to prevent deception or mistake.

The correct answer is "B".

✓ **JUST A SIDE NOTE:** Below is a good example of a deceptive (or at the very least, misleading) country of origin marking…

3. What item is NOT a General Exception to the marking requirements?

A. Articles which are crude substances
B. Articles that are incapable of being marked
C. Products of possessions of the United States
D. Goods of a NAFTA country which are original works of art
E. Products of American fisheries which are not free of duty

 As per 19 CFR 134.32:

134.32 General exceptions to marking requirements.

The articles described or meeting the specified conditions set forth below are excepted from marking requirements (see subpart C of this part for marking of the containers):

(a) Articles that are incapable of being marked;

(b) Articles that cannot be marked prior to shipment to the United States without injury;

(c) Articles that cannot be marked prior to shipment to the United States except at an expense economically prohibitive of its importation;

(d) Articles for which the marking of the containers will reasonably indicate the origin of the articles;

(e) Articles which are crude substances;

... ...

(k) Products of American fisheries which are free of duty;

(l) Products of possessions of the United States;

(m) Products of the United States exported and returned;

(n) Articles exempt from duty under §§10.151 through 10.153, §145.31 or §145.32 of this chapter;

(o) Articles which cannot be marked after importation except at an expense that would be economically prohibitive unless the importer, producer, seller, or shipper failed to mark the articles before importation to avoid meeting the requirements of the law;

(p) Goods of a NAFTA country which are original works of art; and

(q) Goods of a NAFTA country which are provided for in subheading 6904.10 or heading 8541 or 8542 of the Harmonized Tariff Schedule of the United States (HTSUS) (19 U.S.C. 1202).

 Products of American fisheries which are "NOT free of duty" are not exempt. The correct answer is "E".

✔ **INTERESTINGLY ENOUGH:** "American Fisheries" refers to the 200 miles wide belt that runs along the coasts of the United States. This zone is known as the Exclusive Economic Zone (EEZ).

Category II: Power of Attorney

4. Which of the following is NOT a true statement concerning Power of Attorney (POA)?

A. Written notification to the client of the option to pay CBP directly is to be cited within the POA document or be attached to the POA.
B. Brokers are not required to file POA with the Port Director but must retain them and make them available to CBP upon demand.
C. The name of the Broker on the POA must match the name on the Broker's license. If the Broker has been approved to use a trade or fictitious name, the Broker's name must be included on the POA followed by "doing business as" the approved trade or fictitious name.
D. POA must be retained until revoked. Letters of Revocation must be retained for 3 years after the date of revocation or 2 years after the date the client ceases to be an active client.
E. POA issued by a partnership shall be limited to a period not to exceed 2 years from the date of execution.

 As per 19 CFR, 111.29(b), 141.46, 111.30(c), 111.23(b), 141.34:

111.29 (b) Notice to client of method of payment—(1) **All brokers must provide their clients with the following written notification:**

If you are the importer of record, payment to the broker will not relieve you of liability for customs charges (duties, taxes, or other debts owed CBP) in the event the charges are not paid by the broker. Therefore, if you pay by check, ***customs charges may be paid with a separate check payable to the "U.S. Customs and Border Protection"*** *which will be delivered to CBP by the broker.*
... ...
(i) **On, or attached to, any power of attorney** *provided by the broker to a client for execution on or after September 27, 1982; and*

141.46 Power of attorney retained by customhouse broker.
Before transacting Customs business in the name of his principal, a customhouse broker is required to obtain a valid power of attorney to do so. ***He is not required to file the power of attorney with a port director. Customhouse brokers shall retain powers of attorney with their books and papers, and make them available*** *to representatives of the Department of the Treasury as provided in subpart C of part 111 of this chapter.*

111.30(c) Change in name. ... ... The name must not be used until the approval of Headquarters has been received. In the case of a trade or fictitious name, ***the broker must affix his own name in conjunction with each signature of the trade or fictitious name when signing customs documents.***

111.23 (b) Period of retention. The records described in this section, other than powers of attorney, must be retained for at least 5 years after the date of entry. ***Powers of attorney must be retained until revoked, and revoked powers of attorney and letters of revocation must be retained for 5 years after the date of revocation or for 5 years after the date the client ceases to be an "active client"*** *as defined in §111.29(b)(2)(ii), ...*

141.34 Duration of power of attorney.
Powers of attorney issued by a partnership shall be limited to a period not to exceed 2 years *from the date of execution. All other powers of attorney may be granted for an unlimited period.*

 As with most all CBP record retention, 5 years is the requirement. The correct answer is "D".

Using the information provided below, please answer Questions 5 through 9.

Below are two Powers of Attorney (POA). The first was received by Daniel Evans, General Manager, East Coast Freight Forwarder & Logistics, Inc. (a freight forwarder), from General Merchants Corp., on December 31, 2008 (POA1). The second was issued by East Coast Freight Forwarder & Logistics, Inc. to Russell Morris, a customs broker doing business as Quick Brokers, on January 2, 2009 (POA 2). The importing history between the customs broker on behalf of the importer of record demonstrates that entries were made on February 1, 2009; March 1, 2009 and May 22, 2009.

POA 1: East Coast Freight Forwarder & Logistics, Inc. from General Merchants Corp.

CUSTOMS POWER OF ATTORNEY

I hereby authorize East Coast Freight Forwarders & Logistics, Inc. to act as General Merchants Corp. agent and customs broker and to file entry/entry summary for all commercial shipments from January 1, 2009 onwards. General Merchants Corp. authorizes other duly licensed customs brokers to act as Grantor's agent.

(Capacity): BUYER   Date: DECEMBER 31, 2008   (Signature) __(Signed)__

POA 2: East Coast Freight Forwarder & Logistics, Inc. to Russell Morris dba Quick Brokers

---

CUSTOMS POWER OF ATTORNEY

KNOW ALL MEN BY THESE PRESENTS: That GENERAL MERCHANTS CORP doing business as a corporation under the laws of the State of Texas residing or having a place of business at 2960 EL ZAPATO LAREDO, TEXAS hereby constitutes and appoints RUSSELL MORRIS dba QUICK BROKERS, which may act through any of it's licensed officers or employees duly authorized to sign documents by power of attorney as a true and lawful agent and attorney of the grantor named above for and in the name, place, and stead of said grantor from this date and in ALL Customs Ports and in no other name, to make, endorse, sign, declare, or swear to any entry, withdrawal, declaration, certificate, bill of lading, carnet, or other document required by law or regulation in connection with the importation, transportation, or exportation of any merchandise shipped or consigned by or to said grantor; to perform any act or condition which may be required by law or regulation in connection with such merchandise; to receive any merchandise deliverable to said grantor.

To receive, endorse and collect checks issued for Customs duty refunds in grantor's name drawn on the Treasurer of the United States.

This power of attorney is to remain in full force and effect until revocation in writing is duly given to and received by grantee (if the donor of this power of attorney is a partnership, the said power shall in no case have any force or effect in the United States after the expiration 2 years from the dates of its execution);

IN WITNESS WHEREOF: the said GENERAL MERCHANTS CORP. has caused these presents to be sealed and signed:

(Signature) __(Signed)__   (Print Name) __DANIEL EVANS__

(Capacity) __ATTORNEY IN FACT__   Date: __JANUARY 2, 2009__

Witness: (if required) _____ (Signature) _____

If you are the importer of record, payment to the broker will not relieve you of liability for customs charges (duties, taxes, or other debts owed CBP) in the event the charges are not paid by the broker. Therefore, if you pay by check, customs charges may be paid with a separate check payable to U.S. Customs and Border Protection which shall be delivered to CBP by the broker. Importers who wish to utilize this procedure must contact our office in advance to arrange timely receipt of duty checks.

5. Which person or entity may act as the intended importer of record?

A. General Merchants Corp.

B. East Coast Logistics, Inc.

C. The nominal consignee

D. Quick Brokers

E. Daniel Evans A.I.F.

 As per RIGHT TO MAKE ENTRY DIRECTIVE 3530-002a, SECTION 5.1.2 & 5.3.1 & 5.3.2:

*5.1.2 Section 484 provides that **only the "importer of record" has the right to make entry. "Importer of Record" is defined as the owner or purchaser of the goods**, or when designated by the owner, purchaser, or consignee, a licensed Customs broker.*

*5.3.1 The terms "owner" and "purchaser" include any party with a financial interest in a transaction, including, but not limited to, the actual owner of the goods, the actual purchaser of the goods, a buying or selling agent, a person or firm who imports on consignment, a person or firm who imports under loan or lease, a person or firm who imports for exhibition at a trade fair, a person or firm who imports goods for repair or alteration or further fabrication, etc. Any such owner or purchaser may make entry on his own behalf or may designate a licensed Customs broker to make entry on his behalf and may be shown as the importer of record on the CF 7501. **The terms "owner" or "purchaser" would not include a "nominal consignee" who effectively possesses no other right, title, or interest in the goods except as he possessed under a bill of lading, air waybill, or other shipping document.***

5.3.2 Examples of nominal consignees not authorized to file Customs entries are express consignment operators (ECO), freight consolidators who handle consolidated shipments as described in 5.10 below, and Customs brokers who are not permitted to transact business in Customs ports where a shipment is being entered.

 The purchaser, General Merchants Corp., is the intended importer of record (IOR). They have not otherwise designated the customs broker to act as IOR on their behalf. The correct answer is "A".

✔ **JUST A SIDE NOTE:** "5.10" of the above-mentioned directive just refers to "Warehouse entries and withdrawals".

6. Based on the information provided for POA 1, which statement is TRUE?

A.   POA 1 allows the forwarder to create a subagency relationship (i.e., assign the POA to a broker)

B.   POA 1 allows the East Coast Logistics, Inc. to classify and value the imported merchandise, and report the outcome to U.S. Customs and Border Protection

C.   The Vice President of an incorporated business entity must sign the POA 1.

D.   POA 1 is invalid since it does not allow for the service of process.

E.   POA 1 must be on CBP Form 5291 "Power of Attorney"

As per 19 CFR 141.31(a) & 141.32:

141.31   General requirements and definitions.
(a) Limited or general power of attorney. ***A power of attorney may be executed for the transaction by an agent or attorney of a specified part or all the Customs business of the principal.***

141.32   Form for power of attorney.
Customs Form 5291 may be used for giving power of attorney to transact Customs business. ***If a Customs power of attorney is not on a Customs Form 5291, it shall be either a general power of attorney with unlimited authority or a limited power of attorney*** *as explicit in its terms and executed in the same manner as a Customs Form 5291. The following is an example of an acceptable general power of attorney with unlimited authority:*

KNOW ALL MEN BY THESE PRESENTS, THAT

_____
(Name of principal)

_____,

____ (State legal designation, such as corporation, individual, etc.) residing at _____ and doing business under the laws of the State of _____, hereby appoints
_____
(Name, legal designation, and address)

as a true and lawful agent and attorney of the principal named above with full power and authority to do and perform every lawful act and thing the said agent and attorney may deem requisite and necessary to be done for and on behalf of the said principal without limitation of any kind as fully as said principal could do if present and acting, and hereby ratify and confirm all that said agent and attorney shall lawfully do or cause to be done by virtue of these presents until and including _____, (date) or until notice of revocation in writing is duly given before that date.

Date _____, 19__;.

_____
(Principal's signature)

The question's POA 1 is a general (i.e. not limited) POA from the importer that, explicitly in writing, "authorizes other duly licensed customs brokers to act as (their) agent". The correct answer is "A".

✓ **NOTE:** "Customs Form 5291" is no longer an official CBP form. Most companies just create their own by following the above guidelines, and adding a generous portion of their own terms and conditions.

7. Based on the information provided for POA 2, which statement is FALSE?

A. POA 2 identifies a resident principal.

B. POA 2 omits the "notice to client of method of payment".

C. Failure of the broker to retain a valid POA may result in a monetary penalty in an amount not to exceed an aggregate of $30,000.00 for one or more violations.

D. POA 2 may be granted for an unlimited period of time.

E. POA 2 authorizes the broker to sign documents in Puerto Rico.

 As per the question's reference POA 2:

If you are the importer of record, payment to the broker will not relieve you of liability for customs charges (duties, taxes, or other debts owed CBP) in the event the charges are not paid by the broker. Therefore, if you pay by check, **customs charges may be paid with a separate check payable to U.S. Customs and Border Protection** *which shall be delivered to CBP by the broker. Importers who wish to utilize this procedure must contact our office in advance to arrange timely receipt of duty checks.*

 The correct answer is "B".

✔ **JUST A SIDE NOTE:** In reference to the harsh tone of multiple choice "C"... Although a customs broker may be penalized up to a maximum of $30,000 for any violation or aggregate of violations, simply misplacing a single POA would only amount to a $1,000 penalty per POA. Furthermore, this amount could be mitigated down, depending on the circumstances. Appendix C to 19 CFR Part 171 spells this out...
… …

E. Penalties for failure to retain powers of attorney from clients to act in their names.

1. The penalty notice should also cite 19 CFR 141.46 as the regulation violated.

2. Assessment amount—$1,000 for each power of attorney not on file.

3. Mitigation—for a first offense, mitigate to an amount between $250 and $500 unless extraordinary mitigating factors are present, in which case full mitigation should be afforded. An extraordinary mitigating factor would be a fire, theft or other destruction of records beyond broker control. Subsequent offenses—no mitigation unless extraordinary mitigating factors are present.

4. Penalty should be mitigated in full if it can be established that a valid power of attorney had been issued to the broker, but it was misplaced or destroyed through clerical error or mistake.
… …

8. Upon review of both POA's, which statement is FALSE?

A. The customs broker may prepare and present the entry summary to CBP

B. East Coast Freight Forwarder & Logistics, Inc. may authorize the customs broker to forward a completed CBP Form 3461

C. The customs broker shall exercise responsible supervision and control when transacting customs business.

D. The POA may be completed and signed after the merchandise has been released from CBP custody.

E. General Merchants Corp. is a resident corporate principal.

As per 19 CFR 141.46:

141.46 Power of attorney retained by customhouse broker.

<u>Before</u> transacting Customs business in the name of his principal, a customhouse broker is required to obtain a valid power of attorney to do so. *He is not required to file the power of attorney with a port director. Customhouse brokers shall retain powers of attorney with their books and papers, and make them available to representatives of the Department of the Treasury as provided in subpart C of part 111 of this chapter.*

Common sense and Customs say the correct answer is "D".

✓ **JUST A SIDE NOTE:** For practical reasons, a Customs Power of Attorney is usually completed by the importer/client without specifying the length of POA validity. The client, however, can choose to specify that the POA is effective for a single shipment, or only for a defined period of time.

9. The Customs broker shall retain POA 2 for a period of 5 years starting on _____.

A. December 31, 2008

B. January 2, 2009

C. February 1, 2009

D. March 1, 2009

E. May 22, 2009

 As per 19 CFR 111.23(b):

(b) Period of retention. The records described in this section, other than powers of attorney, must be retained for at least 5 years after the date of entry. **Powers of attorney must be retained until revoked, and revoked powers of attorney and letters of revocation must be retained for 5 years after the date of revocation or for 5 years after the date the client ceases to be an "active client"** *as defined in §111.29(b)(2)(ii), whichever period is later. When merchandise is withdrawn from a bonded warehouse, records relating to the withdrawal must be retained for 5 years from the date of withdrawal of the last merchandise withdrawn under the entry.*

 The customs broker last transacted customs business for the client on May 22, 2009. The correct answer is "E".

✓ **JUST A SIDE NOTE:** The revocation of a Customs Power of Attorney must be in writing. Per 19 CFR 141.35:

141.35 Revocation of power of attorney.

Any power of attorney shall be subject to revocation at any time by written notice given to and received by the port director.

Category III: Intellectual Property Rights

10. Which of the following is NOT required when submitting an application to record a trademark?

A. The name, address and citizenship of the trademark owner or owners

B. The name or trade style to be recorded

C. The name and principal business address of each foreign person or business entity authorized or licensed to use the trade name and statement as the use authorized

D. The name of the person submitting the application if different from the owner

E. A description of the merchandise with which the trade name is associated

 As per 19 CFR 133.12:

133.12 Application to record a trade name.

An application to record a trade name shall be in writing addressed to the IPR & Restricted Merchandise Branch, 1300 Pennsylvania Avenue, NW., Washington, DC 20229, and shall include the following information:

*(a) The **name, complete business address, and citizenship of the trade name owner or owners** (if a partnership, the citizenship of each partner; if an association or corporation, the State, country, or other political jurisdiction within which it was organized, incorporated or created);*

*(b) The **name or trade style to be recorded**;*

*(c) The **name and principal business address of each foreign person or business entity authorized or licensed to use the trade name and a statement as to the use authorized**;*

(d) The identity of any parent or subsidiary company, or other foreign company under common ownership or control which uses the trade name abroad (see §133.2(d)); and

*(e) A **description of the merchandise with which the trade name is associated**.*

 The correct answer is "D".

✓ **JUST A SIDE NOTE:** A good example of a trademark is the "Swoosh" logo, a trademark of Nike, Inc.

11. A "counterfeit mark" is a (n)_____ mark that is identical with, or substantially indistinguishable from, a mark registered on the Principal Register of the U.S. Patent and Trademark Office.

A. Authentic

B. Irregular

C. Unreadable

D. Unrecognizable

E. None of the above

 As per 19 CFR 133.21(a):

133.21 Articles suspected of bearing counterfeit marks.

(a) Counterfeit mark defined. A "counterfeit mark" is a spurious mark that is identical with, or substantially indistinguishable from, a mark registered on the Principal Register of the U.S. Patent and Trademark Office.

 The correct answer is "E" (None of the above).

✓ **JUST A SIDE NOTE:** According to Wikipedia's definition, "spurious can refer to: seeming to be genuine but false, based on false ideas or facts".

12. The following, if introduced or attempted to be introduced into the U.S. contrary to law, shall be seized:

A. Merchandise marked intentionally in violation of Title 19, United States Code, section 1304

B. Merchandise, the importation or entry of which is subject to any restriction or prohibition imposed by law relating to health, safety, or conservation and which is not in compliance with the applicable rule, regulation or statute

C. Merchandise whose importation or entry requires a license, permit or other authorization of a U.S. government agency, and which is not accompanied by such license, permit or authorization

D. Merchandise subject to quantitative restrictions, unless appropriate visa, permit license, or similar document, or stamp is presented to CBP

E. Merchandise that is stolen, smuggled, or clandestinely imported or introduced

 As per 19 CFR 162.23:

162.23 Seizure under section 596(c), Tariff Act of 1930, as amended (19 U.S.C. 1595a(c)).

*(a) **Mandatory seizures**. The following, if introduced or attempted to be introduced into the United States contrary to law, shall be seized pursuant to section 596(c), Tariff Act of 1930, as amended (19 U.S.C. 1595a(c)):*

*(1) **Merchandise that is stolen, smuggled, or clandestinely imported or introduced**;*
... ...

*(b) **Permissive seizures**. The following, if introduced or attempted to be introduced into the United States contrary to law, may be seized pursuant to section 596(c), Tariff Act of 1930, as amended (19 U.S.C. 1595a(c)):*

*(1) **Merchandise the importation or entry of which is subject to any restriction or prohibition imposed by law relating to health, safety, or conservation, and which is not in compliance with the applicable rule, regulation or statute;***

*(2) **Merchandise the importation or entry of which requires a license, permit or other authorization of a United States Government agency, and which is not accompanied by such license, permit or authorization;***
... ...

*(5) **Merchandise marked intentionally in violation of 19 U.S.C. 1304**;*
... ...

*(7) **Merchandise subject to quantitative restrictions**, found to bear a counterfeit visa, permit, license, or similar document, or stamp from the United States or from a foreign government or issuing authority pursuant to a multilateral or bilateral agreement (but see paragraph (e), of this section).*

All of the above multiple choice scenarios are subject to seizure. Exam credit was given to all examinees. It appears they misworded multiple choice "D".

13. CBP officers examine a commercial shipment of T-shirts and find that many of the t-shirts bear suspect versions of popular trademarks. Upon further investigation, the officers find that the suspect marks are recorded with CBP. Through the broker, the officers notify the importer in writing that the shipment has been detained and request information that would assist CBP in determining whether the detained merchandise bears counterfeit marks. The importer does not respond to the notice and the trademark owners, when contacted, advise that the suspect marks were not applied with authorization. CBP seizes the merchandise on the basis that it bears counterfeit marks. The importer wishes to challenge CBP's decision. What options does the importer have?

A. Request a change of entry type from formal to informal

B. Re-export the commodity to the country of exportation

C. File an in-bond to another port for entry

D. File a petition for relief

E. Pay the counterfeit duty and enter the shipment anyway

 As per 19 CFR 133.21(g):

*(g) Consent of the mark owner; failure to make appropriate disposition. The owner of the mark, within thirty days from notification of seizure, may provide written consent to the importer allowing the importation of the seized merchandise in its condition as imported **or its exportation**, entry after obliteration of the mark, or other appropriate disposition. Otherwise, the merchandise will be disposed of in accordance with §133.52 of this part,* **subject to the importer's right to petition for relief** *from forfeiture under the provisions of part 171 of this chapter.*

The exam key states that the correct answer is "D". However, we can clearly see from the above paragraph (g), that the owner of the mark may, at the owner's discretion, allow the importer to (among other options) re-export/export the shipment back (i.e. multiple choice "B").

✓ **JUST A SIDE NOTE:** Imported goods that are subsequently exported back to the country of export, or exported to a third country are called "re-exports" by Customs.

Category III: Intellectual Property Rights

Using the information provided below, answer questions **14 – 18**.

On April 12, 2015, an importer in the U.S. receives 500 single action economy stopwatches shipped by air from Munich, Germany. The shipment was entered and released through ABI by CBP on April 8, 2015. The stopwatches are packaged for retail sale and are invoiced at U.S. $ 24 F.O.B per stopwatch. The stopwatches are classified under HTSUS 9102.99.60 e/o nominee. The Watch Information Sheet indicates the following:

Manufacturer: Bern Watch Inc.
Model: A1020 Single Action Stopwatch
Features: * Perfect for industrial use
* Start/stop by crown, reset by 10 o'clock button
* Preset push button
* Long hand 60 sec per turn, 1/100 min. increments
* 30 minute short hand
* Rugged steel case
* 1 year warranty
* Quality movement made in Switzerland

Type of Display:	Mechanical with hands	
Type of Movement:	Mechanical	Value US$ 18.50
Type of Case:	Base Metal, Chrome Plated	Value US$ 5.00
Type of Packaging:	Clear Plastic Blister Pack	Value US$ 0.50
Battery Powered:	No	
Automatic Winding:	No	
Number of jewels in movement:	13	
Country of Origin:	Switzerland	

14. What is the DUTY due on this entry?

A. $ 560.00

B. $ 535.00

C. $ 235.00

D. $ 730.00

E. $ 23.50

 As per HTSUS 9102.99.60:

| 9102.99.60 | 1/ | With movement valued over $15 each............ | 1/ | $1.16 each + 6% on the case |

 The correct answer is "D".

  580.00 (500 watches x $1.16 ea. duty)
+ 150.00 ($5.00 casing x 500 watches x 0.06 duty)
= 730.00

✔ **JUST A SIDE NOTE:** The above assessment is a good example of compound duty. Compound duty is where there are duties on an item based on its 1) value AND on its 2) quantity, or weight, or volume, etc.

15. What is the merchandise processing fee due on this entry?

A. $ 2.00

B. $ 25.00

C. $ 41.57

D. $ 485.00

E. Watches are exempt from MPF.

 As per 19 CFR 24.23(b):

*(b) Fees—(1) Formal entry or release—(i) Ad valorem fee—(A) General. Except as provided in paragraph (c) of this section, **merchandise that is formally entered or released is subject to the payment to CBP of an ad valorem fee of 0.3464 percent.** The 0.3464 ad valorem fee is due and payable to CBP by the importer of record of the merchandise at the time of presentation of the entry summary and is based on the value of the merchandise as determined under 19 U.S.C. 1401a. In the case of an express consignment carrier facility or centralized hub facility, each shipment covered by an individual air waybill or bill of lading that is formally entered and valued at $2,500 or less is subject to a $1.00 per individual air waybill or bill of lading fee and, if applicable, to the 0.3464 percent ad valorem fee in accordance with paragraph (b)(4) of this section.*

*(B) Maximum and minimum fees. Subject to the provisions of paragraphs (b)(1)(ii) and (d) of this section relating to the surcharge and to aggregation of the ad valorem fee respectively, the ad valorem fee charged under paragraph (b)(1)(i)(A) of this section **must not exceed $485 and must not be less than $25.***

 The correct answer is "C".

```
  12,000.00 (Entered value of 500 watches x $24.00 ea.)
x    .003464 (MPF)
=     41.57
```

✔ **NOTE:** As per the above 19 CFR excerpt, for formal entries, such as this one, the MPF minimum is $25 and maximum is $485.

16. What is the International Standard Country Code (ISO) for the country of origin?

A. CF

B. CH

C. CN

D. SZ

E. DE

 As per HTSUS, Annex B (International Standard Country Codes):

Sweden	SE
Switzerland	CH
Syrian Arab Republic	SY

 The correct answer is "B".

✓ **INTERESTINGLY ENOUGH:** According to Wikipedia:

A watch is considered Swiss, according to the Swiss law if:

- *its movement is Swiss and,*
- *its movement is cased up in Switzerland and;*
- *the manufacturer carries out the final inspection in Switzerland*

17. Which statement regarding the plastic blister packaging is TRUE?

A. The packaging is classified with the stopwatches.

B. The packaging is classified separately as articles of plastic.

C. The packaging costs are deducted from the entered value.

D. The packaging must include the importer's name.

E. The packaging must include the manufacturer's name.

 As per HTSUS, GRI 5 (b):

5. In addition to the foregoing provisions, the following rules shall apply in respect of the goods referred to therein:

   (a) Camera cases, musical instrument cases, gun cases, drawing instrument cases, necklace cases and similar containers, specially shaped or fitted to contain a specific article or set of articles, suitable for long-term use and entered with the articles for which they are intended, shall be classified with such articles when of a kind normally sold therewith. This rule does not, however, apply to containers which give the whole its essential character;

   (b) Subject to the provisions of rule 5(a) above, packing materials and packing containers entered with the goods therein shall be classified with the goods if they are of a kind normally used for packing such goods. However, this provision is not binding when such packing materials or packing containers are clearly suitable for repetitive use.

The type of packaging used to contain the stopwatches, "clear plastic blister pack", is clearly NOT suitable for repetitive use. Accordingly, the packaging is NOT classified separately and is instead entered with the stopwatches that they contain. The correct answer is "A".

✓ **INTERESTINGLY ENOUGH:** A "blister pack" is a pre-molded, bubble-like, and semi-rigid plastic packaging that in some forms resemble a skin blister. Ironically, "skin packaging" is different than blister packaging in that it is more of a film-like plastic closely molded onto the product.

18. Six months after the entry summary for the stopwatches was filed, the importer informs the broker he gave a die (purchased from a nonrelated U.S. firm at a cost of U.S. $500) to Bern Watch Inc., without charge, to be used only for the manufacturing of the 500 stopwatches. Transportation and duty costs to the importer to get the die to Bern were an additional U.S. $70. Based on this information, the broker should:

A. Take no action because the entry summary is already projected for liquidation.

B. Submit a SIL to CBP with a check for US $570 because this is a proceed to the seller, Bern Watch Inc.

C. Submit a SIL or a Prior Disclosure to CBP because this is an assist valued at US $500.

D. Submit a SIL or a Prior Disclosure to CBP because this is an assist valued at US $570.

E. Submit as a SIL requesting that the entered value be reduced by the amount of the assist and that the subsequent difference in duty and fees be refunded.

 As per 19 CFR 152.103(d):

(d) Assist. If the value of an assist is to be added to the price actually paid or payable, or to be used as a component of computed value, the port director shall determine the value of the assist and apportion that value to the price of the imported merchandise in the following manner:

(1) If the assist consist of materials, components, parts, or similar items incorporated in the imported merchandise, or items consumed in the production of the imported merchandise, acquired by the buyer from an unrelated seller, the value of the assist is the cost of its acquisition. If the assist were produced by the buyer or a person related to the buyer, its value would be the cost of its production. In either case, the value of the assist would include transportation costs to the place of production.

*(2) **If the assist consists of tools, dies, molds, or similar items used in the production of the imported merchandise, acquired by the buyer from an unrelated seller, the value of the assist is the cost of its acquisition.** If the assist were produced by the buyer or a person related to the buyer, its value would be cost of its production. If the assist has been used previously by the buyer, regardless of whether it had been acquired or produced by him, the original cost of acquisition or production would be adjusted downward to reflect its use before its value could be determined. If the assist were leased by the buyer from an unrelated seller, the value of the assist would be the cost of the lease. **In either case, the value of the assist would include transportation costs to the place of production.** Repairs or modifications to an assist may increase its value.*

 The correct answer is "D".

   500.00 (value of die)
 + 70.00 (transportation and duty costs to place of production)
 = 570.00

✓ **NOTE:** The Supplemental Information Letter (SIL) program is no longer used. Instead, a Post Entry Amendment (PEA) can be submitted up to 20 business days prior to the scheduled liquidation date of the entry. Usually the scheduled liquidation date is 314 calendar days after the customs entry date.

Using the invoice provided below, answer questions **19** through **21**.

COMMERCIAL INVOICE			
EL GORDO de S.A.			
Shipper/Exporter El Gordo's Fajita Shack de S.A.. 2568 Bagdad Matamoros, Tamaulipas Mexico		**No. and Date of Invoice** US001836 Lunes, Julio 14, 2007	
		No. and Date of L/C	
For Account and Risk of Messers Crocketts Cafe 301 Alamo Plaza San Antonio, TX 78205		**L/C Issuing Bank**	
Notify Party R.Person, 956.729.3070		**Remarks** P/O No.: TPS001 Not subject to AD/CVD cases	
Port of Lading Matamoros, Tamaulipas Mexico	**Final Destination** San Antonio		
Carrier	**Departure on or about** July 17, 2007	Marks and Numbers of Pkgs. Fernando's Fire Salsa 25/1. 16 Ounce Jar.	
Description of Goods	**Quantity**	**Unit Price**	**Amount**
1. Country of Origin: Mexico Salsa: Ingredients - Tomato puree, peppers (jalapeno, ancho, cascabel), vinegar, onions, garlic, salt, cottonseed oil, bay leaves, and spices. PN: HOTSAUCEFI One pound jar	10000 pieces	0.35 USD	$3500
2. Country of Origin: Vietnam Shrimp: Peeled, headless weight 33 – 45 per kg., dusted w/flour, quick frozen	400 kgs.	0.90 USD	$360
(2%, Net 15 Days) **TOTAL**			$3,860
Master Bill: 001-63324833 House Bill: COSC56676406 Estimated Entry Date 07/18/07			

19. What is the classification of the salsa?

A. 2002.90.8050   Tomatoes prepared or preserved otherwise than by vinegar or acetic acid>>Other>>Other>>Other

B. 2005.91.9700   Other vegetables prepared or preserved otherwise than by vinegar or acetic acid, not frozen, other than products of heading 2006>>Other vegetables and mixtures of vegetables>>Bamboo Shoots>>Other

C. 2103.20.4020   Sauces and preparations therefore; mixed condiments and mixed seasonings; mustard flour and meal and prepared mustard>>Tomato ketchup and other tomato sauces>>Other>>In containers holding less than 1.4kg

D. 2103.90.9051   Sauces and preparations therefore; mixed condiments and mixed seasonings; mustard flour and meal and prepared mustard>>Other>>Other>>Other>>Tomato-based preparations for sauces>>In containers holding less than 1.4kg

E. 2103.90.9091   Sauces and preparations therefore; mixed condiments and mixed seasonings; mustard flour and meal and prepared mustard>>Other>>Other>>Other>>Other

 As per HTSUS Chapter 21:

Heading/ Subheading	Stat. Suf-fix	Article Description	Unit of Quantity	Rates of Duty 1 General	Rates of Duty 1 Special	2
2103		Sauces and preparations therefore; mixed condiments and mixed seasonings; mustard flour and meal and prepared mustard:				
2103.10.00	00	Soy sauce...........	kg	3%	Free (A, AU, BH, CA, CL, CO, D, E, IL, JO, KR, MA, MX, OM, P, PA, PE, SG)	35%
2103.20		Tomato ketchup and other tomato sauces:				
2103.20.20	00	Tomato ketchup...........	kg	6%	Free (A, AU, BH, CA, CL, CO, D, E, IL, JO, KR, MA, MX, OM, P, PA, PE, SG)	35%
2103.20.40		Other...........		11.6%	Free (A+, BH, CA, CL, CO, D, E, IL, JO, MX, OM, P, PA, PE, SG) 3.3% (KR) See 9912.21.05-9912.21.20 (MA) See 9913.96.57-9913.96.66 (AU)	50%
	20	In containers holding less than 1.4 kg...........	kg			
	40	Other...........	kg			

I'd just like to opine that the person who wrote the exam made a poor selection of an over-ambiguous example to test classification skills in this first classification-type question. Without getting into the Explanatory Notes (EN), let's just say that salsa is defined as a "spicy tomato sauce". As per GRI 3(a), the subheading 2103.20 provision for "tomato sauces" provides the most accurate and complete description of the article, salsa. The correct answer is "C".

✓ **INTERESTINGLY ENOUGH:** "Salsa" in Latin means "salty".

20. Column 31 of the CBP Form 7501 should indicate _____ for the salsa.

A. 4,536 kilograms

B. 10,000 pounds

C. 10,000 pieces

D. 16 ounces

E. 2,2046 kilograms

 As per FORM 7501 INSTRUCTIONS, Column 31:

COLUMN 31) NET QUANTITY IN HTS UNITS

When a unit of measure is specified in the HTS for an HTS number, report the net quantity in the specified unit of measure, *and show the unit of measure after the net quantity figure. Record quantities in whole numbers for statistical purposes unless fractions of units are required for other CBP purposes. Fractions must be expressed as decimals.*

 For the salsa classification 2103.20.4020, a unit of measure of "kg" is specified. The correct answer is "A".

Here's the math…

    10,000 (number of jars of salsa per the commercial invoice)
x 0.453592 kg (each salsa jar = 1 pound = 0.453592 kg)
= 4,536 (rounded to nearest kilogram)

✓ **NOTE:** Best to bring a metric/standard conversion cheat sheet to the exam, just in case a question like this shows up.

21. The shrimp is identified as line item 002 of the Entry Summary. The correct information for identifying line number 002 from the abbreviated Entry Summary at Blocks 27 through 29 is:

A.

27.	28. Description of Merchandise		
Line No.	29. A. HTSUS No. B. ADA/CVD Case No.	30. A. Gross Weight B. Manifest Qty.	31. Net Quantity in HTSUS Units
002 O-VN	SHRIMP, Frozen dusted 1605.20.1030		

B.

27.	28. Description of Merchandise		
Line No.	29. A. HTSUS No. B. ADA/CVD Case No.	31. A. Gross Weight B. Manifest Qty.	31. Net Quantity in HTSUS Units
002 O-MX	SHRIMP, Frozen dusted 0306.23.0040		

C.

27.	28. Description of Merchandise		
Line No.	29. A. HTSUS No. B. ADA/CVD Case No.	32. A. Gross Weight B. Manifest Qty.	31. Net Quantity in HTSUS Units
002	SHRIMP, Frozen dusted 1605.90.6060		

D.

27.	28. Description of Merchandise		
Line No.	29. A. HTSUS No. B. ADA/CVD Case No.	33. A. Gross Weight B. Manifest Qty.	31. Net Quantity in HTSUS Units
002 VN	SHRIMP, Frozen dusted 0306.23.0040		

E.

27.	28. Description of Merchandise		
Line No.	29. A. HTSUS No. B. ADA/CVD Case No.	34. A. Gross Weight B. Manifest Qty.	31. Net Quantity in HTSUS Units
002	SHRIMP, Frozen dusted 1605.20.1030		

 As per FORM 7501 INSTRUCTIONS, Block 10:

When an entry summary covers merchandise from more than one country of origin, record the word "MULTI" in this block. In column 27, directly below the line number, prefixed with the letter "O," indicate the ISO code corresponding to each line item.

The salsa was made in Mexico and the shrimp in Vietnam (i.e. multi-origin). Accordingly, the country of origin for the shrimp, ISO code "VN", will be preceded by the letter "O". The correct answer is "A".

✔ **NOTE:** The HTS numbers in blocks 29 are fictitious, or at least from the sub-heading level. However, there is sufficient information presented in blocks 27 to select the correct answer.

Category V: Broker Compliance

22. If a Customs broker receives payment of duty, taxes and fees from a client after the due date to CBP, the broker must transmit the payment to the Government _____.

A. within 24-48 hours

B. within 5 calendar days

C. within 5 working days

D. within 10 calendar days

E. within 10 working days

 As per 19 CFR 111.29(a):

111.29 Diligence in correspondence and paying monies.

(a) Due diligence by broker. Each broker must exercise due diligence in making financial settlements, in answering correspondence, and in preparing or assisting in the preparation and filing of records relating to any customs business matter handled by him as a broker. Payment of duty, tax, or other debt or obligation owing to the Government for which the broker is responsible, or for which the broker has received payment from a client, must be made to the Government on or before the date that payment is due. **Payments received by a broker from a client after the due date must be transmitted to the Government within 5 working days from receipt by the broker.** *Each broker must provide a written statement to a client accounting for funds received for the client from the Government, or received from a client where no payment to the Government has been made, or received from a client in excess of the Governmental or other charges properly payable as part of the client's customs business, within 60 calendar days of receipt. No written statement is required if there is actual payment of the funds by a broker.*

The correct answer is "C".

✔ **JUST A SIDE NOTE:** Form of payment to CBP may be, among others described in 19 CFR 24.1, U.S. Currency (i.e. cash), cashier's check, certified check, and uncertified check (i.e. personal or business check) if certain conditions are met by the uncertified check writer.

23. How long does the Broker have to submit new employee information to Customs & Border protection?

A. 10 Business days after employment for 30 consecutive days.

B. 30 Calendar days after employment for 30 consecutive days

C. 15 Calendar days after employment initiated.

D. 30 Business days after employment initiated.

E. 10 Calendar days after employment for 30 consecutive days.

 As per 19 CFR 111.28(b):

(b) Employee information—(1) Current employees—(i) General. Each broker must submit, in writing, to the director of each port at which the broker intends to transact customs business, a list of the names of persons currently employed by the broker at that port. The list of employees must be submitted upon issuance of a permit for an additional district under §111.19, or upon the opening of an office at a port within a district for which the broker already has a permit, and before the broker begins to transact customs business as a broker at the port. For each employee, the broker also must provide the social security number, date and place of birth, current home address, last prior home address, and, if the employee has been employed by the broker for less than 3 years, the name and address of each former employer and dates of employment for the 3-year period preceding current employment with the broker. After the initial submission, an updated list, setting forth the name, social security number, date and place of birth, and current home address of each current employee, must be submitted with the status report required by §111.30(d).

*(ii) **New employees. In the case of a new employee, the broker must submit to the port director the written information required under paragraph (b)(1)(i) of this section within 10 calendar days after the new employee has been employed by the broker for 30 consecutive days.***

(2) Terminated employees. Within 30 calendar days after the termination of employment of any person employed longer than 30 consecutive days, the broker must submit the name of the terminated employee, in writing, to the director of the port at which the person was employed.

(3) Broker's responsibility. Notwithstanding a broker's responsibility for providing the information required in paragraph (b)(1) of this section, in the absence of culpability by the broker, Customs will not hold him responsible for the accuracy of any information that is provided to the broker by the employee.

 The correct answer is "E".

✓ **JUST A SIDE NOTE:** As per 19 CFR 111.1: (customs broker) "responsible supervision and control" is defined as:

that degree of supervision and control necessary to ensure the proper transaction of the customs business of a broker, including actions necessary to ensure that an employee of a broker provides substantially the same quality of service in handling customs transactions that the broker is required to provide.

24. Certain documents required for the entry of merchandise must be maintained by brokers for 5 years from the date of entry and must be made available upon reasonable notice for inspection by CBP. The following documents are examples of those that are subject to this requirement, EXCEPT:

A. Evidence of the right to make entry

B. Invoices

C. Packing lists

D. Bond information

E. Export certificates for beef or sugar-containing products subject to tariff-rate quota

As per 19 CFR 163.4(b)(2):

163.4 Record retention period.

(a) General. Except as otherwise provided in paragraph (b) of this section, any record required to be made, kept, and rendered for examination and inspection by Customs under §163.2 or any other provision of this chapter shall be kept for 5 years from the date of entry, if the record relates to an entry, or 5 years from the date of the activity which required creation of the record.

(b) Exceptions. (1) Any record relating to a drawback claim shall be kept until the third anniversary of the date of payment of the claim.

(2) Packing lists shall be retained for a period of 60 calendar days from the end of the release or conditional release period, whichever is later, or, if a demand for return to Customs custody has been issued, for a period of 60 calendar days either from the date the goods are redelivered or from the date specified in the demand as the latest redelivery date if redelivery has not taken place.

(3) A consignee who is not the owner or purchaser and who appoints a customs broker shall keep a record pertaining to merchandise covered by an informal entry for 2 years from the date of the informal entry.

(4) Records pertaining to articles that are admitted free of duty and tax pursuant to 19 U.S.C. 1321(a)(2) and §§10.151 through 10.153 of this chapter, and carriers' records pertaining to manifested cargo that is exempt from entry under the provisions of this chapter, shall be kept for 2 years from the date of the entry or other activity which required creation of the record.

(5) If another provision of this chapter sets forth a retention period for a specific type of record that differs from the period that would apply under this section, that other provision controls.

The correct answer is "C".

✓ **JUST A SIDE NOTE:** A packing list, also sometimes referred to as a packing slip, is a shipping document that lists the contents, quantities, weights and dimensions of each package. In theory, it is a standard shipping document. In practice, however, it is not commonly used at present.

25. An ABI participant who has had his/her ABI privileges revoked, due to fraud or misstatement of material fact, has _____ days to appeal to the Assistant Commissioner, Information and Technology from the date of the written notice of revocation.

A. 0 - appeals are not granted for fraud
B. 10
C. 20
D. 30
E. 60

 As per 19 CFR 143.8:

143.8 Appeal of suspension or revocation.

If the participant files a written appeal with the Assistant Commissioner, Information and Technology, within 10 days following the date of the written notice of action to suspend or revoke participation as provided in §§143.6 and 143.7, the suspension or revocation of participation shall not take effect until the appeal is decided, except in those cases where the Executive Director, Trade Policy and Programs, Office of International Trade, or the Director, User Support Services Division, respectively, determines that participation was obtained through fraud or the misstatement of a material fact, or that continued participation would pose a potential risk of significant harm to the integrity and functioning of the system. The CBP officer who receives the appeal shall stamp the date of receipt of the appeal and the stamped date is the date of receipt for purposes of the appeal. The Assistant Commissioner shall inform the participant of the date of receipt and the date that a response is due under this paragraph. The Assistant Commissioner shall render his decision to the participant, in writing, stating his reasons therefor, by letter mailed within 30 working days following receipt of the appeal, unless this period is extended with due notification to the participant.

 The correct answer is "B".

✔ **JUST A SIDE NOTE:** Sections 143.6 & 143.7 provide for "Failure to maintain performance standards" and "Revocation of ABI participation" respectively. They pertain to the quality and integrity of data transmissions to CBP via Automated Broker Interface (ABI).

26. When a complaint or charge against a broker is investigated, who determines if there is sufficient basis to recommend that charges be preferred against that broker?

A. Commissioner
B. Port director
C. Special agent
D. Import specialist
E. Hearing officer

 As per 19 CFR 111.56:

111.56 Review of report on investigation.

The port director will review the report of investigation to determine if there is sufficient basis to recommend that charges be preferred against the broker. *He will then submit his recommendation with supporting reasons to the Assistant Commissioner for final determination together with a proposed statement of charges when recommending that charges be preferred.*

 The correct answer is "B".

✓ **JUST A SIDE NOTE:** 19 CFR 111.53 lists the possible grounds for customs broker disciplinary action:

(a) The broker has made or caused to be made in any application for any license or permit under this part, or report filed with Customs, any statement which was, at the time and in light of the circumstances under which it was made, false or misleading with respect to any material fact, or has omitted to state in any application or report any material fact which was required;

(b) The broker has been convicted, at any time after the filing of an application for a license under §111.12, of any felony or misdemeanor which:

(1) Involved the importation or exportation of merchandise;

(2) Arose out of the conduct of customs business; or

(3) Involved larceny, theft, robbery, extortion, forgery, counterfeiting, fraudulent concealment, embezzlement, fraudulent conversion, or misappropriation of funds;

(c) The broker has violated any provision of any law enforced by Customs or the rules or regulations issued under any provision of any law enforced by Customs;

(d) The broker has counseled, commanded, induced, procured, or knowingly aided or abetted the violations by any other person of any provision of any law enforced by Customs or the rules or regulations issued under any provision of any law enforced by Customs;

(e) The broker has knowingly employed, or continues to employ, any person who has been convicted of a felony, without written approval of that employment from the Assistant Commissioner;

(f) The broker has, in the course of customs business, with intent to defraud, in any manner willfully and knowingly deceived, misled or threatened any client or prospective client; or ... ...

27. ABC Brokers, Inc. legally changed its name to Zumba Brokers, Inc. Before doing Customs business under the new name, the broker must submit evidence of his authority to use the new name to which of the following offices?

A. Office of the Chief Counsel
B. Office of International Trade
C. Regulatory Audit Division
D. Office of the Commissioner
E. National Finance Center in Indianapolis

 As per 19 CFR 111.30(c):

*(c) Change in name. **A broker who changes his name, or who proposes to operate under a trade or fictitious name** in one or more States within the district in which he has been granted a permit and is authorized by State law to do so, **must submit to the Office of International Trade**, U.S. Customs and Border Protection, Washington, DC 20229, evidence of his authority to use that name. The name must not be used until the approval of Headquarters has been received. In the case of a trade or fictitious name, the broker must affix his own name in conjunction with each signature of the trade or fictitious name when signing customs documents.*

 The correct answer is "B".

✓ **JUST A SIDE NOTE:** Not to be confused with the International Trade Association (or ITA, under Department of Commerce), the Office of International Trade (also referred to as Office of Trade, or OT, under Department of Homeland Security),

consolidates the trade policy, program development, and compliance measurement functions of CBP into one office.

Category VI: Antidumping/Countervailing Duties

28. What duty is levied when imported merchandise receives a bounty or grant when exported with material injury to an U. S. manufacturer?

A. Foreign Export Duties
B. Quota
C. Anti-Dumping Duties
D. Countervailing Duties
E. Marking

 As per the CATAIR, Glossary of Terms:

Cotton Fee	An assessment collected on imported upland cotton and products containing upland cotton. The class code is 056.
Countervailing Duty	Countervailing duty is levied when imported merchandise receives a bounty or grant when exported with material injury to an U.S. manufacturer.
CSMS	Cargo Systems Messaging Service

 The correct answer is "D".

✓ **JUST A SIDE NOTE:** Only about 6 pages in length, the CBP and Trade Automated Interface Requirements (CATAIR) Glossary *identifies document specific and ACS terminology and is provided for reference.* Here's another snapshot of the document that provides some more insight on the variety of terms described in the CATAIR Glossary.

FIRMS Code	Facilities Information and Resources Management System (FIRMS) code identifies the CBP facility where goods are located.
Foreign Trade Zone (FTZ)	Secured areas legally outside of a nation's CBP territory.
FROB	Foreign Remain On Board
GATT	General Agreement on Tariff and Trade
General Order (G.O.)	Premises owned or leased by the U.S. Government and used for the storage of merchandise undergoing CBP examination or under seizure, or pending final release from CBP custody. Unclaimed merchandise stored in such premises is held under "general order".

29. What is the correct collection code for antidumping duties?

A. 499
B. 012
C. 013
D. 501
E. 311

 As per FORM 7501 INSTRUCTIONS, Block 39:

… …

The applicable collection code must be indicated on the same line as the fee or other charge or exaction. Report the fees in the format below:

Fee	Code
AD	012
CVD	013
Tea Fee	038
Misc. Interest	044
Beef Fee	053
Pork Fee	054
Honey Fee	055
Cotton Fee	056
Pecan Fee	057
Sugar Fee	079
Potato Fee	090
Mushroom Fee	103
Watermelon	104
Blueberry Fee	106
Avocado	107
Mango	108
Informal Entry MPF	311
Dutiable Mail Fee	496
Merchandise Processing Fee (MPF)	499
Manual Surcharge	500
Harbor Maintenance Fee (HMF)	501

… …

 The correct answer here is "B".

✓ **JUST A SIDE NOTE:** "Dumping" is when a party sells its product abroad at a price lower than it does in its domestic market. "Anti-dumping" is the imposition of additional duties on that party's imports in an effort to protect the domestic market parties.

30. An entry made on July 18, 2003, is under a statutory suspension of liquidation because it is subject to an antidumping order, and is later liquidated on December 20, 2004. A protest must be filed in order to be considered timely filed.

A. within 180 days of December 20, 2004, the date of liquidation

B. within 90 days of December 20, 2004, the date of liquidation

C. within one year of December 20, 2004, the date of liquidation

D. within one year of July 18, 2003, the date entry

E. 30 days before December 20, 2004, the date of liquidation

 As per 19 CFR 174.12(e):

*(e) Time of filing. **Protests must be filed**, in accordance with section 514, Tariff Act of 1930, as amended (19 U.S.C. 1514), **within 90 days of a decision relating to an entry made before December 18, 2004**, or within 180 days of a decision relating to an entry made on or after December 18, 2004, **after any of the following**:*

*(1) **The date of notice of liquidation** or reliquidation, or the date of liquidation or reliquidation, as determined under §§159.9 or 159.10 of this chapter;*

(2) The date of the decision, involving neither a liquidation nor reliquidation, as to which the protest is made (for example: The date of an exaction; the date of written notice excluding merchandise from entry, delivery or demanding redelivery to CBP custody under any provision of the customs laws; the date of written notice of a denial of a claim filed under section 520(d), Tariff Act of 1930, as amended (19 U.S.C. 1520(d)), or; within 90 days of the date of denial of a petition filed pursuant to section 520(c)(1), Tariff Act of 1930, as amended (19 U.S.C. 1520(c)(1)), relating to an entry made before December 18, 2004); or

(3) The date of mailing of notice of demand for payment against a bond in the case of a surety which has an unsatisfied legal claim under a bond written by the surety.

 The correct answer is "B".

✔ **JUST A SIDE NOTE:** Currently, protests can be filed within 180 days of liquidation. After 180 days, a prior disclosure is the only way to rectify an issue with Customs.

Category VII: Bonds

31. When a resident of France temporarily imports articles under subheading 9813.00.50, HTSUS, and formal entry is made, the importer of record shall be required to file a bond in what amount?

A. An amount equal to 110 percent of estimated duties and fees
B. An amount equal to 110 percent of estimated duties
C. An amount equal to three times the entered value
D. An amount equal to 200 percent of estimated duties and fees, if payable
E. An amount equal to the entered value plus duties, taxes and fees

 As per 19 CFR 10.31(f):

*(f) With the exceptions stated herein, a bond shall be given on CBP Form 301, containing the bond conditions set forth in §113.62 of this chapter, in an amount equal to double the duties, including fees, which it is estimated would accrue (or such larger amount as the port director shall state in writing or by the electronic equivalent to the entrant is necessary to protect the revenue) had all the articles covered by the entry been entered under an ordinary consumption entry. In the case of samples solely for use in taking orders entered under subheading 9813.00.20, HTSUS, motion-picture advertising films entered under subheading 9813.00.25, HTSUS, and **professional equipment, tools of trade and repair components for such equipment or tools entered under subheading 9813.00.50, HTSUS, the bond required to be given shall be in an amount equal to 110 percent of the estimated duties, including fees**, determined at the time of entry. If appropriate a carnet, under the provisions of part 114 of this chapter, may be filed in lieu of a bond on CBP Form 301 (containing the bond conditions set forth in §113.62 of this chapter). Cash deposits in the amount of the bond may be accepted in lieu of sureties. When the articles are entered under subheading 9813.00.05, 9813.00.20, or ... ...*

 The correct answer is "A".

✓ **JUST A SIDE NOTE:** This exam question is a good example of a Temporary Import under Bond (TIB). Here's a snapshot of 9813.00.50 from HTSUS Chapter 98, Subchapter 13/XIII (ARTICLES ADMITTED TEMPORARILY FREE OF DUTY UNDER BOND):

| 9813.00.50 | 1/ | Professional equipment, tools of trade, repair components for equipment or tools admitted under this heading and camping equipment; all the foregoing imported by or for nonresidents sojourning temporarily in the United States and for the use of such nonresidents.................. | .... | Free, under bond, as prescribed in U.S. note 1 to this subchapter | Free (AU, BH, CA, CL, IL, JO, KR, MA, MX, OM, P, PA, PE, SG) |

32. For Government entries secured by stipulation, bond type _____ should be used in conjunction with surety code _____.

A. 8; 998

B. 9; 999

C. 9; 998

D. 0; 999

E. 0; 998

As per 19 CFR 10.101(d) & FORM 7501 INSTRUCTIONS, Block 5:

*19 CFR 10.101(d) Bond. **No bond shall be required in support of an immediate delivery application provided for in this section if a stipulation in the form as set forth below is filed with the port director in connection with the application:***

____ I, ____, ____ (Title), a duly authorized representative of the_____

(Name of United States Government department or agency) stipulate and agree on behalf of such department or agency that all applicable provisions of the Tariff Act of 1930, as amended, and the regulations thereunder, and all other laws and regulations, relating to the release and entry of merchandise will be observed and complied with in all respects.

(Signature)

FORM 7501 INSTRUCTIONS, BLOCK 5) BOND TYPE

Record the single digit numeric code as follows:

0 - U.S. Government or entry types not requiring a bond
8 - Continuous
9 - Single Transaction

Bond type "0" should be used in conjunction with surety code "999" for government entries secured by stipulation *as provided for in 19 C.F.R. § 10.101(d).*

Bond type "8" or "9," as appropriate, should be used in conjunction with surety code "998" when cash or government securities are deposited in lieu of surety.

Bond type "9" should be used in conjunction with surety code "999" when surety has been waived in accordance with 19 C.F.R. § 142.4 (c). A single entry bond should be attached to the entry summary package.

 The correct answer is "D".

✓ **JUST A SIDE NOTE:** In this case, no customs bond is necessary because CBP does not deem the bond necessary in order to secure payment from another U.S. Government department or agency.

33. If the principal gets free release of any serially numbered shipping container classifiable under subheading 9801.00.10 or 9803.00.50, HTSUS, the principal agrees to all of the following, EXCEPT?

A. To advance the value or improve its condition abroad or claim (or make a previous claim) drawback on, any container released under subheading 9801.00.10, HTSUS
B. To pay the initial duty due and otherwise comply with every condition in subheading 9803.00.50, HTSUS, on any container released under that item
C. To mark that container in the manner required by CBP
D. To keep records which show the current status of that container in service and the disposition of that container if taken out of service
E. To remove or strike out the markings on that container when it is taken out of service or when the principal transfers ownership of it

 As per 19 CFR 113.66(b):

(b) Agreement to Comply With the Provisions of subheading 9801.00.10, or 9803.00.50 Harmonized Tariff Schedule of the United States (HTSUS). If the principal gets free release of any serially numbered shipping container classifiable under subheading 9801.00.10 or 9803.00.50, HTSUS, the principal agrees:

(1) __Not to advance the value or improve its condition abroad or claim (or make a previous claim) drawback on, any container released under subheading 9801.00.10__, HTSUS;

(2) To pay the initial duty due and otherwise comply with every condition in subheading 9803.00.50, HTSUS, on any container released under that item;

(3) To mark that container in the manner required by CBP;

(4) To keep records which show the current status of that container in service and the disposition of that container if taken out of service; and

(5) To remove or strike out the markings on that container when it is taken out of service or when the principal transfers ownership of it.

 The correct answer is "A".

✓ **JUST A SIDE NOTE:** The HTSUS subheadings 9801.00.10 & 9803.00.50 provide for free entry, respectively:

9801.00.10   Products of the United States when returned after having been exported, or any other products when returned within 3 years after having been exported, without having been advanced in value or improved in condition by any process of manufacture or other means while abroad

9803.00.50   Substantial containers and holders, if products of the United States (including shooks and staves of United States production when returned as boxes or barrels containing merchandise), or if of foreign production and previously imported and duty (if any) thereon paid, or if of a class specified by the Secretary of the Treasury as instruments of international traffic, repair components for containers of foreign production which are instruments of international traffic, and accessories and equipment for such containers, whether the accessories and equipment are imported with a container to be reexported separately or with another container, or imported separately to be reexported with a container

34. If a port director believes the acceptance of a transaction such as a "03" antidumping entry secured by a continuous bond would place the revenue in jeopardy, or otherwise hamper the enforcement of Customs and Border Protection laws or regulations, he/she shall require additional security according to:

A. 19 C.F.R. § 151.65

B. 19 C.F.R. § 113.13

C. 19 C.F.R. § 152.101

D. 19 C.F.R. § 152.107

E. 19 C.F.R. § 171.1

 As per 19 CFR 113.13(d):

(d) Additional security. Notwithstanding the provisions of this section or any other provision of this chapter, if CBP believes that acceptance of a transaction secured by a continuous bond would place the revenue in jeopardy or otherwise hamper the enforcement of all applicable laws or regulations, CBP may immediately require additional security.

 The correct answer is "B".

✓ **JUST A SIDE NOTE:** If CBP deems the bond amount to be insufficient, the importer, or customs broker on behalf of the importer, will request the surety (i.e. the importer's customs bond insurance company) to increase the bond amount accordingly.

Category VIII: Classification

35. A driver bit is interchangeable and designed to be fitted into hand-operated power drills and impact drivers in order to drive a screw. What is the classification of the driver bit?

A. 8207.90.6000   Interchangeable tools for handtools, whether or not power operated, or for machine-tools (for example, for pressing, stamping, punching, tapping, threading, drilling, boring, broaching, milling, turning or screwdriving), including dies for drawing or extruding metal, and rock drilling or earth boring tools; base metal parts thereof>>Other interchangeable tools, and parts thereof>>Other>>Other>>Not suitable for cutting metal, and parts thereof>>For handtools, and parts thereof

B. 8207.90.7585   Interchangeable tools for handtools, whether or not power operated, or for machine-tools (for example, for pressing, stamping, punching, tapping, threading, drilling, boring, broaching, milling, turning or screwdriving), including dies for drawing or extruding metal, and rock drilling or earth boring tools; base metal parts thereof>>Other interchangeable tools, and parts thereof>>Other>>Other>>Not suitable for cutting metal, and parts thereof>>Other

C. 8204.20.0000   Hand-operated spanners and wrenches (including torque meter wrenches but not including tap wrenches); socket wrenches, with or without handles, drives or extensions; base metal parts thereof>>Socket wrenches, with or without handles, drives and extensions, and parts thereof

D. 8205.40.0000   Handtools (including glass cutters) not elsewhere specified or included; blow torches and similar self-contained torches; vises, clamps and the like, other than accessories for and parts of machine tools; anvils; portable forges; hand- or pedal-operated grinding wheels with frameworks; base metal parts thereof>>Screwdrivers, and parts thereof

E. 8466.10.0175   Parts and accessories suitable for use solely or principally with the machines of headings 8456 to 8465, including work or tool holders, self-opening dieheads, dividing heads and other special attachments for machine tools; tool holders for any type of tool for working in the hand>>Tool holders and self-opening dieheads>>Other

 As per HTSUS Section XVI (Machinery and Electronics Chapters 84 & 85), Note 1(o):

Notes
1. *This section does not cover:*
... ...
(o) **Interchangeable tools of heading 8207** *or brushes of a kind used as parts of machines (heading 9603); similar interchangeable tools are to be classified according to the constituent material of their working part (for example, in chapter 40, 42, 43, 45 or 59 or heading 6804 or 6909);*

Multiple choices "C" (wrenches and wrench parts) and "E" (tool holders and self-opening dieheads) do not describe the product, so let's start by eliminating these two. Moreover, "E" is excluded per the Section XVI note. Now, notice that the item in question, a hand-operated power drill driver bit is "prima facie" (i.e. classifiable under more than one heading/classification). Accordingly, we try to classify using GRI 3(a), which says the most specific classification is preferred to less descriptive classifications. Thus heading 8207 ("A" and "B") is preferred over the "handtools not elsewhere specified" heading of 8205 ("D"). The driver bit is for "handtools", and so we select "A" as the correct answer.

Heading/ Subheading	Stat. Suffix	Article Description	Unit of Quantity	Rates of Duty 1 General	Rates of Duty 1 Special	Rates of Duty 2
8207 (con.)		Interchangeable tools for handtools, whether or not power operated, or for machine-tools (for example, for pressing, stamping, punching, tapping, threading, drilling, boring, broaching, milling, turning or screwdriving), including dies for drawing or extruding metal, and rock drilling or earth boring tools; base metal parts thereof: (con.)				
8207.90		Other interchangeable tools, and parts thereof:				
8207.90.15	00	Files and rasps, including rotary files and rasps, and parts thereof..................	doz..........	1.6%	Free (A, AU, BH, CA, CL, CO, D, E, IL, JO, KR, MA, MX, OM, P, PA, PE, SG)	15%
		Other:				
8207.90.30		Cutting tools with cutting part containing by weight over 0.2 percent of chromium, molybdenum, or tungsten or over 0.1 percent of vanadium...........	....	5%	Free (A, AU, BH, CA, CL, CO, D, E, IL, JO, KR, MA, MX, OM, P, PA, PE, SG)	60%
	30	Hobs and other gear cutting tools................	X			
		For woodworking:				
	75	Cutterheads with interchangeable tools....	X			
	80	Other........................	X			
	85	Other........................	X			
		Other:				
8207.90.45	00	Suitable for cutting metal, and parts thereof....	X................	4.8% 1/	Free (A, AU, BH, CA, CL, CO, D, E, IL, JO, KR, MA, MX, OM, P, PA, PE, SG)	50%
		Not suitable for cutting metal, and parts thereof:				
8207.90.60	00	For handtools, and parts thereof............	X................	4.3%	Free (A, AU, BH, CA, CL, CO, D, E, IL, JO, KR, MA, MX, OM, P, PA, PE, SG)	45%
8207.90.75		Other........................	....	3.7% 1/	Free (A, AU, BH, CA, CL, CO, D, E, IL, JO, KR, MA, MX, OM, P, PA, PE, SG)	35%
	45	Cutterheads with interchangeable tools............	X			
	85	Other........................	X			

36. One 13oz. jar of 100% petroleum jelly labeled as skin protectant is put up for retail sale. How would you classify the petroleum jelly?

A.	3301.29.51	Essential oils (terpeneless or not), including concretes and absolutes; resinoids; extracted oleoresins; concentrates of essential oils in fats, in fixed oils, in waxes or the like, obtained by enfleurage or maceration; terpenic by products of the deterpenation of essential oils; aqueous distillates and aqueous solutions of essential oils>>Essential oils other than those of citrus fruit>>Other>>Other
B.	2712.10.00	Petroleum jelly; paraffin wax, microcrystalline petroleum wax, slack wax, ozokerite, lignite wax, peat wax, other mineral waxes and similar products obtained by synthesis or by other processes, whether or not colored>>Petroleum jelly
C.	3304.99.10	Beauty or make-up preparations and preparations for the care of the skin (other than medicaments), including sunscreen or sun tan preparations; manicure or pedicure preparations>>Other>>Other>>Petroleum jelly put up for retail sale
D.	3403.11.50	Lubricating preparations (including cutting-oil preparations, bolt or nut release preparations, antirust or anticorrosion preparations and mold release preparations, based on lubricants) and preparations of a kind used for the oil or grease treatment of textile materials, leather, furskins or other materials, but excluding preparations containing, as basic constituents, 70 percent or more by weight of petroleum oils or oils obtained from bituminous minerals>>Containing petroleum oils or oils obtained from bituminous minerals>>Preparations for the treatment of textile materials, leather, furskins or other materials>>Other
E.	2711.12.00	Petroleum gases and other gaseous hydrocarbons>>Liquefied>>Propane

 As per HTSUS, Chapter 27, Additional U.S. Note 8:

8. Subheading 2712.10.00 does not include petroleum jelly, suitable for use for the care of the skin, put up in packings of a kind sold at retail for such use (subheading 3304.99.10).

The item in question, 100% petroleum jelly put up for retail sale, is specifically provided for in HTSUS subheading 3304.99.10. Moreover, the above-mentioned Chapter 27 note precludes "B" from consideration. The correct answer is "C".

✓ **NOTE:** The actual HTSUS classifications are 10-digits in length, but have been truncated to 8-digits in this exam question, possibly in an attempt to simplify things.

Heading/ Subheading	Stat. Suf- fix	Article Description	Unit of Quantity	Rates of Duty		
				1		**2**
				General	Special	
3303.00		Perfumes and toilet waters:				
		Not containing alcohol:				
3303.00.10	00	Floral or flower waters.............................	liters......	Free		20%
3303.00.20	00	Other..	kg..........	Free		75%
3303.00.30	00	Containing alcohol..	kg..........	Free		88¢/kg + 75%
3304		Beauty or make-up preparations and preparations for the care of the skin (other than medicaments), including sunscreen or sun tan preparations; manicure or pedicure preparations:				
3304.10.00	00	Lip make-up preparations...........................	X............	Free		75%
3304.20.00	00	Eye make-up preparations...........................	X............	Free		75%
3304.30.00	00	Manicure or pedicure preparations..............	X............	Free		75%
		Other:				
3304.91.00		Powders, whether or not compressed.......		Free		75%
	10	Rouges..	X			
	50	Other...	X			
		Other:				
3304.99.10	00	Petroleum jelly put up for retail sale............	X............	Free		75%
3304.99.50	00	Other...	X............	Free		75%
3305		Preparations for use on the hair:				
3305.10.00	00	Shampoos...	X............	Free		75%
3305.20.00	00	Preparations for permanent waving or straightening........	X............	Free		75%
3305.30.00	00	Hair lacquers..	kg..........	Free		88¢/kg + 75%
3305.90.00	00	Other..	kg..........	Free		88¢/kg + 75%
3306		Preparations for oral or dental hygiene, including denture fixative pastes and powders; yarn used to clean between the teeth (dental floss), in individual retail packages:				
3306.10.00	00	Dentifrices..	X............	Free		75%
3306.20.00	00	Yarn used to clean between the teeth (dental floss)........	kg..........	Free		88¢/kg + 75%
3306.90.00	00	Other..	kg..........	Free		88¢/kg + 75%

37. A two-piece box is constructed of rigid cardboard. Within the box is a paperboard sleeve and plastic "c" clip, upon which a watch will be mounted. Logos and graphics related to the style of watch being sold are printed on the exterior of the box. This packaging will be imported in the United States without watches. Upon importation the watch will be put into the boxes for retail sale. This container is not suitable for long term use. What is classification of the box?

A. 3923.10.0000   Articles for the conveyance or packing of goods, of plastics; stoppers, lids, caps and other closures, of plastics>>Boxes, cases, crates and similar articles

B. 3923.29.0000   Articles for the conveyance or packing of goods, of plastics; stoppers, lids, caps and other closures, of plastics>>Sacks and bags (including cones)>>Of other plastics

C. 4202.92.9015   Trunks, suitcases, vanity cases, attache cases, briefcases, school satchels, spectacle cases, binocular cases, camera cases, musical instrument cases, gun cases, holsters and similar containers; traveling bags, insulated food or beverage bags, toiletry bags, knapsacks and backpacks, handbags, shopping bags, wallets, purses, map cases, cigarette cases, tobacco pouches, tool bags, sports bags, bottle cases, jewelry boxes, powder cases, cutlery cases and similar containers, of leather or of composition leather, of sheeting of plastics, of textile materials, of vulcanized fiber or of paperboard, or wholly or mainly covered with such materials or with paper>>Other>>With outer surface of sheeting of plastic or of textile materials>>Other>>Other>>With outer surface of textile materials>>Other, jewelry boxes of a kind normally sold at retail with their contents

D. 4202.92.9036   Trunks, suitcases, vanity cases, attache cases, briefcases, school satchels, spectacle cases, binocular cases, camera cases, musical instrument cases, gun cases, holsters and similar containers; traveling bags, insulated food or beverage bags, toiletry bags, knapsacks and backpacks, handbags, shopping bags, wallets, purses, map cases, cigarette cases, tobacco pouches, tool bags, sports bags, bottle cases, jewelry boxes, powder cases, cutlery cases and similar containers, of leather or of composition leather, of sheeting of plastics, of textile materials, of vulcanized fiber or of paperboard, or wholly or mainly covered with such materials or with paper>>Other>>With outer surface of sheeting of plastic or of textile materials>>Other>>Other>>With outer surface of textile materials>>Other>>Other

E. 4819.50.4040   Cartons, boxes, cases, bags and other packing containers, of paper, paperboard, cellulose wadding or webs of cellulose fibers; box files, letter trays and similar articles, of paper or paperboard of a kind used in offices, shops or the like>>Other packing containers, including record sleeves>>Other>>Other>>Rigid boxes and cartons

The item in question is a rigid cardboard (i.e. paperboard) box with a paperboard sleeve and plastic clip. Let's go about solving this one via the process of elimination. It is not a plastic "sack" or "bag", so we may disregard "B". It does not have an "outer surface of textile materials", so we may disregard "C" and "D". Now, at this point, we could (with an open mind) say that the item is potentially classifiable under "A" as a box of plastic, or under "E" as a box of cardboard/paperboard. In other words, the item is prima-facie (i.e. classifiable under more than 1 heading). So, we first try to classify by GRI 3(a), which says the most specific classification description is preferred to other classifications. This is not necessarily the case here, so next we try to classify via GRI 3(b), which says to classify the composite item based on its essential character. The cardboard/paperboard, from which the item is mostly constructed of, imparts the essential character of the item, more so than does the relatively insignificant "plastic 'c' clip". The correct answer is "E".

✓ **JUST A SIDE OTE:** Cardboard is "heavy paper pulp–based (paper)board"

Heading/ Subheading	Stat. Suffix	Article Description	Unit of Quantity	Rates of Duty General	Rates of Duty Special	2
4819		Cartons, boxes, cases, bags and other packing containers, of paper, paperboard, cellulose wadding or webs of cellulose fibers; box files, letter trays and similar articles, of paper or paperboard of a kind used in offices, shops or the like:				
4819.10.00		Cartons, boxes and cases, of corrugated paper or paperboard..................................	....	Free		35%
	20	Sanitary food and beverage containers...............	kg			
	40	Other..	kg			
4819.20.00		Folding cartons, boxes and cases, of non-corrugated paper or paperboard..	....	Free		35%
	20	Sanitary food and beverage containers...............	kg			
	40	Other..	kg			
4819.30.00		Sacks and bags, having a base of a width of 40 cm or more...	....	Free		35%
	20	Shipping sacks and multiwall bags, other than grocers' bags...	kg			
	40	Other..	kg			
4819.40.00		Other sacks and bags, including cones.............................	....	Free		35%
	20	Shipping sacks and multiwall bags, other than grocers' bags...	kg			
	40	Other..	kg			
4819.50		Other packing containers, including record sleeves:				
4819.50.20	00	Sanitary food and beverage containers....................	kg	Free		35%
4819.50.30	00	Record sleeves..	kg	Free		19.3¢/kg
4819.50.40		Other..	....	Free		35%
	20	Fiber drums, cans, tubes and similar containers...	kg			
		Other:				
	40	Rigid boxes and cartons..	kg			
	60	Other..	kg			
4819.60.00	00	Box files, letter trays, storage boxes and similar articles, of a kind used in offices, shops or the like........................	kg	Free		35%

38. What is the classification of women's cheerleading briefs made of 100% nylon knit fabric?

A. 6108.29.9000		Women's or girls' slips, petticoats, briefs, panties, night dresses, pajamas, negligees, bathrobes, dressing gowns and similar articles, knitted or crocheted>>Briefs and panties>>Of other textile materials>>Other
B. 6114.30.3070		Other garments, kitted or crocheted>>Of man-made fibers>>Other>>Other>>Women's or girls'
C. 6104.63.2060		Women's or girls' suits, ensembles, suit-type jackets, blazers, dresses, skirts, divided skirts, trousers, bib and brace overalls, breeches and shorts (other than swimwear), knitted or crocheted>>Trousers, big and brace overalls, breeches and shorts>>Of synthetic fibers>>Other>>Other>>Shorts>>Girls'>>Other
D. 6104.69.2060		Women's or girls' suits, ensembles, suit-type jackets, blazers, dresses, skirts, divided skirts, trousers, bib and brace overalls, breeches and shorts (other than swimwear), knitted or crocheted>>Trousers, big and brace overalls, breeches and shorts>>Of other textile materials>>Of artificial fibers>>Trousers, breeches and shorts>>Other>>Shorts
E. 6307.90.9889		Other made up articles, including dress patterns>>Other>>Other>>Other>>Other>>Other

The item in question, "cheerleading briefs" (also known as bloomers), are considered prima facie. Meaning, in the HTSUS, they could potentially be classified as underwear-like "briefs" (heading 6108), "shorts" (heading 6104), or "other garments" (heading 6114)? Since neither GRI 3(a), nor GRI 3(b) are definitively applicable here, we try GRI 3(c), which says to classify based on the heading that occurs last in numerical order. The correct answer is "B".

✓ **NOTE:** The difference between "synthetic" fibers and "artificial" fibers is that "artificial" fibers are made from naturally-occurring substances, such plant cellulose. Both are "man-made". Nylon is a synthetic fiber.

Heading/ Subheading	Stat. Suffix	Article Description	Unit of Quantity	Rates of Duty General	Rates of Duty Special	2
6114 (con.)		Other garments, knitted or crocheted: (con.)				
6114.30 (con.)		Of man-made fibers: (con.)				
6114.30.30		Other...	....	14.9%	Free (AU, BH, CA, CL, CO, IL, JO, KR, MA, MX, OM, P, PA, PE, SG)	90%
		Jumpers:				
	12	Containing 23 percent or more by weight of wool or fine animal hair (459)............................	doz. kg			
	14	Other (659)...	doz. kg			
		Sunsuits, washsuits, one-piece playsuits and similar apparel:				
	20	Boys' (237)...	doz. kg			
	30	Women's or girls' (237).............................	doz. kg			
		Coveralls, jumpsuits and similar apparel: Men's or boys':				
	42	Containing 23 percent or more by weight of wool or fine animal hair (459)...............	doz. kg			
	44	Other (659)...	doz. kg			
		Women's or girls':				
	52	Containing 23 percent or more by weight of wool or fine animal hair (459)...............	doz. kg			
	54	Other (659)...	doz. kg			
		Other:				
	60	Men's or boys' (659)...............................	doz. kg			
	70	Women's or girls' (659)...........................	doz. kg			

39. What is the classification of a men's 100% knit cotton sleeveless muscle shirt?

A.	6105.10.0010	Men's or boy's shirts, knitted or crocheted>>Of cotton>>Men's
B.	6110.20.2069	Sweaters, pullovers, sweatshirts, waistcoats (vests) and similar articles, knitted or crocheted>>Of cotton>>Other>>Other>>Other>>Other
C.	6105.20.2010	Men's or boys' shirts, knitted or crocheted>>Of man-made fibers>>Other>>Boys'
D.	6106.10.0010	Women's or girls' blouses and shirts, knitted or crocheted>>Of cotton>>Women's
E.	6205.20.2066	Men's or boys' shirts>>Of cotton>>Other>>Other>>Other>>Men's

 As per HTSUS Chapter 61, Note 4:

4. Headings 6105 and 6106 do not cover garments with pockets below the waist, with a ribbed waistband or other means of tightening at the bottom of the garment, or garments having an average of less than 10 stitches per linear centimeter in each direction counted on an area measuring at least 10 centimeters by 10 centimeters. **Heading 6105 does not cover sleeveless garments.**

 And, as per HTSUS Chapter 62, Note 1:

1. **This chapter (62)** *applies only to made up articles of any textile fabric other than wadding,* **excluding knitted or crocheted articles** *(other than those of heading 6212).*

An initial assessment of the exam question makes it appear that 6105.10.0010 ("A") is the correct classification. However, as per GRI 1, we must base our classification on heading descriptions AND Section and Chapter Notes. The above-mentioned Chapter 61, Note 4 precludes this heading and choices "A" and "C" from being used for "sleeveless" articles. "D" describes women's clothing, and is thus disregarded. And, as per the above-mentioned Chapter 61, Note 1, we may disregard chapter 62 ("E"). Finally, a reasonable argument could be made that a "muscle shirt" is an article similar to a sweatshirt (i.e. heading 6110), and that accordingly, the correct answer is "B".

✔ **NOTE:** It is our opinion that a more appropriate classification for the item question, a sleeveless muscle shirt, lies in HTSUS 6109.10.0018, which provides for T-Shirts, singlets, **tank tops** and similar garments, knitted or crocheted>>Of cotton>>Men's or boys'>>Tank topes and other singlets>>Men's

Heading/ Subheading	Stat. Suffix	Article Description	Unit of Quantity	Rates of Duty General	Rates of Duty Special	2
6110 (con.)		Sweaters, pullovers, sweatshirts, waistcoats (vests) and similar articles, knitted or crocheted: (con.)				
6110.20 (con.)		Of cotton: (con.)				
6110.20.20		Other...	....	16.5%	Free (AU, BH, CA, CL, CO, IL, JO, MA, MX, OM, P, PA, PE, SG) 8.2% (KR)	50%
	05	Boys' or girls' garments imported as parts of playsuits (237)..................................	doz. kg			
		Other: Sweaters:				
	10	Men's (345)..	doz. kg			
	15	Boys' (345)...	doz. kg			
	20	Women's (345)....................................	doz. kg			
	25	Girls' (345)..	doz. kg			
		Vests, other than sweater vests:				
	30	Men's or boys' (359)...........................	doz. kg			
	35	Women's or girls' (359).......................	doz. kg			
		Sweatshirts:				
	41	Men's (338)..	doz. kg			
	44	Boys' (338)...	doz. kg			
	46	Women's (339)....................................	doz. kg			
	49	Girls' (339)...	doz. kg			
		Other: Men's or boys':				
	67	Knit to shape articles described in statistical note 6 to this chapter (338)...	doz. kg			
	69	Other (338).................................	doz. kg			
		Women's or girls':				
	77	Knit to shape articles described in statistical note 6 to this chapter (339)...	doz. kg			
	79	Other (339).................................	doz. kg			

40. What is the proper classification of a fluorine-based polyether polymer, in primary form? This is also chemically known as trifluoromethyl- poly[oxy-2-(trifluoromethyl)-trifluoroethylene]-poly(oxy- difluoromethylene)-trifluoromethyl ether.

A. 3403.99.0000   Lubricating preparations (including cutting-oil preparations, bolt or nut release preparations, antirust or anticorrosion preparations and mold release preparations, based on lubricants) and preparations of a kind used for the oil or grease treatment of textile materials, leather, furskins or other materials, but excluding preparations containing, as basic constituents, 70 percent or more by weight of petroleum oils or oils obtained from bituminous minerals>>Other>>Other

B. 3907.20.0000   Polyacetals, other polyethers and epoxide resins, in primary forms; polycarbonates, alkyd resins, polyallyl esters and other polyesters, in primary forms>> Other polyethers

C. 9902.23.11/3907.20.0000
   9902.23.11:   1-Propene, 1,1,2,3,3,3-hexafluoro-, oxidized, polymerized (CAS No. 69991-67-9) (provided for in subheading 3904.69.50)
   3907.20.0000: (see above "B")

D. 3907.30.0000   Polyacetals, other polyethers and epoxide resins, in primary forms; polycarbonates, alkyd resins, polyallyl esters and other polyesters, in primary forms>>Epoxide resins

E. 9902.01.85/3907.30.0000
   9902.01.85:   Epoxy molding compounds, of a kind used for encapsulating integrated circuits (provided for in subheading 3907.30.00)
   3907.30.0000: (see above "D")

a We are not chemists. However, with a reasonable degree of certainty, we can say that "A" does not describe the item in question. Nor do 9902.23.11, 3907.30.0000, or 9902.01.85, which eliminates choices "C", "D", and "E". Through this process of elimination we can deduce that the correct answer is "B".

✓ **JUST A SIDE NOTE:** Although rarely used, Chapter 99 of the HTSUS imposes additional duties and/or restrictions on a handful of regular HTSUS classifications found throughout the HTSUS (i.e. Chapter 1 thru. Chapter 98). The regular HTSUS classification will be annotated with a note to refer to a Chapter 99 classification, which will further described, in detail, whether the additional classification in Chapter 99 will be necessary or not.

Heading/ Subheading	Stat. Suffix	Article Description	Unit of Quantity	Rates of Duty General	Rates of Duty 1 Special	Rates of Duty 2
3906		Acrylic polymers in primary forms:				
3906.10.00	00	Poly(methyl methacrylate)...........	kg	6.3%	Free (A, AU, BH, CA, CL, CO, D, E, IL, JO, KR, MA, MX, OM, P, PA, PE, SG)	37%
3906.90		Other:				
3906.90.10	00	Elastomeric............	kg	Free		20%
		Other:				
3906.90.20	00	Plastics...........	kg	6.3% 1/	Free (A, AU, BH, CA, CL, CO, D, E, IL, JO, KR, MA, MX, OM, P, PA, PE, SG)	37%
3906.90.50	00	Other...........	kg	4.2% 2/	Free (A, AU, BH, CA, CL, CO, D, E, IL, JO, K, KR, MA, MX, OM, P, PA, PE, SG)	25%
3907		Polyacetals, other polyethers and epoxide resins, in primary forms; polycarbonates, alkyd resins, polyallyl esters and other polyesters, in primary forms:				
3907.10.00	00	Polyacetals............	kg	6.5%	Free (A, AU, BH, CA, CL, CO, D, E, IL, JO, K, KR, MA, MX, OM, P, PA, PE, SG)	2.2¢/kg + 33.5%
3907.20.00	00	Other polyethers...	kg	6.5% 3/	Free (A, AU, BH, CA, CL, CO, D, E, IL, JO, K, KR, MA, MX, OM, P, PA, PE, SG)	2.2¢/kg + 33.5%
3907.30.00	00	Epoxide resins............	kg	6.1% 4/	Free (A, AU, BH, CA, CL, CO, D, E, IL, JO, K, KR, MA, MX, OM, P, PA, PE, SG)	15.4¢/kg + 47%
3907.40.00	00	Polycarbonates............	kg	5.8%	Free (A, AU, BH, CA, CL, CO, D, E, IL, JO, MA, MX, OM, P, PA, PE, SG) 2.9% (KR)	15.4¢/kg + 45%
3907.50.00	00	Alkyd resins............	kg	6.5%	Free (A, AU, BH, CA, CL, CO, D, E, IL, JO, KR, MA, MX, OM, P, PA, PE, SG)	15.4¢/kg + 45%
3907.60.00		Poly(ethylene terephthalate)............		6.5%	Free (A*, AU, BH, CA, CL, CO, D, E, IL, JO, K, MA, MX, OM, P, PA, PE, SG) 3.2% (KR)	15.4¢/kg + 45%
	30	Packaging grade (bottle grade and other, with an intrinsic viscosity of 0.70 or more but not more than 0.88 deciliters per gram)............	kg			

1/ See heading 9902.24.15.
2/ See heading 9902.02.80.
3/ See headings 9902.02.98, 9902.23.10-9902.23.12, 9902.23.14, 9902.23.15, and 9902.23.17-9902.23.19.
4/ See heading 9902.01.85.

41. A package of trail mix is made up of a loose blend of nut kernels, seeds and candy. It contains raw almonds 26.4% C/O USA; raw cashews 22% C/O Vietnam, India or Brazil; raw pumpkin seeds 17.6% C/O China; raw walnut halves 10% C/O USA; candy coated milk chocolate pieces 15% C/O USA; and raw sunflower seeds 9% C/O USA. All of the ingredients will be imported into Canada, where they will be mixed together in the indicated proportion and packaged for export to the United States. No other processing will be done in Canada. What is the classification of the trail mix?

A. 0813.50.0020   Fruit, dried, other than that of headings 0801 to 0806; mixtures of nuts or dried fruits of this chapter>>Mixtures of nuts or dried fruits of this chapter>>Containing only fruit

B. 0813.50.0040   Fruit, dried, other than that of headings 0801 to 0806; mixtures of nuts or dried fruits of this chapter>>Mixtures of nuts or dried fruits of this chapter>>Containing only nuts

C. 0812.90.1000   Fruit and nuts, provisionally preserved (for example, by sulfur dioxide gas, in brine, in sulfur water or in other preservative solutions), but unsuitable in that state for immediate consumption>>Other>>Mixtures of two or more fruits

D. 0813.50.0060   Fruit, dried, other than that of headings 0801 to 0806; mixtures of nuts or dried fruits of this chapter>>Mixtures of nuts or dried fruits of this chapter>>Other

E. 2008.97.1040   Fruit, nuts and other edible parts of plants, otherwise prepared or preserved, whether or not containing added sugar or other sweetening matter or spirit, not elsewhere specified or included>>Other, including mixtures other than those of subheading 2008.19>>Mixtures>> In airtight containers and not containing apricots, citrus fruits, peaches or pears>>Other

 As per HTSUS Chapter 20, Note 1(a):

*1. **This chapter does not cover:***
*(a) **Vegetables, fruit or nuts, prepared or preserved by the processes specified in chapter** 7, 8 or 11;*

The item in question, essentially raw (i.e. unprepared) mixed nuts, are provided for in heading 0813. Accordingly, and, as per the above-mentioned Chapter 20 Note, we may disregard "E" (i.e. Chapter 20). We assume that the item is suitable for immediate consumption and not provisionally preserved, so we may disregard "C". In addition to nuts, the trail mix contains milk chocolate pieces, so the 0813.50.0060 classification of "other" (than containing only nuts) accurately describes the product. The correct answer is "D".

✔ **JUST A SIDE NOTE:** According to Wikipedia…

A **nut** is a fruit composed of a hard shell and a **seed**, which is generally edible. In a general context, however, a wide variety of dried seeds are called nuts, but in a botanical context, there is an additional requirement that the shell does not open to release the seed (indehiscent).

Heading/ Subheading	Stat. Suffix	Article Description	Unit of Quantity	Rates of Duty General	Rates of Duty Special	2
0813 (con.)		Fruit, dried, other than that of headings 0801 to 0806; mixtures of nuts or dried fruits of this chapter: (con.)				
0813.50.00		Mixtures of nuts or dried fruits of this chapter....................	....	14%	Free (A+, AU, BH, CA, CL, CO, D, E, IL, JO, KR, MA, MX, OM, P, PA, PE, SG)	35%
	20	Containing only fruit..	kg			
	40	Containing only nuts..	kg			
	60	Other...	kg			
0814.00		Peel of citrus fruit or melons (including watermelons), fresh, frozen, dried or provisionally preserved in brine, in sulfur water or in other preservative solutions:				
0814.00.10	00	Orange or citron..	kg	Free		4.4¢/kg
0814.00.40	00	Lime...	kg	1.6¢/kg	Free (A, AU, BH, CA, CL, CO, D, E, IL, JO, KR, MA, MX, OM, P, PA, PE, SG)	4.4¢/kg
0814.00.80	00	Other..	kg	1.6¢/kg	Free (A+, AU, BH, CA, CL, CO, D, E, IL, JO, KR, MA, MX, OM, P, PA, PE, SG)	4.4¢/kg

Exam with Broker Commentary (Oct. 2016) — Study Guide

42. Stainless steel tattooing needles are designed for use in a hand-held tattooing machine which features a self-contained electric motor. The needles are dipped in ink and placed in the handheld machine which utilizes a vibratory action to drive the needle in an up-and-down fashion. This causes the needle tips to pierce the top layer of skin and deposit the ink into the second or dermal skin layer. What is the classification of the tattooing needles?

A. 8207.90.6000 — Interchangeable tools for handtools, whether or not power operated, or for machine-tools (for example, for pressing, stamping, punching, tapping, threading, drilling, boring, broaching, milling, turning or screwdriving), including dies for drawing or extruding metal, and rock drilling or earth boring tools; base metal parts thereof>>Other interchangeable tools, and parts thereof>>Other>>Other>>Not suitable for cutting metal, and parts thereof>>For handtools, and parts thereof

B. 8453.90.5000 — Machinery for preparing, tanning or working hides, skins or leather or for making or repairing footwear or other articles of hides, skins or leather, other than sewing machines; parts thereof>>Parts>>Other

C. 8467.99.0190 — Tools for working in the hand, pneumatic, hydraulic or with self-contained electric or nonelectric motor, and parts thereof>>Parts>>Other>>Other

D. 8479.90.9496 — Machines and mechanical appliances having individual functions, not specified or included elsewhere in this chapter; parts thereof>>Parts>>Other>>Other>>Other

E. 8487.90.0080 — Machinery parts, not containing electrical connectors, insulators, coils, contacts or other electrical features, and not specified or included elsewhere in this chapter>>Other>>Other

 As per HTSUS Section XVI (contains Chapters 84 & 85), Notes 1:

1. This section does not cover:

... ...

(k) Articles of chapter 82 or 83;

... ...

The item in question is a needle, a tool which is for use in a hand-held tattooing machine. The item can be classified using GRI 1, which says to classify based on Headings, Chapter Notes and Section Notes. Section XVI, Note 1 says that if an item can be classified in Chapter 82, then do not classify in Chapters 84. The correct answer is "A".

✓ **JUST A SIDE NOTE:** This exact same question appeared on the 2013 October exam. Recycled questions and answers are certainly not uncommon on the exam.

Heading/ Subheading	Stat. Suf- fix	Article Description	Unit of Quantity	Rates of Duty General	Rates of Duty Special	2
8207 (con.)		Interchangeable tools for handtools, whether or not power operated, or for machine-tools (for example, for pressing, stamping, punching, tapping, threading, drilling, boring, broaching, milling, turning or screwdriving), including dies for drawing or extruding metal, and rock drilling or earth boring tools; base metal parts thereof: (con.)				
8207.90		Other interchangeable tools, and parts thereof:				
8207.90.15	00	Files and rasps, including rotary files and rasps, and parts thereof..	doz.........	1.6%	Free (A, AU, BH, CA, CL, CO, D, E, IL, JO, KR, MA, MX, OM, P, PA, PE, SG)	15%
		Other:				
8207.90.30		Cutting tools with cutting part containing by weight over 0.2 percent of chromium, molybdenum, or tungsten or over 0.1 percent of vanadium............	....	5%	Free (A, AU, BH, CA, CL, CO, D, E, IL, JO, KR, MA, MX, OM, P, PA, PE, SG)	60%
	30	Hobs and other gear cutting tools...............	X			
		For woodworking:				
	75	Cutterheads with interchangeable tools....	X			
	80	Other..	X			
	85	Other..	X			
		Other:				
8207.90.45	00	Suitable for cutting metal, and parts thereof....	X............	4.8% 1/	Free (A, AU, BH, CA, CL, CO, D, E, IL, JO, KR, MA, MX, OM, P, PA, PE, SG)	50%
		Not suitable for cutting metal, and parts thereof:				
8207.90.60	00	For handtools, and parts thereof..................	X............	4.3%	Free (A, AU, BH, CA, CL, CO, D, E, IL, JO, KR, MA, MX, OM, P, PA, PE, SG)	45%
8207.90.75		Other..	....	3.7% 1/	Free (A, AU, BH, CA, CL, CO, D, E, IL, JO, KR, MA, MX, OM, P, PA, PE, SG)	35%
	45	Cutterheads with interchangeable tools..	X			
	85	Other..	X			

43. Certain women's bowling shoes, while imported as a pair, have separate identities. Both shoes have uppers of 100 percent rubber/plastics. The left shoe has an outer sole of rubber/plastics. The right shoe has an outer sole consisting of rubber/plastics and a large textile sliding pad. The textile pad comprises the majority of the surface area facing the ground. The shoes are below-the-ankle, do not have a foxing or foxing-like band, are not protective, and are secured to the foot with laces. What is the classification of this pair of bowling shoes?

A.	6402.19.1541	Other footwear with outer soles and uppers of rubber or plastics>>Sports footwear>>Other>>Having uppers of which over 90 percent of the external surface area … … is rubber or plastics … … >>Other>>For women
B.	6402.91.0500	Other footwear with outer soles and uppers of rubber or plastics>>Sports footwear>>Other footwear>>Covering the ankle>>Incorporating a protective metal toe-cap>> Having uppers of which over 90 percent of the external surface area … … is rubber or plastics … …
C.	6402.99.3165	Other footwear with outer soles and uppers of rubber or plastics>>Other footwear>>Other>>Other>> Having uppers of which over 90 percent of the external surface area … … is rubber or plastics … … >>Other>>Other>>Other>>For women>>Other
D.	6404.19.3960	Footwear with outer soles of rubber, plastics, leather or composition leather and uppers of textile materials>>Footwear with outer soles of rubber or plastics>>Other>> Footwear with open toes or open heels; footwear of the slip-on type, that is held to the foot without the use of laces or buckles or other fasteners, … …
E.	6405.90.9000	Other footwear>>Other>>Other

 As per HTSUS Chapter 64, Note 4(b), and Additional U.S. Note 5:

4. Subject to note 3 to this chapter:

*(b) **The constituent material of the outer sole** shall be taken to be the material having the greatest surface area in contact with the ground, **no account being taken of accessories or reinforcements such as spikes, bars, nails, protectors or similar attachments**.*

5. For the purposes of determining the constituent material of the outer sole pursuant to note 4(b) of this chapter, no account shall be taken of textile materials which do not possess the characteristics usually required for normal use of an outer sole, including durability and strength.

The exam key lists "E" as the correct answer. We disagree, and believe "A" to be the correct classification. Based on the above Chapter 64 Note and Chapter 64 Additional U.S. Note, the right shoe's textile sliding pad should NOT be taken into account. Coincidentally, credit was given to all examinees for this question.

✓ **JUST A SIDE NOTE:** "Foxing", according to the Footwear Distributors and Retailers of America (FDRA),

is a strip of material, separate from the sole and upper, that secures the joint where the upper and sole meet.

Subheading	Suffix	Article Description	Unit of Quantity	1 General	1 Special	2
6402		Other footwear with outer soles and uppers of rubber or plastics:				
		Sports footwear:				
6402.12.00	00	Ski-boots, cross-country ski footwear and snowboard boots..	prs.	Free		35%
6402.19		Other:				
		Having uppers of which over 90 percent of the external surface area (including any accessories or reinforcements such as those mentioned in note 4(a) to this chapter) is rubber or plastics (except footwear having foxing or a foxing-like band applied or molded at the sole and overlapping the upper and except footwear designed to be worn over, or in lieu of, other footwear as a protection against water, oil, grease or chemicals or cold or inclement weather):				
6402.19.05		Golf shoes..		6%	Free (AU, BH, CA, CL, CO, D, E, IL, JO, KR, MA, MX, OM, P, PA, PE, R, SG)	35%
	30	For men..	prs.			
	60	For women...	prs.			
	90	Other...	prs.			
6402.19.15		Other...		5.1%	Free (AU, BH, CA, CL, CO, D, E, IL, JO, KR, MA, MX, OM, P, PA, PE, R, SG)	35%
	20	For men..	prs.			
	41	For women...	prs.			
	61	Other...	prs.			
		Other:				
6402.19.30		Valued not over $3/pair...........................		Free		84%
	31	For men..	prs.			
	61	Other...	prs.			
6402.19.50		Valued over $3 but not over $6.50/pair.........		76¢/pr. + 32%	Free (AU, BH, CA, CL, CO, D, E, IL, JO, KR, MA, MX, OM, P, PA, PE, R, SG)	$1.58/pr. + 66%
	31	For men..	prs.			
	61	Other...	prs.			
6402.19.70		Valued over $6.50 but not over $12/pair........		76¢/pr. + 17%	Free (AU, BH, CA, CL, CO, D, E, IL, JO, KR, MA, MX, OM, P, PA, PE, R, SG)	$1.58/pr. + 35%
	31	For men..	prs.			
	61	Other...	prs.			
6402.19.90		Valued over $12/pair.................................		9%	Free (AU, BH, CA, CL, CO, D, E, IL, JO, KR, MA, MX, OM, P, PA, PE, R, SG)	35%
	31	For men..	prs.			
	61	Other...	prs.			
6402.20.00	00	Footwear with upper straps or thongs assembled to the sole by means of plugs (zoris)....................	prs.	Free		35%

44. What is the classification of a woman's handbag with outer surface of textile materials and with a fiber content of 30% nylon, 30% cotton and 40% rayon?

A. 4202.22.4040 — Trunks, suitcases, vanity cases, attache cases, … …, handbags, … … similar containers, of leather or of composition leather, of sheeting of plastics, of textile materials, of vulcanized fiber or … …>>Handbags, whether or not with a shoulder strap, including those without handle>>With outer surface of sheeting of plastic or of textile materials>>With outer surface of textile materials>>Wholly or in part of braid>>Other>>Other>>Other

B. 4202.22.6000 — Trunks, suitcases, vanity cases, attache cases, … …, handbags, … … similar containers, of leather or of composition leather, of sheeting of plastics, of textile materials, of vulcanized fiber or … …>>Handbags, whether or not with a shoulder strap, including those without handle>>With outer surface of sheeting of plastic or of textile materials>>With outer surface of textile materials>>Other>> Of vegetable fibers and not of pile or tufted construction>>Other

C. 4202.22.8030 — Trunks, suitcases, vanity cases, attache cases, … …, handbags, … … similar containers, of leather or of composition leather, of sheeting of plastics, of textile materials, of vulcanized fiber or … …>>Handbags, whether or not with a shoulder strap, including those without handle>>With outer surface of sheeting of plastic or of textile materials>>With outer surface of textile materials>>Other>>Other>>Other>>Of cotton

D. 4202.22.8050 — Trunks, suitcases, vanity cases, attache cases, … …, handbags, … … similar containers, of leather or of composition leather, of sheeting of plastics, of textile materials, of vulcanized fiber or … …>>Handbags, whether or not with a shoulder strap, including those without handle>>With outer surface of sheeting of plastic or of textile materials>>With outer surface of textile materials>>Other>>Other>>Other>>Of man-made fibers

E. 4202.22.8080 — Trunks, suitcases, vanity cases, attache cases, … …, handbags, … … similar containers, of leather or of composition leather, of sheeting of plastics, of textile materials, of vulcanized fiber or … …>>Handbags, whether or not with a shoulder strap, including those without handle>>With outer surface of sheeting of plastic or of textile materials>>With outer surface of textile materials>>Other>>Other>>Other>>Other

The item in question is a textile handbag consisting of different materials in 30% nylon, 30% cotton and 40% rayon, and is considered "prima facie" (i.e. potentially classifiable under more than one heading) here. Simply put, once at GRI 3(b), we can mathematically say that the man-made fibers (i.e. nylon and rayon) impart the essential (textile) character of the handbag. The correct answer is "D".

✓ **JUST A SIDE NOTE:** "Vegetable fibers", according to Wikipedia,

are generally based on arrangements of cellulose, often with lignin: examples include cotton, hemp, jute, flax… …

Heading/ Subheading	Stat. Suffix	Article Description	Unit of Quantity	Rates of Duty General	Rates of Duty Special	2
4202 (con.)		Trunks, suitcases, vanity cases, attache cases, briefcases, school satchels, spectacle cases, binocular cases, camera cases, musical instrument cases, gun cases, holsters and similar containers; traveling bags, insulated food or beverage bags, toiletry bags, knapsacks and backpacks, handbags, shopping bags, wallets, purses, map cases, cigarette cases, tobacco pouches, tool bags, sports bags, bottle cases, jewelry boxes, powder cases, cutlery cases and similar containers, of leather or of composition leather, of sheeting of plastics, of textile materials, of vulcanized fiber or of paperboard, or wholly or mainly covered with such materials or with paper: (con.) Handbags, whether or not with shoulder strap, including those without handle: (con.)				

4202.22 (con.)		With outer surface of sheeting of plastic or of textile materials: (con.)
		  With outer surface of textile materials: (con.)
		   Other:
		    Of vegetable fibers and not of pile or tufted construction:				

4202.22.45	00	Of cotton (369)	No. kg	6.3%	Free (AU, BH, CA, CL, CO, IL, JO, KR, MA, MX, OM, P, PA, PE, SG) 4.9% (E)	40%
4202.22.60	00	Other (871)	No. kg	5.7%	Free (AU, BH, CA, CL, CO, IL, JO, KR, MA, MX, OM, P, PA, PE, SG) 4.4% (E)	40%
		Other:				
4202.22.70	00	Containing 85 percent or more by weight of silk or silk waste	No. kg	7%	Free (AU, BH, CA, CL, CO, D, E, IL, JO, KR, MA, MX, OM, P, PA, PE, SG)	65%
4202.22.80		Other		17.6%	Free (AU, BH, CA, CL, CO, IL, JO, KR, MA, MX, OM, P, PA, PE, SG) 16.6% (E)	65%
	30	Of cotton (369)	No. kg			
	50	Of man-made fibers (670)	No. kg			
	70	Of paper yarn	No. kg			
	80	Other (871)	No. kg			

45. How would you classify a glass jar of spread that includes both peanut butter and grape jelly? The peanut butter and jelly each comprise 50% of the product.

A. The item would be classified as peanut butter.	(2008.11)
B. The item would be classified as grape jelly.	(2007.99.7500)
C. The item would be classified as a glass jar.	(7010.90.50)
D. The item would be classified as a 'mixed condiment/seasoning'.	(2103.90)
E. The item must be classified using the tariff numbers for both peanut butter and grape jelly.	

 As per HTSUS GRI 2(b) and 3(a), 3(b), and 3(c):

2.
… …

(b) Any reference in a heading to a material or substance shall be taken to include a reference to mixtures or combinations of that material or substance with other materials or substances. Any reference to goods of a given material or substance shall be taken to include a reference to goods consisting wholly or partly of such material or substance. The classification of goods consisting of more than one material or substance shall be according to the principles of rule 3.

3. When, by application of rule 2(b) or for any other reason, goods are, prima facie, classifiable under two or more headings, classification shall be effected as follows:

(a) The heading which provides the most specific description shall be preferred to headings providing a more general description. However, when two or more headings each refer to part only of the materials or substances contained in mixed or composite goods or to part only of the items in a set put up for retail sale, those headings are to be regarded as equally specific in relation to those goods, even if one of them gives a more complete or precise description of the goods.

(b) Mixtures, composite goods consisting of different materials or made up of different components, and goods put up in sets for retail sale, which cannot be classified by reference to 3(a), shall be classified as if they consisted of the material or component which gives them their essential character, insofar as this criterion is applicable.

(c) When goods cannot be classified by reference to 3(a) or 3(b), they shall be classified under the heading which occurs last in numerical order among those which equally merit consideration.

a The item in question, a spread consisting of 50% peanut butter and 50% grape jelly, is prima facie. As per GRI 2(b), mixtures are implied, meaning one classification can be used for an item containing a mixture of multiple items. So, we may disregard "E".

Next in order, we try to classify based on GRI 3(a), which says the heading with the most specific description is preferred to less descriptive headings. Heading 2103 provides for the relatively vague description of "mixed condiments", so we may disregard "D" here.

Next in order, we move on to GRI 3(b), which says to classify based on the material that gives the item its essential character. Well, neither the peanut butter nor the grape jelly clearly give the product its essential character over the other. The glass jar definitely does not give the product its essential character, so we may disregard "C" at this point.

Finally, we're forced to move on the GRI 3(c), which says to classify using the heading that numerically occurs last. 2008 (peanut butter heading) occurs after 2007 (grape jelly heading). The correct answer is "A".

✓ **NOTE:** GRI 5(b) also dictates that containers, such as the glass jars in this exam question, are to be classified with the goods they contain.

Heading/ Subheading	Stat. Suffix	Article Description	Unit of Quantity	Rates of Duty General	Rates of Duty Special	2
2008		Fruit, nuts and other edible parts of plants, otherwise prepared or preserved, whether or not containing added sugar or other sweetening matter or spirit, not elsewhere specified or included: Nuts, peanuts (ground-nuts) and other seeds, whether or not mixed together:				
2008.11	00	Peanuts (ground-nuts): Peanut butter and paste:				
2008.11.02	00	Described in general note 15 of the tariff schedule and entered pursuant to its provisions..............	kg	Free		15¢/kg
2008.11.05	00	Described in additional U.S. note 5 to this chapter and entered pursuant to its provisions..............	kg	Free		15¢/kg
2008.11.15	00	Other 1/................	kg	131.8%	Free (BH, CL, JO, MX, SG) 35.10% (P) 61.5% (PE) 65.9% (KR) 87.8% (CO) 131.8% (PA)(s) See 9912.12.05, 9912.12.20 (MA) See 9913.12.05, 9913.12.20 (AU) See 9915.20.05-9915.20.20 (P+) See 9916.12.05, 9916.12.20 (OM)	155%
2008.11.22	00	Blanched peanuts: Described in general note 15 of the tariff schedule and entered pursuant to its provisions........	kg	6.6¢/kg	Free (A+, AU, BH, CA, CL, CO, D, E, IL, JO, KR, MA, MX, OM, P, PA, PE, SG)	15¢/kg
2008.11.25	00	Described in additional U.S. note 2 to chapter 12 and entered pursuant to its provisions........	kg	6.6¢/kg	Free (A, BH, CA, CL, CO, D, E, IL, JO, KR, MA, OM, P, PA, PE, SG)	15¢/kg
2008.11.35	00	Other 2/................	kg	131.8%	Free (BH, CL, JO, MX, SG) 61.5% (PE) 65.9% (KR) 70.60% (P) 87.8% (CO) 131.8% (PA)(s) See 9908.12.01 (IL) See 9912.12.05, 9912.12.20 (MA) See 9913.12.05, 9913.12.20 (AU) See 9915.12.05, 9915.12.20, 9915.12.40 (P+) See 9916.12.05, 9916.12.20 (OM)	155%

46. Which statement is False?

A. For legal purposes, the classification of goods in the subheadings of a heading shall be determined according to the terms of those subheadings and any related subheading notes and, mutatis mutandis, to the above rules, on the understanding that only subheadings at the same level are comparable. For the purposes of this rule, the relative section, chapter and subchapter notes also apply, unless the context otherwise requires.

B. Subject to the provisions in section 213 of the Caribbean Basin Economic Recovery Act, goods which are imported from insular possessions of the United States shall receive duty treatment no less favorable than the treatment afforded such goods when they are imported from a beneficiary country under such Act.

C. Goods of Canada, when marked or eligible to be marked with their country of origin, that comply with the terms of the Automotive Products Trade Act are exempt from the Merchandise Processing Fee (MPF) when entered with the Special Program Indicator (SPI) "B#" prefacing the 10-digit HTS number.

D. Instruments of international traffic, such as containers, lift vans, rail cars and locomotives, truck cabs and trailers, etc. are exempt from formal entry procedures but are required to be accounted for when imported and exported into and out of the United States, respectively, through the manifesting procedures required for all international carriers by the United States Customs Service. Fees associated with the importation of such instruments of international traffic shall be reported and paid on a periodic basis as required by regulations issued by the Secretary of the Treasury and in accordance with 1956 Customs Convention on Containers (20 UST 30; TIAS 6634).

E. Schedule C provides a list of U.S. Customs districts, the ports included under each district, and the corresponding numeric codes used in compiling the U.S. foreign trade statistics. The Schedule contains a code for each official U.S. Customs district and port, with some additional codes provided to meet specific compiling requirements of the foreign trade statistics program.

 As per HTSUS Annex C:

ANNEX C
Schedule D - Classification of U.S. Customs Districts and Ports *for U.S. Foreign Trade Statistics*
... ...

Schedule C (a.k.a. HTSUS Annex A) provides a list of numeric "classifications of country and territory designations for U.S. foreign trade statistics". For example, Canada's Schedule C code is 122.0.

Schedule D (a.k.a. HTSUS Annex C) provides a list of U.S. "customs district and port codes". For example, Baltimore, Maryland's port code is 1303. The false statement, and correct answer is "E".

✓ **JUST A SIDE NOTE:** The HTSUS contains 3 annexes. Annex A (Schedule C numeric country codes), Annex B (alpha country codes [e.g. "CA" for Canada]), and Annex C (Schedule D district & port codes).

Harmonized Tariff Schedule of the United States (2017)
Annotated for Statistical Reporting Purposes

STATISTICAL ANNEXES

Annex A -- Schedule C, Classification of Country and Territory Designations for U.S. Import Statistics

Annex B -- International Standard Country Codes

Annex C -- Schedule D, Customs District and Port Codes

47. What is the classification of a steel piston designed for a reciprocating positive displacement liquid pump that is used in the oil industry?

A. 8413.91.90	Pumps for liquids, whether or not fitted with a measuring device; liquid elevators; part thereof>>Parts>>Of pumps>>Other
B. 7326.90.85	Other articles of iron or steel>>Other>>Other>>Other
C. 9015.90.00	Surveying (including photogrammetrical surveying), hydrographic, oceanographic, hydrological, meteorological or geophysical instruments and appliances, excluding compasses; rangefinders; parts and accessories thereof>>Parts and accessories
D. 8413.50.00	Pumps for liquids, whether or not fitted with a measuring device; liquid elevators; part thereof>>Other reciprocating positive displacement pumps
E. 8414.90.90	Air or vacuum pumps, air or other gas compressors and fans; ventilating or recycling hoods incorporating a fan, whether or not fitted with filters; parts thereof>>Parts>>Other

 As per HTSUS Section XVI (contains Chapters 84 & 85), Note 2:

*2. Subject to note 1 to this section, note 1 to chapter 84 and to note 1 to chapter 85, **parts of machines** (not being parts of the articles of heading 8484, 8544, 8545, 8546 or 8547) **are to be classified according to the following rules:***

(a) Parts which are goods included in any of the headings of chapter 84 or 85 (other than headings 8409, 8431, 8448, 8466, 8473, 8487, 8503, 8522, 8529, 8538 and 8548) are in all cases to be classified in their respective headings;

*(b) **Other parts, if suitable for use solely or principally with a particular kind of machine, or with a number of machines of the same heading** (including a machine of heading 8479 or 8543) **are to be classified with the machines of that kind or in heading** 8409, 8431, 8448, 8466, 8473, 8503, 8522, 8529 or 8538 as appropriate. However, parts which are equally suitable for use principally with the goods of headings 8517 and 8525 to 8528 are to be classified in heading 8517;*

(c) All other parts are to be classified in heading 8409, 8431, 8448, 8466, 8473, 8503, 8522, 8529 or 8538 as appropriate or, failing that, in heading 8487 or 8548.

This exam question is a good example of the classification of "parts", and especially relevant for Chapters 84 (mechanical items, generally speaking) and 85 (electrical items, generally speaking). THE BIG QUESTION ABOUT PARTS IS… do we classify the part as a stand-alone item (e.g. a steel piston), or as a "part of" another item (e.g. part of a pump). Well, the answer and procedure for doing so can be found in the applicable Section and/or Chapter Notes. As per the above Section XVI Note 2(a), (except for a small group of headings) parts are to be classified by as a stand-alone item if they are provided for in a heading. There is no such heading for these "steel pistons", so we move on to Section XVI, Note 2(b), which says if 2(a) does not apply, AND if the part is designed for a particular machine, then classify as a "part of" that machine. That is the case in this scenario. The correct answer is "A".

✓ **JUST A SIDE NOTE:** Here's another, yet different example of the classification of parts… As referenced in the above Section XVI, Note 2(a), (excluded) heading 8544 provides for cables and wires. As dictated in the note, essentially all cables and wires, even if parts of a greater product, are to remain classified in heading 8544.

Heading/ Subheading	Stat. Suf- fix	Article Description	Unit of Quantity	Rates of Duty		
				1		2
				General	Special	
8413 (con.)		Pumps for liquids, whether or not fitted with a measuring device; liquid elevators; part thereof: (con.)				
8413.70		Other centrifugal pumps:				
8413.70.10	00	Stock pumps imported for use with machines for making cellulosic pulp, paper or paperboard.............	No............	Free		35%
8413.70.20		Other...		Free		35%
	04	Submersible pumps................................	No.			
		Other:				
		Single-stage, single-suction, close-coupled:				
	05	With discharge outlet under 5.08 cm in diameter...	No.			
	15	With discharge outlet 5.08 cm or over in diameter...	No.			
		Single-stage, single-suction, frame- mounted:				
	22	With discharge outlet under 7.6 cm in diameter...	No.			
	25	With discharge outlet 7.6 cm or over in diameter...	No.			
	30	Single-stage, double-suction............................	No.			
	40	Multi-stage, single- or double-suction............	No.			
	90	Other...	No.			
		Other pumps; liquid elevators:				
8413.81.00		Pumps...		Free		35%
	20	Turbine pumps..	No.			
	30	Household water systems, self-contained; and windmill pumps..	No.			
	40	Other...	No.			
8413.82.00	00	Liquid elevators...	No............	Free		35%
		Parts:				
8413.91		Of pumps:				
8413.91.10	00	Of fuel-injection pumps for compression-ignition engines...	X................	2.5%	Free (A, AU, B, BH, C, CA, CL, CO, D, E, IL, JO, MA, MX, OM, P, PA, PE, SG) 1.2% (KR)	35%
8413.91.20	00	Of stock pumps imported for use with machines for making cellulosic pulp, paper or paperboard...	X................	Free		35%
8413.91.90		Other...		Free		35%
	10	Of subheading 8413.30.90............................	X			
	50	Of hydraulic fluid power pumps.....................	X			
	80	Other...	X			
8413.92.00	00	Of liquid elevators..	X................	Free		35%

Category IX: Drawback

48. Merchandise or articles that for commercial purposes are identical and interchangeable in all situations are called:

A. Multiple products

B. Fungible merchandise or articles

C. Commercially interchangeable merchandise

D. Designated merchandise

E. Substituted merchandise or articles

 As per 19 CFR 191.2(o):

(o) Fungible merchandise or articles. ***Fungible merchandise or articles means merchandise or articles which for commercial purposes are identical and interchangeable in all situations****.*

 The correct answer is "B".

✔ **JUST A SIDE NOTE:** The word "fungibility" comes from Latin "fungibilis" from "fungi", meaning "to perform", related to "function" and "defunct". Examples of fungible items are cash, salt, etc.

49. How long must records pertaining to the filing of a drawback claim be kept?

A. Five years from the date of entry

B. Ten years from the date the claim is filed

C. Indefinitely

D. At least until the third anniversary of the date of payment of the claim

E. At least until the fifth anniversary of the date of payment of the claim

 As per 19 CFR 163.4(b):

*(b) Exceptions. **(1) Any record relating to a drawback claim shall be kept until the third anniversary of the date of payment of the claim.***

(2) Packing lists shall be retained for a period of 60 calendar days from the end of the release or conditional release period, whichever is later, or, if a demand for return to Customs custody has been issued, for a period of 60 calendar days either from the date the goods are redelivered or from the date specified in the demand as the latest redelivery date if redelivery has not taken place.

(3) A consignee who is not the owner or purchaser and who appoints a customs broker shall keep a record pertaining to merchandise covered by an informal entry for 2 years from the date of the informal entry.

(4) Records pertaining to articles that are admitted free of duty and tax pursuant to 19 U.S.C. 1321(a)(2) and §§10.151 through 10.153 of this chapter, and carriers' records pertaining to manifested cargo that is exempt from entry under the provisions of this chapter, shall be kept for 2 years from the date of the entry or other activity which required creation of the record.

(5) If another provision of this chapter sets forth a retention period for a specific type of record that differs from the period that would apply under this section, that other provision controls.

 The correct answer is "D".

✓ **JUST A SIDE NOTE:** "Drawback", as per CBP's website, is described as

the refund of certain duties, internal revenue taxes and certain fees collected upon the importation of goods. Such refunds are only allowed upon the exportation or destruction of goods under U.S. Customs and Border Protection supervision.

50. To comply with manufacturing drawback (direct identification and substitution), the use of domestic merchandise taken in exchange for imported merchandise of the same kind and quality shall be treated as use of the imported merchandise if no certificate of delivery is issued covering the transfer of the imported merchandise. The provision is known as a/an_____?

A. Interchange

B. Fungibility

C. Trade Good

D. Exchange Merchandise

E. Tradeoff

 As per 19 CFR 191.11(a):

191.11 Tradeoff.

*(a) Exchanged merchandise. To comply with §§191.21 and 191.22 of this part, **the use of domestic merchandise taken in exchange for imported merchandise of the same kind and quality** (as defined in §191.2(x)(1) of this part for purposes of 19 U.S.C. 1313(b)) **shall be treated as use of the imported merchandise if no certificate of delivery is issued covering the transfer of the imported merchandise. This provision shall be known as tradeoff** and is authorized by §313(k) of the Act, as amended (19 U.S.C. 1313(k)).*

 The correct answer is "E".

✓ **JUST A SIDE OTE:** As of October 2016, all drawback claims must be submitted electronically, via ACE (Automated Commercial Environment) instead of ACS/ABI. Manual drawback claims can still be submitted, but ACE claims will be given processing priority over manual claims.

51. A drawback claimant proposes to destroy unmerchantable distilled spirits, wine, or beer and must return the merchandise to CBP custody. The returned merchandise must be destroyed under the supervision of a CBP officer and the completed destruction shall be documented on _____ .

A. CBP Form 7551
B. CBP Form 7553
C. CBP Form 7501
D. CBP Form 3495
E. CBP Form 3461

 As per 19 CFR 191.166(b):

191.166 Destruction of merchandise.

(a) Action by the importer. A drawback claimant who proposes to destroy rather than export the distilled spirits, wine, or beer shall state that fact on Customs Form 7551.

(b) Action by Customs. **Distilled spirits, wine, or beer returned to Customs custody at the place approved by the drawback office where the drawback entry was filed shall be destroyed under the supervision of the Customs officer who shall certify the destruction on Customs Form 7553.**

 The correct answer is "B".

✓ **JUST A SIDE NOTE:** CBP's Information Center has the following notice about drawback refunds:

If you have exported or intend to export goods previously imported with duty paid, there is a possibility you can get a refund of the duty. Drawback is a mechanism that Customs and Border Protection (CBP) has to enable importers to get a refund of duty paid on imported goods when they are exported or destroyed. **Be aware the process of filing for drawback can be involved and the time it takes to receive refunds can be lengthy.**

You must have proof of the export or destruction, as well as proof that duty was originally paid. A bill of sale or airway bill is valid proof of export and a CBP Officer must witness the destruction of the goods. Without proof of export or the destruction, the claim is not substantiated.

Category X: Free Trade Agreements

52. Which of the following is NOT true about the North American Free Trade Agreement (NAFTA) Certificate of Origin?

A. The Certificate must be signed by the exporter or the exporter's authorized agent having knowledge of the relevant facts.

B. The Certificate must be in the possession of the importer at the time preferential treatment is claimed, unless waived by the Port Director pursuant to 19 CFR 181.22(d)(1).

C. A Certificate which is photocopied, faxed, or scanned on a computer disc is acceptable.

D. A Certificate is required for each importation on which NAFTA is claimed, but does not need to accompany each shipment.

E. A producer who is not an exporter may prepare and sign a Certificate, relieving the exporter of his/her obligation to do so.

 As per 19 CFR 181.11(b):

*(b) Preparation of Certificate in the United States. An exporter in the United States who completes and signs a Certificate of Origin for the purpose set forth in paragraph (a) of this section shall use Customs Form 434, or its electronic equivalent or such other medium or format as approved by the Canadian or Mexican customs administration for that purpose. **Where the U.S. exporter is not the producer of the good, that exporter may complete and sign a Certificate on the basis of:***

(1) Its knowledge of whether the good qualifies as an originating good;

(2) Its reasonable reliance on the producer's written representation that the good qualifies as an originating good; or

(3) A completed and signed Certificate for the good voluntarily provided to the exporter by the producer.

Although not explicitly stated in the regulations, it's common sense that a signed NAFTA certificate provided to the exporter by the producer does not relieve the exporter of his or her obligations of the certificate. The correct answer is "E".

✓ **JUST A SIDE NOTE:** If an item eligible for NAFTA is not originally claimed at the time of the importation, CBP will allow post-importation NAFTA claims for refunds within one year after the date of importation.

53. The phrase "goods wholly obtained or produced entirely in the territory of Canada, Mexico and/or the United States" refers to all of the following goods, EXCEPT:

A. mineral goods extracted in the territory of one or more of the NAFTA parties

B. live animals born and raised in the territory of one or more of the NAFTA parties

C. goods obtained from hunting, trapping or fishing in the territory of one or more of the NAFTA parties

D. goods produced on board factory ships from the goods referred to in subdivision (n)(v) provided such factory ships are registered or recorded with that NAFTA party and fly its flag;

E. vegetable goods, as such goods are defined in this schedule, imported in the territory of one or more of the NAFTA parties

 As per HTSUS, General Note 12 (NAFTA) (n):

(n) As used in subdivision (b)(i) of this note, the phrase "goods wholly obtained or produced entirely in the territory of Canada, Mexico and/or the United States" means--

(i) mineral goods extracted in the territory of one or more of the NAFTA parties;

(ii) vegetable goods, as such goods are defined in this schedule, harvested in the territory of one or more of the NAFTA parties;

(iii) live animals born and raised in the territory of one or more of the NAFTA parties;

(iv) goods obtained from hunting, trapping or fishing in the territory of one or more of the NAFTA parties;

(v) goods (fish, shellfish and other marine life) taken from the sea by vessels registered or recorded with a NAFTA party and flying its flag;

(vi) goods produced on board factory ships from the goods referred to in subdivision (n)(v) provided such factory ships are registered or recorded with that NAFTA party and fly its flag;

(vii) goods taken by a NAFTA party or a person of a NAFTA party from the seabed or beneath the seabed outside territorial waters, provided that a NAFTA party has rights to exploit such seabed;

(viii) goods taken from outer space, provided such goods are obtained by a NAFTA party or a person of a NAFTA party and not processed outside the NAFTA parties;

(ix) waste and scrap derived from-- ... ...

"Imported" (i.e. not harvested) vegetable goods are not meant to qualify as "goods wholly obtained or produced entirely in the territory Canada, Mexico and/or the United States" (i.e. NAFTA). The correct answer is "E".

54. Which Country would qualify under the African Growth and Opportunity Act (AGOA)?

A. Barbados

B. Republic of Togo

C. Trinidad

D. Tobago

E. Jordon

 As per HTSUS, General Note 16 (AGOA) (a):

16 <u>Products of Countries Designated as Beneficiary Countries under the African Growth and Opportunity Act (AGOA).</u>

(a) The following sub-Saharan African countries, having been designated as beneficiary sub-Saharan African countries for purposes of the African Growth and Opportunity Act (AGOA), have met the requirements of the AGOA and, therefore, are to be afforded the tariff treatment provided in this note, shall be treated as beneficiary sub-Saharan African countries for purposes of this note:

Republic of Angola
Republic of Benin
Republic of Botswana
Burkina Faso

Republic of Cameroon
Republic of Cape Verde Federal
Republic of Chad
Union of the Comoros
Republic of Congo
Republic of Côte d'Ivoire
Republic of Djibouti
Ethiopia
Gabonese Republic
Republic of Ghana
Republic of Guinea
Republic of Kenya
Kingdom of Lesotho
Republic of Liberia
Republic of Madagascar (Madagascar)
Republic of Mali (Mali)

Republic of Malawi
Islamic Republic of Mauritania
Republic of Mauritius
Republic of Mozambique
Republic of Namibia
Republic of Niger
Republic of Nigeria
Republic of Rwanda
Democratic Republic of Sao Tome and Principe
Republic of Senegal
Republic of Seychelles
Republic of Sierra Leone
Republic of South Africa
Republic of Guinea-Bissau (Guinea-Bissau)
United Republic of Tanzania
Republic of Togo
Republic of Uganda
Republic of Zambia

 All AGOA qualifying countries are listed here. The correct answer is "B".

✓ **JUST A SIDE NOTE:** The AGOA, a U.S. government program, was enacted in the year 2000, and has been renewed until at least 2025.

187

55. With respect to Mexico, the term territory means all of the following except:

A. the states of the Federation and the Federal District

B. the islands, including the reefs and keys, in adjacent seas

C. the islands of Cayman and Revillagigedo situated in the Pacific Ocean

D. the continental shelf and the submarine shelf of such islands, keys and reefs

E. the waters of the territorial seas, in accordance with international law, and its interior maritime waters

 As per HTSUS, General Note 12 (NAFTA) (q):

*(q) For purposes of this note, the term **"territory" means**--*
... ...
*(ii) **with respect to Mexico**,*

(A) the states of the Federation and the Federal District,
(B) the islands, including the reefs and keys, in adjacent seas,
*(C) **the islands of Guadalupe and Revillagigedo situated in the Pacific Ocean,***
(D) the continental shelf and the submarine shelf of such islands, keys and reefs,
(E) the waters of the territorial seas, in accordance with international law, and its interior maritime waters,
(F) the space located above the national territory, in accordance with international law, and
(G) any areas beyond the territorial seas of Mexico within which, in accordance with international law, including the United Nations Convention on the Law of the Sea, and its domestic law, Mexico may exercise rights with respect to the seabed and subsoil and their natural resources; and
... ...

NAFTA Mexican territory includes the islands of "Guadalupe" and "Revillagigedo", NOT the "Cayman" Islands. The correct answer is "C".

✓ **JUST A SIDE NOTE:** The Cayman Islands are located in the Caribbean Sea, and are considered a territory of Great Britain.

56. How long does the importer have to claim preferential tariff treatment on an originating good if preferential tariff treatment was not claimed at importation?

A. Within 5 days after the date of importation

B. Within 90 days after the date of importation

C. Within one year after the date of importation

D. Within 60 days after the date of importation

E. Within 30 days after the date of importation

 As per 19 CFR 181.31:

Notwithstanding any other available remedy, including the right to amend an entry so long as liquidation of the entry has not become final, **where a good would have qualified as an originating good when it was imported into the United States but no claim for preferential tariff treatment on that originating good was made at that time under §181.21(a) of this part, the importer of that good may file a claim for a refund of any excess duties at any time within one year after the date of importation** *of the good in accordance with the procedures set forth in §181.32 of this part. Subject to the provisions of §181.23 of this part, Customs may refund any excess duties by liquidation or reliquidation of the entry covering the good in accordance with §181.33(c) of this part.*

The exam question does not specify for which free trade program the post-importation duty refund claim would be for. The above-mentioned CFR excerpt refers to NAFTA, however the one year post-importation claim window applies also to the free trade agreements for Chile, Dominican Republic, Oman, Peru, Korea, Panama, and Colombia. The correct answer is "C".

✓ **NOTE:** Generally speaking, the post-importation claim should include the four following elements.

(1) A written or electronic declaration or statement stating that the good was an originating good at the time of importation and setting forth the number and date of the entry or entries covering the good;

(2) A copy of a written or electronic certification demonstrating that the good qualifies for preferential tariff treatment;

(3) A written statement indicating whether the importer of the good provided a copy of the entry summary or equivalent documentation to any other person. If such documentation was so provided, the statement must identify each recipient by name, CBP identification number, and address and must specify the date on which the documentation was provided; and

(4) A written statement indicating whether or not any person has filed a protest relating to the good under any provision of law; and if any such protest has been filed, the statement must identify the protest by number and date.

57. The NAFTA de minimis provision allows for non-originating materials that do not satisfy the required tariff shift when incorporated into a finished textile product to be disregarded when determining NAFTA eligibility, IF:

A. The value of the materials is not more than 7 percent of the value of the good.

B. The total weight of those components or materials is not more than 7 percent of the total weight of the good.

C. The value of the materials is more than 7 percent of the value of the good.

D. The total weight of those components or materials is more than 7 percent of the total weight of the good.

E. The value of the materials is more than 15 percent of the value of the goods

 As per 19 CFR 102.13(c):

102.13 De Minimis.
... ...
(c) Foreign components or materials that do not undergo the applicable change in tariff classification set out in §102.21 or satisfy the other applicable requirements of that section when incorporated into a textile or apparel product covered by that section shall be disregarded in determining the country of origin of the good if the total weight of those components or materials is not more than 7 percent of the total weight of the good.

Generally speaking, the De Minimis level (i.e. the allowable percentage of non-originating materials) for textile products is 7% of "weight", and for non-textile products 7% "value". The correct answer is "B".

✔ **JUST A SIDE NOTE:** "Textile or Apparel Products" means ANY item classified in Chapters 50 thru. 63 (i.e. HTSUS Section XI), AND other miscellaneous items, such as textile bags, textile footwear, etc., classified under the following headings and sub-headings:

3005.90	6501
3921.12.15	6502
3921.13.15	6504
3921.90.2550	6505.90
4202.12.40-80	6601.10-99
4202.22.40-80	7019.19.15
4202.32.40-95	7019.19.28
4202.92.04-08	7019.40-59
4202.92.15-30	8708.21
4202.92.60-90	8804
6405.20.60	9113.90.40
6406.10.77	9404.90
6406.10.90	9612.10.9010
6406.99.15	

Category XI: Valuation

58. Which of the following is considered an assist and should be included in the entered value of headphones?

A. The cost of engineering plans produced in Las Vegas, Nevada for a headphone.

B. The cost of wiring purchased at full price by the foreign producer of headphones in Shenzhen, China.

C. The cost of copier paper supplied free of charge by the U.S. importer to the foreign producer of headphones in Shenzhen, China, for wedding invitations.

D. The cost of plastic earpiece components supplied free of charge by a U.S. importer to the foreign producer of headphones in Shenzhen, China.

E. The cost of computer training classes supplied free of charge by a U.S. importer to the foreign producer of headphones for use in training employees how to track time worked and leave.

 As per 19 CFR 152.102 (a):

(a) Assist. (1) "Assist" means any of the following if supplied directly or indirectly, and free of charge or at reduced cost, by the buyer of imported merchandise for use in connection with the production or the sale for export to the United States of the merchandise:

(i) Materials, components, parts, and similar items incorporated in the imported merchandise.

(ii) Tools, dies, molds, and similar items used in the production of the imported merchandise.

(iii) Merchandise consumed in the production of the imported merchandise.

(iv) Engineering, development, artwork, design work, and plans and sketches that are undertaken elsewhere than in the United States and are necessary for the production of the imported merchandise.

Of the five options provided, the plastic earpiece components are the only free-of-charge/discounted, non-US design work items directly attributable to the production of the headphones. The correct answer is "D".

✓ **JUST A SIDE NOTE:** The purpose, in spirit, of adding any assist value to an import's invoice value is to help prevent the under-valuation of the import.

59. Which statement is true?

A. Interest on overdue bills will be assessed on the delinquent principal amount by 60-day periods. No interest charge will be assessed for the 60-day period in which the payment is actually received at the "Send Payment To" location designated on the bill.

B. Imported merchandise may not be appraised on the basis of, the price of merchandise in the domestic market of the country of exportation.

C. For the purpose of the entry of theatrical scenery, properties and apparel under subheading 9817.00.98, Harmonized Tariff Schedule of the United States, animals imported for use or exhibition in theaters or menageries may not be classified as theatrical properties.

D. A person transacting business in connection with entry or clearance of vessels or other regulation of vessels under the navigation laws is required to be licensed as a broker.

E. For purposes of administering quotas, "official office hours" shall mean 8:30 a.m. to 4:30 a.m. in all time zones.

As per 19 CFR 152.108(c):

152.108 Unacceptable bases of appraisement.

*For the purposes of this subpart, **imported merchandise may not be appraised on the basis of:***

(a) The selling price in the United States of merchandise produced in the United States;

(b) A system that provides for the appraisement of imported merchandise at the higher of two alternative values;

*(c) **The price of merchandise in the domestic market of the country of exportation**;*

(d) A cost of production, other than a value determined under §152.106 for merchandise that is identical merchandise, or similar merchandise, to the merchandise being appraised;

(e) The price of merchandise for export to a country other than the United States;

(f) Minimum values for appraisement;

(g) Arbitrary or fictitious values.

In regards to multiple choice "A", interest on overdue bills will be assessed on the delinquent principal amount by 30-day periods (Ref: 19 CFR 24.3a(c)). In regards to "C", neither the Chapter 98 Notes, nor the subheading 9817.00.98 state that animals may not be classified as theatrical properties (Ref: HTSUS Chapter 98). In regards to "D", a person transacting business in connection with entry or clearance of vessels or other regulation of vessels under the navigation laws is not required to be licensed as a broker (Ref: 19 CFR 111.2(a)). In regards to "E", CBP "hours of business" are 8:30 to 5:00 (Ref: 19 CFR 101.6). The correct answer is "B".

60. Which of the following is NOT an assist?

A. Materials, components, parts, and similar items incorporated in the imported merchandise that are supplied directly and free of charge by the buyer of the imported merchandise.

B. Tools, dies, molds, and similar items used in the production of the imported merchandise that are supplied indirectly and at a reduced cost by the buyer of the imported merchandise.

C. Engineering, development, artwork, design work, and plans and sketches that are undertaken elsewhere than in the United States and are necessary for the production of the imported merchandise that are supplied directly and free of charge by the buyer of the imported merchandise.

D. Merchandise consumed in the production of the imported merchandise that are supplied indirectly and at a reduced cost by the buyer of the imported merchandise.

E. Merchandise consumed in the production of the imported merchandise that are supplied directly and free of charge by the seller of the imported merchandise.

 As per 19 CFR 152.102 (a):

(a) Assist. (1) "Assist" means any of the following if supplied directly or indirectly, and free of charge or at reduced cost, by the buyer of imported merchandise for use in connection with the production or the sale for export to the United States of the merchandise:

(i) Materials, components, parts, and similar items incorporated in the imported merchandise.

(ii) Tools, dies, molds, and similar items used in the production of the imported merchandise.

(iii) Merchandise consumed in the production of the imported merchandise.

(iv) Engineering, development, artwork, design work, and plans and sketches that are undertaken elsewhere than in the United States and are necessary for the production of the imported merchandise.

"Seller"-provided (as opposed to importer-provided) items used in production are NOT considered assists. Such costs are just regular seller/exporter cost of goods sold. The correct answer is "E".

✓ **JUST A SIDE NOTE:** Import "assists" are not at all illegal. However, they must be reported by being added to the transaction value (i.e. the price actually paid or payable) of the import.

61. "Generally accepted accounting principles" refers to any generally recognized consensus or substantial authoritative support regarding all of the following, EXCEPT:

A. Which economic resources and obligations should be recorded as assets and liabilities

B. Which changes in assets and liabilities should be recorded

C. How the assets and liabilities and changes in them should be measured

D. What information should not be disclosed and how it should be disclosed

E. Which financial statements should be prepared

 As per 19 CFR 152.102 (c):

*(c) Generally accepted accounting principles. (1) **"Generally accepted accounting principles" refers to any generally recognized consensus or substantial authoritative support regarding:***

(i) Which economic resources and obligations should be recorded as assets and liabilities;

(ii) Which changes in assets and liabilities should be recorded;

(iii) How the assets and liabilities and changes in them should be measured;

*(iv) **What information should be disclosed and how it should be disclosed**; and*

(v) Which financial statements should be prepared.

 The key word is the "not" in multiple choice and correct answer "D".

✓ **JUST A SIDE NOTE:** Generally Accepted Accounting Principles (GAAP) are the international standard guidelines for the practice of accounting.

Category XII: Fine and Penalties

62. Which is NOT a valid element to a prior disclosure per 19 CFR 162.74?

A. Specifies the material false statements, omissions or acts including an explanation as to how and when they occurred.

B. Identification of the class or kind of merchandise involved in the violation.

C. Actual loss of duties, taxes, and fees must be tendered.

D. Provide any information or data unknown at the time of disclosure within 60 days of the initial disclosure date.

E. Identifies the importation or drawback claim included in the prior disclosure.

 As per 19 CFR 162.74(b):

162.74 Prior disclosure.
... ...

(b) Disclosure of the circumstances of a violation. **The term "discloses the circumstances of a violation" means the act of providing to Customs a statement orally or in writing that:**

(1) Identifies the class or kind of merchandise involved in the violation;

(2) Identifies the importation or drawback claim included in the disclosure by entry number, drawback claim number, or by indicating each concerned Customs port of entry and the approximate dates of entry or dates of drawback claims;

(3) Specifies the material false statements, omissions or acts including an explanation as to how and when they occurred; and

(4) Sets forth, to the best of the disclosing party's knowledge, the true and accurate information or data that should have been provided in the entry or drawback claim documents, **and states that the disclosing party will provide any information or data unknown at the time of disclosure within 30 days of the initial disclosure date.** *Extensions of the 30-day period may be requested by the disclosing party from the concerned Fines, Penalties, and Forfeitures Officer to enable the party to obtain the information or data.*

 The correct answer is "D".

✓ **JUST A SIDE NOTE:** The reason for the 30 day grace period is that timing is of the essence when it comes to the submittal of a prior disclosure. A prior disclosure affords the disclosing party favorable government treatment in the case of a violation, but the prior disclosure must be presented to CBP before the importer's knowledge of an investigation. A fully detailed report to CBP can be drafted after the initial prior disclosure communication.

63. Section 592(d) demands for actual losses of duty ordinarily are issued in connection with a _____ action.

A. Liquidated damages

B. Seizure remission decision

C. Liquidation Notice

D. Penalty

E. Bill

 As per 19 CFR 171 Appendix B, (J) Section 592(d) Demands:

Section 592(d) demands for actual losses of duty ordinarily are issued in connection with a penalty action, or as a separate demand without an associated penalty action. In either case, information must be present establishing a violation of section 592(a). In those cases where the appropriate Customs field officer determines that issuance of a penalty under section 592 is not warranted (notwithstanding the presence of information establishing a violation of section 592(a)), but that circumstances do warrant issuance of a demand for payment of an actual loss of duty pursuant to section 592(d), the Customs field officer shall follow the procedures set forth in section 162.79b of the Customs Regulations (19 CFR 162.79b). Except in cases where less than one year remains before the statute of limitations may be raised as a defense, information copies of all section 592(d) demands should be sent to all concerned sureties and the importer of record if such party is not an alleged violator. Also, except in cases where less than one year remains before the statute of limitations may be raised as a defense, Customs will endeavor to issue all section 592(d) demands to concerned sureties and non-violator importers of record only after default by principals.

 The correct answer is "D".

✓ **JUST A SIDE NOTE:** "Section 592" refers to "Section 592 of the Tariff Act of 1930", the act which "prohibits persons, by fraud, gross negligence or negligence, from entering or introducing, attempting to enter or introduce, or aiding and abetting the entry or introduction of merchandise into the commerce of the United States."

Appendix B to Part 171 is titled "Customs Regulations, Guidelines for the Imposition and Mitigation of Penalties for Violations of 19 U.S.C. 1592". This "19 U.S.C. 1592" provides for laws for penalties for fraud, gross negligence, and negligence

"U.S.C. stands for United States Code". New laws are assigned a number and recorded in the U.S.C. The CFR, on the other hand, is subsequently created or amended to explain in detail these laws and how they will be implemented and enforced.

64. A broker counsels a client that certain gemstones are absolutely free of duty and need not be declared upon entry into the United States. The client arrives in the United States and fails to declare a quantity of gemstones worth $45,000. A penalty of $30,000 may be imposed against the broker for such counseling, yet not to exceed $30,000. What personal penalty would the client incur, under the provision of title 19, United States Code, section 1497?

A. None

B. $10,000

C. $15,000

D. $30,000

E. $45,000

 As per 19 CFR 171, Appendix C, VI. Section 1641(d)(1)(D)—Counseling, Commanding, Inducing, Procuring or Knowingly Aiding and Abetting Violations by Any Other Person of Any Law Enforced by the Customs Service:

A. If the law violated by another moves only against property, a monetary penalty equal to the domestic value of such property or $30,000 whichever is less, may be imposed against the broker who counsels, commands or knowingly aids and abets such violation.

B. If the law violated provides for only a personal penalty against the actual violator, a penalty may be imposed against the broker in an amount equal to that assessed against the violator, but in no case can the penalty exceed $30,000.

C. If the broker is assessed a penalty under the statute violated by the other person, he may be assessed a penalty under this section in addition to any other penalties.

D. Examples of violations of this subsection:

1. A broker counsels a client that certain gemstones are absolutely free of duty and need not be declared upon entry into the United States. The client arrives in the United States and fails to declare a quantity of gemstones worth $45,000. A penalty of $30,000 may be imposed against the broker for such counseling. The client would incur a personal penalty of $45,000 under the provisions of title 19, United States Code, section 1497, but the penalty against the broker cannot exceed $30,000.

... ...

The exam question is taken from the regulations example verbatim. The correct answer is "E".

 **JUST A SIDE NOTE:** Appendix C to Part 171 is titled "Customs Regulations Guidelines for the Imposition and Mitigation of Penalties for Violations of 19 U.S.C. 1641". This "19 U.S.C. 1641" provides for laws governing customs brokers.

65. The port director may review transactions for correctness and take action under his general authority to correct errors, including those in appraisement where appropriate, at the time of all the below except.

A. Liquidation of an entry

B. Voluntary reliquidation completed within 90 days after liquidation

C. Voluntary correction of an exaction within 180 days after the exaction was made

D. Reliquidation made pursuant to a valid protest covering the particular merchandise as to which a change is in order

E. Modification, pursuant to a valid protest, of a transaction or decision which is neither a liquidation nor reliquidation.

 As per 19 CFR 173.2:

The port director may review transactions for correctness, and take appropriate action under his general authority to correct errors, including those in appraisement where appropriate, at the time of:

(a) Liquidation of an entry;

(b) Voluntary reliquidation completed within 90 days after liquidation;

(c) Voluntary correction of an exaction within 90 days after the exaction was made;

(d) Reliquidation made pursuant to a valid protest covering the particular merchandise as to which a change is in order; or

(e) Modification, pursuant to a valid protest, of a transaction or decision which is neither a liquidation or reliquidation.

 An exaction by CBP may be corrected within "90 days" (i.e. NOT 180 days). The correct answer is "C".

✓ **JUST A SIDE NOTE:** Charges and exactions are "specific sums of money (other than ordinary customs duties) on imported merchandise".

Category XIII: Entry

66. The following motor vehicles may be imported by any person and do not have to be shown to be in compliance with emission requirements or modified before entitled to admissibility, except for which of the following:

A. **Gasoline-fueled light-duty trucks and light-duty motor vehicles manufactured before January 1, 1968**

B. **Diesel-fueled light-duty motor vehicles manufactured before January 1, 1979**

C. **Diesel-fueled light-duty trucks manufactured before January 1, 1976**

D. **Motorcycles manufactured before January 1, 1978**

E. **Gasoline-fueled and diesel-fueled heavy-duty engines manufactured before January 1, 1970**

 As per 19 CFR 12.73(e):

*(e) Exemptions and exclusions from emission requirements based on age of vehicle. **The following motor vehicles, except as shown, may be imported by any person and do not have to be shown to be in compliance with emission requirements or modified before entitled to admissibility:***

(1) Gasoline-fueled light-duty trucks and light-duty motor vehicles manufactured before January 1, 1968;

*(2) **Diesel-fueled light-duty motor vehicles manufactured before January 1, 1975;***

(3) Diesel-fueled light-duty trucks manufactured before January 1, 1976;

(4) Motorcycles manufactured before January 1, 1978;

(5) Gasoline-fueled and diesel-fueled heavy-duty engines manufactured before January 1, 1970; and

(6) Motor vehicles not otherwise exempt from EPA emission requirements and more than 20 years old. Age is determined by subtracting the year of production (as opposed to model year) from the year of importation. The exemption under this subparagraph is available only if the vehicle is imported by an ICI.

 The exemption cut-off year for diesel-fueled light-duty vehicles is 1975, not 1979. The correct answer is "B".

✔ **JUST A SIDE NOTE:** This Section 73 of 19 CFR Part 12 works in the U.S. Environmental Protection Agency (EPA) emission requirements. The EPA's complete regulations are separately found in Title 40 CFR.

67. Where in 19 CFR would you find information relation to importations prohibited by Section 307, Tariff Act of 1930?

A. 19 CFR 10.107

B. 19 CFR 12.42

C. 19 CFR 127.32

D. 19 CFR 141.112

E. 19 CFR 192.12

 As per 19 CFR 12.42:

Merchandise Produced By Convict, Forced, or Indentured Labor

§12.42 Findings of Commissioner of Customs.

*(a) **If any port director or other principal Customs officer has reason to believe that any class of merchandise that is being, or is likely to be, imported** into the United States is being produced, whether by mining, manufacture, or other means, in any foreign locality with the use of convict labor, forced labor, or indentured labor under penal sanctions, including forced child labor or indentured child labor under penal sanctions, **so as to come within the purview of section 307, Tariff Act of 1930**, he shall communicate his belief to the Commissioner of Customs. Every such communication shall contain or be accompanied by a statement of substantially the same information as is required in paragraph (b) of this section, if in the possession of the port director or other officer or readily available to him.*

… …

 The correct answer is "B".

✓ **JUST A SIDE NOTE:** "Section 307 of the Tariff Act of 1930" (19 U.S.C. 1307) is for the purpose of reducing child labor and forced labor.

68. All of the following articles are articles that may NOT be designated as an eligible article for purposes of the GSP, EXCEPT:

A. Watches, except as determined by the President pursuant to section 503(c)(1)(8) of the Trade Act of 1974, as amended

B. Import-sensitive steel articles

C. Import-sensitive electronic articles

D. Any agricultural product of chapters 2 through 52, inclusive, that is subject to a tariff-rate quota, if entered in a quantity in excess of the in-quota quantity for such product;

E. Textile and apparel articles which were eligible articles for purposes of this note on January 1, 1994

 As per HTSUS General Note 4(c) (Generalized System of Preferences):

(c) Articles provided for in a provision for which a rate of duty of "Free" appears in the "Special" subcolumn followed by the symbols "A" or "A*" in parentheses are those designated by the President to be eligible articles for purposes of the GSP pursuant to section 503 of the Trade Act of 1974. **The following articles may not be designated as an eligible article for purposes of the GSP:**

(i) textile and apparel articles which were NOT eligible articles for purposes of this note on January 1, 1994;

(ii) watches, except as determined by the President pursuant to section 503(c)(1)(B) of the Trade Act of 1974, as amended;

(iii) import-sensitive electronic articles;

(iv) import-sensitive steel articles;

(v) footwear, handbags, luggage, flat goods, work gloves and leather wearing apparel, the foregoing which were not eligible articles for purposes of the GSP on April 1, 1984;

(vi) import-sensitive semimanufactured and manufactured glass products;

(vii) any agricultural product of chapters 2 through 52, inclusive, that is subject to a tariff-rate quota, if entered in a quantity in excess of the in-quota quantity for such product; and

(viii) any other articles which the President determines to be import-sensitive in the context of the GSP.

 "NOT" is the key word that determines that the correct answer is "E".

✓ **INTERESTINGLY ENOUGH:** On this date, January 1, 1994, GSP eligibility for Mexico was replaced by NAFTA eligibility.

69. Which statement is TRUE?
A. "Guaranteeing association" means an association approved by the Office of Trade to guarantee the payment of obligations under carnets covering merchandise entering the Customs territory of the United States under a Customs Convention or multilateral Agreement to which the United States has acceded.
B. The importation into the United States of plants and plant products is subject to regulations and orders of the Food and Drug Administration. Customs officers and employees shall perform such functions as are necessary or proper to carry out such regulations and orders.
C. Any packages containing merchandise subject to an absolute quota, which is filled shall be returned to the postmaster for return to the sender immediately as undeliverable mail.
D. Unless a formal entry or entry by appraisement is required, a mail entry on Customs Form 7501 shall be issued and forwarded with the package to the postmaster for delivery to the addressee.
E. Under the Trade Facilitation and Trade Enforcement Act of 2015, the port director shall pass free of duty and tax any shipment of merchandise, as defined in § 101.1, imported by one person per week and having a fair retail value, in the country of shipment not exceeding $200, unless he has reason to believe that the shipment is one of several lots covered by a single order or contract and that it was sent separately for the express purpose of securing free entry therefore or of avoiding compliance with any pertinent law or regulation.

 As per 19 CFR 114.1(c), 19 CFR 12.10, 19 CFR 132.22, 19 CFR 132.24, & 19 CFR 10.151:

114.1 Definitions.
... ...
*(c) Guaranteeing association. "Guaranteeing association" means an association **approved by the Commissioner** to guarantee the payment of obligations under carnets covering merchandise entering the Customs territory of the United States under a Customs Convention **or bilateral Agreement** to which the United States has acceded.*

12.10 Regulations and orders of the Department of Agriculture.
*The importation into the United States of plants and plant products is subject to regulations and orders of the **Department of Agriculture** restricting or prohibiting the importation of such plants and plant products. ... ...*

132.22 When quota is filled.
Any packages containing merchandise subject to an absolute quota which is filled shall be returned to the postmaster for return to the sender immediately as undeliverable mail. The addressee will be notified on Customs Form 3509 or in any other appropriate manner that entry has been denied because the quota is filled.

132.24 Entry.
*Unless a formal entry or entry by appraisement is required, a mail entry on **Customs Form 3419** shall be issued and forwarded with the package to the postmaster for delivery to the addressee and collection of any duties in the same manner as for any other mail package subject to Customs treatment.*

10.151 Importations not over $800.
*Subject to the conditions in §10.153 of this part, the port director shall pass free of duty and tax any shipment of merchandise, as defined in §101.1 of this chapter, imported by one person **on one day** having a fair retail value, as evidenced by an oral declaration or the bill of lading (or other document filed as the entry) or manifest listing each bill of lading, in the country of shipment **not exceeding $800**, ...*

 The only correct statement and answer is multiple choice "C".

70. If merchandise is withheld from release by CBP due to an active withhold release order, an importer has up to _____ after the article was imported to provide information to CBP to contend that its goods were not mined, produced, or manufactured with any form of labor specified in section 307, Tariff Act of 1930.

A. 1 month
B. 6 months
C. 3 months
D. 2 months
E. 12 months

As per 19 CFR 12.43(a):

2.43 Proof of admissibility.

(a) If an importer of any article detained under §12.42(e) or (g) desires to contend that the article was not mined, produced, or manufactured in any part with the use of a class of labor specified in section 307, Tariff Act of 1930, **he shall submit to the Commissioner of Customs within 3 months after the date the article was imported a certificate of origin***, or its electronic equivalent, in the form set forth below, signed by the foreign seller or owner of the article. If the article was mined, produced, or manufactured wholly or in part in a country other than that from which it was exported to the United States, an additional certificate, or its electronic equivalent, in such form and signed by the last owner or seller in such other country, substituting the facts of transportation from such other country for the statements with respect to shipment from the country of exportation, shall be so submitted.*

Certificate of Origin
I, _____, *foreign seller or owner of the merchandise hereinafter described, certify that such merchandise, consisting of* _____ *(Quantity) of* _____ *(Description) in* _____ *(Number and kind of packages) bearing the following marks and numbers* _____ *was mined, produced, or manufactured by* _____ *(Name) at or near* _____*, and was laden on board* _____ *(Carrier to the United States) at* _____ *(Place of lading) (Place of final departure from country of exportation) which departed from on* _____*; (Date); and that* _____ *(Class of labor specified in finding) was not employed in any stage of the mining, production, or manufacture of the merchandise or of any component thereof.*

Dated _____

(Signature)

The importer has 3 months to certify that the goods were not obtained through child or forced labor. The correct answer is "C".

✓ JUST A SIDE OTE: As per 19 CFR 12.42(h):

(h) The following findings made under the authority of section 307, Tariff Act of 1930 are currently in effect with respect to the merchandise listed below:

Merchandise	Country	T.D.
Furniture, clothes hampers, and palm leaf bags	Ciudad Victoria, Tamaulipas, Mexico	53408 54725

71. Importation is prohibited, except as authorized by the issuance of a permit by the Director, U.S. Fish and Wildlife Service, for all the below, EXCEPT:

A. Any species of European rabbit the genus Oryctolagus
B. Any species of Indian wild dog, red dog, or dhole of the genus Cuon
C. Any live specimens or egg of the species of so-called "pink starling" or "rosy pastor" Sturnus roseus
D. Any live fish or viable eggs of the family Clariidae
E. Any species of the so-called Bumblebee bat

As per 19 CFR 12.26(a):

12.26 Importations of wild animals, fish, amphibians, reptiles, mollusks, and crustaceans; prohibited and endangered and threatened species; designated ports of entry; permits required.

(a)(1) The importation into the United States, the Commonwealth of Puerto Rico, and the territories and possessions of the United States of live specimens of:

(i) Any species of the so-called "flying fox" or fruit bat of the genus Pteropus;

(ii) Any species of mongoose or meerkat of the genera Atilax, Cynictis, Helogale, Herpestes, Ichneumia, Mungos, and Suricata;

*(iii) **Any species of European rabbit the genus Oryctolagus;***

*(iv) **Any species of Indian wild dog, red dog, or dhole of the genus Cuon;***

(v) Any species of multimammate rat or mouse of the genus Mastomys;

*(vi) **Any live specimens or egg of the species of so-called "pink starling" or "rosy pastor" Sturnus roseus;***

(vii) The species of dioch (including the subspecies black-fronted, red-billed, or Sudan dioch) Quelea quelea;

(viii) Any species of Java sparrow, Padda oryzivora;

(ix) The species of red-whiskered bulbul, Pycnonotus jocosus;

*(x) **Any live fish or viable eggs of the family Clariidae;***

(xi) Any other species of wild mammals, wild birds, fish (including mollusks and crustacea), amphibians, reptiles, or the offspring or eggs of any of the foregoing which the Secretary of the Interior may prescribe by regulations to be injurious to human beings, to the interest of agriculture, horticulture, forestry, or to wildlife or the wildlife resources of the United States, is prohibited, except as may be authorized by the issuance of a permit by the Director, U.S. Fish and Wildlife Service, U.S. Department of the Interior, Washington, DC ... ...

The importation of the bumblebee bat is not prohibited. However, unless otherwise authorized, the U.S. Fish and Wildlife Service Form 3-177 will be required at the port of entry. The correct answer is "E".

✓ **JUST A SIDE NOTE:** The Fish and Wildlife Service regulations are contained in Title 50 of the CFR.

72. In the case of nonconsumable vessel stores and equipment returned to the United States under subheading 9801.00.10, HTSUS, the entry summary may be made on CBP Form 3311, or its electronic equivalent. The entry summary on CBP Form 3311, or its electronic equivalent, must be executed in duplicate by the entrant and supported by the entry documentation required by §142.3 of this chapter. Before an entry summary on CBP Form 3311, or its electronic equivalent, may be accepted for nonconsumable vessel stores and equipment, the CBP officer must be satisfied with all of the following, EXCEPT:

A. The articles are products of the United States.

B. The articles have not been improved in condition or advanced in value while abroad

C. No drawback has been or will be paid

D. No duty equal to an internal revenue tax is payable under subheading 9801.00.80, HTSUS.

E. Duty equal to an internal revenue tax is payable under subheading 9801.00.80, HTSUS

 As per 19 CFR 10.1(h):

(h) Nonconsumable vessel stores and equipment. (1) In the case of nonconsumable vessel stores and equipment returned to the United States under subheading 9801.00.10, HTSUS, the entry summary may be made on CBP Form 3311, or its electronic equivalent. The entry summary on CBP Form 3311, or its electronic equivalent, must be executed in duplicate by the entrant and supported by the entry documentation required by §142.3 of this chapter. Before an entry summary on CBP Form 3311, or its electronic equivalent, may be accepted for nonconsumable vessel stores and equipment, the CBP officer must be satisfied that:

(i) The articles are products of the United States.

(ii) The articles have not been improved in condition or advanced in value while abroad.

(iii) No drawback has been or will be paid, and

*(iv) **No duty equal to an internal revenue tax is payable under subheading 9801.00.80, HTSUS.***

... ...

 The correct answer is "E".

✓ **JUST A SIDE NOTE:** CBP Form 3311 is the "Declaration for Free Entry of Returned American Products" statement.

73. A radiation generator unit is sent to Japan for repair under warranty and returned. The value of the equipment prior to repair is $45000. The value of the repairs is $4000. The equipment is properly classified under subheading 9022.90.0050, HTSUS, and subheading 9802.00.4040, HTSUS, is properly claimed. What is the merchandise processing fee?

A. $0.00

B. $169.74

C. $25.00

D. $155.88

E. $13.86

 As per 19 CFR 24.23(c):

*(c) Exemptions and limitations. (1) **The ad valorem fee, surcharge**, and specific fees provided for under paragraphs (b)(1) and (b)(2) **of this section will not apply to:***

*(i) Except as provided in paragraph (c)(2) of this section, **articles provided for in chapter 98**, Harmonized Tariff Schedule of the United States (HTSUS; 19 U.S.C. 1202);*

(ii) Products of insular possessions of the U.S. (General Note 3(a)(iv), HTSUS);

(iii) Products of beneficiary countries under the Caribbean Basin Economic Recovery Act (General Note 7, HTSUS);

(iv) Products of least-developed beneficiary developing countries (General Note 4(b)(i), HTSUS); and

(v) Merchandise described in General Note 19, HTSUS, merchandise released under 19 U.S.C. 1321, and merchandise imported by mail.
... ...

Although "duty" will be assessed for the $4000 in repairs at the duty rate applicable to the classification 9022.90.0050, the "Merchandise Processing Fee" for this Chapter 98 customs entry will not be assessed due to the above-mentioned exemption. The correct answer is "A".

✓ **JUST A SIDE NOTE:** The chapter 98 classifications that are not exempt from the Merchandise Processing Fee (MPF) rate of .003464 are HTSUS 9802.00.60 and 9802.00.80, which provide for articles of metal exported for further processing, and certain articles exported for simple assembly abroad respectively.

74. The person claiming a certification of exemption from entry for undeliverable articles under General Note 3(e), HTSUS, is subject to the following conditions, EXCEPT:

A. The merchandise was intended to be exported to a foreign country
B. The merchandise is being returned within 45 days of departure from the United States
C. The merchandise did not leave the custody of the carrier or foreign customs
D. The merchandise is being returned to the United States because it was undeliverable to the foreign consignee.
E. The merchandise was sent abroad to receive benefit from, or fulfill obligations to, the United States as a result of exportation.

 As per 19 CFR 141.4(c):

(c) Undeliverable articles. The exemption from entry for undeliverable articles under General Note 3(e), HTSUS, is subject to the following conditions:

(1) The person claiming the exemption must submit a certification (documentary or electronic) that:

(i) The merchandise was intended to be exported to a foreign country;

(ii) The merchandise is being returned within 45 days of departure from the United States;

(iii) The merchandise did not leave the custody of the carrier or foreign customs;

(iv) The merchandise is being returned to the United States because it was undeliverable to the foreign consignee; and

*(v) **The merchandise was not sent abroad to receive benefit from, or fulfill obligations to, the United States as a result of exportation.***

(2) Upon request by CBP, the person claiming the exemption shall provide evidence required to support the claim for exemption.

 Yet another "NOT" gotcha attempt by exam writer. The correct answer is "E".

✓ **JUST A SIDE NOTE:** Below is an excerpt from the above-referenced HTSUS General Note 3(e):

(e) Exemptions. For the purposes of general note 1--

(i) corpses, together with their coffins and accompanying flowers,

(ii) telecommunications transmissions,

(iii) records, diagrams and other data with regard to any business, engineering or exploration operation whether on paper, cards, photographs, blueprints, tapes or other media,

(iv) articles returned from space within the purview of section 484a of the Tariff Act of 1930,

(v) articles exported from the United States which are returned within 45 days after such exportation from the United States as undeliverable and which have not left the custody of the carrier or foreign customs service, ...

75. Which of the following operations performed abroad would not be regarded as an assembly operation?

A. Laminating
B. Sewing
C. Mixing or Combining of liquids
D. Gluing
E. Welding

 As per 19 CFR 10.16(a):

10.16 Assembly abroad.

(a) Assembly operations. The assembly operations performed abroad may consist of any method used to join or fit together solid components, such as welding, soldering, riveting, force fitting, gluing, laminating, sewing, or the use of fasteners, and may be preceded, accompanied, or followed by operations incidental to the assembly as illustrated in paragraph (b) of this section. ***The mixing or combining of liquids, gases, chemicals, food ingredients, and amorphous solids with each other or with solid components is not regarded as an assembly.***

Example 1. A television yoke is assembled abroad from American-made magnet wire. In the foreign assembly plant the wire is despooled and wound into a coil, the wire cut from the spool, and the coil united with other components, including a terminal panel and housing which are also American-made. The completed article upon importation would be subject to the ad valorem rate of duty applicable to television parts upon the value of the yoke less the cost or value of the American-made wire, terminal panel and housing, assembled therein. The winding and cutting of the wire are either assembly steps or steps incidental to assembly.

Example 2. An aluminum electrolytic capacitor is assembled abroad from American-made aluminum foil, paper, tape, and Mylar film. In the foreign assembly plant the aluminum foil is trimmed to the desired width, cut to the desired length, interleaved with paper, which may or may not be cut to length or despooled from a continuous length, and rolled into a cylinder wherein the foil and paper are cut and a section of sealing tape fastened to the surface to prevent these components from unwinding. Wire or other electric connectors are bonded at appropriate intervals to the aluminum foil of the cylinder which is then inserted into a metal can, and the ends closed with a protective washer. As imported, the capacitor is subject to the ad valorem rate of duty applicable to capacitors upon the value less the cost or value of the American-made foil, paper, tape, and Mylar film. The operations performed on these components are all either assembly steps or steps incidental to assembly.

Example 3. The manufacture abroad of cloth on a loom using thread or yarn exported from the United States on spools, cops, or pirns is not considered an assembly but a weaving operation, and the thread or yarn does not qualify for the exemption. However, American-made thread used to sew buttons or garment components is qualified for the exemption because it is used in an operation involving the assembly of solid components.

 The simple mixing or combining of materials is not regarded as "assembly" abroad. The correct answer is "C".

✓ **JUST A SIDE NOTE:** Articles assembled abroad from U.S. components are eligible for partial exemption from duties by utilization of HTSUS 9802.00.80 (i.e. "a duty upon the full value of the imported article, less the cost or value of such products of the United States").

76. Any person outside the Customs Service who has reason to believe that any merchandise produced whether by mining, manufacture, or other means, in any foreign locality with the use of convict labor, forced labor, or indentured labor under penal sanctions, is likely to be, imported into the United States and that merchandise of the same class is being produced in the United States in such quantities as to meet the consumptive demands of the United States may communicate his belief to any port director or the Commissioner of Customs. Every such communication shall contain, or be accompanied by all of the below, EXCEPT:

A. a full statement of the reasons for the belief

B. a detailed description or sample of the merchandise

C. all pertinent facts obtainable as to the production of the merchandise abroad

D. if the foreign merchandise is believed to be mined, produced or manufactured with forced labor or indentured labor under penal sanctions include detailed information as to the production and consumption of the particular class of merchandise in the United States and the names and addresses of domestic producers likely to be interested in the matter

E. location of foreign mining, production or manufacture at issue

 As per 19 CFR 12.42(b):

(b) Any person outside the Customs Service who has reason to believe that merchandise produced in the circumstances mentioned in paragraph (a) of this section is being, or is likely to be, imported into the United States and, if the production is with the use of forced labor or indentured labor under penal sanctions, that merchandise of the same class is being produced in the United States in such quantities as to meet the consumptive demands of the United States may communicate his belief to any port director or the Commissioner of Customs. Every such communication shall contain, or be accompanied by, (1) a full statement of the reasons for the belief, (2) a detailed description or sample of the merchandise, and (3) all pertinent facts obtainable as to the production of the merchandise abroad. If the foreign merchandise is believed to be mined, produced, or manufactured with the use of forced labor or indentured labor under penal sanctions, such communication shall also contain (4) detailed information as to the production and consumption of the particular class of merchandise in the United States and the names and addresses of domestic producers likely to be interested in the matter.

Reporting to CBP of the location of foreign mining, production or manufacture at issue is not required. The correct answer is "E".

✓ **JUST A SIDE NOTE:** Uncommon to all previous exams, this year's exam makes regular reference to the regulations pertaining to merchandise produced by convict, forced, or indentured labor (i.e. 19 CFR 12.42 & 12.43).

CATERGORY XIV: Foreign Trade Zones

77. After merchandise is warehoused, the importer has 5 years from what DATE to remove the merchandise, provided an extension was not granted by the port director?

A. Release Date

B. Entry Summary Date

C. Exportation Date

D. Importation Date

E. Liquidation Date

 As per 19 CFR 146.64(d):

(d) Time limit. **Merchandise may neither be placed nor remain in a Customs bonded warehouse after 5 years from the date of importation** *of the merchandise.*

 The correct answer is "D".

✓ **JUST A SIDE NOTE:** Merchandise in a Foreign Trade Zone (FTZ) may be transferred from an FTZ for 1) exportation, 2) transport to a different port, 3) consumption (entry), or 4) (bonded) warehouse.

78. What is the time limit for physical removal from a foreign trade zone of merchandise that has been permitted for transfer to Customs territory?

A. Within 30 business days of issuance of a Customs permit.

B. Within 5 calendar days of issuance of a Customs permit.

C. Within 90 business days of issuance of a Customs permit.

D. Within 5 business days of issuance of a Customs permit.

E. None of the above.

 As per 19 CFR 146.71(c):

*(c) Time limit. Except in the case of articles for use in a zone, merchandise for which a Customs permit for transfer to Customs territory has been issued must be physically removed from the zone **within 5 working days of issuance of that permit**. The port director, upon request of the operator, may extend that period for good cause. Merchandise awaiting removal within the required time limit will not be further manipulated or manufactured in the zone, but will be segregated or otherwise identified by the operator as merchandise that has been constructively transferred to Customs territory.*

 The correct answer is "D".

✓ **JUST A SIDE NOTE:** CBP's website describes, in general, what products and activities are allowed in FTZ's:

The Foreign-Trade Zones Board may exclude from a zone any merchandise that is in its judgment detrimental to the public interest, health, or safety. The Board may place restrictions on certain types of merchandise, which would limit the zone status allowed, the kind of operation on the merchandise in a zone, the entry of the merchandise into the commerce, or similar transactions or activities.

Many products subject to an internal revenue tax may not be manufactured in a zone. These products include alcoholic beverages, products containing alcoholic beverages except domestic denatures distilled spirits, perfumes containing alcohol, tobacco products, firearms, and sugar. In addition, the manufacture of clock and watch movements is not permitted in a zone.

No retail trade of foreign merchandise may be conducted in a FTZ. However, foreign and domestic merchandise may be stored, examined, sampled, and exhibited in a zone.

79. The person with the right to make entry shall file a Customs entry or file an application for admission of the merchandise to the foreign trade zone on Customs Form 214 within _____ days after identifying an OVERAGE.

A. 5

B. 7

C. 10

D. 15

E. 30

 As per 19 CFR 146.53(d):

*(d) Overage. The person with the right to make entry shall file, **within 5 days after identification of an overage**, an application for admission of the merchandise to the zone on Customs Form 214 or file a Customs entry for the merchandise. If a Customs Form 214 or a Customs entry is not timely filed, and the port director has not granted an extension of the time provided, the merchandise shall be sent to general order.*

 The correct answer is "A".

✓ **JUST A SIDE NOTE:** For regular, non-FTZ merchandise, if an import shipment has been sitting at the port for more than 15 days without a customs entry or in-bond transfer assigned to it, the import will enter into General Order (GO) status. If still unclaimed after 6 months in General Order, the shipment will legally be made available for public auction.

80. A CBP Form 7512 must be presented to CBP for .

A. merchandise to be withdrawn from a bonded warehouse for consumption

B. admission into a foreign trade zone

C. presentation of quota class merchandise withdrawn from continuous customs custody

D. a drawback claimant to claim manufacturing drawback on merchandise transferred from continuous customs custody

E. merchandise to be withdrawn from a bonded warehouse for immediate transportation, immediate exportation, or transportation and exportation

 As per 19 CFR 18.10:

18.10 Kinds of entry.

(a) The following entries and withdrawals may be made for merchandise to be transported in bond:

(1) Entry for immediate transportation without appraisement.

*(2) Warehouse or rewarehouse **withdrawal for transportation**.*

*(3) Warehouse or rewarehouse **withdrawal for exportation or for transportation and exportation**.*

(4) Entry for transportation and exportation.

(5) Entry for exportation.

*(b) The copy of each entry or withdrawal made in any of the classes named in paragraph (a) of this section which is retained in the office of the forwarding port director shall be signed by the party making the entry or withdrawal. In the case of shipments to the Virgin Islands (U.S.) under paragraph (a), (3), (4), or (5) of this section, one additional copy of the entry or withdrawal on **Customs Form 7512 shall be filed** and shall be mailed by the receiving port director to the port director, Charlotte Amalie, St. Thomas, Virgin Island (U.S.). Before shipping merchandise in bond to another port for the purpose of warehousing or rewarehousing, the shipper should ascertain whether warehouse facilities are available at the intended port of destination.*

 The correct answer is "E".

✓ **JUST A SIDE NOTE:** Essentially, CBP Form 7512 is a carrier's request to CBP to move in-bond items to another port or to export.

Book 1 Part 10

Exam with Broker Commentary
April 2016 Customs Broker License Examination

This section of the study guide analyzes an actual customs broker exam. It presents the actual question and its multiple choices. For HTSUS classification questions, the author of this book has included abbreviated HTSUS Article Descriptions notated directly to the right of each multiple choice classification for the student's convenience and ease of reference purposes. As necessary, and in proportion to the complexity of each particular exam question, an analysis of the question and path to the correct answer has been provided. Direct excerpts from the HTSUS, 19 CFR, etc. are also included as supporting points of reference for each answer as necessary. This exam (without commentary, etc.) and its answer key, as well as other previous customs exams can be downloaded directly from Customs' website at...

http://www.cbp.gov/document/publications/past-customs-broker-license-examinations-answer-keys

Exam Refs: Harmonized Tariff Schedule of the United States
Title 19, Code of Federal Regulations
Customs and Trade Automated Interface Requirements (CATAIR)
   * Appendix B - Valid Codes
   * Appendix D - Metric Conversion
   * Appendix E - Valid Entry Numbers
   * Appendix G - Common Errors
   * Glossary of Terms
Instructions for Preparation of CBP Form 7501
Right to Make Entry Directive, 3530-002A

Exam Breakdown by Subject:

Category I –	Practical Exercises	Questions 1-3
Category II –	Powers of Attorney	Questions 4-6
Category III –	Entry	Questions 7-16
Category IV –	Foreign Trade Zones	Questions 17-20
Category V –	Classification	Questions 21-32
Category VI –	Valuation	Questions 33-38
Category VII –	Free Trade Agreements	Questions 39-44
Category VIII –	Drawback	Questions 45-49
Category IX –	Antidumping/Countervailing	Questions 50-52
Category X –	Marking	Questions 53-57
Category XI –	Broker Compliance	Questions 58-65
Category XII –	Fines and Penalties	Questions 66-71
Category XIII –	Bonds	Questions 72-76
Category XIV –	Intellectual Property Rights	Questions 77-80

Category I: Practical Exercises

Please use the table below to answer questions 1-3.

DEPARTMENT OF HOMELAND SECURITY
U.S. Customs and Border Protection
ENTRY SUMMARY

Form Approved OMB No. 1651-0022
EXP. 10-31-2017

1. Filer Code/Entry No.	BMB-1007201-5
2. Entry Type	03 ABI/P
3. Summary Date	06/17/2015
4. Surety No.	201
5. Bond Type	8
6. Port Code	5301
7. Entry Date	06/17/2015
8. Importing Carrier	OOCL CANADA
9. Mode of Transport	11
10. Country of Origin	TW
11. Import Date	06/10/2015
12. B/L or AWB No.	OOLU 2534567390
13. Manufacturer ID	TWCHACHU301TAI
14. Exporting Country	TW
15. Export Date	05/28/2015
16. I.T. No.	V1622934183
17. I.T. Date	
18. Missing Docs	
19. Foreign Port of Lading	52809
20. U.S. Port of Unlading	2709
21. Location of Goods/G.O. No.	S639 BNSF HOUSTON
22. Consignee No.	99-887766500
23. Importer No.	99-887766500
24. Reference No.	23-456789100

25. Ultimate Consignee Name and Address
City _____ State DE Zip _____

26. Importer of Record Name and Address
PLASTIC CORPORATION OF NOWHERE
7804 MARKET ST
City OCEANBREEZE State FL Zip 45678

27. Line No.	28. Description of Merchandise / 29. A. HTSUS No. B. ADA/CVD No.	30. A. Grossweight B. Manifest Qty.	31. Net Quantity in HTSUS Units	32. A. Entered Value B. CHGS C. Relationship	33. A. HTSUS Rate B. ADA/CVD Rate C. IRC Rate D. Visa No.	34. Duty and I.R. Tax Dollars Cents
001 TW	2000 PCS POLY(VINYL ALCOHOLS) 3905.30.0000 TSCA:P A-583-841-001 MERCHANDISE PROCESSING FEE I.V. 98760.00 -NDC 5783.85 E.V. 92976.15	41600 BLOCK 39 SUMMARY MERCHANDISE PROCESSING FEE HARBOR MAINT. FEE	40000 KG	92976 C5784 0.0308 499 322.07 501 116.22	3.2% 0.3464%	2975.23 2863.66 322.07

Other Fee Summary for Block 39	35. Total Entered Value
2863.66 ANTIDUMPING DUTY	$ 92976.00
	Total Other Fees $ 3301.95

CBP USE ONLY

A. LIQ CODE	B. Ascertained Duty	37. Duty 2975.23
REASON CODE	C. Ascertained Tax	38. Tax
	D. Ascertained Other	39. Other 3301.95
	E. Ascertained Total	40. Total 6277.18

38. DECLARATION OF IMPORTER OF RECORD (OWNER OR PURCHASER) OR AUTHORIZED AGENT

I declare that I am the ☐ importer of record and that the actual owner, purchaser, or consignee for CBP purposes is as shown above, OR ☐ owner or purchaser or agent thereof. I further declare that the merchandise ☐ was obtained pursuant to a purchase or agreement to purchase and that the prices set forth in the invoices are true, OR ☐ was not obtained pursuant to a purchase or agreement to purchase and the statements in the invoices as to value or price are true to the best of my knowledge and belief. I also declare that the statements in the documents herein filed fully disclose to the best of my knowledge and belief the true prices, values, quantities, rebates, drawbacks, fees, commissions, and royalties and are true and correct, and that all goods or services provided to the seller of the merchandise either free or at reduced cost are fully disclosed.
I will immediately furnish to the appropriate CBP officer any information showing a different statement of facts.

41. DECLARANT NAME _____ TITLE _____ SIGNATURE _____ DATE _____

42. Broker/Filer Information (Name, address, phone number)

43. Broker/Importer File No.

CBP Form 7501 (06/09)

1) In Block 2, "Entry Type", what does ABI/P represent?

a) ABI statement paid by check or cash
b) ABI statement paid via Automated Clearinghouse (ACH)
c) ABI statement paid on a periodic monthly basis
d) ABI summary not paid on statement
e) ABI statement paid via ACH for a "live" entry/entry summary

 As per CBP Form 7501 Instructions, BLOCK 2) ENTRY TYPE:

... ...

Automated Broker Interface (ABI) processing requires an ABI status indicator. This indicator must be recorded in the entry type code block. It is to be shown for those entry summaries with ABI status only, and must be shown in one of the following formats:

ABI/S = ABI statement paid by check or cash
ABI/A = ABI statement paid via Automated Clearinghouse (ACH)
ABI/P = ABI statement paid on a periodic monthly basis
ABI/N = ABI summary not paid on a statement

"ABI" stands for Automated Broker Interface. The "P" stands for Periodic (Monthly Statement). The correct answer is "c".

✓ **JUST A SIDE NOTE:** Periodic Monthly Statement (PMS) is a feature in Automated Commercial Environment (ACE) that allows importers and brokers flexibility to pay for all entries released in a month as a single payment, and as late as the 15th working day of the following month, interest free.

Exam with Broker Commentary (Apr. 2016) Study Guide

2) In "Other Fee Summary for Block 39", what is the collection code for Antidumping Duties?

a) 012
b) 013
c) 044
d) 055
e) 103

 As per CBP Form 7501 Instructions, OTHER FEE SUMMARY FOR BLOCK 39:

The applicable collection code must be indicated on the same line as the fee or other charge or exaction. Report the fees in the format below:

AD 012
CVD 013
Tea Fee 038
Misc. Interest 044
Beef Fee 053
Pork Fee 054
Honey Fee 055
Cotton Fee 056
Pecan Fee 057
Sugar Fee 079
Potato Fee 090
Mushroom Fee 103
Watermelon 104
Blueberry Fee 106
Avocado 107
Mango 108
Informal Entry MPF 311
Dutiable Mail Fee 496
Merchandise Processing Fee (MPF) 499
Manual Surcharge 500
Harbor Maintenance Fee (HMF) 501

The "Other Fee Summary for Block 39" line should read "2863.66   012   ANTIDUMPING DUTY". The correct answer is "a".

✓ **JUST A SIDE NOTE:** The Merchandise Processing Fee (MPF) and Harbor Maintenance Fee (HMF) are also usually included in the same "Other Fee Summary for Block 39", though they are not for this exam entry summary.

3) If refunds, bills, or notices of extension or suspension of liquidation are sent to an individual or firm other than the importer of record, which block would be used to record the IRS, EIN, SSN, or CBP assigned number?

a) Block 13
b) Block 15
c) Block 22
d) Block 23
e) Block 24

 As per CBP Form 7501 Instructions, BLOCK 24) REFERENCE NUMBER:

BLOCK 24) REFERENCE NUMBER

***Record the IRS EIN, SSN, or CBP assigned number of the individual or firm to whom refunds, bills, or notices of extension or suspension of liquidation are to be sent (if other than the importer of record** and only when a CBP Form 4811 is on file). Proper format is listed under the instructions for Consignee Number. Do not use this block to record any other information.*

 The answer is "e".

✓ **JUST A SIDE NOTE:** The above-referenced CBP Form 4811 is simply a "Special Address Notification" form. Snapshot of which is below for your reference.

Category II: Powers of Attorney

4) What form is used for giving power of attorney to transact Customs business?

a) CBP Form 5291
b) CBP Form 3347
c) CBP Form 4647
d) CBP Form 368
e) CBP Form 7501

As per 19 CFR 141.32:

141.32 Form for power of attorney.

Customs Form 5291 may be used for giving power of attorney to transact Customs business. *If a Customs power of attorney is not on a Customs Form 5291, it shall be either a general power of attorney with unlimited authority or a limited power of attorney as explicit in its terms and executed in the same manner as a Customs Form 5291. The following is an example of an acceptable general power of attorney with unlimited authority:*

KNOW ALL MEN BY THESE PRESENTS, THAT

_____

(Name of principal)

_____,

(State legal designation, such as corporation, individual, etc.) residing at _____ and doing business under the laws of the State of _____, hereby appoints

(Name, legal designation, and address)

as a true and lawful agent and attorney of the principal named above with full power and authority to do and perform every lawful act and thing the said agent and attorney may deem requisite and necessary to be done for and on behalf of the said principal without limitation of any kind as fully as said principal could do if present and acting, and hereby ratify and confirm all that said agent and attorney shall lawfully do or cause to be done by virtue of these presents until and including _____, (date) or until notice of revocation in writing is duly given before that date.

Date _____, 20__;.

(Principal's signature)

The answer is "a".

✓ **JUST A SIDE NOTE:** Although the above-mentioned form may be used to assign a customs power of attorney for an importer, most customs brokerage operations create their own unique form and include their terms and conditions with the form.

5) Where a limited partnership is the Grantor of a power of attorney, _____ must accompany the power of attorney.

a) a copy of the partnership agreement
b) CBP Form 7501
c) a nonnegotiable check for duties due to U.S. Customs and Border Protection
d) a copy of the articles of incorporation
e) fingerprint cards and proof of citizenship of the partners

 As per 19 CFR 141.39(a)(2):

141.39 Partnerships.

(a)(1) General. A power of attorney granted by a partnership shall state the names of all members of the partnership. One member of the partnership may execute a power of attorney in the name of the partnership for the transaction of all its Customs business.

(2) Limited partnership. A power of attorney granted by a limited partnership need only state the names of the general partners who have authority to bind the firm unless the partnership agreement provides otherwise. ***A copy of the partnership agreement must accompany the power of attorney.*** *For this purpose, a partnership or limited partnership means any business association recognized as such under the laws of the state where the association is organized.*

 The correct answer is "a".

✓ **JUST A SIDE NOTE:** Simply put, a "partnership agreement" (a.k.a. articles of partnership) is a legal contract between two or more parties that spells out the rights and obligations of the parties entering into the agreement.

6) A Customs Power of Attorney issued by a partnership shall be limited to _____ year(s).

a) 1
b) 5
c) 2
d) 10
e) unlimited

 As per 19 CFR 141.34:

141.34 Duration of power of attorney.

***Powers of attorney issued by a partnership shall be limited to a period not to exceed 2 years from the date of execution.** All other powers of attorney may be granted for an unlimited period.*

 The correct answer is "c".

✓ **JUST A SIDE NOTE:** Although a Power of Attorney (POA) for a non-partnership organization may be granted for a limited time period, for a defined time period, or for a specific shipment referenced within the POA.

Category III: Entry

7) Absolute quota merchandise imported in excess of the admissible quantity may NOT be_____.

a) held in a Foreign Trade Zone (FTZ) for the opening of the next quota period
b) held in a warehouse for the opening of the next quota period
c) exported
d) destroyed under CBP supervision
e) entered at a higher rate of duty

 As per 19 CFR 132.5(c):

(c) Disposition of excess merchandise. **Merchandise imported in excess of either an absolute or a tariff-rate quota may be held for the opening of the next quota period by placing it in a foreign-trade zone or by entering it for warehouse, or it may be exported or destroyed under Customs supervision.**

There are several options for handling an import in excess of an "absolute quota", though entering it in at a higher duty rate is not one of those options. Entering a quota shipment in at a higher duty rate is only an option for a "tariff rate quota." The correct answer is "e".

✔ **JUST A SIDE NOTE:** An "absolute quota" is also referred to, and is the same thing as a "quantitative quota."

8) A work of fine art arrived at the Port of Miami and was admitted temporarily into the United States under chapter 98, subchapter XIII of the Harmonized Tariff Schedule of the United States. Eleven months later, the importer wants the work of art to remain in the United States under Chapter 98, Subchapter XIII for eight additional months and to be exported from the Port of Boston. What course of action should the importer take?

a) File a consumption entry
b) File a written application for extension on CBPF 3173 to the Commissioner of CBP
c) File a written application for extension on CBPF 3173 to the Port Director of Miami before the initial twelve months has lapsed
d) File a written application for extension on CBPF 3173 after the twelve months has lapsed to the Director of Field Operations for the Port of Miami
e) File a written application for extension on CBPF 3173 to the Port Director of Boston

 As per 19 CFR 10.37:

10.37 Extension of time for exportation.

***The period of time during which merchandise entered under bond under chapter 98, subchapter XIII, Harmonized Tariff Schedule of the United States (19 U.S.C. 1202), may remain in the customs territory of the United States, may be extended for not more than two further periods of 1 year each, or such shorter period as may be appropriate. Extensions may be granted by the director of the port where the entry was filed upon written application on CBP Form 3173**, provided the articles have not been exported or destroyed before the receipt of the application, and liquidated damages have not been assessed under the bond before receipt of the application. Any untimely request for an extension of time for exportation shall be referred to the Director, Commercial and Trade Facilitation Division, Office of International Trade, CBP Headquarters, for disposition. Any request for relief from a liquidated damage assessment in excess of a Fines, Penalties, and Forfeitures Officer's delegated authority shall be referred to the Director, Border Security and Trade Compliance Division, Office of International Trade, CBP Headquarters, for disposition. No extension of the period for which a carnet is valid shall be granted.*

 The correct answer is "c".

✓ **JUST A SIDE NOTE:** HTSUS 9813.00.70 is the classification for:

Works of the free fine arts, engravings, photographic pictures and philosophical and scientific apparatus brought into the United States by professional artists, lecturers or scientists arriving from abroad for use by them for exhibition and in illustration, promotion and encouragement of art, science or industry in the United States.

9) For merchandise entered under any temporary monthly entry program established by CBP before July 1, 1989, for the purpose of testing entry processing improvements, provided that those importations involve the same importer and exporter, the fee for processing merchandise for each day's importations at an individual port will be the lesser of the 0.3464 percent ad valorem merchandise processing fee and:

a) $25.00
b) $400.00
c) $425.00
d) $485.00
e) $500.00

 As per 19 CFR 24.23(d)(1):

*(d) Aggregation of ad valorem fee. (1) **Notwithstanding any other provision of this section, in the case of entries of merchandise made under any temporary monthly entry program established by CBP before July 1, 1989, for the purpose of testing entry processing improvements, the ad valorem fee charged under paragraph (b)(1)(i) of this section for each day's importations at an individual port will be the lesser of the following,** provided that those importations involve the same importer and exporter:*

(i) $400; or

(ii) The amount determined by applying the ad valorem rate under paragraph (b)(1)(i)(A) of this section to the total value of such daily importations.

 The correct answer is "b".

✓ **NOTE:** The above-referenced "paragraph (b)(1)(i)(A)" refers to the MPF rate of 0.3464 percent.

✓ **JUST A SIDE NOTE:** "Ad Valorem" means the duties or fees percentage rate is multiplied against the entered value of the item (as opposed to duty based on weight or surface area).

10) Bills resulting from dishonored checks or dishonored Automated Clearinghouse (ACH) transactions are due _____.

a) within 2 days of the date of issuance of the bill
b) within 10 days of the date of issuance of the bill
c) within 15 days of the date of issuance of the bill
d) within 20 days of the date of issuance of the bill
e) within 30 days of the date of issuance of the bill

 As per 19 CFR 24.3(e):

(e) Except for bills resulting from dishonored checks or dishonored Automated Clearinghouse (ACH) transactions, all other bills for duties, taxes, fees, interest, or other charges are due and payable within 30 days of the date of issuance of the bill. **Bills resulting from dishonored checks or dishonored ACH transactions are due within 15 days of the date of issuance of the bill.**

 The correct answer is "c".

✓ **JUST A SIDE NOTE:** Automated Clearinghouse (ACH) is simply a electronic method of payment between two parties. An ACH payment is relatively cheap and multiple payments can be batched together, as opposed to a wire transfer. If an entry is processed as an Automated Broker Interface (ABI) entry, then duties and fees may be paid by the customs broker or importer by ACH.

11) A prospective participant interested in transmitting data electronically through the Automated Broker Interface (ABI) must submit which of the following documents to CBP?

a) Power of attorney
b) Letter of intent
c) Custom's bond
d) Hold harmless agreement
e) Broker's license number

 As per 19 CFR 143.2:

143.2 Application.

A prospective participant in ABI shall submit a letter of intent to the port director closest to his principal office, with a copy to the Assistant Commissioner, Information and Technology, or designee. The letter of intent shall set forth a commitment to develop, maintain and adhere to the performance requirements and operational standards of the ABI system in order to ensure the validity, integrity and confidentiality of the data transmitted. The letter of intent must also contain the following, as applicable:

 The correct answer is "b".

✓ **JUST A SIDE NOTE:** The Letter of Intent must include the following items, as listed in section 143.2:

(a) A description of the computer hardware, communications and entry processing systems to be used and the estimated completion date of the programming;

(b) If the participant has offices in more than one location, the location of each office and the estimated start-up date for each office listed;

(c) The name(s) of the participant's principal management and contact person(s) regarding the system;

(d) If the system is being developed or supported by a data processing company, the data processing company's name and the contact person;

(e) The software vendor's name and the contact person; and

(f) The participant's entry filer code and average monthly volume.

12) Any person, whose protest has been denied, in whole or in part, may contest the denial by _____.

a) filing a request for accelerated disposition with U.S. Customs and Border Protection
b) filing a request for further review of the protest
c) submitting an amended protest with the Port Director of New York within 180 days of the protest denial
d) filing a civil action in the United States Court of International Trade
e) filing a protest with U.S. Customs and Border Protection after 180 days of the protest denial

 As per 19 CFR 174.31:

Any person whose protest has been denied, in whole or in part, may contest the denial by filing a civil action in the United States Court of International Trade in accordance with 28 U.S.C. 2632 within 180 days after—

 The correct answer is "d".

✔ **JUST A SIDE NOTE:** Protests may be filed within 180 days after the entry liquidation date, or within 180 days after the Customs action that is being protested.

13) What is the timeframe to submit the adjusted summary along with payment of duties, taxes and fees once the quota has gone on hold and Headquarters has authorized release of merchandise?

a) within 5 working days after presentation
b) within 10 working days after presentation
c) within 5 working days after authorized release
d) within 10 working days after authorized release
e) any time after the authorization from Headquarters

 As per 19 CFR 132.13(a):

132.13 Quotas after opening.
(a) Procedure when nearing fulfillment. To secure for each importer the rightful quota priority and status for his quota-class merchandise, and to close the quota simultaneously at all ports of entry:

... ...

(iii) Quota Proration. When it is determined that entry summaries for consumption or withdrawals for consumption must be amended to permit only the quantity of tariff-rate and absolute quota merchandise determined to be within the quota, the entry summaries for consumption or withdrawals for consumption must be returned to the importer for adjustment. The time of presentation for quota purposes in that event shall be the same as the time of the initial presentation of the entry summaries for consumption or withdrawals for consumption or their electronic equivalents, provided:

*(A) **An adjusted entry summary for consumption, or withdrawals for consumption, or their electronic equivalents, with estimated duties attached, is deposited within 5 working days after Headquarters authorizes release of the merchandise**, and*

 The correct answer is "c".

✓ **JUST A SIDE NOTE:** In general, when a quota reaches the threshold of 95% of its limit, Customs puts a hold on the quota. This is done to provide more of an equal opportunity for affected importers to make entry prior to the closing of the quota.

14) Which of the following circumstances requires a separate entry for any portion of a split shipment?

a) The importer pre-filed an entry with U.S. Customs and Border Protection
b) The portion of the shipment that arrived six calendar days after the first portion
c) The portion of the shipment that arrived at a different port and was transported in-bond to the port of destination where entry was made for the other portions of the shipment
d) The portion of merchandise that arrives twelve calendar days after the first portion
e) The portion arriving after the importer of record filed and was granted a special permit for immediate delivery when the first portion arrived

 As per 19 CFR 141.57(b):

141.57 Single entry for split shipments.

(a) At election of importer of record. At the election of the importer of record, **Customs may process a split shipment**, *pursuant to section 484(j)(2), Tariff Act of 1930 (19 U.S.C. 1484(j)(2)),* **under a single entry, as prescribed under the procedures set forth in this section.**

(b) Split shipment defined. A "split shipment", for purposes of this section, means a shipment:

(1) Which may be accommodated on a single conveyance, and which is delivered to and accepted by a carrier in the exporting country under one bill of lading or waybill, and is thus intended by the importer of record to arrive in the United States as a single shipment;

(2) Which is thereafter divided by the carrier, acting on its own, into different portions which are transported and consigned to the same party in the United States; and

(3) Of which the first portion and all succeeding portions arrive at the same port of entry in the United States, as listed in the original bill of lading or waybill; and all the succeeding portions arrive at the port of entry within 10 calendar days of the date of the first portion. If any portion of the shipment arrives at a different port, such portion must be transported in-bond to the port of destination where entry of the shipment is made.

The later portion of a split shipment must arrive within 10 days of the first portion in order for Customs to process both portions under a single entry. The multiple choice "d" scenario has the later portion arriving 12 days after the first portion, thus requiring a separate entry. The correct answer is "d".

✓ **JUST A SIDE NOTE:** A "split shipment" most often occurs when an airline does not have sufficient space to carry the entire shipment on one flight.

15) Dutiable merchandise imported and afterwards exported, even though duty thereon may have been paid on the first importation, is liable to duty on every subsequent importation into the Customs territory of the United States for:

a) Personal and household effects taken abroad by a resident of the United States and brought back on his or her return to this country
b) Automobiles and other vehicles taken abroad for noncommercial use
c) Articles exported for exhibition under certain conditions
d) Domestic animals taken abroad for temporary pasturage purposes and returned within 11 months
e) Articles exported under lease to a foreign manufacturer

 As per 19 CFR 141.2:

141.2 Liability for duties on reimportation.

Dutiable merchandise imported and afterwards exported, even though duty thereon may have been paid on the first importation, is liable to duty on every subsequent importation into the Customs territory of the United States, but this does not apply to the following:

(a) Personal and household effects taken abroad by a resident of the United States and brought back on his return to this country (see §148.31 of this chapter);

(b) Professional books, implements, instruments, and tools of trade, occupation, or employment taken abroad by an individual and brought back on his return to this country (see §148.53 of this chapter);

(c) Automobiles and other vehicles taken abroad for noncommercial use (see §148.32 of this chapter);

... ...

(f) Articles exported for exhibition under certain conditions (see §§10.66 and 10.67 of this chapter);

*(g) **Domestic animals taken abroad for temporary pasturage purposes and returned within 8 months** (see §10.74 of this chapter);*

(h) Articles exported under lease to a foreign manufacturer (see §10.108 of this chapter); or

(i) Any other reimported articles for which free entry is specifically provided.

Domestic animals taken abroad (e.g. Canada) for temporary pasturage for 8 months or less are not liable for duty on subsequent importations. If they are taken abroad for more than 8 months, as in the scenario for multiple choice "d", then they are dutiable. The correct answer is "d".

✓ **NOTE:** The actual exam copy was incorrectly written with the word "EXCEPT" at the end of this question, rendering the problem invalid. Thus, we have removed the word from this rendition of the exam problem.

Exam with Broker Commentary (Apr. 2016) — Study Guide

16) What is the Shipping/Packaging Unit Code for Bulk Liquid?

a) BL
b) BJ
c) BU
d) LG
e) VL

 As per CATAIR – Appendix B, Shipping/Packaging Unit Codes:

TZ	Tubes, In Bundle/Bunch/Truss
VA	Vat
VG	Bulk Gas (At 1031 MBAR and 15 degrees Celsius)
VI	Vial
VL	**Bulk Liquid**
VO	Bulk, Solid, Large Particles ("Nodules")
VP	Vacuum-packed
VQ	Bulk, Liquified Gas (At Normal Temperature)
VR	Bulk, Solid, Granular Particles ("Grains")
VY	Bulk, Solid, Fine Particles ("Powders")
WB	Wicker bottle

 The correct answer is "e".

✓ **JUST A SIDE NOTE:** "CATAIR" stands for Customs (or CBP) and Trade Automated Interface Requirements. Basically speaking, it spells out how a customs broker can communicate electronically with CBP. It is technical in nature and mainly for persons working with customs brokerage-type software development.

Category IV: Foreign Trade Zones

17) What is the correct entry type code to be entered on an entry summary filed for Foreign Trade Zone (FTZ) consumption merchandise?

a) 03
b) 06
c) 21
d) 23
e) 61

 As per Form 7501 Instructions, BLOCK 2) ENTRY TYPE:

BLOCK 2) ENTRY TYPE

Record the appropriate entry type code by selecting the two-digit code for the type of entry summary being filed. The first digit of the code identifies the general category of the entry (i.e., consumption = 0, informal = 1, warehouse = 2). The second digit further defines the specific processing type within the entry category. The following codes shall be used:

Consumption Entries
    Free and Dutiable   *01*
    Quota/Visa   *02*
    Antidumping/Countervailing Duty (AD/CVD)   *03*
    Appraisement   *04*
    Vessel Repair   *05*
    Foreign Trade Zone Consumption   **06**
    Quota/Visa and AD/CVD combinations   *07*
    Duty Deferral   *08*

Informal Entries
    Free and Dutiable   *11*
    Quota Other than textiles   *12*

Warehouse Entries
    Warehouse   *21*
    Re-Warehouse   *22*
    Temporary Importation Bond   *23*
    … …

 The correct answer is "b".

✓ **JUST A SIDE NOTE:** A "Foreign Trade Zone", though directly supervised by Customs, is considered to be outside U.S. Customs territory. It is also commonly referred to as a "Free Trade Zone".

18) Prior to any action within a Foreign Trade Zone (FTZ), the operator shall file with the port director an application for permission to manipulate, manufacture, exhibit, or destroy merchandise. Which Customs Form is used for that purpose?

a) Customs Form 214
b) Customs Form 216
c) Customs Form 300
d) Customs Form 4607
e) Customs Form 7512

 As per 19 CFR 146.52(a):

146.52 Manipulation, manufacture, exhibition or destruction; Customs Form 216.

(a) Application. **Prior to any action, the operator shall file with the port director an application (or blanket application) on Customs Form 216 for permission to manipulate, manufacture, exhibit, or destroy merchandise in a zone.** *After Customs approves the application (or blanket application), the operator will retain in his recordkeeping system the approved application.*

 The correct answer is "b".

✓ **JUST A SIDE NOTE:** Here's a snapshot of the above-mentioned CBP Form 216.

19) XYZ Corp. operates a manufacturing facility within a Foreign Trade Zone (FTZ). XYZ Corp. manufactures bottles using raw materials imported from Asia and admitted into the FTZ as non-privileged foreign merchandise on a Form 214. The finished bottles are then sold and delivered daily to U.S. beverage companies. Which of the following is true?

a) XYZ Corp. does not need to file entry, as the bottles are considered products of the United States.
b) XYZ Corp. may enter all of its merchandise on their reconciliation report.
c) XYZ Corp. is not allowed to file pro forma invoices for this merchandise.
d) XYZ Corp. may file weekly entries.
e) XYZ Corp. does not need to file entry, as the entry was made when the raw materials were admitted into the FTZ.

 As per 19 CFR 146.63(c):

146.63 Entry for consumption.

... ...

(c) Estimated production—(1) Weekly entry. **When merchandise is manufactured or otherwise changed in a zone (exclusive of packing) to its physical condition as entered within 24 hours before physical transfer from the zone for consumption, the port director may allow the person making entry to file an entry on Customs Form 3461, or its electronic equivalent, for the estimated removals of merchandise during the calendar week.** *The Customs Form 3461, or its electronic equivalent, must be accompanied by a pro forma invoice or schedule showing the number of units of each type of merchandise to be removed during the week and their zone and dutiable values. Merchandise covered by an entry made under the provisions of this section will be considered to be entered and may be removed only when the port director has accepted the entry on Customs Form 3461, or its electronic equivalent. If the actual removals will exceed the estimate for the week, the person making entry shall file an additional Customs Form 3461, or its electronic equivalent, to cover the additional units before their removal from the zone. Notwithstanding that a weekly entry may be allowed, all merchandise will be dutiable as provided in §146.65. When estimated removals exceed actual removals, that excess merchandise will not be considered to have been entered or constructively transferred to the Customs territory.*

 The correct answer is "d".

✓ **JUST A SIDE NOTE:** "Privileged Foreign Status" means that the merchandise will be classified and assessed duty based on its condition when admitted into the FTZ (front end). "Non-privileged Foreign Status" means the merchandise will be classified and assessed duty based on its condition when it formally leaves the FTZ (back end). The difference here is significant because often items are manufactured within the FTZ, transforming them into merchandise with different classifications and duty rates.

20) On November 15, 2015, a shipment of t-shirts enters an FTZ, and does not undergo any manipulation or manufacturing while in the FTZ. On April 20, 2016, the owner of the t-shirts decides to enter 5,000 of them for sale at the local swap meet. Which form is required to enter the t-shirts?

a) Form 3495
b) Form 214
c) Form 301
d) Form 7523
e) Form 7501

 As per 19 CFR 146.62(b):

146.62 Entry.

... ...

*(b) Documentation. (1) **Customs Form 7501, or its electronic equivalent, or the entry summary will be accompanied by the entry documentation**, including invoices as provided in parts 141 and 142 of this chapter. The person with the right to make entry shall submit any other supporting documents required by law or regulations that relate to the transferred merchandise and provide the information necessary to support the admissibility, the declared values, quantity, and classification of the merchandise. If the declared values are predicated on estimates or estimated costs, that information must be clearly stated in writing at the time an entry or entry summary is filed.*

 The correct answer is "e".

✓ **JUST A SIDE NOTE:** Another commonly used FTZ-related term is "zone-restricted merchandise". Zone-restricted merchandise means that the designated merchandise in the FTZ cannot be entered for consumption, and is considered exported. Essentially, it cannot be touched except to export or to destroy.

Category V: Classification

21) Which of the following products is NOT covered in Chapter 26: Ores, Slag & Ash?

a) Iron ores and concentrates, including roasted iron pyrites
b) Copper Ores and Concentrates
c) Slag wool, rock wool or similar mineral wools
d) Nickel Ores and Concentrates
e) Cobalt ores and concentrates

 As per HTSUS Chapter 26, Note 1:

Notes

1. This chapter does not cover:

(a)   *Slag or similar industrial waste prepared as macadam (heading 2517);*
(b)   *Natural magnesium carbonate (magnesite), whether or not calcined (heading 2519);*
(c)   *Sludges from the storage tanks of petroleum oils, consisting mainly of such oils (heading 2710);*
(d)   *Basic slag of chapter 31;*
(e)   **Slag wool, rock wool or similar mineral wools (heading 6806);**
(f)   *Waste or scrap of precious metal or of metal clad with precious metal; other waste or scrap containing precious metal or precious metal compounds, of a kind used principally for the recovery of precious metal (heading 7112); or*
(g)   *Copper, nickel or cobalt mattes produced by any process of smelting (section XV).*

Here's a relatively easy classification question. If there are items that a particular HTSUS Section or Chapter DO NOT cover, then those items will be listed in that Section's Note 1 or Chapter's Note 1.

 The correct answer is "c".

✓ **JUST A SIDE NOTE:** "Slag" is the by-product of smelting a metal from that metal's raw ore.

22) Which of the following rules does NOT apply if merchandise is entered duty free into the U.S. under Harmonized Tariff Schedule of the United States (HTSUS) number 9802.00.5010 or 9802.00.8040?

a) The country of origin must be the U.S. or a CBI country.
b) The country of export must be a CBI country.
c) The additional tariff number must be reported with the 9802 number and the number cannot begin with 2709 or 2710.
d) The additional HTS number cannot be associated with a textile category number unless the number is from chapter 62.
e) None of the above

 As per CATAIR, Appendix B, CBTPA NOTES:

The following must apply if merchandise is entered duty free into the U.S. under HTS number 9802.00.5010 or 9802.00.8040.

- *The country of origin must be the U.S. or a CBI country.*

- *The country of export must be a CBI country.*

- *An additional tariff number must be reported with the 9802 number and the number cannot begin with 2709 or 2710.*

- *The additional HTS number **cannot be associated with a textile category number unless the number is from chapter 64**.*

In our humble opinion, this is not at all a practical exam question. This is a classification question, so the examinee would naturally be searching in HTSUS Chapter 98 for the answer. Instead, the answer is found in the CATAIR on page 31 (of 43 pages).

Nevertheless, the correct answer here is "d".

✓ **JUST A SIDE NOTE:** The Caribbean Basin Trade Partnership Act (CBTPA) is a trade preference program that includes beneficiary countries such as Costa Rica, Guatemala, and Panama. The Caribbean Basin Initiative (CBI) program preceded the CBTPA and essentially includes the same list of countries.

23) Textile or apparel product is any good classifiable in Chapters 50 through 63 of the Harmonized Tariff Schedule of the United States (HTSUS), and any good classifiable under which one of the following HTSUS headings or subheadings?

a) 9113.90.40
b) 1213.00
c) 2833
d) 4407.10
e) None of the above

 As per 19 CFR 102.21(b):

102.21   Textile and apparel products.

… …

(b) Definitions. *The following terms will have the meanings indicated when used in this section:*
… …

(5) Textile or apparel product. A textile or apparel product is any good classifiable in Chapters 50 through 63, Harmonized Tariff Schedule of the United States (HTSUS), and any good classifiable under one of the following HTSUS headings or subheadings:

3005.90	6501
3921.12.15	6502
3921.13.15	6504
3921.90.2550	6505.90
4202.12.40-80	6601.10-99
4202.22.40-80	7019.19.15
4202.32.40-95	7019.19.28
4202.92.04-08	7019.40-59
4202.92.15-30	8708.21
4202.92.60-90	8804
6405.20.60	**9113.90.40**
6406.10.77	9404.90

… …

Here's another obscure exam classification question. Who would think to look in Part 102 (Rules of origin) of 19 CFR to look this up?

Nonetheless, the correct answer is "a". Hang in there—they're not all this complicated.

✓ **JUST A SIDE NOTE:**   HTSUS 9113.90.40 is the classification for watch straps of textile material.

24) What is the classification for the 10th copy of a bronze statue cast from an original mold created twenty (20) years after the original artist has died?

a) 7419.91.0050   Other articles of copper>>Other>>Cast, molded, stamped or forged, but not further worked>>Other

b) 7419.99.5050   Other articles of copper>>Other>>Other>>Other>>Other

c) 8306.21.0000   Bells, gongs and the like, nonelectric, of base metal; statuettes and other ornaments, of base metal; photograph, picture or similar frames, of base metal; mirrors of base metal; and base metal parts thereof>>Statuettes and other ornaments, and parts thereof>>Plated with precious metal, and parts thereof

d) 9703.00.0000   Original sculptures and statuary, in any material.

e) None of the above

As per HTSUS Chapter 97, Additional U.S. Note 1:

Additional U.S. Notes

1. Heading 9703 covers not only original sculpture made by the sculptor, but also the first 12 castings, replicas or reproductions made from a sculptor's original work or model, by the sculptor himself or by another artist, with or without a change in scale and whether or not the sculptor is alive at the time the castings, replicas or reproductions are completed.

The item in question, a bronze cast statue, is a prima facie item (i.e. classifiable under more than one heading). As far as we know, no single heading differentiates itself from the others as being more specific, so the item cannot be classified by application of GRI 3(a). The item is not a composite or set item, so GRI 3(b) (essential character) cannot be applied. Hence, as the last option for classifying a prima facie item, GRI 3(c), we choose the classification that occurs numerically last in the HTSUS, which is 9703.00.0000. The correct answer is "d".

✓ **NOTE:** GRI 1(notes and headings) is also applied here as the Chapter 97 Additional U.S. Note 1 specifies that the bronze statue in question is considered by the HTSUS to be an "original" statue.

Heading/ Subheading	Stat. Suffix	Article Description	Unit of Quantity	Rates of Duty 1 General	Rates of Duty 1 Special	Rates of Duty 2
9701		Paintings, drawings and pastels, executed entirely by hand, other than drawings of heading 4906 and other than hand-painted or hand-decorated manufactured articles; collages and similar decorative plaques; all the foregoing framed or not framed:				
9701.10.00	00	Paintings, drawings and pastels............................	X...........	Free		Free
9701.90.00	00	Other..	X...........	Free		Free
9702.00.00	00	Original engravings, prints and lithographs, framed or not framed..	X...........	Free		Free
9703.00.00	00	Original sculptures and statuary, in any material.............	X...........	Free		Free
9704.00.00	00	Postage or revenue stamps, stamp-postmarks, first-day covers, postal stationery (stamped paper) and the like, used or unused, other than those of heading 4907...........................	X...........	Free		Free
9705.00.00		Collections and collectors' pieces of zoological, botanical, mineralogical, anatomical, historical, archeological, paleontological, ethnographic or numismatic interest........................		Free		Free
		Numismatic (collector's) coins:				
	30	Gold..	Au g			
	60	Other..	X			
	70	Archaeological, historical, or ethnographic pieces.............	X			
	91	Other..	X			
9706.00.00		Antiques of an age exceeding one hundred years................		Free		Free
	20	Silverware..	X			
	40	Furniture..	X			
	60	Other..	X			

25) The Miami Sound Machine music store is importing cellos from a manufacturer in Spain for a client in Orlando, FL. Included in the shipment are forty of each of the following: cellos, black and red cello cases, and bows. The store will sell each cello, case, and bow as a unit to the Florida client. Which of the following statements describes how these items will be classified?

a) The cellos, cases, and bows all must be separately classified.
b) The cases and bows shall be classified with the cellos.
c) The bows shall be classified with the cellos, but the cases must be separately classified.
d) The bows shall be classified with the cases, but the cellos must be separately classified.
e) The cases shall be classified with the cellos, but the bows must be separately classified.

 As per HTSUS, General Rules of Interpretation (GRI) 3(b) & GRI 5(a):

*GRI 3(b) Mixtures, **composite goods** consisting of different materials or made up of different components, and goods put up in sets for retail sale, which cannot be classified by reference to 3(a), **shall be classified as if they consisted of the material or component which gives them their essential character**, insofar as this criterion is applicable.*

*GRI 5(a) Camera cases, **musical instrument cases**, gun cases, drawing instrument cases, necklace cases and similar containers, specially shaped or fitted to contain a specific article or set of articles, suitable for long-term use and **entered with the articles for which they are intended, shall be classified with such articles when of a kind normally sold therewith. This rule does not, however, apply to containers which give the whole its essential character.***

a The item in question, a cello with bow and case, should be entered as a single HTS classification. Using GRI 3(b) we can say that the cello, not the bow, gives the shipment its essential character. Using GRI 5(a) we can say that the case should be classified with the cello as well. The correct answer is "b".

✓ **NOTE:** The question states that the store is "importing cellos", so from that we may safely assume here that the cello cases do not impart the essential character.

Heading/ Subheading	Stat. Suffix	Article Description	Unit of Quantity	Rates of Duty General	Rates of Duty Special	2
9202		Other string musical instruments (for example, guitars, violins, harps):				
9202.10.00	00	Played with a bow..	No............	3.2%	Free (A, AU, BH, CA, CL, CO, E, IL, JO, KR, MA, MX, OM, P, PA, PE, SG)	37.5%
9202.90		Other: Guitars:				
9202.90.20	00	Valued not over $100 each, excluding the value of the case..	No............	4.5%	Free (A, AU, BH, CA, CL, CO, E, IL, JO, KR, MA, MX, OM, P, PA, PE, SG)	40%
9202.90.40	00	Other..	No............	8.7%	Free (A, AU, BH, CA, CL, CO, E, IL, JO, KR, MA, MX, OM, P, PA, PE, SG)	40%
9202.90.60	00	Other..	No............	4.6%	Free (A, AU, BH, CA, CL, CO, E, IL, JO, KR, MA, MX, OM, P, PA, PE, SG)	40%

26) **A clothing set for a child measures 85 centimeters, consists of a 100 percent cotton woven dress, and coordinates 100 percent cotton knit diaper cover. The items are imported together, presented as a set, and intended to be worn together by the same person. What is (are) the classification(s) for this clothing set?**

a) **6111.20.6030/6209.20.1000**
    6111.20.6030 Babies' garments and clothing accessories, knitted or crocheted>>Of cotton>>Other>>Other>>Other>>Imported as parts of sets
    6209.20.1000 Babies' garments and clothing accessories>>Of cotton>>Dresses

b) **6111.20.6070/6209.20.1000**
    6111.20.6070 Babies' garments and clothing accessories, knitted or crocheted>>Of cotton>>Other>>Other>>Other>>Other
    6209.20.1000 Babies' garments and clothing accessories>>Of cotton>>Dresses

c) **6111.20.6030/6209.20.5045**
    6111.20.6030 Babies' garments and clothing accessories, knitted or crocheted>>Of cotton>>Other>>Other>>Other>>Imported as parts of sets
    6209.20.5045 Babies' garments and clothing accessories>>Of cotton>>Other>>Other>>Imported as parts of sets

d) **6111.20.6020**   Babies' garments and clothing accessories, knitted or crocheted>>Of cotton>>Other>>Other>>Sets

e) **6209.20.5035**   Babies' garments and clothing accessories>>Of cotton>>Other>>Other>>Sets

As per HTSUS Section XI (includes Textile Chapters 50 thru. 63), Note 14:

14. Unless the context otherwise requires, textile garments of different headings are to be classified in their own headings even if put up in sets for retail sale. For the purposes of this note, the expression "textile garments" means garments of headings 6101 to 6114 and headings 6201 to 6211.

The item in question is a child's outfit set consisting of a diaper cover (heading 6111) and a dress (heading 6209). As per the above-mentioned Section Note, the two items in the set are to be classified separately since they each belong to different headings. Accordingly, we may disregard multiple choice options "d" and "e".

Multiple choice "c" classification 6209.20.5045 is for Other (than dresses), so we may disregard it. Multiple choice "b" classification 6111.20.6070 is for Other (than Imported as parts of sets), so we may disregard it. Multiple choice "a" is the only option that, without any contradictions, correctly describes the clothing set. The correct answer is "a".

✓ **NOTE:** Here's a good example of just applying GRI 1 to classify. We classified based on the Section Note (GRI 1), and based on the heading terms (also GRI 1).

Heading/ Subheading	Stat. Suffix	Article Description	Unit of Quantity	Rates of Duty General	Rates of Duty 1 Special	Rates of Duty 2
6111		Babies' garments and clothing accessories, knitted or crocheted:				
6111.20		Of cotton:				
6111.20.10	00	Blouses and shirts, except those imported as parts of sets (239).............................	doz............ kg	19.7%	Free (AU, BH, CA, CL, CO, IL, JO, KR, MA, MX, OM, P, PA, PE, SG)	90%
6111.20.20	00	T-shirts, singlets and similar garments, except those imported as parts of sets (239)....................	doz............ kg	14.9%	Free (AU, BH, CA, CL, CO, IL, JO, KR, MA, MX, OM, P, PA, PE, SG)	90%
6111.20.30	00	Sweaters, pullovers, sweatshirts, waistcoats (vests) and similar articles, except those imported as parts of sets (239)...................................	doz............ kg	14.9%	Free (AU, BH, CA, CL, CO, IL, JO, KR, MA, MX, OM, P, PA, PE, SG)	90%
6111.20.40	00	Dresses (239)...	doz............ kg	11.5%	Free (AU, BH, CA, CL, CO, IL, JO, KR, MA, MX, OM, P, PA, PE, SG)	45%
		Other:				
6111.20.50	00	Trousers, breeches and shorts, except those imported as parts of sets (239)............................	doz............ kg	14.9%	Free (AU, BH, CA, CL, CO, IL, JO, KR, MA, MX, OM, P, PA, PE, SG)	90%
6111.20.60		Other..		8.1%	Free (AU, BH, CA, CL, CO, IL, JO, KR, MA, MX, OM, P, PE, SG) See 9822.09.65, 9919.61.01- 9919.61.02 (PA)	90%
	10	Sunsuits, washsuits and similar apparel (239)...	doz. kg			
	20	Sets (239)...	doz. kg			
		Other:				
	30	Imported as parts of sets (239)..........	doz. kg			
	50	Babies' socks and booties (239)...............	doz.pr. kg			
	70	Other (239)...	doz. kg			

Heading/ Subheading	Stat. Suffix	Article Description	Unit of Quantity	Rates of Duty General	Rates of Duty Special	2
6209		Babies' garments and clothing accessories:				
6209.20		Of cotton:				
6209.20.10	00	Dresses (239)..	doz. kg	11.8%	Free (AU, BH, CA, CL, CO, IL, JO, KR, MA, MX, OM, P, PA, PE, SG)	90%
6209.20.20	00	Blouses and shirts, except those imported as parts of sets (239)..	doz. kg	14.9%	Free (AU, BH, CA, CL, CO, IL, JO, KR, MA, MX, OM, P, PA, PE, SG)	37.5%
		Other:				
6209.20.30	00	Trousers, breeches and shorts, except those imported as parts of sets (239).......................	doz. kg	14.9%	Free (AU, BH, CA, CL, CO, IL, JO, KR, MA, MX, OM, P, PA, PE, SG)	90%
6209.20.50		Other...		9.3%	Free (AU, BH, CA, CL, CO, IL, JO, KR, MA, MX, OM, P, PA, PE, SG)	90%
	30	Sunsuits, washsuits and similar apparel (239)..	doz. kg			
	35	Sets (239)..	doz. kg			
		Other:				
	45	Imported as parts of sets (239)...............	doz. kg			
	50	Other (239)...	doz. kg			

(This Page Intentionally Left Blank)

27) For the purposes of subheading 2601.11.0060, the term "coarse" refers to iron ores with a majority of individual particles having a diameter _____.

a) less than 3.50 mm
b) between 1 to 2 mm
c) exceeding 4.75mm
d) between 2 to 3 mm
e) less than 4.50 mm

 As per HTSUS Chapter 26, Statistical Note 2:

Statistical Notes

1. The quantity of metal content to be reported shall be the assay quantity without deductions.

2. For the purposes of subheading 2601.11.0060, the term "coarse" refers to iron ores with a majority of individual particles having a diameter exceeding 4.75 mm.

 As per the above-mentioned Chapter 26 note, "c" is clearly the correct answer.

✓ **NOTE:** The HTSUS Section and Chapter Notes may include four separately named "notes". They are the "Notes", "Subheading Notes", "Additional U.S. Notes", and "Statistical Notes". As their names suggest, they somewhat differ in their breadth of applicability. The main things to remember is that they are all potentially helpful in the classification process, and that they are all also fair game on the exam.

Heading/ Subheading	Stat. Suffix	Article Description	Unit of Quantity	Rates of Duty General	Rates of Duty 1 Special	Rates of Duty 2
2601		Iron ores and concentrates, including roasted iron pyrites:				
		Iron ores and concentrates, other than roasted iron pyrites:				
2601.11.00		Non-agglomerated............	....	Free		Free
	30	Concentrates............	t			
		Ores:				
	60	Coarse............	t			
	90	Other............	t			
2601.12.00		Agglomerated............	....	Free		Free
	30	Pellets............	t			
	60	Briquettes............	t			
	90	Other............	t			
2601.20.00	00	Roasted iron pyrites............	t	Free		Free
2602.00.00		Manganese ores and concentrates, including ferruginous manganese ores and concentrates with a manganese content of 20 percent or more, calculated on the dry weight............	....	Free		2.2¢/kg on manganese content
	40	Containing less than 47 percent by weight of manganese............	kg Mn kg			
	60	Containing 47 percent or more by weight of manganese...	kg Mn kg			
2603.00.00		Copper ores and concentrates............	....	1.7¢/kg on lead content	Free (A, AU, BH, CA, CL, CO, E, IL, JO, KR, MA, MX, OM, P, PA, PE, SG)	8.8¢/kg on copper content + 3.3¢/kg on lead content + 3.7¢/kg on zinc content
	10	Copper content............	Cu kg 1/			
	20	Lead content............	Pb kg 1/			
	30	Zinc content............	Zn kg 1/			
	40	Silver content............	Ag g 1/			
	50	Gold content............	Au g 1/			
2604.00.00		Nickel ores and concentrates............	....	Free		Free
	40	Nickel content............	Ni kg 1/			
	80	Other metal content............	kg 1/			
2605.00.00	00	Cobalt ores and concentrates............	kg Co kg	Free		Free
2606.00.00		Aluminum ores and concentrates............	....	Free		$1/t
		Bauxite, calcined:				
	30	Refractory grade............	t			
	60	Other............	t			
	90	Other............	t			

28) Bitrex, also known as Denatonium Benzoate, is an aromatic, cyclic amide indicated for use as a denaturant and bittering agent. It is imported from Singapore and classified in HTS 2924.29.7100. The importer has provided the Chemical Abstract Service (CAS) number, 3734-33-6, and certified that it is not listed in the Chemical Appendix to the Tariff Schedule. What is the rate of duty for Bitrex?

a) 0%
b) 3.7%
c) 5.9%
d) 6.5%
e) 15.4%/kg + 58%

 As per HTSUS General Note (GN) 13 (Pharmaceutical products):

13. Pharmaceutical products. Whenever a rate of duty of "Free" followed by the symbol "K" in parentheses appears in the "Special" subcolumn for a heading or subheading, any product (by whatever name known) classifiable in such provision which is the product of a country eligible for tariff treatment under column 1 shall be entered free of duty, provided that such product is included in the pharmaceutical appendix to the tariff schedule. Products in the pharmaceutical appendix include the salts, esters and hydrates of the ... ...

 AND as per the HTSUS Pharmaceutical Appendix:

... ...
DENAGLIPTIN   483369-58-0
DENATONIUM BENZOATE   **3734-33-6**
DENAVERINE   3579-62-2
... ...

The HTSUS number 2924.29.7100 includes Special Program Indicator (SPI) "K". Accordingly, the item in question, Denatonium Benzoate, may potentially be eligible for duty free treatment under the Agreement on Trade in Pharmaceutical Products program. In searching the HTSUS Pharmaceutical Appendix, Denatonium Benzoate is found to be listed. Thus, as per General Note 13, the shipment may be entered duty free. The correct answer is "a".

✔ **NOTE:** The above GN 13 Note includes the condition "which is the product of a country eligible for tariff treatment under column 1". Singapore is an eligible country. Only the countries Cuba and North Korea are column 2 countries (i.e. not column 1).

✔ **NOTE:** As referenced in the classification article description, Additional U.S. Note 3: to Section VI says:
3. The term "products described in additional U.S. note 3 to section VI" refers to any product not listed in the Chemical Appendix to the Tariff Schedule and--

(a) For which the importer furnishes the Chemical Abstracts Service (C.A.S.) registry number and certifies that such registry number is not listed in the Chemical Appendix to the Tariff Schedule; or ... ...

✔ **JUST A SIDE NOTE:** A "denaturant" is added to alcohol to render it undrinkable, particularly for the purpose of discouraging recreational drinking.

Heading/ Subheading	Stat. Suf- fix	Article Description	Unit of Quantity	Rates of Duty General	Rates of Duty Special	2
2924 (con.)		Carboxyamide-function compounds; amide-function compounds of carbonic acid: (con.) Cyclic amides (including cyclic carbamates) and their derivatives; salts thereof: (con.)				
2924.29 (con.)		Other: (con.) Aromatic: (con.) Other: (con.) Other:				
2924.29.65	00	5-Bromoacetyl-2-salicylamide............	kg...........	6.5%	Free (A, AU, BH, CA, CL, CO, E, IL, JO, KR, MA, MX, OM, P, PA, PE, SG)	15.4¢/kg + 58%
2924.29.71	00	Other: Products described in additional U.S. note 3 to section VI............	kg...........	6.5% 114/	Free (A+, AU, BH, CA, CL, CO, D, E, IL, JO, K, KR, L, MA, MX, OM, P, PA, PE, SG)	15.4¢/kg + 58%
2924.29.76		Other..................................		6.5% 115/	Free (A+, AU, BH, CA, CL, CO, D, E, IL, JO, K, KR, L, MA, MX, OM, P, PA, PE, SG)	15.4¢/kg + 58%
	10	Acetoacetanilide.................	kg			
	20	Acetoacet-2,5-dimethoxy-4-chloroanilide........................	kg			
	30	p-Aminobenzamide................	kg			
	90	Other..............................	kg			
		Other:				
2924.29.80	00	2,2-Dimethylcyclopropylcarboxamide............	kg...........	Free		30.5%
2924.29.95	00	Other..................................	kg...........	6.5%	Free (A, AU, BH, CA, CL, CO, E, IL, JO, K, KR, MA, MX, OM, P, PA, PE, SG)	30.5%

29) What is the classification for 48 hair combs, worn in the hair, made of silver (a precious metal), valued at $22 per dozen pieces?

a) 9615.19.2000 — Combs, hair-slides and the like; hairpins, curling pins, curling grips, hair-curlers and the like, other than those of heading 8516, and parts thereof>>Combs, hair-slides and the like>>Other>>Combs>>Valued not over $4.50 per gross

b) 7113.11.2080 — Articles of jewelry and parts thereof, of precious metal or of metal clad with precious metal>>Of precious metal whether or not plated or clad with precious metal>>Of silver, whether or not plated or clad with other precious metal>>Other>>Valued not over $18 per dozen pieces or parts

c) 9615.11.1000 — Combs, hair-slides and the like; hairpins, curling pins, curling grips, hair-curlers and the like, other than those of heading 8516, and parts thereof>>Combs, hair-slides and the like>>Of hard rubber or plastics>>Combs>>Valued not over $4.50 per gross

d) 7113.11.5080 — Articles of jewelry and parts thereof, of precious metal or of metal clad with precious metal>>Of precious metal whether or not plated or clad with precious metal>>Of silver, whether or not plated or clad with other precious metal>>Other>>Other>>Other

e) 9615.19.4000 — Combs, hair-slides and the like; hairpins, curling pins, curling grips, hair-curlers and the like, other than those of heading 8516, and parts thereof>>Combs, hair-slides and the like>>Other>>Combs>>Valued over $4.50 per gross

 As per HTSUS Chapter 96, Note 4:

4. Articles of this chapter, other than those of headings 9601 to 9606 or 9615, remain classified in the chapter whether or not composed wholly or partly of precious metal or metal clad with precious metal, of natural or cultured pearls, or precious or semiprecious stones (natural, synthetic or reconstructed). However, headings 9601 to 9606 and 9615 include articles in which natural or cultured pearls, precious or semiprecious stones (natural, synthetic or reconstructed), precious metal or metal clad with precious metal constitute only minor constituents.

 And As per HTSUS Chapter 71, Note 9:

9. For the purposes of heading 7113, the expression "articles of jewelry" means:

*(a) Any small objects of personal adornment (for example, rings, bracelets, necklaces, brooches, earrings, watch chains, fobs, pendants, tie pins, cuff links, dress studs, religious or other medals and insignia); and
... ...*

Per the Chapter 96, Note 4, items of precious metal that DON"T constitute only minor constituents should be classified elsewhere than in heading 9615. The item is made of silver, so we may disregard heading 9615 options "a", "c", and "e".

The item is valued at over $18 per dozen, so we eliminate option "b". The correct answer is "d".

✔ **JUST A SIDE NOTE:** The unit of measure "gross" means 12 dozen (i.e. 144). So, in using the exam question as an example, $22 per dozen ÷ 12 = 1.833 grosses.

Heading/ Subheading	Stat. Suffix	Article Description	Unit of Quantity	Rates of Duty 1 General	Rates of Duty 1 Special	Rates of Duty 2
		III. JEWELRY, GOLDSMITHS' AND SILVERSMITHS' WARES AND OTHER ARTICLES				
7113		Articles of jewelry and parts thereof, of precious metal or of metal clad with precious metal:				
		Of precious metal whether or not plated or clad with precious metal:				
7113.11		Of silver, whether or not plated or clad with other precious metal:				
7113.11.10	00	Rope, curb, cable, chain and similar articles produced in continuous lengths, all the foregoing, whether or not cut to specific lengths and whether or not set with imitation pearls or imitation gemstones, suitable for use in the manufacture of articles provided for in this heading..........	X	6.3%	Free (A, AU, BH, CA, CL, CO, E, IL, JO, KR, MA, MX, OM, P, PA, PE, SG)	80%
		Other:				
7113.11.20		Valued not over $18 per dozen pieces or parts..........		13.5%	Free (A, AU, BH, CA, CL, CO, E, IL, JO, KR, MA, MX, OM, P, PA, PE, SG)	110%
	15	Containing jadeite or rubies..........	X			
	80	Other..........	X			
7113.11.50		Other..........		5%	Free (A*, AU, BH, CA, CL, CO, E, IL, JO, KR, MA, MX, OM, P, PA, PE, SG)	80%
	15	Containing jadeite or rubies..........	X			
	80	Other..........	X			

30) What is the classification of a woman's 70% rayon (artificial) / 30% wool knit suit comprised of a divided skirt and a suit coat? The skirt and suit coat are of the same fabric construction, color, composition, style and size.

a) 6204.19.2000 — Women's or girls' suits, ensembles, suit-type jackets, blazers, dresses, skirts, divided skirts, trousers, bib and brace overalls, breeches and shorts (other than swimwear)>>Suits>>Of other textile materials>>Of artificial fibers>>Other

b) 6104.13.1000 — Women's or girls' suits, ensembles, suit-type jackets, blazers, dresses, skirts, divided skirts, trousers, bib and brace overalls, breeches and shorts (other than swimwear), knitted or crocheted>>Suits>>Of synthetic fibers>>Containing 23% or more by weight of wool or fine animal hair

c) 6104.19.1000 — Women's or girls' suits, ensembles, suit-type jackets, blazers, dresses, skirts, divided skirts, trousers, bib and brace overalls, breeches and shorts (other than swimwear), knitted or crocheted>>Suits>>Of other textile materials>>Of artificial fibers>>Containing 23% or more by weight of wool or fine animal hair

d) 6204.39.3010 — Women's or girls' suits, ensembles, suit-type jackets, blazers, dresses, skirts, divided skirts, trousers, bib and brace overalls, breeches and shorts (other than swimwear)>>Suit-type jackets and blazers>>Of other textile materials>>Of artificial fibers>>Other>>Women's

e) 6104.19.1500 — Women's or girls' suits, ensembles, suit-type jackets, blazers, dresses, skirts, divided skirts, trousers, bib and brace overalls, breeches and shorts (other than swimwear), knitted or crocheted>>Suits>>Of other textile materials>>Of artificial fibers>>Other

 As per HTSUS Chapter 61, Note 3(a):

3. For the purposes of headings 6103 and 6104:

(a) The term "suit" means a set of garments composed of two or three pieces made up, in respect of their outer surface, in identical fabric and comprising:
- one suit coat ... ... and
- one garment designed to cover the lower part of the body and consisting of trousers, breeches or shorts (other than swim- wear), a skirt or a divided skirt, having neither braces nor bibs.
All of the components of a "suit" must be of the same fabric construction, color and composition; they must also be of the same style and of corresponding or compatible size. ... ...

First off, the item in question is a "knit" suit, so we'll disregard heading 6204 (i.e. the non-knitted heading) choices "a" and "d". The suit is made of "artificial" fibers, not "synthetic", so we disregard "b". The suit is 30% wool, so we choose "c" and not "e". The correct answer is "c".

✓ **JUST A SIDE NOTE:** Chapter 54 (man-made filaments) defines "synthetic fibers" and "artificial fibers" as:

Synthetic Fibers: *By polymerization of organic monomers to produce polymers such as polyamides, polyesters, polyolefins or polyurethanes, or by chemical modification of polymers produced by this process (for example, poly(vinyl alcohol) prepared by the hydrolysis of poly(vinyl acetate)).*

Artificial Fibers: *By dissolution or chemical treatment of natural organic polymers (for example, cellulose) to produce polymers such as cuprammonium rayon (cupro) or viscose rayon, or by chemical modification of natural organic polymers (for example, cellulose, casein and other proteins, or alginic acid), to produce polymers such as cellulose acetate or alginates.*

Heading/ Subheading	Stat. Suffix	Article Description	Unit of Quantity	Rates of Duty General	Rates of Duty 1 Special	Rates of Duty 2
6104		Women's or girls' suits, ensembles, suit-type jackets, blazers, dresses, skirts, divided skirts, trousers, bib and brace overalls, breeches and shorts (other than swimwear), knitted or crocheted:				
		Suits:				
6104.13		Of synthetic fibers:				
6104.13.10	00	Containing 23 percent or more by weight of wool or fine animal hair (444)..................	No........ kg	Free		54.5%
6104.13.20	00	Other (644)...................	No........ kg	14.9%	Free (AU, BH, CA, CL, CO, IL, JO, KR, MA, MX, OM, P, PA, PE, SG)	72%
6104.19		Of other textile materials:				
		Of artificial fibers:				
6104.19.10	00	Containing 23 percent or more by weight of wool or fine animal hair (444)...................	No........ kg	8.5%	Free (AU, BH, CA, CL, CO, IL, JO, KR, MA, MX, OM, P, PA, PE, SG)	54.5%
6104.19.15	00	Other (644)...................	No........ kg	Free		72%
6104.19.40	00	Containing 70 percent or more by weight of silk or silk waste (744)....................	No........ kg	0.9%	Free (AU, BH, CA, CL, CO, E, IL, JO, KR, MA, MX, OM, P, PA, PE, SG)	60%
6104.19.50	00	Of wool or fine animal hair (444).................	No........ kg	13.6%	Free (AU, BH, CA, CL, CO, IL, JO, KR, MA, MX, P, PA, PE, SG) 2.7% (OM)	54.5%
6104.19.60		Of cotton...................		9.4%	Free (AU, BH, CA, CL, CO, IL, JO, KR, MA, MX, OM, P, PA, PE, SG)	90%
	10	Jackets imported as parts of suits (335).........	doz. kg			
	20	Skirts and divided skirts imported as parts of suits (342).....................	doz. kg			
	30	Trousers, breeches and shorts imported as parts of suits (348).....................	doz. kg			
	40	Waistcoats imported as parts of suits (359)....	doz. kg			

31) What is the classification for leather golf bags?

a) **4202.92.4500** — Trunks, suitcases, vanity cases, attache cases, briefcases, school satchels, spectacle cases, … …, sports bags, bottle cases, jewelry boxes, powder cases, cutlery cases and similar containers, of leather or of composition leather, … …>>Other>>With outer surface of sheeting of plastic or of textile materials>>Travel, sports and similar bags>>Other

b) **6305.90.0000** — Sacks and bags, of a king used for the packing of goods>>Of other textile materials

c) **9506.39.0080** — Articles and equipment for general physical exercise, gymnastics, athletics, other sports (including table-tennis) or outdoor games, not specified or included elsewhere in this chapter; swimming pools and wading pools; parts and accessories thereof>>Golf clubs and other golf equipment; parts and accessories thereof>>Other

d) **4202.91.0010** — Trunks, suitcases, vanity cases, attache cases, briefcases, school satchels, spectacle cases, … …, sports bags, bottle cases, jewelry boxes, powder cases, cutlery cases and similar containers, of leather or of composition leather, … …>>Other>>With outer surface of leather or of composition leather>>Golf bags

e) **9506.99.6080** — Articles and equipment for general physical exercise, gymnastics, athletics, other sports (including table-tennis) or outdoor games, not specified or included elsewhere in this chapter; swimming pools and wading pools; parts and accessories thereof>>Other>>Other>>Other>>Other

 As per HTSUS Chapter 95, Note 1(d):

Notes

1. This chapter does not cover:
… …
(d) Sports bags or other containers of heading 4202, 4303 or 4304;

To begin with, as per the above-mentioned Chapter 95 note, the sports bag in question is to be classified in heading 4202 here, so we eliminate multiple choice options "b", "c", and "e".

Next, since "a" is for golf bags made of plastic or textile material, we eliminate it. The correct classification for the leather golf bags and the answer is in multiple choice "d".

✓ **JUST A SIDE NOTE:** The Chapter 95 note makes reference to headings 4303 and 4304, which are for articles of (real) fur and artificial fur respectively.

Heading/ Subheading	Stat. Suffix	Article Description	Unit of Quantity	Rates of Duty		
				1		**2**
				General	Special	
4202 (con.)		Trunks, suitcases, vanity cases, attache cases, briefcases, school satchels, spectacle cases, binocular cases, camera cases, musical instrument cases, gun cases, holsters and similar containers; traveling bags, insulated food or beverage bags, toiletry bags, knapsacks and backpacks, handbags, shopping bags, wallets, purses, map cases, cigarette cases, tobacco pouches, tool bags, sports bags, bottle cases, jewelry boxes, powder cases, cutlery cases and similar containers, of leather or of composition leather, of sheeting of plastics, of textile materials, of vulcanized fiber or of paperboard, or wholly or mainly covered with such materials or with paper: (con.) Other:				
4202.91.00		With outer surface of leather or of composition leather............	....	4.5%	Free (AU, BH, CA, CL, CO, D, IL, JO, KR, MA, MX, OM, P, PA, PE, R, SG) 3.5% (E)	35%
	10	Golf bags............	No.			
	30	Travel, sports and similar bags............	No.			
	90	Other............	No.			
4202.92		With outer surface of sheeting of plastic or of textile materials: Insulated food or beverage bags: With outer surface of textile materials:				
4202.92.04	00	Beverage bags whose interior incorporates only a flexible plastic container of a kind for storing and dispensing potable beverages through attached flexible tubing............	No............ kg	7%	Free (A, AU, BH, CA, CL, CO, E, IL, JO, KR, MA, MX, OM, P, PA, PE, SG)	40%
4202.92.08		Other............	....	7%	Free (AU, BH, CA, CL, CO, E, IL, JO, KR, MA, MX, OM, P, PA, PE, SG)	40%
	05	Of cotton (369)............	No. kg			
	07	Of man-made fibers (670)............	No. kg			
	09	Other (870)............	No. kg			
4202.92.10	00	Other............	No............ kg	3.4%	Free (A, AU, BH, CA, CL, CO, E, IL, JO, KR, MA, MX, OM, P, PA, PE, SG)	80%

32) A pneumatic handheld impact riveter is imported by a civil aircraft manufacturer in Philadelphia. The riveter is specially designed and is used for attaching metal sheeting on aircraft. What is the classification of the riveter?

a) 8705.10.0010   Special purpose motor vehicles, other than those principally designed for the transport of persons or goods (for example, wreckers, mobile cranes, fire fighting vehicles, concrete mixers, road sweepers, spraying vehicles, mobile workshops, mobile radiological units)>>Mobile cranes>>Cable operated

b) 8803.20.0030   Parts of goods of heading 8801 or 8802>>Undercarriages and parts thereof>>For use in civil aircraft>>Other

c) 8467.21.0010   Tools for working in the hand, pneumatic, hydraulic or with self-contained electric or nonelectric motor, and parts thereof>>With self-contained electric motor>>Drills of all kinds>>Rotary>>Battery powered

d) 8467.19.1000   Tools for working in the hand, pneumatic, hydraulic or with self-contained electric or nonelectric motor, and parts thereof>>Pneumatic>>Other>>Suitable for metal working

e) 8203.30.0000   Metal cutting shears and similar tools, and parts thereof

 As per HTSUS Section XVII (Chapters 86 thru. 89), Note 2(e):

2. The expressions "parts" and "parts and accessories" do not apply to the following articles, whether or not they are identifiable as for the goods of this section:
… …
(e) Machines or apparatus of headings 8401 to 8479, or parts thereof; articles of heading 8481 or 8482 or, provided they constitute integral parts of engines or motors, articles of heading 8483;

 AND as per HTSUS Section XV (Chapters 72 thru. 83), Note 1(f):

1. This section does not cover:
… …
(f) Articles of section XVI (Chapters 84 & 85);

Just based on the heading / classification descriptions of each multiple choice option, the examinee could possibly arrive at the correct answer. However, for the sake of practice, we'll acknowledge the related section notes and address each classification here.

The item in question, a pneumatic handheld impact riveter, is definitely not a mobile crane, so we disregard multiple choice "a". We may disregard "b" as per the Section XVII, machines for (use on) the goods of Chapters 86 thru. 89 are to be classified in Chapter 84. We may disregard "c" as the item in question is pneumatic (i.e. air powered), not battery powered. We may also disregard "e" as the Section XV note precludes it from consideration. Therefore, by application of GRI 1 (notes and heading descriptions) and by the process of elimination, we deduce that the correct answer is "d".

✓ **JUST A SIDE NOTE:** Headings 8801 and 8802 are for non-powered aircraft (e.g. hot air balloons) and powered aircraft (e.g. airplanes) respectively.

Heading/ Subheading	Stat. Suf- fix	Article Description	Unit of Quantity	Rates of Duty General	Rates of Duty 1 Special	2
8467		Tools for working in the hand, pneumatic, hydraulic or with self-contained electric or nonelectric motor, and parts thereof: Pneumatic:				
8467.11		Rotary type (including combined rotary-percussion):				
8467.11.10		Suitable for metal working....................................	....	4.5%	Free (A, AU, BH, CA, CL, CO, E, IL, JO, KR, MA, MX, OM, P, PA, PE, SG)	30%
	40	Grinders, polishers and sanders....................	No.			
	80	Other..	No.			
8467.11.50		Other..	....	Free		27.5%
	10	Rock drills...	No.			
	20	Drills, other than rock drills; screwdrivers and nut runners..	No.			
	40	Wrenches, other than nut runners...................	No.			
	90	Other..	No.			
8467.19		Other:				
8467.19.10	00	Suitable for metal working....................................	No............	4.5%	Free (A, AU, BH, CA, CL, CO, E, IL, JO, KR, MA, MX, OM, P, PA, PE, SG)	30%
8467.19.50		Other..	....	Free		27.5%
	30	Pneumatic, hand-held force feed lubricating equipment...	No.			
	60	Designed for use in construction or mining.......	No.			
	90	Other..	No.			

Exam with Broker Commentary (Apr. 2016) — Study Guide

Category VI: Valuation

33) ABC Steel purchased carbon steel bars from a manufacturer in Ontario, Canada. ABC Steel paid $19,000, ex-factory, in Canadian dollars. The steel bars arrived at the Detroit Port of Entry via semi-tractor trailer on 5/6/2015, and the shipment was released the same day. The applicable currency exchange rate is .793021. The invoice price does not include duty at 2.9%, merchandising processing fee at .3464%, or freight charges of $1,628. What is the entered value of this shipment?

a) $17,372
b) $19,000
c) $15,067
d) $13,017
e) $18,403

As per 19 CFR 152.103(a):

152.103 Transaction value.

(a) Price actually paid or payable—(1) General. In determining transaction value, the price actually paid or payable will be considered without regard to its method of derivation. It may be the result of discounts, increases, or negotiations, or may be arrived at by the application of a formula, such as the price in effect on the date of export in the London Commodity Market. The word "payable" refers to a situation in which the price has been agreed upon, but actual payment has not been made at the time of importation. ... ...

 Here's a fairly straightforward and practical exam question. The Transaction Value, which excludes duties, fees, freight, insurance, etc., for this shipment is the ex-factory/ex-works value of 19,000.00 in Canadian Dollars. To calculate the Entered Value (EV), which must be in U.S. Dollars (USD), we can simply take this value (in foreign currency) and multiply it by the applicable exchange rate.

19,000.00 CAD x 0.793021 (exchange rate) = $15,067.40 USD

The entered value is rounded to $15,067.00. The correct answer is "c".

✓ **JUST A SIDE NOTE:** In many cases, the "Certified Quarterly Rate" is used to convert commercial invoices in foreign currencies to U.S. Dollars. 19 CFR 159.34 explains:

159.34 Certified quarterly rate.

(a) Countries for which quarterly rate is certified. For the currency of each of the following foreign countries, there will be published in the Customs Bulletin, for the quarter beginning January 1, and for each quarter thereafter, the rate or rates first certified by the Federal Reserve Bank of New York for such foreign currency for a day in that quarter:

Australia, Austria, Belgium, Brazil, Canada, Denmark, Finland, France, Germany, Hong Kong, India, Iran, Ireland, Italy, Japan, Malaysia, Mexico, Netherlands, New Zealand, Norway, People's Republic of China, Philippines, Portugal, Republic of South Africa, Singapore, Spain, Sri Lanka (Ceylon), Sweden, Switzerland, Thailand, United Kingdom, Venezuela.

(b) When certified quarterly rate is used. The certified quarterly rate established under paragraph (a) of this section shall be used for Customs purposes for any date of exportation within the quarter, ...

34) What is the amount of duties and fees for goods entered in the U.S. for a shipment with the following characteristics?

- **Contains seven (7) 31mm ball bearings with integral shafts**
- **Is manufactured by XYZ Company from Germany with a value of $7,598.00.**
- **Has an applicable anti-dumping duty deposit rate is 68.89%, HTS 8482.10.1080 @2.4% duty rate and MPF.3464%**

a) $5260.57
b) $5234.26
c) $5416.61
d) $5442.93
e) $208.66

a Here we just take the value of the shipment and multiply it against each of the listed duties and fees rates, and then add the resulting totals.

```
 5234.26 (7598 x .6889)
+ 182.35 (7598 x 0.024)
+  26.32 (7598 x 0.003464)
= 5442.93
```

The correct answer is "d".

✓ **NOTE:** The exam states that the total is $5442.92. This is incorrect, so we revised "d" to $5442.93.

35) Which of the following individuals is NOT considered when determining a related party transaction, as defined in the Tariff Act of 1930?

a) Employer and Employee

b) Members of the same family, including brothers and sisters (whether by whole or half-blood), spouse, ancestors, and lineal descendants

c) Any officer or director of an organization and such organization

d) Any person, directly or indirectly, owning, controlling or holding with power to vote, less-than four percent of the outstanding voting stock or shares of any organization and such organization.

e) An officer or director of an organization and an officer or director of another organization, who is also an officer or director in the other organization.

 As per 19 CFR 152.102(g):

(g) Related persons. ***"Related persons" means****: (1) Members of the same family, including brothers and sisters (whether by whole or half-blood), spouse, ancestors, and lineal descendants.*

(2) Any officer or director of an organization, and that organization.

(3) An officer or director of an organization and an officer or director of another organization, if each individual also is an officer or director in the other organization.

(4) Partners.

(5) Employer and employee.

*(6) **Any person directly or indirectly owning, controlling, or holding with power to vote, five percent or more of the outstanding voting stock or shares of any organization, and that organization.***

(7) Two or more persons directly or indirectly controlling, controlled by, or under common control with, any person.

The correct answer is "d". Owning "five percent or more" of the outstanding shares is the related persons threshold.

✓ **JUST A SIDE NOTE:** Customs may somewhat scrutinize "related persons" transactions to ensure that the relationship does not influence customs values.

36) Which of the following is an exclusion from transaction value?

a) The packing costs incurred by the buyer with respect to the imported merchandise
b) The transportation cost of the merchandise after its importation, when identified separately from the price actually paid or payable
c) A mold used in the production of the imported goods, supplied free of charge by the buyer to the manufacturer
d) The price actually paid or payable for the imported merchandise
e) A selling commission incurred by the buyer with respect to the imported merchandise

 As per 19 CFR 152.103(b):

*(b) Additions to price actually paid or payable. (1) **The transaction value of imported merchandise is the price actually paid or payable for the merchandise when sold for exportation to the United States, plus amounts equal to:***

(i) The packing costs incurred by the buyer with respect to the imported merchandise;

(ii) Any selling commission incurred by the buyer with respect to the imported merchandise;

(iii) The value, apportioned as appropriate, of any assist;

(iv) Any royalty or license fee related to the imported merchandise that the buyer is required to pay, directly or indirectly, as a condition of the sale of the imported merchandise for exportation to the United States; and

(v) The proceeds of any subsequent resale, disposal, or use of the imported merchandise that accrue, directly or indirectly, to the seller.

 Freight is not included as part of the price actually paid or payable. The correct answer is "b".

✓ **NOTE:** An easy-to-remember and worth-repeating tool on what to add to the price actually paid or payable is to remember the acronym **"C.R.A.P.P."** (Commissions, Royalties, Assists, Packaging, Proceeds).

37) The foreign commercial invoice before you shows a value of $7200 with an addition of $800 for "distributor fee", for a total invoice value of $8000. The nature of the fee charged by the seller was to compensate the exclusive U. S. distributor who, by agreement with the foreign seller, receives 10% of all sales in the U. S. as a commission. They receive this regardless of whether or not they actually make the sale. What is the $800?

a) Not part of Transaction Value
b) A buying commission to be added to the price actually paid or payable
c) A buying commission; part of the price actually paid or payable
d) A selling commission to be added to the price actually paid or payable
e) A selling commission; part of the price actually paid or payable

 As per 19 CFR 152.103(b):

*(b) Additions to price actually paid or payable. (1) **The transaction value of imported merchandise is the price actually paid or payable for the merchandise when sold for exportation to the United States, plus amounts equal to:***

(i) The packing costs incurred by the buyer with respect to the imported merchandise;

*(ii) **Any selling commission incurred by the buyer with respect to the imported merchandise;***

(iii) The value, apportioned as appropriate, of any assist;

(iv) Any royalty or license fee related to the imported merchandise that the buyer is required to pay, directly or indirectly, as a condition of the sale of the imported merchandise for exportation to the United States; and

(v) The proceeds of any subsequent resale, disposal, or use of the imported merchandise that accrue, directly or indirectly, to the seller.

 The correct answer is "d".

✔ **JUST A SIDE NOTE:** Generally speaking, a buying commission is a payment made by the importer to their agent. On the other hand, a selling commission is a payment made by the exporter to their agent.

38) A U.S. television manufacturer contracts with a manufacturer in China to produce 500 bare printed circuit boards at a cost of $50 per board. The U.S. television manufacturer also contracts with a design company in New York to prepare the schematics for use in the production of the bare printed circuit boards at a cost of $20,000. Upon completion, the bare printed circuit boards are exported from China to Malaysia for further processing into printed circuit board assemblies for televisions at a cost of $200 per assembly. The completed printed circuit board assemblies are shipped to the U.S. television manufacturer and an invoice from the Malaysia manufacturer in the amount of $100,000 is included in the shipment at the time of importation. What is the transaction value of this shipment?

a) $20,000
b) $100,000
c) $120,000
d) $125,000
e) $145,000

 As per 19 CFR 152.102(a):

(a) Assist. (1) "Assist" means any of the following if supplied directly or indirectly, and free of charge or at reduced cost, by the buyer of imported merchandise for use in connection with the production or the sale for export to the United States of the merchandise:

... ...

(iv) Engineering, development, artwork, design work, and plans and sketches that are undertaken elsewhere than in the United States and are necessary for the production of the imported merchandise.

(2) No service or work to which paragraph (a)(1)(iv) of this section applies will be treated as an assist if the service or work:

(i) Is performed by an individual domiciled within the United States;

The Malaysian invoice value is $100,000 (500 boards x $200 ea.) for the imported printed circuit board assemblies. However, the assist for the initial Chinese manufacturing of $25,000 (500 boards x $50 ea.) must be added to this to make market value. $100,000 + $25,000 = $125,000.

We do not add the cost of $20,000 for the NY company's preparation of the schematics. Costs for engineering work and design work, etc. are only added as an assist to the transaction value if such work was done outside of the United States. The correct answer is "d".

✔ **JUST A SIDE NOTE:** "Make Market Value" (MMV) is the term used for adding dutiable values to the Invoice Value (IV) to calculate the Entered Value (EV) on the annotated commercial invoice. Using the above-scenario as an example:

Invoice Value $100,000
MMV $25,000

Entered Value $125,000

VII: Free Trade Agreements

39) Which of the following elements determine whether a particular good qualifies under the Generalized System of Preferences (GSP) value content requirement?

a)   **Cost or value of originating materials**
b)   **Direct cost of processing**
c)   **Cost or value of originating materials plus direct costs of processing that are greater than or equal to 35% of the appraised value of the good**
d)   **Cost or value of originating materials plus direct costs of processing that are less than 35% of the appraised value of the goods.**
e)   **Cost or value of originating materials plus direct costs of processing that are greater than or equal to 45% of the appraised value of the good.**

 As per GN 4:

The symbol "A" indicates that all beneficiary developing countries are eligible for preferential treatment with respect to all articles provided for in the designated provision. The symbol "A*" indicates that certain beneficiary developing countries, specifically enumerated in subdivision (d) of this note, are not eligible for such preferential treatment with regard to any article provided for in the designated provision. **Whenever an eligible article which is the growth, product, or manufacture of a designated beneficiary developing country listed in subdivision (a) of this note is imported into the customs territory of the United States directly from such country or territory, such article shall be eligible for duty-free treatment** *as set forth in the "Special" subcolumn, unless excluded from such treatment by subdivision (d) of this note;* **provided that, in accordance with regulations promulgated by the Secretary of the Treasury the sum of (1) the cost or value of the materials produced in the beneficiary developing country or any 2 or more countries which are members of the same association of countries which is treated as one country under section 507(2) of the Trade Act of 1974, plus (2) the direct costs of processing operations performed in such beneficiary developing country or such member countries is not less than 35 percent of the appraised value** *of such article at the time of its entry into the customs territory of the United States. No article or material of a beneficiary developing country shall be eligible for such treatment by virtue of having merely undergone simple combining or packing operations, or mere dilution with water or mere dilution with another substance that does not materially alter the characteristics of the article.*

a Basically, if qualifying Materials + Processing ≥ 35% then the item probably qualifies for GSP. The correct answer is "c".

✓ **NOTE:** Here's a snapshot of just a few of the GSP beneficiary developing countries as listed in HTSUS General Note 4(a):

<u>Independent Countries</u>

Afghanistan	Grenada	Republic of Yemen
Albania	Guinea	Rwanda
Algeria	Guinea-Bissau	Saint Lucia
Angola	Guyana	Saint Vincent and the
Armenia	Haiti	Grenadines
Azerbaijan	India	Samoa
Belize	Indonesia	Sao Tomé and
Benin	Iraq	Principe
Bhutan	Jamaica	Senegal
Bolivia	Jordan	Serbia
… …		

40) A Merchandise Processing Fee (MPF) is exempt for originating goods from which Free Trade Agreement listed below?

a) Jordan JOFTA
b) Australia AUFTA
c) Morocco MAFTA
d) China CHFTA
e) Egypt QIZ

 As per 19 CFR 24.23(c):

24.23   Fees for processing merchandise.
... ...

(c) Exemptions and limitations. (1) **The ad valorem fee, surcharge, and specific fees provided for under** *paragraphs (b)(1) and (b)(2) of* **this section will not apply to:**

... ...

(8) The ad valorem fee, surcharge, and specific fees provided under paragraphs (b)(1) and (b)(2)(i) of this section will not apply to goods that qualify as originating goods under §203 of **the United States-Australia Free Trade Agreement** *Implementation Act (see also General Note 28, HTSUS) that are entered, or withdrawn from warehouse for consumption, on or after January 1, 2005.*

 The correct answer is "b".

✓ **JUST A SIDE NOTE:** Many other Free Trade Agreements (FTA) are also exempt from the Merchandise Processing Fee (MPF), such as NAFTA, Singapore FTA, Chile FTA, Korea FTA, Panama TPA (Trade Promotion Agreement).

✓ **JUST A SIDE NOTE:** Currently there is no such thing as a China FTA, as referenced in the above exam question.

41) Where no claim for preferential treatment under the North American Free Trade Agreement was made at the time of importation, an importer may file a claim for preferential treatment under NAFTA within _____.

a) 1 year from the date of exportation of the goods
b) 1 year from the date of the importation of the goods
c) 1 year from the date of liquidation of the entry
d) 80 days from the date of liquidation of the entry
e) 314 days from the date of exportation of the goods

 As per 19 CFR 181.31 (NAFTA Post-importation):

181.31 Right to make post-importation claim and refund duties.

*Notwithstanding any other available remedy, including the right to amend an entry so long as liquidation of the entry has not become final, **where a good would have qualified as an originating good when it was imported into the United States but no claim for preferential tariff treatment on that originating good was made at that time under §181.21(a) of this part, the importer of that good may file a claim for a refund of any excess duties at any time within one year after the date of importation** of the good in accordance with the procedures set forth in §181.32 of this part. Subject to the provisions of §181.23 of this part, Customs may refund any excess duties by liquidation or reliquidation of the entry covering the good in accordance with §181.33(c) of this part.*

 The correct answer is "b".

✓ **JUST A SIDE NOTE:** A NAFTA Certificate of Origin (CBP Form 434) is required to support a NAFTA preferential tariff treatment claim. A snapshot of what the form looks like included below:

42) The NAFTA Certificate of Origin must be retained in the _____.

a) U.S. by the importer until notification of liquidation is received from CBP
b) NAFTA country of origin by the producer for one year after liquidation
c) NAFTA country of origin by the producer for five years after liquidation
d) U.S. for five years after entry of the good with all relevant documentation
e) NAFTA country of origin for five years after date of liquidation

 As per 19 CFR 181.22(a):

181.22 Maintenance of records and submission of Certificate by importer.

(a) Maintenance of records. **Each importer claiming preferential tariff treatment for a good imported into the United States shall maintain in the United States, for five years after the date of entry of the good, all documentation relating to the importation of the good. Such documentation shall include a copy of the Certificate of Origin and any other relevant records** as specified in §163.1(a) of this chapter.

 The correct answer is "d".

✓ **JUST A SIDE NOTE:** A NAFTA Certificate of Origin may be made for a single shipment, or it may be made to cover multiple shipments on what's commonly referred to as a "blanket certificate", valid up to 1 year.

43) When an importer is making a claim of preferential tariff treatment under the United States-Australia Free Trade Agreement, the importer indicates their claim on the CBP Form 7501. Which of the following special program indicator should be used?

a) A+
b) MX
c) AU
d) CL
e) K

 As per HTSUS GN 3(c):

(c) Products Eligible for Special Tariff Treatment.

  *(i) Programs **under which special tariff treatment may be provided, and the corresponding symbols for such programs as they are indicated in the "Special" subcolumn, are as follows:***

Generalized System of Preferences	A, A* or A+
United States-Australia Free Trade Agreement	**AU**
Automotive Products Trade Act	B
United States-Bahrain Free Trade Agreement Implementation Act	BH
Agreement on Trade in Civil Aircraft	C
North American Free Trade Agreement:	
Goods of Canada, under the terms of general note 12 to this schedule	CA
Goods of Mexico, under the terms of general note 12 to this schedule	MX
United States-Chile Free Trade Agreement	CL
African Growth and Opportunity Act	D
Caribbean Basin Economic Recovery Act	E or E*
United States-Israel Free Trade Area	IL
United States-Jordan Free Trade Area Implementation Act	JO
Agreement on Trade in Pharmaceutical Products	K
Dominican Republic-Central America-United States Free Trade Agreement	P or P+
Uruguay Round Concessions on Intermediate Chemicals for Dyes	L
United States-Caribbean Basin Trade Partnership Act	R
United States-Morocco Free Trade Agreement Implementation Act	MA
United States-Singapore Free Trade Agreement	SG
United States-Oman Free Trade Agreement Implementation Act	OM
United States-Peru Trade Promotion Agreement Implementation Act	PE
United States-Korea Free Trade Agreement Implementation Act	KR
United States-Colombia Trade Promotion Agreement Implementation Act	CO
United States-Panama Trade Promotion Agreement Implementation Act	PA

 The correct answer is "c".

✓ **JUST A SIDE NOTE:** If "AU" precedes the HTS number on the Entry Summary (CBP Form 7501), that means the Australia FTA is being claimed for that Entry Summary line. If, instead, "0AU" (zero-A-U) precedes the HTS number on the Entry Summary, that means the country of origin is Australia for that Entry Summary line, and no Australia FTA is being claimed.

44) Which of the following is NOT a direct cost of processing operations performed in the beneficiary developing country?

a) All actual labor costs involved in the growth, production, manufacture, or assembly of the specific merchandise, including fringe benefits, on-the-job-training, and the cost of engineering, supervisory, quality control, and similar personnel
b) General expenses of doing business which are either not allocable to the specific merchandise or are not related to the growth, production, manufacture, or assembly of merchandise, such as administrative salaries, casualty and liability insurance, advertising, and salaries, commissions, or expenses
c) Dies, molds, tooling, and depreciation on machinery and equipment which are allocable to the specific merchandise
d) Costs of inspecting and testing the specific merchandise
e) Research, development, design, engineering, and blueprint costs insofar as they are allocable to the specific merchandise

 As per 19 CFR 10.178:

10.178 Direct costs of processing operations performed in the beneficiary developing country.

*(a) Items included in the direct costs of processing operations. As used in §10.176, the words **"direct costs of processing operations"** means those costs either directly incurred in, or which can be reasonably allocated to, the growth, production, manufacture, or assembly of the specific merchandise under consideration. Such costs include, but are not limited to:*

*(1) **All actual labor costs** involved in the growth, production, manufacture, or assembly of the specific merchandise, including fringe benefits, on-the-job training, and the cost of engineering, supervisory, ...*

*(2) **Dies, molds, tooling, and depreciation** on machinery and equipment which are allocable to the specific merchandise;*

*(3) **Research, development,** design, engineering, and blueprint costs insofar as they are allocable to the specific merchandise; and*

*(4) **Costs of inspecting and testing** the specific merchandise.*

*(b) Items not included in the direct costs of processing operations. **Those items which are not included within the meaning of the words "direct costs of processing operations" are those which are not directly attributable to the merchandise under consideration or are not "costs" of manufacturing the product. These include, but are not limited to:***

*(1) **Profit**; and*

*(2) **General expenses of doing business** which are either not allocable to the specific merchandise or are not related to the growth, production, manufacture, or assembly of the merchandise, such as administrative salaries, casualty and liability insurance, advertising, and salesmen's salaries, commissions, or expenses.*

 The correct answer is "b".

✓ **JUST A SIDE NOTE:** Direct costs, such as manufacturing labor, are traceable to the finished product. On the other hand, other expenses that are naturally fixed, such as telephone bills, are not considered direct costs.

VIII: Drawback

45) Which form must be presented to CBP to request exportation of merchandise that is intended for a rejected merchandise drawback claim?

a) CBP Form 7512
b) CBP Form 7551
c) CBP Form 7553
d) CBP Form 7523
e) CBP Form 7533

 As per 19 CFR 191.42 (c):

*(c) Notice. **A notice of intent to export or destroy merchandise which may be the subject of a rejected merchandise drawback claim** (19 U.S.C. 1313(c)) must be provided to the Customs Service to give Customs the opportunity to examine the merchandise. **The claimant, or the exporter (for destruction, see §191.44), must file at the port of intended redelivery to Customs custody a Notice of Intent to Export, Destroy, or Return Merchandise for Purposes of Drawback on Customs Form 7553** at least 5 working days prior to the date of intended return to Customs custody. Waiver of prior notice for exportations under 19 U.S.C. 1313(j) (see §191.91 of this part) is inapplicable to exportations under 19 U.S.C. 1313(c).*

 The correct answer is "c".

✓ **JUST A SIDE NOTE:** See below snapshot of what the relatively rarely used CBP Form 7553 looks like:

46) A person may be certified in the drawback compliance program after meeting the core requirements established under this program. In order to be certified as a participant in the drawback compliance program or negotiated alternative drawback compliance program, the party must be able to demonstrate all of the following EXCEPT:

a) Understanding of the legal requirements for filing claims, including the nature of the records that are required to be maintained and produced and the time period involved

b) Having established procedures explain the Customs requirements to those employees involved in the preparation of claims, and the maintenance and production of required records.

c) Having a dependable individual(s) who will be responsible for compliance under the program, and maintenance and production of required records.

d) Having an established a record maintenance program approved by Customs regarding original records or, if approved by Customs, alternative records or recordkeeping formats for other than the original records.

e) Having procedures for notifying the importer of variances in, or violations of, the drawback compliance or other alternative negotiated drawback compliance program, and for taking corrective action when notified by the importer of violations and problems regarding such program.

As per 19 CFR 191.192(b):

(b) Core requirements of program. ***In order to be certified as a participant in the drawback compliance program or negotiated alternative drawback compliance program, the party must be able to demonstrate that it:***

(1) ***Understands the legal requirements for filing claims****, including the nature of the records that are required to be maintained and produced and the time periods involved;*

(2) ***Has in place procedures that explain the Customs requirements*** *to those employees involved in the preparation of claims, and the maintenance and production of required records;*

(3) Has in place procedures regarding the preparation of claims and maintenance of required records, and the production of such records to Customs;

(4) ***Has designated a dependable individual*** *or individuals who will be responsible for compliance under the program, and maintenance and production of required records;*

(5) ***Has in place a record maintenance program approved by Customs*** *regarding original records, or if approved by Customs, alternative records or recordkeeping formats for other than the original records; and*

(6) ***Has procedures for notifying Customs of variances*** *in, or violations of, the drawback compliance or other alternative negotiated drawback compliance program, and for taking corrective action when notified by Customs of violations and problems regarding such program.*

Multiple choice "e" says "procedures for notifying 'the importer' of variances." Whereas, 19 CFR 191.192(b)(6) states "procedures for notifying 'Customs' of variances." The correct answer is "e".

✓ **JUST A SIDE NOTE:** The Drawback Compliance Program is a voluntary certification program open to importers and customs brokers. Its benefits include, but may not be limited to, reduced penalties and reduced warnings from Customs.

47) The method by which fungible merchandise or articles are identified on the basis of calculation by recordkeeping of the amount of drawback that may be attributed to each unit of merchandise or articles in the inventory. Which of the following approved accounting method is utilized by Customs and Border Protection?

a) Average
b) Inventory turn-over for limited purposes
c) Low-to-High
d) Last-in, first out
e) First-in, first out

 As per 19 CFR 191.14(c):

... ...

(4) Average—(i) General. **The average method is the method by which fungible merchandise or articles are identified on the basis of the calculation by recordkeeping of the amount of drawback that may be attributed to each unit of merchandise or articles in the inventory.** *In this method, the ratio of:*

(A) The total units of a particular receipt of the fungible merchandise in the inventory at the time of a withdrawal to;

(B) The total units of all receipts of the fungible merchandise (including each receipt into inventory) at the time of the withdrawal;

(C) Is applied to the withdrawal, so that the withdrawal consists of a proportionate quantity of units from each particular receipt and each receipt is correspondingly decreased. Withdrawals and corresponding decreases to receipts are rounded to the nearest whole number.

Actually, all five multiple choice options are actual accounting methods approved and utilized by CBP, depending on the company and situation. In this scenario, the "average method" is utilized. The correct answer is "a".

✓ **JUST A SIDE NOTE:** "Fungibility" means the interchangeability of identical items. It is a Latin-based word and related to the word "function". A good example of fungible merchandise is salt, and is defined by Customs as:

Fungible merchandise or articles means merchandise or articles which for commercial purposes are identical and interchangeable in all situations.

48) Upon review of a drawback claim, if the claim is determined to be incomplete, the claim will be rejected and Customs will notify the filer in writing. The filer shall then have the opportunity to complete the claim subject to the requirement for filing a complete claim within _____.

a) 2 days
b) 30 days
c) 1 years
d) 2 years
e) 3 years

 As per 19 CFR 191.52(a):

191.52 Rejecting, perfecting or amending claims.

(a) Rejecting the claim. Upon review of a drawback claim, if the claim is determined to be incomplete (see §191.51(a)(1)), the claim will be rejected and Customs will notify the filer in writing. The filer shall then have the opportunity to complete the claim subject to the requirement for filing a complete claim within 3 years.

 The correct answer is "e".

✔ **JUST A SIDE NOTE:** A (duty) drawback is the (partial or in full) refund of import duties on an item subsequently exported or destroyed.

49) Which of the following parties does NOT have authority to sign drawback documents?

a) Owner of a sole proprietorship
b) An individual acting on his/her behalf
c) Licensed Customs broker without a power of attorney
d) A full partner of a partnership
e) President, Vice President, Secretary, Treasurer, or any employee legally authorized to bind the corporation

 As per 19 CFR 191.6(a):

191.6 Authority to sign drawback documents.

(a) Documents listed in paragraph (b) of this section shall be signed only by one of the following:

(1) The president, a vice-president, secretary, treasurer, or any other employee legally authorized to bind the corporation;

(2) A full partner of a partnership;

(3) The owner of a sole proprietorship;

(4) Any employee of the business entity with a power of attorney;

(5) An individual acting on his or her own behalf; or

(6) A licensed Customs broker with a power of attorney.

A licensed customs broker WITHOUT a power of attorney does not have such authority. The correct answer is "c".

✓ **JUST A SIDE NOTE:** A licensed customs broker CAN, without a power of attorney, file a "Section 321" entry for an importer. Basically, a Section 321 entry is a simplified entry with very little document requirements, and can be done on most imports valued at $800 or less (previously $200 or less). This is also known as a Low Value Shipment (LVS).

IX: Antidumping and Countervailing Duties

50) Qualifying expenditures which may be offset by a distribution of assessed antidumping and countervailing duties must fall within the categories described below with the exception of?

"These expenditures must be incurred after the issuance, and prior to the termination, of the antidumping duty order or finding or countervailing duty order under which the distribution is sought. Further, these expenditures must be related to the production of the same product that is the subject of the related order or finding, with the exception of expenses incurred by associations which must relate to a specific case."

a) Manufacturing facilities
b) Housing
c) Personnel training
d) Health Care Benefits for employees paid for by the employer
e) Equipment

 As per 19 CFR 159.61(c):

(c) Qualifying expenditures. Qualifying expenditures which may be offset by a distribution of assessed antidumping and countervailing duties must fall within the categories described in paragraphs (c)(1) through (c)(10) of this section. ... ...

(1) **Manufacturing facilities;**

(2) **Equipment;**

(3) Research and development;

(4) **Personnel training;**

(5) Acquisition of technology;

(6) **Health care benefits for employees paid for by the employer;**

(7) Pension benefits for employees paid for by the employer;

(8) Environmental equipment, training, or technology;

(9) Acquisition of raw materials and other inputs; and

(10) Working capital or other funds needed to maintain production.

 Employee housing expenses are not eligible for antidumping payments. The correct answer is "b".

✓ **JUST A SIDE NOTE:** "Affected domestic producers" are eligible to receive subsidy payments pulled from Customs collected antidumping and countervailing duty receipts.

51) Which entry types(s) may be used for merchandise subject to antidumping/countervailing duties (AD/CVD)?

a) 03
b) 07
c) 34
d) 38
e) All of the above

 As per CBP Form 7501 Instructions, BLOCK 2) ENTRY TYPE:

BLOCK 2) ENTRY TYPE

Record the appropriate entry type code by selecting the two-digit code for the type of entry summary being filed. The first digit of the code identifies the general category of the entry (i.e., consumption = 0, informal = 1, warehouse = 2). The second digit further defines the specific processing type within the entry category. The following codes shall be used:

Consumption Entries
- *Free and Dutiable* — *01*
- *Quota/Visa* — *02*
- **Antidumping/Countervailing Duty (AD/CVD)** **03**
- *Appraisement* — *04*
- *Vessel Repair* — *05*
- *Foreign Trade Zone Consumption* — *06*
- **Quota/Visa and AD/CVD combinations** — **07**
- *Duty Deferral* — *08*

Informal Entries
- *Free and Dutiable* — *11*
- *Quota Other than textiles* — *12*

Warehouse Entries
- *Warehouse* — *21*
- *Re-Warehouse* — *22*
- *Temporary Importation Bond* — *23*
- *Trade Fair* — *24*
- *Permanent Exhibition* — *25*
- *Foreign Trade Zone Admission* — *26*

Warehouse Withdrawal
- *For Consumption* — *31*
- *Quota/Visa* — *32*
- **AD/CVD** — **34**
- **Quota/Visa and AD/CVD combinations** — **38**

... ...

 The correct answer is "e".

✓ **JUST A SIDE NOTE:** Antidumping/Countervailing Duty entry type "03" is by far the most common of all AD/CVD entry types filed.

277

52) _____ is required prior to liquidation of an entry subject to an antidumping/countervailing duty order or those duties will be doubled upon liquidation.

a) A Certificate of manufacturing
b) A sales receipt
c) A reimbursement certificate
d) Meeting with Import Specialists
e) An Invoice

 As per 19 CFR 351.402 (f):

... ...

(2) Certificate. **The importer must file prior to liquidation a certificate in the following form** with the appropriate District Director of Customs:

> *I hereby certify that I (have) (have not) entered into any agreement or understanding for the payment or for the refunding to me, by the manufacturer, producer, seller, or exporter, of all or any part of the antidumping duties or countervailing duties assessed upon the following importations of (commodity) from (country): (List entry numbers) which have been purchased on or after (date of publication of antidumping notice suspending liquidation in the Federal Register) or purchased before (same date) but exported on or after (date of final determination of sales at less than fair value).*

... ...

 The correct answer is "c".

✓ **JUST A SIDE NOTE:** The above-mentioned certificate and statement is also known as an Antidumping/Countervailing Duty Non-Reimbursement Certificate. It can be completed for a single shipment or as a one year-blanket certificate. Basically, it makes the importer certify that they will not receive compensation from the foreign supplier to help off-set the antidumping duties that CBP levies on the import.

Category X: Marking

53) Which of the following parties CANNOT request a county-of-origin advisory ruling or final determination?

a) A foreign Manufacturer, producer, or exporter, or a United States importer of the merchandise

b) A manufacturer, producer, or wholesaler in the United States of a like product

c) United States members of a labor organization or other association of workers whose members are employed in the manufacture, production, or wholesale in the United States of a like product

d) A trade or business association a majority of whose members manufacture, produce, or wholesale a like product in the United States

e) The Port Director to where the merchandise has arrived

 As per 19 CFR 177.23:

177.23 Who may request a country-of-origin advisory ruling or final determination.

A country-of-origin advisory ruling or final determination may be requested by:

*(a) **A foreign manufacturer, producer, or exporter, or a United States importer** of merchandise,*

*(b) **A manufacturer, producer, or wholesaler in the United States of a like product**,*

*(c) **United States members of a labor organization** or other association of workers whose members are employed in the manufacture, production, or wholesale in the United States of a like product, or*

*(d) **A trade or business association** a majority of whose members manufacture, produce, or wholesale a like product in the United States.*

 The correct answer is "e".

✓ **JUST A SIDE NOTE:** Such country of origin rulings and classification rulings are recorded and indexed at CBP's Customs Rulings Online Search System (CROSS). This CBP website is an excellent free resource for importers and customs brokers. Currently there are over 190,000 searchable Customs rulings here.

www.rulings.cbp.gov

54) How many days does CBP have before it is required to notify the importer that it is detaining goods to determine admissibility relative to possible counterfeit trademarks?

a) 5 business days
b) 5 calendar days
c) 7 calendar days
d) 10 business days
e) 10 calendar days

 As per 19 CFR 133.21(b):

(b) Detention, notice, and disclosure of information—(1) Detention period. CBP may detain any article of domestic or foreign manufacture imported into the United States that bears a mark suspected by CBP of being a counterfeit version of a mark that is registered with the U.S. Patent and Trademark Office and is recorded with CBP pursuant to subpart A of this part. The detention will be for a period of up to 30 days from the date on which the merchandise is presented for examination. In accordance with 19 U.S.C. 1499(c), if, after the detention period, the article is not released, the article will be deemed excluded for the purposes of 19 U.S.C. 1514(a)(4).

(2) Notice of detention to importer and disclosure to owner of the mark—(i) Notice and seven business day response period. **Within five business days from the date of a decision to detain suspect merchandise, CBP will notify the importer in writing of the detention** *as set forth in §151.16(c) of this chapter and 19 U.S.C. 1499. CBP will also inform the importer that for purposes of assisting CBP in determining whether the detained merchandise bears counterfeit marks:*
... ...

 The correct answer is "a".

✓ **JUST A SIDE NOTE:** 19 CFR 133.21(a) defines a "counterfeit mark" as "a spurious mark that is identical with, or substantially indistinguishable from, a mark registered on the Principal Register of the U.S. Patent and Trademark Office."

55) What is the fee for recording a trademark with CBP for a United States Patent and Trademark Office (USPTO) registration that includes four classes of goods?

a) $190
b) $0
c) $300
d) $760
e) $380

 As per 19 CFR 133.3(b):

*(b) Fee. The application shall be accompanied by a fee of $190 for each trademark to be recorded. However, **if the trademark is registered for more than one class of goods** (based on the class, or classes, first stated on the certificate of registration, without consideration of any class, or classes, also stated in parentheses) **the fee for recordation shall be $190 for each class** for which the applicant desires to record the trademark with the United States Customs Service. For example, to secure recordation of a trademark registered for three classes of goods, a fee of $570 is payable. A check or money order shall be made payable to the United States Customs Service.*

 $190 x 4 classes = $760. The correct answer is "d".

✓ **JUST A SIDE NOTE:** There are currently 45 trademark classes, as organized by the World Intellectual Property Organization. Trade mark classes include goods such as paints, pharmaceuticals, vehicles, etc., as well as services such as advertising, transportation, education, etc.

56) Which article is NOT exempt from country of origin marking requirements when imported into the United States?

a) A unicycle that was manufactured in 1953
b) A clothes dryer machine made in Wisconsin
c) An original oil painting produced in France
d) A printed poster produced in Italy
e) A set of glasses to be used by the importer

 As per 19 CFR 134.32:

134.32 General exceptions to marking requirements.

The articles described or meeting the specified conditions set forth below are excepted from marking requirements *(see subpart C of this part for marking of the containers):*

(a) Articles that are incapable of being marked;

*(b) **Articles that cannot be marked prior to shipment to the United States without injury**;*

(c) Articles that cannot be marked prior to shipment to the United States except at an expense economically prohibitive of its importation;

(d) Articles for which the marking of the containers will reasonably indicate the origin of the articles;

(e) Articles which are crude substances;

*(f) **Articles imported for use by the importer** and not intended for sale in their imported or any other form;*
... ...

*(i) **Articles which were produced more than 20 years prior** to their importation into the United States;*
... ...

*(m) **Products of the United States** exported and returned;*
... ...

 The correct answer is "d".

✓ **NOTE:** The following section, 19 CFR 134.33 contains the "J-List", which is a more specific list of items exempt from country of origin requirements. Excerpt below:

Articles
Art, works of.
Articles classified under subheadings 9810.00.15, 9810.00.25, 9810.00.40 and 9810.00.45, Harmonized Tariff Schedule of the United States
Articles entered in good faith as antiques and rejected as unauthentic.

57) Additional duties will be assessed at _____ for failure to mark the article (or container) to indicate the English name of the country of origin of the article or to include words or symbols required to prevent deception or mistake.

a) 5%
b) 10%
c) 15%
d) 20%
e) 100%

 As per 19 CFR 134.2:

134.2 Additional duties.

Articles not marked as required by this part shall be subject to additional duties of 10 percent of the final appraised value *unless exported or destroyed under Customs supervision prior to liquidation of the entry, as provided in 19 U.S.C. 1304(f). The 10 percent additional duty is assessable for failure either to mark the article (or container) to indicate the English name of the country of origin of the article or to include words or symbols required to prevent deception or mistake.*

 The correct answer is "b".

✔ **NOTE:** Country of origin markings must be reasonably legible, durable, and noticeable enough for the ultimate purchaser.

Category XI: Broker Compliance

58) The license of a broker that is a corporation or association can be revoked by operation of law if it fails for _____ continuous days to have at least one officer of the corporation or association who holds a valid individual broker license.

a) 30
b) 60
c) 120
d) 160
e) 180

 As per 19 CFR 111.45(a):

111.45 Revocation by operation of law.

(a) License. ***If a broker that is a partnership, association, or corporation fails to have, during any continuous period of 120 days, at least one member of the partnership or at least one officer of the association or corporation who holds a valid individual broker's license, that failure will, in addition to any other sanction that may be imposed under this part, result in the revocation by operation of law of the license*** *and any permits issued to the partnership, association, or corporation. The Assistant Commissioner or his designee will notify the broker in writing of an impending revocation by operation of law under this section 30 calendar days before the revocation is due to occur.*

 The correct answer is "c".

✓ **JUST A SIDE NOTE:** "120 days" means 120 calendar days. If Customs explicitly specifies "working days", that means weekends and federal holidays are not included in the counting of days.

59) **The negligent failure to produce entry documents required by law or regulation for the entry of merchandise after a lawful demand by CBP, will subject the person who is required to maintain the documents to a penalty, per release of merchandise. What is the maximum penalty?**

a) $100,000 or an amount equal to 75% of the appraised value of the merchandise, whichever is less
b) $25,000 and 50% of the appraised value of the merchandise
c) $10,000 or an amount equal to 40% of the appraised value of the merchandise, whichever amount is less
d) $1,000,000 or an amount equal to 75% of the appraised value of the merchandise, whichever amount is less
e) **No penalty applicable**

 As per 19 CFR 163.6(b):

(b) Failure to produce entry records—(1) Monetary penalties applicable. The following penalties may be imposed if a person fails to comply with a lawful demand for the production of an entry record and is not excused from a penalty pursuant to paragraph (b)(3) of this section:

(i) If the failure to comply is a result of the willful failure of the person to maintain, store, or retrieve the demanded record, such person shall be subject to a penalty, for each release of merchandise, not to exceed $100,000, or an amount equal to 75 percent of the appraised value of the merchandise, whichever amount is less; or

*(ii) **If the failure to comply is a result of negligence of the person in maintaining, storing, or retrieving the demanded record, such person shall be subject to a penalty, for each release of merchandise, not to exceed $10,000, or an amount equal to 40 percent of the appraised value** of the merchandise, whichever amount is less.*
… …

 The correct answer is "c".

✓ **JUST A SIDE NOTE:** "Entry Records" usually include the CBP Form 7501 (entry summary), CBP Form 3461 (release), Commercial Invoice, Bill of Lading (or Air Waybill), and any applicable certificates.

60) Requests for alternative methods of storage for records, other than those that are required to be maintained as original records under laws and regulations administered by other Federal government agencies, must be made from which of the following offices?

a) Port Director, in the port where the records will be stored
b) Broker Management Office, Washington, DC
c) Regulatory Audit, Charlotte, NC
d) Director of Field Operations, in the District where the records will be stored
e) National Finance Office, Indianapolis, IN

 As per 19 CFR 163.5(b):

*(b) Alternative method of storage—(1) General. **Any of the persons listed in §163.2 may maintain any records, other than records required to be maintained as original records under laws and regulations administered by other Federal government agencies, in an alternative format, provided that the person gives advance written notification of such alternative storage method to the Regulatory Audit**, U.S. Customs and Border Protection, 2001 Cross Beam Dr., Charlotte, North Carolina 28217, and provided further that the Director of Regulatory Audit, Charlotte office does not instruct the person in writing as provided herein that certain described records may not be maintained in an alternative format. The written notice to the Director of Regulatory Audit, Charlotte office must be provided at least 30 calendar days before implementation of the alternative storage method, must identify the type of alternative storage method to be used, and must state that the alternative storage method complies with the standards set forth in paragraph (b)(2) of this section. If an alternative storage method covers records that pertain to goods under CBP seizure or detention or that relate to a matter that is currently the subject of an inquiry or investigation or administrative or court proceeding, the appropriate CBP office may instruct the person in writing that those records must be maintained as original records and therefore may not be converted to an alternative format until specific written authorization is received from that CBP office. A written instruction to a person under this paragraph may be issued during the 30-day advance notice period prescribed in this section or at any time thereafter, must describe the records in question with reasonable specificity but need not identify the underlying basis for the instruction, and shall not preclude application of the planned alternative storage method to other records not described therein.*

(2) Standards for alternative storage methods. Methods commonly used in standard business practice for storage of records include, but are not limited to, machine readable data, CD ROM, and microfiche. Methods that are in compliance with generally accepted business standards will generally satisfy CBP requirements, provided that the method used allows for retrieval of records requested within a reasonable time after the request and provided that adequate provisions exist to prevent alteration, destruction, or deterioration of the records. The following standards must be applied by recordkeepers when using alternative storage methods:
... ...

 The correct answer is "c".

✓ **JUST A SIDE NOTE:** Entry documents are required to be kept for 5 years after the customs entry date.

61) Which of the following is NOT "Customs Business" as defined in the Code of Federal Regulations?

a) The payment of duties, taxes and fees
b) Corporate compliance activity
c) Determining the admissibility of merchandise
d) Determining the classification and valuation of merchandise
e) The preparation and filing of CBP Form 7501

 As per 19 CFR 111.1:

*Customs business. "Customs business" means those activities involving transactions with CBP concerning the entry and admissibility of merchandise, its classification and valuation, the payment of duties, taxes, or other charges assessed or collected by CBP on merchandise by reason of its importation, and the refund, rebate, or drawback of those duties, taxes, or other charges. "Customs business" also includes the preparation, and activities relating to the preparation, of documents in any format and the electronic transmission of documents and parts of documents intended to be filed with CBP in furtherance of any other customs business activity, whether or not signed or filed by the preparer. However, **"customs business" does not include the mere electronic transmission of data received for transmission to CBP and does not include a corporate compliance activity.***

 The correct answer is "b".

✓ **JUST A SIDE NOTE:** The regulations' definition of "customs broker" means a licensed customs broker. However, outside of the regulations, the term "customs broker" does not necessarily mean the individual is licensed by CBP.

62) When a broker is employed for the transaction of customs business by an unlicensed person, who is not the actual importer, the broker must transmit _____.

a) the entry in ACS immediately, as this type of transaction is new and only accepted in ACS

b) the entry in ACE immediately, as this type of transaction is new and only accepted in ACE

c) a copy of the importer's bill for services rendered or a copy of the entry

d) Customs Form 5106 for the unlicensed person

e) a Power of Attorney to Customs and Border Protection on behalf of the unlicensed person

 As per 19 CFR 111.36(a):

111.36 Relations with unlicensed persons.

(a) Employment by unlicensed person other than importer. **When a broker is employed for the transaction of customs business by an unlicensed person who is not the actual importer, the broker must transmit to the actual importer either a copy of his bill for services rendered or a copy of the entry**, *unless the merchandise was purchased on a delivered duty-paid basis or unless the importer has in writing waived transmittal of the copy of the entry or bill for services rendered.*

 The correct answer is "c".

✓ **JUST A SIDE NOTE:** Many freight forwarding companies do not possess their own customs brokerage departments. So, when such a freight forwarder imports a shipment into the U.S., they will often contract out the customs clearance to a 3rd party customs broker, and include that customs broker's invoice and the customs entry packet with their own freight forwarding services invoice to the importer.

63) XYC Brokerage is located in New York. It is permitted to conduct Customs business in the ports of New York, Florida, California, and Alabama. The individual qualifying the permit in New York leaves the brokerage. Which statement is correct?

a) The broker has only 120 days to replace the individual qualifying the permit in New York.

b) The broker may demonstrate to the Port Director in New York that the licensed individual qualifying the Alabama permit can exercise responsible supervision and control over the business conducted in New York.

c) A waiver from the requirements of CR 111.11 can be granted because that is where the corporate license was issued.

d) There is no requirement to replace the licensed individual in New York as long as it is shown that the quality of work rendered by the employees in New York is the same as that rendered by the licensed individual.

e) XYC Brokerage has only 180 days to replace the individual qualifying the permit in New York.

 As per 19 CFR 111.45(b):

*(b) Permit. **If a broker who has been granted a permit for an additional district fails, for any continuous period of 180 days, to employ within that district** (or region, as defined in §111.1, if an exception has been granted pursuant to §111.19(d))* ***at least one person who holds a valid individual broker's license, that failure will****, in addition to any other sanction that may be imposed under this part,* ***result in the revocation of the permit by operation of law.***

 The correct answer is "e".

✓ **JUST A SIDE NOTE:** When a customs broker receives their license from their port director, they are also eligible to receive a permit for the district in which that port is located. Essentially, this is their primary permit. After receipt of which, they may apply for additional district permits or for a national permit.

64) If a broker that is a partnership, association, or corporation fails to have at least one member or officer who holds a valid individual broker's license during any continuous period of _____, the license and any permits will be revoked by operation of law.

a) 30 days
b) 60 days
c) 120 days
d) 180 days
e) 360 days

 As per 19 CFR 111.45(a):

*(a) License. **If a broker that is a partnership, association, or corporation fails to have, during any continuous period of 120 days, at least one member of the partnership or at least one officer of the association or corporation who holds a valid individual broker's license, that failure will**, in addition to any other sanction that may be imposed under this part, **result in the revocation by operation of law of the license and any permits issued to the partnership, association, or corporation**. The Assistant Commissioner or his designee will notify the broker in writing of an impending revocation by operation of law under this section 30 calendar days before the revocation is due to occur.*

 The correct answer is "c".

✓ **JUST A SIDE NOTE:** This type of exam question that asks how long a business may operate without a licensed customs broker is frequently asked on the exams. Just try to remember the answer is "120" days for the license question, and "180" days for additional permit question.

65) What is the deadline for a Licensed Customs Broker to file a status report?

a) March 31st of the reporting year
b) January 1st of each year
c) February 1st of each third year
d) December 31st of each third year
e) April 30th of each second year

 As per 19 CFR 111.30(d):

(d) Status report—(1) General. **Each broker must file a written status report with Customs on February 1, 1985, and on February 1 of each third year after that date.** *The report must be accompanied by the fee prescribed in §111.96(d) and must be addressed to the director of the port through which the license was delivered to the licensee (see §111.15). A report received during the month of February will be considered filed timely. No form or particular format is required.*

 The correct answer is "c".

✔ **JUST A SIDE NOTE:** Currently, the above-mentioned (triennial) status report fee is $100, which can be paid in the form of a company or personal check, and enclosed in envelope with the status report.

Category XII: Fines and Penalties

66) From June 2015 to September 2015, an importer entered five shipments of widgets as consumption entries despite his Customs attorney having advised him the widgets are subject to an antidumping case. In October 2015, CBP determined that the widgets should have been entered as antidumping entries and that the appropriate cash deposit rate for the widgets at the time of entry was 0.00%. Which of the following best describes the culpability of the importer for a penalty under 19 U.S.C. § 1592?

a) The importer is not culpable because there was no loss of revenue.
b) The importer is not culpable because, as the cash deposit rate is 0.00%, he is not liable for antidumping duties.
c) The importer is not culpable because CBP had previously released five shipments of the same merchandise, which is a contributory Customs error.
d) The importer may be culpable because the error affects CBP's determination of whether an unfair trade practice has been committed.
e) The importer is culpable, but he will not receive a penalty if his customs attorney can show that his advice was given prior to the commencement of any CBP investigation.

 As per 19 CFR 171, APPENDIX B:

(B) Definition of Materiality Under Section 592

*A document, statement, act, or **omission is material if it has the natural tendency to influence or is capable of influencing agency action including, but not limited to a Customs action regarding**: (1) Determination of the classification, appraisement, or admissibility of merchandise (e.g., whether merchandise is prohibited or restricted); (2) determination of an importer's liability for duty (including marking, antidumping, and/or countervailing duty); (3) collection and reporting of accurate trade statistics; (4) determination as to the source, origin, or quality of merchandise; (5) **determination of whether an unfair trade practice has been committed under the anti-dumping or countervailing duty laws or a similar statute**; (6) determination of whether an unfair act has been committed involving patent, trademark, or copyright infringement; or (7) the determination of whether any other unfair trade practice has been committed in violation of federal law. The "but for" test of materiality is inapplicable under section 592.*

 The correct answer is "d".

✔ **JUST A SIDE NOTE:** "Culpable" means a person being held responsible for something the person did or did not do.

67) A prior disclosure must _____.

a) disclose the circumstances of the exportation violation

b) include the disclosing party's calculation of the loss of revenue

c) specify the material false statements, omissions or acts and explain how and when they occurred

d) be submitted in response to a government issued notice of formal investigation

e) not involve entries subject to a drawback claim

 As per 19 CFR 162.74(b):

(b) Disclosure of the circumstances of a violation. **The term "discloses the circumstances of a violation" means the act of providing to Customs a statement orally or in writing that:**

(1) Identifies the class or kind of merchandise involved in the violation;

(2) Identifies the importation or drawback claim included in the disclosure by entry number, drawback claim number, or by indicating each concerned Customs port of entry and the approximate dates of entry or dates of drawback claims;

(3) **Specifies the material false statements, omissions or acts including an explanation as to how and when they occurred**; *and*

(4) Sets forth, to the best of the disclosing party's knowledge, the true and accurate information or data that should have been provided in the entry or drawback claim documents, and states that the disclosing party will provide any information or data unknown at the time of disclosure within 30 days of the initial disclosure date. Extensions of the 30-day period may be requested by the disclosing party from the concerned Fines, Penalties, and Forfeitures Officer to enable the party to obtain the information or data.

 The correct answer is "c".

✓ **JUST A SIDE NOTE:** A prior disclosure may be initiated either orally or in writing. If a conversation took place, however, it should be documented and sent to the appropriate CBP office within 10 days of the oral disclosure. As a wise man once said, if it isn't in writing, it didn't happen.

68) When filing a prior disclosure, the disclosing party may choose to make the tender of actual loss of duties, taxes, and fees, or actual loss of revenue. When must the disclosing party make the tender of actual loss of duties, taxes, and fees, or actual loss of revenue?

a) Within 1 year of filing the prior disclosure

b) At the time of the claimed prior disclosure or within 30 days after Customs notifies the person in writing of Customs calculation of the actual loss of duties, taxes and fees or actual loss of revenue

c) At the time of the claimed prior disclosure or within 90 days after Customs notifies the person in writing of Customs calculation of the actual loss of duties, taxes and fees or actual loss of revenue

d) Within 1 year of filing the prior disclosure or within 30 days after Customs notifies the person in writing of Customs calculation of the actual loss of duties, taxes and fees or actual loss of revenue

e) Within 90 days after Customs notifies the person in writing of Customs calculation of the actual loss of duties, taxes and fees or actual loss of revenue

 As per 19 CFR 162.74(c):

(c) Tender of actual loss of duties, taxes and fees or actual loss of revenue. A person who discloses the circumstances of the violation shall tender any actual loss of duties, taxes and fees or actual loss of revenue. **The disclosing party may choose to make the tender either at the time of the claimed prior disclosure, or within 30 days after CBP notifies the person in writing of CBP calculation of the actual loss of duties, taxes and fees or actual loss of revenue.** *The Fines, Penalties, and Forfeitures Officer may extend the 30-day period if there is good cause to do so.*

... ...

Failure to tender the actual loss of duties, taxes and fees or actual loss of revenue finally calculated by CBP shall result in denial of the prior disclosure.

 The correct answer is "b".

✓ **JUST A SIDE NOTE:** One reason a company might decide to submit a prior disclosure without accompanying duties is to secure prior disclosure status prior to the initiation of a CBP investigation.

69) **Petition for relief must be filed within _____ from the date of mailing to the bond principal the notice of claim for liquidated damages or penalty secured by a bond.**

a) 2 days
b) 10 days
c) 30 days
d) 60 days
e) 90 days

 As per 19 CFR 172.3(b):

(b) When filed. **Petitions for relief must be filed within 60 days from the date of mailing to the bond principal** *the notice of claim for liquidated damages or penalty secured by a bond.*

 The correct answer is "d".

✓ **JUST A SIDE NOTE:** "Liquidated damages" are demands for payment by CBP to a principal's (e.g. importer's) surety (i.e. customs bond company). Petitions and supplemental petitions for relief are requests to have the penalties mitigated (i.e. reduced).

70) An error in the liquidation of an entry covering household or personal effects may be corrected by the port director even though a timely protest was not filed if entry was made before December 18, 2004 and an application for refund is filed with the port director _____ and no waiver of compliance with applicable regulations is involved other than a waiver which the port director has authority to grant. Where the port director has no authority to grant the waiver, the application will be referred to the Commissioner of CBP.

a) Within 10 days after the date of entry
b) Within 30 days after the date of entry
c) Within 60 days after the date of entry
d) Within 90 days after the date of entry
e) Within 1 year after the date of entry

 As per 19 CFR 173.5:

173.5 Review of entry covering household or personal effects.

An error in the liquidation of an entry covering household or personal effects may be corrected by the port director even though a timely protest was not filed if entry was made before December 18, 2004 and an application for refund is filed with the port director within 1 year after the date of the entry and no waiver of compliance with applicable regulations is involved other than a waiver which the port director has authority to grant. Where the port director has no authority to grant the waiver, the application will be referred to the Commissioner of CBP.

 The correct answer is "e".

✓ **JUST A SIDE NOTE:** Part 173 of these customs regulations is titled "ADMINISTRATIVE REVIEW IN GENERAL". It provides procedures and authority for CBP to review and relatively casually amend errors associated with old entries.

Exam with Broker Commentary (Apr. 2016) — Study Guide

71) If the Fines, Penalties, and Forfeitures Officer has reasonable cause to believe that a violation of section 592, Tariff Act of 1930, as amended (19 U.S.C. 1592), has occurred, and determines that further proceedings are warranted, he shall issue to the person concerned a notice of his intent to issue a claim for a monetary penalty. The prepenalty notice shall be issued whether or not a seizure has been made. The prepenalty notice shall contain all of the below EXCEPT:

a) Description of merchandise
b) State the actual loss of duties, if any and demand payment immediately
c) Specify all laws and regulations allegedly violated
d) Disclose all material facts which established the alleged violation
e) State whether the alleged violations occurred as the result of fraud, gross negligence or negligence

 As per 19 CFR 162.77(b):

*(b) Contents—(1) Facts of violation. **The prepenalty notice shall**:*

(i) Describe the merchandise,

(ii) Set forth the details of the entry or introduction, the attempted entry or introduction, or the aiding or abetting of the entry, introduction, or attempt,

(iii) Specify all laws and regulations allegedly violated,

(iv) Disclose all material facts which establish the alleged violation,

(v) State whether the alleged violation occurred as the result of fraud, gross negligence, or negligence, and

*(vi) **State the estimated loss of duties, if any, and, taking into account all circumstances, the amount of the proposed monetary penalty.***

 The prepenalty notice will state the "estimated" (i.e. not "actual") loss of duties, etc. The correct answer is "b".

✓ **JUST A SIDE NOTE:** "Section 592 of Tariff Act of 1930" provides for penalties for errors in statements to CBP.

Category XIII: Bonds

72) If the principal gets free release of any serially numbered shipping container classifiable under subheading 9801.00.10 or 9803.00.50, Harmonized Tariff Schedule of the United States (HTSUS), the principal agrees to all of the following EXCEPT:

a) To advance the value and improve its condition abroad or claim (or make a previous claim) drawback on any container released under subheading 9801.00.10, HTSUS.
b) To pay the initial duty due and otherwise comply with every condition in subheading 9803.00.50, HTSUS, on any container released under that item
c) To mark that container in the manner required by Customs
d) To keep records which show the current status of that container in service and the disposition of that container if taken out of service
e) To remove or strike out the markings on that container when it is taken out of service or when the principal transfers ownership of it

 As per 19 CFR 113.66(b):

(b) Agreement to Comply With the Provisions of subheading 9801.00.10, or 9803.00.50 Harmonized Tariff Schedule of the United States (HTSUS). **If the principal gets free release of any serially numbered shipping container classifiable under subheading 9801.00.10 or 9803.00.50, HTSUS, the principal agrees:**

(1) **Not** *to advance the value or improve its condition abroad or claim (or make a previous claim) drawback on, any container released under subheading 9801.00.10, HTSUS;*

(2) To pay the initial duty due and otherwise comply with every condition in subheading 9803.00.50, HTSUS, on any container released under that item;

(3) To mark that container in the manner required by CBP;

(4) To keep records which show the current status of that container in service and the disposition of that container if taken out of service; and

(5) To remove or strike out the markings on that container when it is taken out of service or when the principal transfers ownership of it.

 With the release, the importer agrees "NOT to advance the value" of the container. The correct answer is "a".

✓ **JUST A SIDE NOTE:** The above-referenced subheadings 9801.00.10 and 9803.00.50 provide for:

9801.00.10   *Products of the United States when returned after having been exported, without having been advanced in value or improved in condition by any process of manufacture or other means while abroad.*

9803.00.50   *Substantial containers and holders, if products of the United States (including shooks and staves of United States production when returned as boxes or barrels containing merchandise), or if of foreign production and previously imported and duty (if any) thereon paid ... ...*

73) With regards to the disposition of merchandise on a basic custodial bond, the principal agrees to all of the following EXCEPT:

a) If a bonded carrier, to report promptly the arrival of merchandise at the destination port by delivering to CBP the manifest or other approved notice.

b) If a cartage or lighterage business, to deliver promptly and safely to CBP any merchandise placed in the principal's custody together with any related cartage and lighterage ticket and manifest.

c) To dispose of merchandise in a manner authorized by CBP Regulations.

d) To file timely with CBP any report required by CBP Regulations.

e) In the case of Class 9 warehouses, to provide reasonable assurance of exportation of only merchandise subject to excise taxes that is withdrawn under the sales ticket procedure of §144.37(h) of this chapter.

 As per 19 CFR 113.63(c):

(c) Disposition of Merchandise. The principal agrees:

(1) If a bonded carrier, to report promptly the arrival of merchandise at the destination port by delivering to CBP the manifest or other approved notice;

(2) If a cartage or lighterage business, to deliver promptly and safely to CBP any merchandise placed in the principal's custody together with any related cartage and lighterage ticket and manifest;

(3) To dispose of merchandise in a manner authorized by CBP regulations; and

(4) To file timely with CBP any report required by CBP regulations.

*(5) **In the case of Class 9 warehouses, to provide reasonable assurance of exportation of merchandise withdrawn under the sales ticket** procedure of §144.37(h) of this chapter.*

Assurance of exportation for all (i.e. not just excise tax-type) merchandise withdrawn under the referenced procedure. The correct answer is "e".

✓ **JUST A SIDE NOTE:** A "Class 9 warehouse" is a duty-free store. A "sales ticket" is the duty-free store's sales receipt to their customer that provides Customs' required details of the transaction such as description and quantity of goods sold, etc.

74) The principal agrees to comply with all Importer Security Filing requirements set forth in part 149 of this chapter, including but not limited to, providing security filing information to Customs and Border Protection in the manner and in the time period prescribed by regulation. If the principal defaults with regard to any obligation, the principal and surety (jointly and severally) must pay liquidated damages of _____ for each violation.

a) $1,000
b) $2,000
c) $5,000
d) $10,000
e) $15,000

 As per 19 CFR 113.62(j):

*(j) The principal agrees to comply with all Importer Security Filing requirements set forth in part 149 of this chapter including but not limited to providing security filing information to CBP in the manner and in the time period prescribed by regulation. **If the principal defaults with regard to any obligation, the principal and surety (jointly and severally) agree to pay liquidated damages of $5,000 for each violation.***

 The correct answer is "c".

✔ **JUST A SIDE NOTE:** "Severally" means separately, as the examinee can possibly deduce from the context of the paragraph.

75) A bond is not required on an importation of a vehicle when:

a) A vehicle that conforms to the EPA & DOT standards is purchased by a U.S. Citizen for resale in the United States within one year of importation.

b) The vehicle is imported by a U.S. military employee on commission for another person.

c) The vehicle conforms to the EPA & DOT standards and was recently purchased abroad by a nonresident already living in the United States who had the vehicle shipped directly from the foreign factory to his U.S address for his personal use while employed in the United States.

d) An EPA & DOT conforming vehicle is imported in connection with the arrival of a nonresident, to be used in the United States only for his or her personal transportation, and will not be resold within 1 year after the date of importation.

e) A bond is required on all types of vehicle importations.

 As per 19 CFR 142.4(a):

142.4 Bond requirements.

(a) At the time of entry. **Except as provided in §10.101(d) of this chapter, or paragraph (c) of this section, merchandise shall not be released from Customs custody at the time Customs receives the entry documentation or the entry summary documentation which serves as both the entry and the entry summary, as required by §142.3 unless a single entry or continuous bond** *on Customs Form 301, containing the bond conditions set forth in §113.62 of this chapter, executed by an approved corporate surety, or secured by cash deposits or obligations of the United States, as provided for in §113.40 of this chapter,* **has been filed***. When any of the imported merchandise is subject to a tariff-rate quota and is to be released at a time when the applicable quota is filled, the full rates shall be used in computing the estimated duties to determine the amount of the bond.*

 The correct answer is "e".

✓ **NOTE:** The CBP states that the correct answer is "d", however we respectfully disagree on this one.

✓ **NOTE:** 19 CFR 10.101(d) is for U.S. Government entries. 19 CFR 142.4(c) is for informal entries.

76) Too Loud Audio imported three speakers as samples for use in taking orders under a Temporary Importation Bond (TIB) on June 1, 2012, subheading classification 9813.00.20. They have extended the expiration period by two one-year time periods. In May, 2015 the broker notifies the importer that the TIB is about to reach its expiration date. The importer has indicated that it will not be able to export or destroy the speakers by the TIB's expiration date. What is the importer's best option?

a) Extend the TIB for an additional one-year time period

b) File an anticipatory breach and pay liquidated damages of 110% of all duties and the merchandise processing fee

c) Export similar speakers of the same value

d) File an anticipatory breach and pay liquidated damages for double the duties and the merchandise processing fee

e) Sell the speakers

 As per 19 CFR 10.39(e) & (f):

... ...

*(4) Upon the payment of an amount equal to double the duty which would have accrued on the articles had they been entered under an ordinary consumption entry, or **equal to 110 percent of such duties where that percentage is prescribed in §10.31(f)**, if such amount is determined to be less than the full amount of the bond.*

*(f) Anticipatory breach. **If an importer anticipates that the merchandise entered under a Temporary Importation Bond will not be exported or destroyed in accordance with the terms of the bond, the importer may indicate to Customs in writing before the bond period has expired of the anticipatory breach.** At the time of written notification of the breach, the importer shall pay to Customs the full amount of liquidated damages that would be assessed at the time of breach of the bond, and the entry will be closed. The importer shall notify the surety in writing of the breach and payment. By this payment, the importer waives his right to receive a notice of claim for liquidated damages as required by §172.1(a) of this chapter.*

 The correct answer is "b".

✓ **JUST A SIDE NOTE:** Temporary imports under bond are to be exported within 1 year of their importation. However, if approved, the TIB may be extended twice, 1 year each for each extension. This means the total time allowed for a TIB may not exceed 3 years.

Category XIV: Intellectual Property Rights

77) Which of the following is NOT provided for in 19 CFR 133 to dispose of merchandise seized for infringement of a trademark recorded with U.S. Customs and Border Protection?

a) Forfeiture followed by destruction of the infringing merchandise
b) Release of the infringing merchandise by way of a gift to a charitable institution having a need for the same when there is consent of the trademark owner, obliteration of the offending mark, and a determination by CBP that the merchandise is not unsafe or hazardous
c) Exportation of the infringing merchandise without obliteration of the offending mark when it is one other than a counterfeit
d) Release of the infringing merchandise after obliteration when the offending mark is counterfeit
e) None of the above

 As per 19 CFR 133.51(b) & 133.52(c):

133.51 Relief from forfeiture or liquidated damages.

... ...

(b) Conditioned relief. In appropriate cases, **except for articles bearing a counterfeit trademark, relief** *from a forfeiture may be granted pursuant to a petition for relief upon the following conditions* *and such other conditions as may be specified by the appropriate Customs authority:*

(1) **The unlawfully imported or prohibited articles are exported or destroyed under Customs supervision and at no expense to the Government***;*

(2) **All offending trademarks or trade names are removed or obliterated prior to release of the articles***:*
... ...

133.52 Disposition of forfeited merchandise.

... ...

(c) **Articles bearing a counterfeit trademark***. Merchandise forfeited for violation of the trademark laws shall be destroyed, unless it is determined that the merchandise is not unsafe or a hazard to health and the Commissioner of Customs or his designee has the written consent of the U.S. trademark owner, in which case the Commissioner of Customs or his designee may dispose of the merchandise,* **after obliteration of the trademark, where feasible,** *by:*

(1) Delivery to any Federal, State, or local government agency that, in the opinion of the Commissioner or his designee, has established a need for the merchandise; or

(2) **Gift to any charitable institution that, in the opinion of the Commissioner or his designee, has established a need for the merchandise***; or*

19 CFR 133.51 explains that articles may be released if trademarks are removed "except for articles bearing a 'counterfeit' trademark". The correct answer is "d".

✓ **NOTE:** The exam questions mentions an "infringement" of a trademark, which is not necessarily a "counterfeit" of a trademark. All counterfeits are infringements, though not all infringements are counterfeit (i.e. fraudulent) cases.

78) **If a violation of the trademark or copyright laws is not discovered until after entry and deposit of estimated duty, the entry shall be endorsed with an appropriate notation and the duty refunded as an erroneous collection upon exportation or destruction of the prohibited articles in accordance with _____ of this chapter.**

a) 19CFR 10.581 or 10.709
b) 19CFR 24.3 or 24.3a
c) 19CFR 158.41 or 158.45
d) 19CFR 174.2 or 174.12
e) 19CFR 191.176 or 191.183

 As per 19 CFR 133.53:

133.53 Refund of duty.

*If a violation of the trademark or copyright laws is not discovered until after entry and deposit of estimated duty, the entry shall be endorsed with an appropriate notation and the duty refunded as an erroneous collection upon exportation or destruction of the prohibited articles **in accordance with §158.41 or §158.45 of this chapter.***

 The correct answer is "c".

✓ **JUST A SIDE NOTE:** 19 CFR Sections 158.41 and 158.45 cover the destruction of prohibited merchandise and the exportation of the merchandise, respectively.

79) Which of the following is appropriate to challenge the seizure of merchandise for a violation of 19 USC 1526(e), as implemented by 19 CFR 133.21(d)?

a) Filing a protest under 19 CFR 174
b) Filing a petition under 19 CFR 172
c) Filing a ruling request under 19 CFR 177
d) All of the above
e) None of the above

 As per 19 CFR 133.21(g):

*(g) Consent of the mark owner; failure to make appropriate disposition. The owner of the mark, within thirty days from notification of seizure, may provide written consent to the importer allowing the importation of the seized merchandise in its condition as imported or its exportation, entry after obliteration of the mark, or other appropriate disposition. Otherwise, the merchandise will be disposed of in accordance with §133.52 of this part, **subject to the importer's right to petition for relief from forfeiture under the provisions of part 171 of this chapter.***

Petition for relief from forfeiture is located in part 171 (FINES, PENALTIES, AND FORFEITURES). The correct answer is "e" (none of the above).

✓ **NOTE:** The exam question says "as implemented by 19 CFR 133.21**(d)**", though we believe this must be a typo, and was meant to read "as implemented by 19 CFR 133.21**(g)**".

✓ **JUST A SIDE NOTE:** "19 USC 1526(e)" is, in a way, the United States Code (USC) equivalent of Title 19 Code of Federal Regulations (CFR) 133.52 (Disposition of forfeited merchandise). New laws are assigned a number and recorded in the USC. The CFR is subsequently created or amended to explain in detail these laws and how they will be implemented.

80) Which of the following is TRUE with respect to imported merchandise after the U.S. International Trade Commission (ITC) finds a violation of section 337 of the Tariff Act (19 USC 1337) and issues an exclusion order, as implemented by CBP under 19 CFR 12.39?

a) The exclusion order is not effective until 60 days after issuance, at which point merchandise subject to the exclusion order no longer may be entered.

b) Merchandise subject to the exclusion order may be entered under a single entry bond, in an amount set by the ITC, from the time the exclusion order issues until the time it expires.

c) Merchandise subject to the exclusion order may be entered under bond, in an amount set by the ITC that is secured by the importer's basic importation bond.

d) Merchandise subject to the exclusion order may be entered under bond as provided for in 19 CFR 113, until the determination of a violation becomes final.

e) Merchandise subject to the exclusion order may not be entered after the exclusion order has issued.

 As per 19 CFR 12.39(b):

(b) Exclusion from entry; entry under bond; notice of exclusion order. (1) If the Commission finds a violation of section 337, or reason to believe that a violation exists, it may direct the Secretary of the Treasury to exclude from entry into the United States the articles concerned which are imported by the person violating or suspected of violating section 337. The Commission's exclusion order remains in effect until the Commission determines, and notifies the Secretary of the Treasury, that the conditions which led to the exclusion no longer exist, or until the determination of the Commission on which the order is based is disapproved by the President.

*(2) **During the period the Commission's exclusion order remains in effect, excluded articles may be entered under a single entry bond** in an amount determined by the International Trade Commission to be sufficient to protect the complainant from any injury. **On or after the date that the Commission's determination of a violation of section 337 becomes final**, as set forth in paragraph (a) of this section, **articles covered by the determination will be refused entry**. If a violation of section 337 is found, the bond may be forfeited to the complainant under terms and conditions prescribed by the Commission. To enter merchandise that is the subject of a Commission exclusion order, importers must:*

(i) File with the port director prior to entry a bond in the amount determined by the Commission that contains the conditions identified in the special importation and entry bond set forth in appendix B to part 113 of this chapter; and

(ii) Comply with the terms set forth in 19 CFR 210.50(d) in the event of a forfeiture of this bond.
... ...

 The correct answer is "d".

✓ **JUST A SIDE NOTE:** "19 USC 1337" covers "Unfair Practices in Import Trade".

Book 1 Part 11

Exam with Broker Commentary
Oct. 2015 Customs Broker License Examination

This section of the study guide analyzes an actual customs broker exam. It presents the actual question and its multiple choices. For HTSUS classification questions, the author of this book has included abbreviated HTSUS Article Descriptions notated directly to the right of each multiple choice classification for the student's convenience and ease of reference purposes. As necessary, and in proportion to the complexity of each particular exam question, an analysis of the question and path to the correct answer has been provided. Direct excerpts from the HTSUS, 19 CFR, etc. are also included as supporting points of reference for each answer as necessary. This exam (without commentary, etc.) and its answer key, as well as other previous customs exams can be downloaded directly from Customs' website at...

http://www.cbp.gov/document/publications/past-customs-broker-license-examinations-answer-keys

Exam Refs: Harmonized Tariff Schedule of the United States
Title 19, Code of Federal Regulations
Customs and Trade Automated Interface Requirements (CATAIR)
 * Appendix B - Valid Codes
 * Appendix D - Metric Conversion
 * Appendix E - Valid Entry Numbers
 * Appendix G - Common Errors
 * Glossary of Terms
Instructions for Preparation of CBP Form 7501
Right to Make Entry Directive, 3530-002A

Exam Breakdown by Subject:

Category I –	Practical Exercises	Questions 1-10
Category II –	Powers of Attorney	Questions 11-13
Category III –	Entry	Questions 14-21
Category IV –	Foreign Trade Zones	Questions 22-25
Category V –	Classification	Questions 26-39
Category VI –	Valuation	Questions 40-44
Category VII –	Free Trade Agreements	Questions 45-50
Category VIII –	Drawback	Questions 51-54
Category IX –	Antidumping/Countervailing	Questions 55-57
Category X –	Marking	Questions 58-61
Category XI –	Broker Compliance	Questions 62-66
Category XII –	Fines and Penalties	Questions 67-71
Category XIII –	Bonds	Questions 72-75
Category XIV –	Intellectual Property Rights	Questions 76-80

Exam with Broker Commentary (Oct. 2015) — Study Guide

Category I: Practical Exercises

Practical Exercise 1:

Using the one line entry summary provided below, answer questions 1 through 3.

27. Line No.	28. Description of Merchandise			32.	33.	34. Duty and I.R. Tax	
	29. A. HTSUS No. B. ADA/CVD Case No.	30. A. Gross Weight B. Manifest Qty.	31. Net Quantity in HTSUS Units	A. Entered Value B. CHGS C. Relationship	A. HTSUS Rate B. ADA/CVD Rate C. IRC Rate D. Visa No.	Dollars	Cents

001	M
	Iron nickel alloy strip
	  2 CT
	Invoice Number - 4
	FLT-RLD, MORE THAAN COLD ROLLED
	7226.99.0180 528 467 KG
	
	A533-817-000
	C533-818-000
	Merchandise Processing Fee
	   I.V. 17041.90 USD @ 1.000000
	   E.V. 17041.90 As 17042
				2 CT
				
				NOT-RELATED
				17042
				C 3148
					
					FREE
					00
					29.71%
					12.82%
					.3464%
						0.00	

Other Fee Summary for Block 39	35. Total Entered Value $	CBP USE ONLY		TOTALS	
		A. LIQ CODE	B. Ascertained Duty	37. Duty	
	Total Other Fees $	REASON CODE	C. Ascertained Tax	38. Tax	
36. DECLARATION OF IMPORTER OF RECORD (OWNER OR PURCHASER) OR AUTHORIZED AGENT			D. Ascertained Other	39. Other	
I declare that I am the ☐ Importer of record and that the actual owner, purchaser, or consignee for CBP purposes is as shown above, OR ☒ owner			E. Ascertained Total	40. Total	

308

Exam with Broker Commentary (Oct. 2015) — Study Guide

1) Which of the following free trade agreements is claimed?
(Refer to Practical Exercise 1)

A) U.S. – Colombia Free Trade Agreement
B) U.S. – Chile Free Trade Agreement
C) U.S. – Korea Free Trade Agreement
D) North American Free Trade Agreement
E) There is no free trade agreement claimed

 As per CBP Form 7501 Instructions, Column 27 (Line Number):

*... **The special program indicator (SPI) should be right justified on the same line and immediately preceding the HTS number to which it applies.** If more than one HTS number is required for a line item, place the SPI on the same line as the HTS number upon which the rate of duty is based. If more than one SPI is used, the primary indicator that establishes the rate of duty is shown first, followed by a period and the secondary SPI immediately following.*

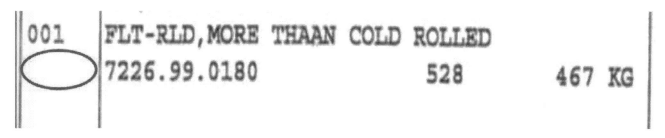

Immediately to the left of the HTS number (in column 27), there is no Special Program Indicator (SPI) such as "KR" (Korea FTA) or "MX" (NAFTA / Mexico). Accordingly, no Free Trade Agreement (FTA) is being claimed on the Entry Summary example. "E" is the correct answer.

✓ **INTERESTINGLY ENOUGH:** NAFTA began in 1994, replacing the already existing Canada—United States Free Trade Agreement, and incorporating Mexico into the multi-lateral trade agreement.

2) What is the correct value for Block 35, "Total Entered Value"?
(Refer to Practical Exercise 1)

A) $5,063.18
B) $7,247.96
C) $17,042.00
D) $2,184.78
E) $17,101.03

 As per CBP Form 7501 Instructions:

BLOCK 35) TOTAL ENTERED VALUE

Report the total entered value for all line items. This information is required on all entry summaries.

| 7226.99.0180 | 528 | 467 KG | 17042 |

The premise of this Entry Summary exercise is that it is a "one-line entry summary". This means that the single "Line Item Entered Value" of $17042 from Column 32 (see above) is also going to be the "Total Entered Value" to be entered in Block 35. The correct answer is "C".

✓ **JUST A SIDE NOTE:** The number "528", which is immediately to the right (in Column 30) of the HTS number, is the gross weight of the item in kilograms.

3) What is the correct value for Block 39, "Other"?

A) $2,184.78
B) $59.03
C) $7,247.96
D) $7,306.99
E) None of the above

 As per CBP Form 7501 Instructions:

BLOCK 39) OTHER

Record the total estimated AD/CVD or other fees, ...

A533-817-000	29.71%
C533-818-000	12.82%
Merchandise Processing Fee	.3464%

"Block 39" on the Entry Summary is for the total amount of any Anti-Dumping and/or Countervailing Duty duties and other fees that may apply such as the Merchandise Processing Fee (MPF) and the Harbor Maintenance Fee (HMF). To do this here, we simply multiply the value of the merchandise ($17042) by the AD, CVD, and MPF, etc. rates, then add them together.

5063.18 (17042 x .2971)
+2184.78 (17042 x .1282)
+   59.03 (17042 x .003464)

=$7,306.99

The answer is "D".

✓ **JUST A SIDE NOTE:** MPF is 0.3464% of entered value. However, the minimum MPF due for formal entries is $25. The maximum is $485.

Practical Exercise 2:
Using the invoice provided below, answer questions 4 through 6.

COMMERCIAL INVOICE Mario's Foods				
1) **Shipper/Exporter** Mario's Foods Atlixco 100B Mexico City Mexico			2) **No. and Date of Invoice** US001836 Monday, January 13, 2014	
:::			3) **No. and Date of L/C**	
4) **For Account and Risk of Messers** Jones Cafe 301 Texan Plaza Dallas, TX 78205			5) **L/C Issuing Bank**	
6) **Notify Party** 7) R.Schaub, 231-423-1234			8) **Remarks** P/O No.: TPS001 Not subject to AD/CVD cases	
9) **Port of Lading** Mexico City, Mexico	10) **Final Destination** Dallas	:::	
11) **Carrier**	12) **Departure on or about** January 20, 2014	:::	
:::	:::	Marks and Numbers of Pkgs. Fernando's Pickles 25/1. 16 Ounce Jar.	
13) **Description of Goods**	14) **Quantity**	15) **Unit Price**	16) **Amount**	
Country of Origin: Mexico Pickled cucumbers $7,000 One pound jar	10000 pieces	0.70 USD		
TOTAL $7,000			
Master Bill: 001-63324833 House Bill: COSC56676406 Estimated Entry Date 01/20/2014			

312

Exam with Broker Commentary (Oct. 2015) — Study Guide

4) If Dallas, TX, is the port of entry, what is the port code?

A) 2101
B) 5311
C) 5501
D) 5507
E) 6420

 As per HTSUS (Statistical) Annex C:

Harmonized Tariff Schedule of the United States (2015)
Annotated for Statistical Reporting Purposes

Code Number, Customs District and Port	Code Number, Customs District and Port
51. VIRGIN ISLANDS OF THE UNITED STATES 01. Charlotte Amalie, VI 02. Cruz Bay, VI 03. Coral Bay, VI 04. Christiansted, VI 05. Frederiksted, VI 52. MIAMI, FLORIDA 01. Miami, FL 02. Key West, FL 03. Port Everglades, FL 04. West Palm Beach, FL 05. Fort Pierce, FL 06. Miami Intl Airport 10. Ft. Lauderdale -Hollywood Intl Airp 70. Int. Courier Ass. 72. MIA/CFS Exp Consig Facil 73. UPS, Miami Intl Airp, FL 95. UPS Courier Hub, Miami, FL 96. DHL Worldwide Express, Miami, FL 97. FEDEX, Courier Hub, Miami, FL 98. IBC Courier Hub, FL	53. HOUSTON-GALVESTON, TEXAS 01. Houston TX 06. Texas City, TX 09. Houston Intercontinental AIRP, TX 10. Galveston, TX 11. Freeport, TX 12. Corpus Christi, TX 13. Port Lavaca, TX 81. Sugar Land Reg, AIRP Sugar Land, TX 54. WASHINGTON, DC 01. Washington, DC 02. Alexandria, VA 55. DALLAS-FORT WORTH, TEXAS 01. Dallas-Fort Worth, TX 02. Amarillo, TX 03. Lubbock, TX 04. Oklahoma City, OK 05. Tulsa, OK 06. Austin, TX 07. San Antonio, TX 82. Midland Intl Airport, Midland, TX 83. Fort Worth Alliance Airp, TX 84. Addison Airport, Addison, TX 88. Dallas Love Field User Fee AIRP, Dallas, TX

 The correct answer is "C".

✓ **INTERESTINGLY ENOUGH:** The Dallas-Fort Worth metropolitan area consists of 12 Texas counties, and is the largest land-locked (i.e. not bordering coastal waters) metropolitan area in the U.S.

5) Block 31 of the CBP Form 7501 should indicate _____ for the pickles.

A) 16 ounces
B) 10,000 pounds
C) 10,000 pieces
D) 10,000 kilograms
E) 4,536 kilograms

 As per the HTSUS Chapter 20:

Heading/ Subheading	Stat. Suffix	Article Description	Unit of Quantity
2001		Vegetables, fruit, nuts and other edible parts of plants, prepared or preserved by vinegar or acetic acid:	
2001.10.00	00	Cucumbers including gherkins...................	kg.......

The correct HTSUS classification for pickled cucumbers is 2001.10.0000. The reporting unit of quantity (column) of which is in "kg" (kilograms). So, the number input into block 31 of CBP Form 7501 for this specific entry should accordingly be in "kg". The commercial invoice provided quantifies the merchandise as 10,000 pieces of "one pound jar". This equals a total of 10,000 pounds. Convert the 10,000 pounds into kilograms by dividing the 10,000 by 2.20462 to equal 4536 (rounded to the nearest whole number) kg. "E" is the correct answer.

✓ **JUST A SIDE NOTE:** A "gherkin" is a small type of cucumber. What Americans call a "pickle", the British generically call a "gherkin".

Exam with Broker Commentary (Oct. 2015) — Study Guide

6) The Manufacturer's Identification Code is:

A) MXELGOR2568MEX
B) MXGORDES2BAGTA
C) MXMARFOO100MEX
D) NAFTAMARFOOMX
E) TAELGOR2568MAT

As per CBP Form 7501 Instructions, Appendix 2 (RULES FOR CONSTRUCTING THE MANUFACTURER IDENTIFICATION CODE):

These instructions provide for the construction of an identifying code for a manufacturer or shipper from its name and address. The code can be up to 15 characters in length, with no inserted spaces.
To begin, for the first 2 characters, use the ISO code for the actual country of origin of the goods. *The exception to this rule is Canada. "CA" is NOT a valid country for the manufacturer code; instead, show as one of the appropriate province codes listed below:*
… …
Next, use the first three characters from the first two "words" of the name. *If there is only one "word" in the name, then use only the first three characters from the first name. For example, Amalgamated Plastics Corp. would be "AMAPLA;" Bergstrom would be "BER."*
If there are two or more initials together, treat them as a single word. For example, A.B.C. Company or A B C Company would yield "ABCCOM." O.A.S.I.S. Corp. would yield "OASCOR." Dr. S.A. Smith yields "DRSA," Shavings B L Inc. yields "SHABL."
In the manufacturer name, ignore the English words a, an, and, of, and the. For example, "The Embassy of Spain" would yield "EMBSPA."
Portions of a name separated by a hyphen are to be treated as a single word. For example, "Rawles-Aden Corp." or "Rawles – Aden Corp." would both yield "RAWCOR."
Some names will include numbers. For examples, "20th Century Fox" would yield "20TCEN" and "Concept 2000" yields "CON200."
Some words in the title of the foreign manufacturer's name should not be used for the purpose of constructing the MID. For example, most textile factories in Macau start with the same words, "Fabrica de Artigos de Vestuario" which means "Factory of Clothing." For a factory named "Fabrica de Artigos de Vestuario JUMP HIGH Ltd," the portion of the factory name that identifies it as a unique entity is "JUMP HIGH." This is the portion of the name that should be used to construct the MID. Otherwise, all of the MIDs from Macau would be the same, using "FABDE," which is incorrect.
Similarly, many factories in Indonesia begin with the prefix PT, such as "PT Morich Indo Fashion." In Russia, other prefixes are used, such as "JSC," "OAO," "OOO," and "ZAO." These prefixes should be eliminated for the purpose of constructing the MID.
Next, find the largest number on the street address line and use up to the first four numbers. *For example, "11455 Main Street Suite 9999" would yield "1145." A suite number or a post office box should be used if it contains the largest number. For example, "232 Main Street Suite 1234" would yield "1234." If the numbers in the street address are spelled out, such as "One Thousand Century Plaza," there will be no numbers in this section of the MID. However, if the address is "One Thousand Century Plaza Suite 345," this would yield "345." When commas or hyphens separate numbers, ignore all punctuation and use the number that remains. For examples, "12,34,56 Alaska Road" and "12-34-56 Alaska Road" would yield "1234." When numbers are separated by a space, the space is a delimiter and the larger of the two numbers should be selected. For example, "Apt. 509 2727 Cleveland St." yields "2727."*
Finally, use the first three alpha characters from the city name. *"Tokyo" would be "TOK," "St. Michel" would be "STM," "18-Mile High" would be "MIL," and "The Hague" would be "HAG." Notice that numerals in the city line are to be ignored.*
For city-states, use the country name to compose the first three alpha characters. For examples, Hong Kong would be "HON," Singapore would be "SIN," and Macau would be "MAC."
General Rules:

Ignore all punctuation, such as commas, periods, apostrophes and ampersands. Ignore all single character initials, such as the "S" in "Thomas S. Delvaux Company." Ignore leading spaces in front of any name or address.

a. The Manufacturer ID Code for the Shipper "Mario's Foods, Atlixco 100B, Mexico City, Mexico" is "MXMARFOO100MEX". The correct answer is "C".

✓ **INTERESTINGLY ENOUGH:** Mexico City is "officially" known as "Mexico, D.F.". D.F. stands for Distrito (district) Federal.

Exam with Broker Commentary (Oct. 2015)   Study Guide

Practical Exercise 3:
Using the entry summary above, please answer questions 7 and 8.

Form Approved OMB No. 1651-0022
EXP. 10-31-2017

DEPARTMENT OF HOMELAND SECURITY U.S. Customs and Border Protection ENTRY SUMMARY			1. Filer Code/Entry No. TPB-00109957	2. Entry Type 01	3. Summary Date 08/07/2015
			4. Surety No. 089	5. Bond Type 8	6. Port Code 2704	7. Entry Date 07/31/2015

8. Importing Carrier Patriot 127E	9. Mode of Transport 11	10. Country of Origin China	11. Import Date 07/24/2015
12. B/L or AWB No. PRES 496023	13. Manufacturer ID CNSUPCHI807SHA	14. Exporting Country China	15. Export Date 07/08/2015
16. I.T. No.	17. I.T. Date	18. Missing Docs	19. Foreign Port of Lading 5700	20. U.S. Port of Unlading 2704
21. Location of Goods/G.O. No. L492	22. Consignee No. 00-610881400	23. Importer No. 74-611991500	24. Reference No.

25. Ultimate Consignee Name and Address	26. Importer of Record Name and Address
Same	Trade Processes International
City State Zip	City Long Beach State CA Zip 90302

27. Line No.	28. Description of Merchandise			32.	33.	34. Duty and I.R. Tax
	29. A. HTSUS No. B. ADA/CVD No.	30. A. Grossweight B. Manifest Qty.	31. Net Quantity in HTSUS Units	A. Entered Value B. CHGS C. Relationship	A. HTSUS Rate B. ADA/CVD Rate C. IRC Rate D. Visa No.	Dollars Cents

317

7) What type of bond was used for this entry summary?

A) Single Entry Bond
B) Continuous Bond
C) Carriers Bond
D) Transfer Bond
E) Warehouse Bond

 As per CBP Form 7501 Instructions:

BLOCK 5) BOND TYPE

Record the single digit numeric code as follows:
0 - U.S. Government or entry types not requiring a bond
8 - Continuous
9 - Single Transaction
Bond type "0" should be used in conjunction with surety code "999" for government entries secured by stipulation as provided for in 19 C.F.R. § 10.101(d).
Bond type "8" or "9," as appropriate, should be used in conjunction with surety code "998" when cash or government securities are deposited in lieu of surety.
Bond type "9" should be used in conjunction with surety code "999" when surety has been waived in accordance with 19 C.F.R. § 142.4 (c). A single entry bond should be attached to the entry summary package.

As per the above snapshot of this particular Entry Summary's Block 5, the Bond Type code is "8", which means a "Continuous Bond" was used. The correct answer is "B".

✓ **JUST A SIDE NOTE:** An importer can purchase a customs bond through their customs broker or directly from a surety company. As per CBP.gov:
A continuous (customs) bond is 10% of duties, taxes and fees paid for the 12 month period. The minimum amount is $50,000.00. Current bond formulas can be found on www.CBP.gov. A single entry bond is generally in an amount not less than the total entered value, plus any duties, taxes and fees.

8) What is the mode of transportation?

A) Vessel; container
B) Trucker; container
C) Mail
D) Vessel; non-container
E) Rail; container

 As per CBP Form 7501 Instructions:

BLOCK 9) MODE OF TRANSPORT

Record the mode of transportation by which the imported merchandise entered the U.S. port of arrival from the last foreign country utilizing the following two digit numeric codes:

10 - Vessel, non-container (including all cargo at first U.S. port of unlading aboard a vessel regardless of later disposition; lightered, land bridge and LASH all included). If container status unknown, but goods did arrive by vessel, use this code.
11 - Vessel, container
12 - Border, Waterborne (used in cases where vessels are used exclusively to ferry automobiles, trucks, and/or rail cars, carrying passengers and baggage and/or cargo and merchandise, between the U.S. and a contiguous country).
20 - Rail, non-container
21 - Rail, container
30 - Truck, non-container
31 - Truck, container
32 - Auto
33 - Pedestrian
34 - Road, other
40 - Air, non-container
41 - Air, container
50 - Mail
60 - Passenger, hand-carried
70 - Fixed transport installation (includes pipelines, powerhouse, etc.)

For merchandise arriving in the customs territory from a U.S. FTZ, leave blank.

As per the above snapshot of this particular Entry Summary's Block 9, the Mode of Transport code is showing as "11", which means a "Containerized Vessel" was used. The correct answer is "A".

✓ **JUST A SIDE NOTE:** Container Vessel capacity is measured in terms of twenty-foot equivalent units (TEU). A typical 40 foot long ocean container equals 2 TEU's.

Exam with Broker Commentary (Oct. 2015) Study Guide

Practical Exercise 4:
Using the edited 7501 below, please answer questions 9 and 10.

27. Line No.	28. Description of Merchandise			32.	33.	34.
	29. A. HTSUS No. B. ADA/CVD No.	30. A. Grossweight B. Manifest Qty.	31. Net Quantity in HTSUS Units	A. Entered Value B. CHGS C. Relationship	A. HTSUS Rate B. ADA/CVD Rate C. IRC Rate D. Visa No.	Duty and I.R. Tax Dollars Cents
001	24 CTNS OTHR IRN/STL WIRE ARTIC, HA 7326.20.0020	1586kg	35000 NO	NOT RELATED 6726 C1211	3.9%	

Other Fee Summary for Block 39	35. Total Entered Value	CBP USE ONLY		TOTALS	
499 501	$ 6,726.00	A. LIQ CODE	B. Ascertained Duty	37. Duty	
	Total Other Fees $	REASON CODE	C. Ascertained Tax	38. Tax	
36. DECLARATION OF IMPORTER OF RECORD (OWNER OR PURCHASER) OR AUTHORIZED AGENT			D. Ascertained Other	39. Other	
I declare that I am the ☐ Importer of record and that the actual owner, purchaser, or consignee for CBP purposes is as shown above, OR ☐ owner or purchaser or agent thereof. I further declare that the merchandise ☐ was obtained pursuant to a purchase or agreement to purchase and that the prices set forth in the invoices are true, OR ☐ was not obtained pursuant to a purchase or agreement to purchase and the statements in the invoices as to value or price are true to the best of my knowledge and belief. I also declare that the statements in the documents herein filed fully disclose to the best of my knowledge and belief the true prices, values, quantities, rebates, drawbacks, fees, commissions, and royalties and are true and correct, and that all goods or services provided to the seller of the merchandise either free or at reduced cost are fully disclosed.			E. Ascertained Total	40. Total	

9) **What is the Merchandise Processing Fee amount for Block 39?**

A) $23.30
B) $25.00
C) $36.28
D) $151.30
E) $485.00

 As per 19 CFR 24.23(b):

*(b) Fees—(1) Formal entry or release—(i) Ad valorem fee—(A) General. Except as provided in paragraph (c) of this section, **merchandise that is formally entered or released is subject to the payment to CBP of an ad valorem fee of 0.3464 percent.** The 0.3464 ad valorem fee is due and payable to CBP by the importer of record of the merchandise at the time of presentation of the entry summary and is based on the value of the merchandise as determined under 19 U.S.C. 1401a. In the case of an express consignment carrier facility or centralized hub facility, each shipment covered by an individual air waybill or bill of lading that is formally entered and valued at $2,500 or less is subject to a $1.00 per individual air waybill or bill of lading fee and, if applicable, to the 0.3464 percent ad valorem fee in accordance with paragraph (b)(4) of this section.*

*(B) Maximum and minimum fees. Subject to the provisions of paragraphs (b)(1)(ii) and (d) of this section relating to the surcharge and to aggregation of the ad valorem fee respectively, the ad valorem fee charged under paragraph (b)(1)(i)(A) of this section **must not exceed $485 and must not be less than $25.***

The Merchandise Processing Fee (MPF) is calculated by multiplying the Total Entered Value by 0.003464. We can tell that this is a formal entry because value exceeds $2,500.00. For formal entries, the maximum MPF is 485 and the minimum MPF is 25.

6726.00 x 0.003464 = 23.30

The calculated amount is less than the minimum, so the minimum MPF of $25 will be used in this case. The answer is "B".

✓ **JUST A SIDE NOTE:** The Harbor Maintenance Fee (HMF), which is basically a fee due for ocean cargo at a rate of 0.00125 of entered value, has neither a minimum nor a maximum amount.

10) What duty amount should be in Block 37?

A) $0.00
B) $161.29
C) $262.31
D) $485.00
E) $6,726.00

 As per CBP Form 7501 Instructions:

BLOCK 37) DUTY

Record the total estimated duty paid (excluding AD/CVD).

| 7326.20.0020 | 1586kg | 35000 NO | 6726 | 3.9% |

 Customs duty is calculated by multiplying the Total Entered Value by the HTS duty rate.

6726.00 x 0.039 = 262.31

The answer is "C".

✓ **JUST A SIDE NOTE:** The HTS number for this example is for garment hangers.

7326.20.00		Articles of iron or steel wire..	....	3.9%
	10	Belts and belting..	kg	
	20	Garment hangers..	No.	
	30	Sod staples, U staples, irrigation staples, ground staples, and ground pins..............................	X	
	40	Double loop bar ties and double loop wire ties............	X	
	71	Other..	X	

Category II: Power of Attorney

11) When may a power of attorney be revoked?

A) At any time by written notice given to and received by the Port Director
B) It may not be revoked
C) Within 30 days from execution
D) Upon written approval by the Port Director
E) Prior to being submitted to CBP

As per 19 CFR 141.35:

141.35 Revocation of power of attorney.

Any power of attorney shall be subject to revocation at any time by written notice given to and received by the port director.

The answer is "A".

✓ **JUST A SIDE NOTE:** The term "Attorney-in-fact", as seen printed on CBP Form 7501, is not the same as "attorney-at-law". "Attorney-in-fact" simply means an agent is acting on behalf of another party, for which a power of attorney is on file.

Exam with Broker Commentary (Oct. 2015) — Study Guide

12) What is the penalty, as stated by the CBP Mitigation Guidelines, for each power of attorney that a broker does not have on file?

A) $250
B) $500
C) $1,000
D) $1,500
E) $2,000

As per 19 C.F.R. 171 App C (V)(E):

E. *Penalties for failure to retain powers of attorney from clients to act in their names.*

1. *The penalty notice should also cite 19 CFR 141.46 as the regulation violated.*

2. *Assessment amount—$1,000 for each power of attorney not on file.*

The correct answer is "C".

JUST A SIDE NOTE: Customs provides an example of a Customs Power of Attorney in Part 141.32:

141.32 Form for power of attorney.

Customs Form 5291 may be used for giving power of attorney to transact Customs business. If a Customs power of attorney is not on a Customs Form 5291, it shall be either a general power of attorney with unlimited authority or a limited power of attorney as explicit in its terms and executed in the same manner as a Customs Form 5291.

The following is an example of an acceptable general power of attorney with unlimited authority:

KNOW ALL MEN BY THESE PRESENTS, THAT

_____
   (Name of principal)

_____,
(State legal designation, such as corporation, individual, etc.) residing at _____ and doing business under the laws of the State of _____, hereby appoints

(Name, legal designation, and address)
as a true and lawful agent and attorney of the principal named above with full power and authority to do and perform every lawful act and thing the said agent and attorney may deem requisite and necessary to be done for and on behalf of the said principal without limitation of any kind as fully as said principal could do if present and acting, and hereby ratify and confirm all that said agent and attorney shall lawfully do or cause to be done by virtue of these presents until and including _____, (date) or until notice of revocation in writing is duly given before that date.
Date _____, 19__;.

(Principal's signature)

13) ABC Brokers has authorized its unlicensed employee Joe to sign Customs documents on its behalf and has executed a valid Power of Attorney for this purpose. Which of the following reflects Joe's legal authority to sign documents?

A) Joe is unlicensed, and even with a valid Power of Attorney, he cannot sign Customs documents.
B) Joe can sign Customs documents without a valid Power of Attorney.
C) ABC Brokers cannot execute a valid Power of Attorney because Joe is unlicensed, and therefore cannot sign Customs documents.
D) ABC Brokers, upon request from Customs, must furnish proof of the existence of the Power of Attorney.
E) Joe is required to file the Power of Attorney with the port director.

 As per 19 CFR 111.2(a):

111.2 License and district permit required.

(a) License—(1) General. Except as otherwise provided in paragraph (a)(2) of this section, a person must obtain the license provided for in this part in order to transact customs business as a broker.

(2) Transactions for which license is not required—(i) For one's own account. An importer or exporter transacting customs business solely on his own account and in no sense on behalf of another is not required to be licensed, nor are his authorized regular employees or officers who act only for him in the transaction of such business.

(ii) As employee of broker—(A) General. ***An employee of a broker, acting solely for his employer, is not required to be licensed where:***

(1) Authorized to sign documents. *The broker has authorized the employee to sign documents pertaining to customs business on his behalf, and has executed a power of attorney for that purpose. The broker is not required to file the power of attorney with the port director, but must provide proof of its existence to Customs upon request; or*

 The correct answer is "D".

✓ **JUST A SIDE NOTE:** There is no official CBP or government form for the Customs Broker Triennial Status Report. Thankfully, however, Customs provides an unofficial form for the customs broker community to use and can be found at the following. It contains all the necessary information required from the triennially due report.

http://www.cbp.gov/sites/default/files/documents/triennial_report_form_p.pdf

14) In the following scenario, what is the date of entry for the imported merchandise if it is approved to be released under the immediate delivery procedure?

Eight automobiles made in Canada were purchased by an auto dealership in the United States on May 1, 2015. The automobiles were loaded onto a tractor-trailer at the Canadian assembly plant on May 5, 2015. The truck cargo was examined by CBP at the U.S. border and released into the United States on May 7, 2015. The tractor-trailer arrived at the U.S. dealership on May 8, 2015, and the automobiles were unloaded. The automobiles qualify for duty free status under NAFTA, and the entry summary with estimated duties was submitted to CBP on May 15, 2015.

A) May 1, 2015
B) May 5, 2015
C) May 7, 2015
D) May 8, 2015
E) May 15, 2015

 As per 19 CFR 141.68(c)

(c) When merchandise is released under the immediate delivery procedure. The time of entry of merchandise released under the immediate delivery procedure will be the time the entry summary is filed in proper form, with estimated duties attached.

 The correct answer is "E".

✔ **JUST A SIDE NOTE:** The term "released under the immediate delivery procedure" refers to the CBP Form 3461 release.

15) You have a shipment of merchandise that reports 0.48 gross kilograms. What is the reportable gross shipping weight of less than 1 kilogram on the CBP Form 7501 in column 30?

A) 1 KG
B) 0 KG
C) 0.48 KG
D) 0.50 KG
E) 11 KG

 (exam reference material citation not available for this question)

 The correct answer is "A".

✔ **JUST A SIDE NOTE:** The above rule of thumb is also used for exports. When filing an exporter Electronic Export Information (EEI, and formerly known as SED), commodity weights of less than 1 kilogram are rounded up to 1 kilogram.

16) A licensed broker is preparing an entry using a foreign manufacturer's invoice that shows only foreign currency. The importer stated they did not have an agreement prior to exportation concerning the currency conversion rate. Which date should the broker use to determine the rate of exchange for calculation of the entered value?

A) Date the goods are ready to leave the factory
B) Date of export
C) Date that duty is paid
D) Date of entry
E) Date the importer paid for the goods

 As per 19 CFR 159.32:

159.32 Date of exportation.

The date of exportation for currency conversion *shall be fixed in accordance with §152.1(c) of this chapter.*

 The correct answer is "B".

✓ **NOTE:** 19 CFR 152.1(c) defines "date of exportation" as follows:
(c) Date of exportation. "Date of exportation," or the "time of exportation" referred to in section 402, Tariff Act of 1930, as amended (19 U.S.C. 1401a), means the actual date the merchandise finally leaves the country of exportation for the United States. If no positive evidence is at hand as to the actual date of exportation, the port director shall ascertain or estimate the date of exportation by all reasonable ways and means in his power, and in so doing may consider dates on bills of lading, invoices, and other information available to him.

The following question is to be used for answers 17 through 19.

17) For a consumption entry made on July 18, 2014, the statutory 1-year period for liquidation may be extended by a port director for a period not to exceed _____.

A) 3 years
B) 2 years
C) 1 year
D) 180 days
E) 90 days

 As per 19 CFR 159.12(a):

159.12 Extension of time for liquidation.

(a) Reasons—(1) Extension. **The port director may extend the 1-year statutory period for liquidation for an additional period not to exceed 1 year if:**

Although multiple extensions may total as many as 3 years, each individual extension period may not exceed 1 year. The correct answer is "C".

✓ **JUST A SIDE NOTE:** Importers are notified of suspended entry liquidation (for pending anti-dumping case reasons, etc.) by CBP via a mailed CBP Form 4333A.

18) The total time for which extensions may be granted may not exceed _____.

A) 1 year
B) 2 years
C) 3 years
D) 4 years
E) 5 years

As per 19 CFR 159.12(e):

*(e) Limitation on extensions. **The total time for which extensions may be granted by the port director may not exceed 3 years.***

The correct answer is "C".

19) Hence, if CBP does not actively liquidate the entry in question by _____, it will be deemed liquidated by operation of law on said date.

A) July 18, 2016
B) July 18, 2017
C) July 18, 2018
D) July 18, 2020
E) July 18, 2019

As per 19 CFR 159.12(f):

*(f) Time limitation—(1) Generally. **An entry not liquidated within 4 years from either the date of entry, or the date of final withdrawal of all the merchandise covered by a warehouse entry, will be deemed liquidated** by operation of law at the rate of duty, value, quantity, and amount of duty asserted by the importer at the time of filing the entry summary for consumption in proper form, with estimated duties attached, or the withdrawal for consumption in proper form, with estimated duties attached, unless liquidation continues to be suspended by statute or court order. CBP will endeavor to provide a courtesy notice of liquidation, in accordance with §159.9(d), in addition to the bulletin notice specified in §159.9(c)(2)(ii).*

This particular entry, for which liquidation has presumably been extended to the max, will be considered liquidated at least by July 18, 2018, which is four years from date of original entry. The correct answer is "C".

20) Which of the following is NOT a valid reason for extension of liquidation?

A) Liquidation is suspended as required by statute
B) Additional information is required by CBP for proper appraisement of merchandise
C) The importer's merchandise is before Customs Court pending litigation
D) Additional information is required by CBP for proper classification of merchandise
E) The importer requests an extension in writing showing good cause

 As per 19 CFR 159.12(a):

159.12 Extension of time for liquidation.

(a) Reasons—(1) Extension. **The port director may extend the 1-year statutory period for liquidation for an additional period not to exceed 1 year if:**

(i) Information needed by CBP. **Information needed by CBP for the proper appraisement or classification** *of the merchandise is not available, or*

(ii) Importer's request. **The importer requests an extension in writing before the statutory period expires and shows good cause why the extension should be granted.** *"Good cause" is demonstrated when the importer satisfies the port director that more time is needed to present to CBP information which will affect the pending action, or there is a similar question under review by CBP.*

(2) Suspension. **The 1-year liquidation period may be suspended as required by statute or court order.**

 And as per 19 CFR 159.51:

159.51 General.

Liquidation of entries shall be suspended only when provided by law or regulation, or when directed by the Commissioner of Customs. **Liquidation of entries shall not be suspended simply because issues involved therein may be before the Customs Court in pending litigation,** *since the importer may seek relief by protesting the entries after liquidation.*

Unless there is a court order, which is an official proclamation by a judge, an entry may not be suspended (i.e. extended). The correct answer is "C".

✓ **JUST A SIDE NOTE:** 19 CFR 159.1 defines liquidation as "the final computation or ascertainment of duties on entries for consumption or drawback entries".

21) A nonresident corporation can enter merchandise for consumption if it has _____.

A) an ultimate consignee located somewhere in the United States
B) a resident agent anywhere in the United States
C) a broker located in the United States to clear its merchandise
D) a resident agent in the port of entry who is authorized to accept process against that corporation
E) a resident agent in the port of entry who is authorized to accept process against that corporation and files a bond with conditions set forth in 113.62 CFR

 As per 19 CFR 141.18:

141.18 Entry by nonresident corporation.

A nonresident corporation (i.e., one which is not incorporated within the customs territory of the United States or in the Virgin Islands of the United States) may not enter merchandise for consumption unless it:

(a) Has a resident agent in the State where the port of entry is located who is authorized to accept service of process against that corporation or, in the case of an entry filed from a remote location pursuant to subpart E of part 143 of this chapter, has a resident agent authorized to accept service of process against that corporation either in the State where the port of entry is located or in the State from which the remote location filing originates; and

(b) Files a bond on CBP Form 301, containing the bond conditions set forth in §113.62 of this chapter having a resident corporate surety to secure the payment of any increased and additional duties which may be found due.

 The correct answer is "E".

✓ **JUST A SIDE NOTE:** Customs Bonds (CBP Form 301) are issued by surety companies. These surety companies are accordingly licensed by the U.S. Treasury Department.

Category IV: Foreign Trade Zones

22) _____ is the procedure for delivery of merchandise to a zone without prior application and approval on Customs Form 214.

A) Constructive Transfer
B) Activation
C) Transfer
D) Admit
E) Direct Delivery

 As per 19 CFR 146.39(a):

146.39 Direct delivery procedures.

(a) General. **This procedure is for delivery of merchandise to a zone without prior application and approval on Customs Form 214.**

 The correct answer is "E".

JUST A SIDE NOTE: Benefits of Foreign Trade Zone (FTZ) utilization for high-volume importers include:

- Inverted tariff (i.e. pay duties only on the FTZ manufactured goods) benefits
- Duty payment deferment
- Improved inventory management capabilities

23) What CBP Form is used to admit merchandise into a Foreign Trade Zone (FTZ)?

A) CBP Form 7501
B) CBP Form 214
C) CBP Form 3499
D) CBP Form 3461
E) CBP Form 6043

 As per 19 CFR 146.32(a):

(a)(1) Application on CBP Form 214 and permit. **Merchandise may be admitted into a zone only upon application on a uniquely and sequentially numbered CBP Form 214** *("Application for Foreign Trade Zone Admission and/or Status Designation") and the issuance of a permit by the port director. Exceptions to the CBP Form 214 requirement are for merchandise temporarily deposited (§146.33), transiting merchandise (§146.34), or domestic merchandise admitted without permit (§146.43). The applicant for admission shall present the application to the port director and shall include a statistical copy on CBP Form 214-A for transmittal to the Bureau of Census, unless the applicant has made arrangements for the direct transmittal of statistical information to that agency.*

 The correct answer is "B".

✓ **INTERESTINGLY ENOUGH:** There are two separate sets of U.S. regulations that cover Foreign Trade Zones. The first is Title 19 (Customs). The other is Title 15 (Commerce and Foreign Trade), which also includes regulations for the Bureau of Industry and Security (BIS), the agency that controls non-arms-related exports.

24) Absolute quota merchandise imported in excess of the admissible quantity may NOT be_____.

A) held in an FTZ for the opening of the next quota period
B) held in a warehouse for the opening of the next quota period
C) exported under CBP supervision
D) destroyed under CBP supervision
E) entered at a higher rate of duty

 As per 19 CFR 132.5:

132.5 Merchandise imported in excess of quota quantities.

(a) Absolute quota merchandise. Absolute quota merchandise imported in excess of the quantity admissible under the applicable quota must be disposed of in accordance with paragraph (c) of this section.

(b) Tariff-rate quota merchandise. Merchandise imported in excess of the quantity admissible at the reduced quota rate under a tariff-rate quota is permitted entry at the higher duty rate. However, it may be disposed of in accordance with paragraph (c) of this section.

(c) Disposition of excess merchandise. Merchandise imported in excess of either an absolute or a tariff-rate quota may be held for the opening of the next quota period by placing it in a foreign-trade zone or by entering it for warehouse, or it may be exported or destroyed under Customs supervision.

Only tariff-rate quote merchandise may be entered at a higher duty rate after quote limits have been reached. The same is not true for absolute quote merchandise after quota limits have been reached. Basically, that's the difference between the two quota types. The correct answer is "E".

✓ **JUST A SIDE NOTE:** 19 CFR 132.1 defines both quota types:

(a) Absolute (or quantitative) quotas. "Absolute (or quantitative) quotas" are those which permit a limited number of units of specified merchandise to be entered or withdrawn for consumption during specified periods. Once the quantity permitted under the quota is filled, no further entries or withdrawals for consumption of merchandise subject to quota are permitted. Some absolute quotas limit the entry or withdrawal of merchandise from particular countries (geographic quotas) while others are global quotas and limit the entry or withdrawal of merchandise not by source but by total quantity.

(b) Tariff-rate quotas. "Tariff-rate quotas" permit a specified quantity of merchandise to be entered or withdrawn for consumption at a reduced duty rate during a specified period.

25) An FTZ Operator shall prepare a reconciliation report within ___ days of the end of the zone/sub zone year unless the port director authorizes an extension for reasonable cause.

A) 30
B) 60
C) 90
D) 120
E) 180

 As per 19 CFR 146.25(a):

146.25 Annual reconciliation.

(a) Report. **The operator shall prepare a reconciliation report within 90 days after the end of the zone/subzone year** *unless the port director authorizes an extension for reasonable cause. The operator shall retain that annual reconciliation report for a spot check or audit by Customs, and need not furnish it to Customs unless requested. There is no form specified for the preparation of the report.*

 The correct answer is "C".

✔ **JUST A SIDE NOTE:** As per 19 CFR 146.25(c), "The operator shall submit to the port director within 10 working days after the annual reconciliation report, a letter signed by the operator certifying that the annual reconciliation has been prepared, is available for Customs review, and is accurate."

Category V: Classification

26) Where would a women's knitted sweater from Ireland with a fiber content of 50% merino wool and 50% man-made rayon be classified in the Harmonized Tariff Schedule of the United States (HTSUS)?

A) 6110.30.1520   Sweaters, pullovers, sweatshirts, waistcoats (vests) and similar articles, knitted or crocheted>>Of man-made fibers>>Other>>Containing 23% or more by weight of wool or fine animal hair>>Sweaters>>Women's or girls

B) 6110.20.2020   Sweaters, pullovers, sweatshirts, waistcoats (vests) and similar articles, knitted or crocheted>>Of cotton>>Other>>Other>>Sweaters>>Women's

C) 6110.30.1020   Sweaters, pullovers, sweatshirts, waistcoats (vests) and similar articles, knitted or crocheted>>Of man-made fibers>>Containing 25% or more by weight of leather>>Sweaters>>Women's or girls

D) 6110.19.0030   Sweaters, pullovers, sweatshirts, waistcoats (vests) and similar articles, knitted or crocheted>>Of wool or fine animal hair>>Other>>Sweaters>>Women's

E) 6105.20.1000   Men's or boys' shirts, knitted or crocheted>>Of man-made fibers>>Containing 23% or more by weight of wool or fine animal hair

 As per HTSUS Section XI (Textiles and Textile Articles), Note 2(A):

2. (A) Goods classifiable in chapters 50 to 55 or in heading 5809 or 5902 and of a mixture of two or more textile materials are to be classified as if consisting wholly of that one textile material which predominates by weight over each other single textile material.

When no one textile material predominates by weight, the goods are to be classified as if consisting wholly of that one textile material which is covered by the heading which occurs last in numerical order among those which equally merit consideration.

 And as per HTSUS Section XI (Textiles and Textile Articles), Subheading Note 2(A):

2. (A) Products of chapters 56 to 63 containing two or more textile materials are to be regarded as consisting wholly of that textile material which would be selected under note 2 to this section for the classification of a product of chapters 50 to 55 or of heading 5809 consisting of the same textile materials.

As per the above-mentioned Section Notes, if no textile material predominates over other textile materials, we are to classify the item using the classification that occurs numerically last in the HTS. This is also in line with GRI 3(c).

The sweater is of 50% man-made fibers (multiple choice "A") and 50% wool (multiple choice D"). The HTS number for "A" occurs numerically after that of "D". Thus, the correct answer is "A".

✓ **JUST A SIDE NOTE:** Examples of man-made textile fibers include nylon, polyester, rayon, and spandex. All of which were invented before 1960.

Heading/ Subheading	Stat. Suffix	Article Description	Unit of Quantity	Rates of Duty General	Rates of Duty 1 Special	Rates of Duty 2
6110		Sweaters, pullovers, sweatshirts, waistcoats (vests) and similar articles, knitted or crocheted (con.):				
6110.30		Of man-made fibers:				
6110.30.10		Containing 25 percent or more by weight of leather.....	....	6%	Free (AU, BH, CA, CL, CO, IL, JO, KR, MA, MX, OM, P, PA, PE, SG)	35%
		Sweaters:				
	10	Men's or boys' (645)................	doz. kg			
	20	Women's or girls' (646)................	doz. kg			
		Vests, other than sweater vests:				
	30	Men's or boys' (659)................	doz. kg			
	40	Women's or girls' (659)................	doz. kg			
		Other:				
	50	Men's or boys' (638)................	doz. kg			
	60	Women's or girls' (639)................	doz. kg			
		Other:				
6110.30.15		Containing 23 percent or more by weight of wool or fine animal hair................	....	17%	Free (AU, BH, CA, CL, CO, IL, JO, KR, MA, MX, OM, P, PA, PE, SG)	54.5%
		Sweaters:				
	10	Men's or boys' (445)................	doz. kg			
	20	Women's or girls' (446)................	doz. kg			
		Vests, other than sweater vests:				
	30	Men's or boys' (459)................	doz. kg			
	40	Women's or girls' (459)................	doz. kg			
		Other:				
	50	Men's or boys' (438)................	doz. kg			
	60	Women's or girls' (438)................	doz. kg			

27) Daisy's Dairy Delights wishes to import ice cream. They are a new importer with a limited importing history and the low rate quota for ice cream is closed. They are importing samples, in shipments exceeding 5 kilograms, to determine which flavors they will carry in their line and request you classify it under 2105.00.0500 which references GN 15. They do not have any written approvals or licenses from the Department of Agriculture. The product is of a type subject to tariff-rate quota and is subject to the provisions of Subchapter IV of Chapter 99. Which of the following is NOT a reason this classification can be used?

A) They are not importing such products for the account of any agency of the U.S. Government.

B) The products are not being imported for personal use.

C) Such products, which will not enter the commerce of the United States, are imported as samples for taking orders; for exhibition, display or sampling at a trade fair; for research; for use by embassies of foreign governments; or for testing of equipment, provided that written approval from the Secretary of Agriculture or his/her designated representative of the United States Department of Agriculture (USDA) is presented at the time of entry.

D) The shipment of the product exceeds 5 kilograms.

E) This tariff number can only be used when the low rate quota is open but the importer has not been importing long enough to obtain a dairy license from USDA.

 As per HTSUS Chapter 21:

| 2105.00.05 | 00 | Described in general note 15 of the tariff schedule and entered pursuant to its provisions.................................. | kg.............. | 20% |

 And as per HTSUS General Note 15:

15 Exclusions.

Whenever any agricultural product of chapters 2 through 52, inclusive, is of a type (i) subject to a tariff-rate quota and (ii) subject to the provisions of subchapter IV of chapter 99, entries of such products described in this note shall not be counted against the quantity specified as the in-quota quantity for any such product in such chapters:

(a) such products imported by or for the account of any agency of the U.S. Government;

(b) such products imported for the personal use of the importer, provided that the net quantity of such product in any one shipment does not exceed 5 kilograms;

(c) such products, which will not enter the commerce of the United States, imported as samples for taking orders, for exhibition, display or sampling at a trade fair, for research, for use by embassies of foreign governments or for testing of equipment, provided that written approval of the Secretary of Agriculture or his designated representative the United States Department of Agriculture (USDA) is presented at the time of entry;

(d) blended syrups containing sugars derived from sugar cane or sugar beets, capable of being further processed or mixed with similar or other ingredients, and not prepared for marketing to the ultimate consumer in the identical form and package in which imported, provided that, subject to approval of the Foreign Trade Zones Board, such syrups are manufactured in and entered from a U.S. foreign trade zone by a foreign trade zone user whose facilities were in operation on June 1, 1990, to the extent that the annual quantity entered into the customs territory from such zone does not contain a quantity of sugar of nondomestic origin greater than that authorized by the Foreign Trade Zones Board for processing in the zones during calendar year 1985; and

(e) cotton entered under the provisions of U.S. note 6 to subchapter III of chapter 99 and subheadings 9903.52.00 through 9903.52.26, inclusive. In applying to USDA for approval under subdivision (c) of this note, the importer must identify the product, quantity and intended use of the goods for which exemption is sought. USDA may seek additional information and specify such conditions of entry as it deems necessary to ensure that the product will not enter the commerce of the United States.

The Secretary of Agriculture shall carry out the provisions of this note in consultation with the United States Trade Representative.

 The correct answer is "E".

✓ **JUST A SIDE NOTE:** HTSUS Chapter 99, Subchapter IV imposes additional safeguard duties on agricultural products. These safeguard measures are intended to protect domestic producers from foreign competition. However, they protect only a few select industries, and result in higher prices for consumers.

28) An article composed of two different base metals, with the exception of ferroalloys and master alloys, is classified based on which of the following?

A) The metal component that imparts the essential character of the article
B) The metal that possesses the chief value
C) The metal that contributes the most toward marketing the article
D) The metal that is referenced last (in numerical order) in the Harmonized Tariff Schedule
E) The metal that predominates by weight

 As per HTSUS Section XV (Base Metals and Articles of Base Metal), Note 5:

5. *Classification of alloys (other than ferroalloys and master alloys as defined in chapters 72 and 74):*

(a) An alloy of base metals is to be classified as an alloy of the metal which predominates by weight over each of the other metals.

(b) An alloy composed of base metals of this section and of elements not falling within this section is to be treated as an alloy of base metals of this section if the total weight of such metals equals or exceeds the total weight of the other elements present.

(c) In this section the term "alloys" includes sintered mixtures of metal powders, heterogeneous intimate mixtures obtained by melting (other than cermets) and intermetallic compounds.

 The correct answer is "E".

✓ **JUST A SIDE NOTE:** Basically, an alloy is a metal formed by the mixture of different metals. A ferrous metal is a metal that contains iron, the element symbol of which is Fe.

29) What is the tariff classification of a single dinnerware plate that is made of stoneware, measures 15.3 cm in diameter, and is offered for sale in the same pattern as all of the other articles listed in Chapter 69 Additional U.S. Note 6(b), with the aggregate value of all those articles listed in that note being $37?

A) 6911.10.3710 Tableware, kitchenware, other household articles and toilet articles, of porcelain or china>>Tableware and kitchenware>>Other>>Other>>Available in specified sets>>In any pattern for which the aggregate value of the articles listed in additional U.S. note 6(b) of this chapter is over $56>>Aggregate value not over $200>>Plates not over 27.9 cm in maximum dimension, teacups and saucers; mugs; soups, fruits and cereals, the foregoing not over 22.9 cm in maximum dimension

B) 6911.10.5200 Tableware, kitchenware, other household articles and toilet articles, of porcelain or china>>Tableware and kitchenware>>Other>>Other>>Other>>Cups valued over $8 but not over $29 per dozen; saucers valued over $5.25 but not over $18.75 per dozen; soups, oatmeals and cereals valued over $9.30 but not over $33 per dozen; plates not over 22.9 cm in maximum diameter and valued over $8.50 but not over $31 per dozen; plates over 22.9 but not over 27.9 cm in maximum diameter and valued over $11.50 but not over $41 per dozen; platters or chop dishes valued over $40 but not over $143 per dozen; sugars valued over $23 but not over $85 per dozen; creamers valued over $20 but not over $75 per dozen; and beverage servers valued over $50 but not over $180 per dozen

C) 6912.00.3510 Ceramic tableware, kitchenware, other household articles and toilet articles, other than of porcelain or china>>Tableware and kitchenware>>Other>>Other>>Available in specified sets>>In any pattern for which the aggregate value of the articles listed in additional U.S. note 6(b) of this chapter is not over $38>>Plates not over 27.9 cm in maximum dimensions; teacups and saucers; mugs; soups, fruits and cereals, the foregoing not over 22.9 cm in maximum dimension

D) 6912.00.4500 Ceramic tableware, kitchenware, other household articles and toilet articles, other than of porcelain or china>>Tableware and kitchenware>>Other>>Other>>Other>>Cups valued over $5.25 per dozen; saucers valued over $3 per dozen; soups, oatmeals and cereals valued over $6 per dozen; plates not over 22.9 cm in maximum diameter and valued over $6 per dozen; plates over 22.9 but not over 27.9 cm in maximum diameter and valued over $8.50 per dozen; platters or chop dishes valued over $35 per dozen; sugars valued over $21 per dozen; reamers valued over $15 per dozen; and beverage servers valued over $42 per dozen

E) 6912.00.4810 Ceramic tableware, kitchenware, other household articles and toilet articles, other than of porcelain or china>>Tableware and kitchenware>>Other>>Other>>Other>>Other>>Suitable for food or drink contact

As per HTSUS Chapter 69, Additional U.S. Note 6:

*(a) **The term "available in specified sets" embraces plates, cups, saucers and other articles principally used for preparing, serving or storing food or beverages, or food or beverage ingredients, which are sold or offered for sale in the same pattern,** but no article is classifiable as being "available in specified sets" unless it is of a pattern in which at least the articles listed below in (b) of this note are sold or offered for sale.*

*(b) **If each of the following articles is sold or offered for sale in the same pattern, the classification hereunder in subheadings 6911.10.35, 6911.10.37, 6911.10.38, 6912.00.35 or 6912.00.39, of all articles of such pattern shall be governed by the aggregate value of the following articles in the quantities indicated**, as determined by the appropriate customs officer under section 402 of the Tariff Act of 1930, as amended, whether or not such articles are imported in the same shipment:*

12 plates of the size nearest to 26.7 cm in maximum dimension, sold or offered for sale,
12 plates of the size nearest to 15.3 cm in maximum dimension, sold or offered for sale,
12 tea cups and their saucers, sold or offered for sale,
12 soups of the size nearest to 17.8 cm in maximum dimension, sold or offered for sale,
12 fruits of the size nearest to 12.7 cm in maximum dimension, sold or offered for sale,
1 platter or chop dish of the size nearest to 38.1 cm in maximum dimension, sold or offered for sale,
1 open vegetable dish or bowl of the size nearest to 25.4 cm in maximum dimension, sold or offered for sale,
1 sugar of largest capacity, sold or offered for sale,
1 creamer of largest capacity, sold or offered for sale.

 AND as per HTSUS Chapter 69, Additional U.S. Note 5(a):

*(a) The terms "porcelain", "china" and "chinaware" embrace ceramic ware (other than stoneware), whether or not glazed or decorated, having a fired white body (unless artificially colored) which will not absorb more than 0.5 percent of its weight of water and is translucent in thicknesses of several millimeters. **The term "stoneware" as used in this note, embraces ceramic ware** which contains clay as an essential ingredient, is not commonly white, will absorb not more than 3 percent of its weight of water, and is naturally opaque (except in very thin pieces) even when absorption is less than 0.1 percent.*

The item in question is made of stoneware, which is a ceramic. It is not, however, considered as porcelain or china, so we may disregard multiple choices "A" and "B".

The item in question is a single plate, but it is also available in sets. The question states that the item is "is offered for sale in the same pattern as all of the other articles listed in Chapter 69 Additional U.S. Note 6(b)", and so we will classify under subheading 6912.00.35. The item is a plate measuring 15.3 cm in diameter. Accordingly, the correct answer is "C".

✓ **JUST A SIDE NOTE:** This HTSUS Chapter 69 does not cover *Articles of chapter 97 (for example, works of art)*.

Heading/ Subheading	Stat. Suffix	Article Description	Unit of Quantity	Rates of Duty General	Rates of Duty 1 Special	Rates of Duty 2
6912.00		Ceramic tableware, kitchenware, other household articles and toilet articles, other than of porcelain or china: Tableware and kitchenware:				
6912.00.10	00	Of coarse-grained earthenware, or of coarse- grained stoneware; of fine-grained earthenware, whether or not decorated, having a reddish-colored body and a lustrous glaze which, on teapots, may be any color, but which, on other articles, must be mottled, streaked or solidly colored brown to black with metallic oxide or salt..	doz.pcs.....	0.7%	Free (A, AU, BH, CA, CL, CO, E, IL, JO, KR, MA, MX, OM, P, PA, PE, SG)	25%
		Other:				
6912.00.20	00	Hotel or restaurant ware and other ware not household ware..	doz.pcs.....	28%	Free (A+, AU, BH, CA, CL, CO, D, E, IL, JO, MA, MX, P, PE, SG) 8.4% (OM) 16.8% (KR)	55%
		Other: Available in specified sets:				
6912.00.35		In any pattern for which the aggregate value of the articles listed in additional U.S. note 6(b) of this chapter is not over $38....	....	9.8%	Free (A, AU, BH, CA, CL, CO, E, IL, JO, KR, MA, MX, OM, P, PA, PE, SG)	55%
	10	Plates not over 27.9 cm in maximum dimension; teacups and saucers; mugs; soups, fruits and cereals, the foregoing not over 22.9 cm in maximum dimension........................	doz.pcs.			
	50	Other..	doz.pcs.			
6912.00.39		In any pattern for which the aggregate value of the articles listed in additional U.S. note 6(b) of this chapter is over $38........	....	4.5%	Free (A+, AU, BH, CA, CL, CO, D, E, IL, JO, MA, MX, P, PA, PE, SG) 1.3% (OM) 2.7% (KR)	55%
	10	Plates not over 27.9 cm in maximum dimension; teacups and saucers; mugs; soups, fruits and cereals, the foregoing not over 22.9 cm in maximum dimension........................	doz.pcs.			
	50	Other..	doz.pcs.			

30) You are reviewing a spec sheet for a cutting machine die which your client continually refers to as "porcelain ceramic." According to the specs, the die, which was fired after shaping, has a hardness of 7.1 on the Mohs scale and will absorb .8% of its weight in water. What is the tariff classification for the cutting machine die?

A) 6909.11.2000   Ceramic wares for laboratory, chemical or other technical uses; ceramic troughs, tubs and similar receptacles of a kind used in agriculture; ceramic pots, jars and similar articles of a kind used for the conveyance or packing of goods>>Ceramic wares for laboratory, chemical or other technical uses>>Of porcelain or china>>Machinery parts

B) 6909.11.4000   Ceramic wares for laboratory, chemical or other technical uses; ceramic troughs, tubs and similar receptacles of a kind used in agriculture; ceramic pots, jars and similar articles of a kind used for the conveyance or packing of goods>>Ceramic wares for laboratory, chemical or other technical uses>>Of porcelain or china>>Other

C) 6909.12.0000   Ceramic wares for laboratory, chemical or other technical uses; ceramic troughs, tubs and similar receptacles of a kind used in agriculture; ceramic pots, jars and similar articles of a kind used for the conveyance or packing of goods>>Ceramic wares for laboratory, chemical or other technical uses>>Articles having a hardness equivalent to 9 or more on the Mohs scale

D) 6909.19.5095   Ceramic wares for laboratory, chemical or other technical uses; ceramic troughs, tubs and similar receptacles of a kind used in agriculture; ceramic pots, jars and similar articles of a kind used for the conveyance or packing of goods>>Ceramic wares for laboratory, chemical or other technical uses>>Other>>Other>>Other

E) 6909.90.0000   Ceramic wares for laboratory, chemical or other technical uses; ceramic troughs, tubs and similar receptacles of a kind used in agriculture; ceramic pots, jars and similar articles of a kind used for the conveyance or packing of goods>>Other

 As per HTSUS Chapter 69, Additional U.S. Note 5(a):

*(a) **The terms "porcelain"**, "china", and "chinaware" **embrace ceramic ware** (other than stoneware), whether or not glazed or decorated, having a fired white body (unless artificially colored) **which will not absorb more than 0.5 percent of its weight of water** and is translucent in thicknesses of several millimeters. The term "stoneware" as used in this note, embraces ceramic ware which contains clay as an essential ingredient, is not commonly white, will absorb not more than 3 percent of its weight of water, and is naturally opaque (except in very thin pieces) even when absorption is less than 0.1 percent.*

The client describes the item as "porcelain ceramic", however, the item "will absorb .8% of its weight in water", which based on the above-mentioned Additional U.S. Note 5(a), precludes it from being defined as "porcelain". This we eliminate multiple choices "A" and "B". "C" may also be eliminated due to the conflicting Mohs scale value. Finally, "D" provides a more specific true description of the item than does "E". Hence, we can conclude that the correct answer is "D".

✔ **NOTE:** The exam key states that "A" is the correct answer, but we disagree with this as per our above-mentioned analysis.

Heading/ Subheading	Stat. Suffix	Article Description	Unit of Quantity	Rates of Duty 1 General	Rates of Duty 1 Special	Rates of Duty 2
6909		Ceramic wares for laboratory, chemical or other technical uses; ceramic troughs, tubs and similar receptacles of a kind used in agriculture; ceramic pots, jars and similar articles of a kind used for the conveyance or packing of goods:				
		Ceramic wares for laboratory, chemical or other technical uses:				
6909.11		Of porcelain or china:				
6909.11.20	00	Machinery parts............................	X	Free		40%
6909.11.40	00	Other..	X	4.5%	Free (A, AU, BH, CA, CL, CO, E, IL, JO, KR, MA, MX, OM, P, PA, PE, SG)	60%
6909.12.00	00	Articles having a hardness equivalent to 9 or more on the Mohs scale.........................	X	4%	Free (A, AU, BH, CA, CL, CO, E, IL, JO, KR, MA, MX, OM, P, PA, PE, SG)	45%
6909.19		Other:				
6909.19.10	00	Ferrite core memories..................	X	Free		35%
6909.19.50		Other..		4%	Free (A, AU, BH, CA, CL, CO, E, IL, JO, KR, MA, MX, OM, P, PA, PE, SG)	45%
	10	Ceramic bearings........................	No.			
	95	Other..	X			
6909.90.00	00	Other..	X	4%	Free (A, AU, BH, CA, CL, CO, E, IL, JO, KR, MA, MX, OM, P, PA, PE, SG)	45%
6910		Ceramic sinks, washbasins, washbasin pedestals, baths, bidets, water closet bowls, flush tanks, urinals and similar sanitary fixtures:				
6910.10.00		Of porcelain or china...............................		5.8%	Free (A*, AU, BH, CA, CL, CO, E, IL, JO, KR, MA, MX, OM, P, PA, PE, SG)	60%
	05	Water closet bowls, flushometer type..............	No.			
	10	Water closet bowls with tanks, in one piece.......	No.			
	15	Flush tanks..................................	No.			
	20	Other water closet bowls.............	No.			
	30	Sinks and lavatories....................	No.			
	50	Other..	No.			
6910.90.00	00	Other..	No.	5.7%	Free (A*, AU, BH, CA, CL, CO, E, IL, JO, KR, MA, MX, OM, P, PA, PE, SG)	60%

31) What is the tariff classification of Valacyclovir Hydrochloride (CAS 124832-27-5) imported in 500 mg tablets in measured dosage form? Each tablet contains 1 gram of Valacyclovir Hydrochloride mixed with other inactive ingredients (carnauba wax, colloidal silicon dioxide, microcrystalline cellulose and polyethylene glycol). Valacyclovir Hydrochloride is an anti-viral drug used for the treatment of herpes zoster and cold sores. It slows the growth and spread of the herpes virus so that the body can fight off the infection.

A)	3004.20.0060	Medicaments (excluding goods of heading 3002, 3005 or 3006) consisting of mixed or unmixed products for therapeutic or prophylactic uses, put up in measured doses (including those in the form of transdermal administration systems) or in forms or packings for retail sale>>Containing other antibiotics>>Other>>Other
B)	2933.59.3600	Heterocyclic compounds with nitrogen hetero-atom(s) only>> Compounds containing a pyrimidine ring (whether or not hydrogenated) or piperazine ring in the structure>>Other>>Drugs>>Aromatic or modified aromatic>>Anti-infective agents>>Other
C)	3004.90.9110	Medicaments (excluding goods of heading 3002, 3005 or 3006) consisting of mixed or unmixed products for therapeutic or prophylactic uses, put up in measured doses (including those in the form of transdermal administration systems) or in forms or packings for retail sale>>Other>>Other>>Other>>Anti-infective medicaments>>Other
D)	3824.90.5500	Prepared binders for foundry molds or cores; chemical products and preparations of the chemical or allied industries (including those consisting of mixtures of natural products), not elsewhere specified or included>>Other>>Other>>Other>>Mixtures of halogenated hydrocarbons>>Other
E)	3003.90.0000	Medicaments (excluding goods of heading 3002, 3005 or 3006) consisting of two or more constituents which have been mixed together for therapeutic or prophylactic uses, not put up in measured doses or in forms or packings for retail sale>>Other

 As per HTSUS Section VI (encompasses Chapters 28 thru. 38), Note 2:

*2. Subject to note 1 above, **goods classifiable in heading 3004, 3005, 3006, 3212, 3303, 3304, 3305, 3306, 3307, 3506, 3707 or 3808 by reason of being put up in measured doses or for retail sale are to be classified in those headings and in no other heading of the tariff schedule.***

As per the above-mentioned Section Note, the item in question (which is in measured dosage form), is to be classified in the Note's named headings only. Headings 2933 and 3824 are not listed here, so we may disregard multiple choices "B" and "D". "A" may be eliminated as a choice as the drug is "anti-viral", and there is no mention of any "antibiotics". "E" may also be disregarded as it references "not put up in measured doses".

The correct answer is "C".

✔ **NOTE:** In regards to a few terms used in the classifications for this question: A "medicament" is simply a substance used for medical treatment. "Prophylactic" means a preventative medicine.

Heading/ Subheading	Stat. Suffix	Article Description	Unit of Quantity	Rates of Duty General	Rates of Duty 1 Special	Rates of Duty 2
3004 (con.)		Medicaments (excluding goods of heading 3002, 3005 or 3006) consisting of mixed or unmixed products for therapeutic or prophylactic uses, put up in measured doses (including those in the form of transdermal administration systems) or in forms or packings for retail sale: (con.)				
3004.90		Other:				
3004.90.10	00	Containing antigens or hyaluronic acid or its sodium salt..................	kg	Free		Free
3004.90.91		Other..................		Free		30%
	03	For veterinary use..................	kg			
		Other: Anti-infective medicaments:				
	05	Sulfonamides..................	kg			
	10	Other..................	kg			
	15	Antineoplastic and immunosuppressive medicaments..................	kg			
	20	Cardiovascular medicaments..................	kg			
		Medicaments primarily affecting the central nervous system: Analgesics, antipyretics and nonhormonal anti-inflammatory agents:				
	22	Tolmetin..................	kg			
	24	Tolmetin sodium dihydrate..................	kg			
	26	Tolmetin sodium (anhydrous)..................	kg			
	28	Other..................	kg			
	30	Anticonvulsants, hypnotics and sedatives..................	kg			
	35	Antidepressants, tranquilizers, and other psychotherapeutic agents..................	kg			
	40	Other..................	kg			
	45	Dermatological agents and local anesthetics..................	kg			
		Medicaments primarily affecting the digestive system:				
	50	Laxatives..................	kg			
	55	Antacids..................	kg			
	60	Other..................	kg			
		Preparations primarily affecting the electrolytic, caloric or water balance:				
	65	Diuretics..................	kg			
	70	Other..................	kg			
		Medicaments primarily affecting the eyes, ears or respiratory system:				
	76	Cough and cold preparations..................	kg			
		Other:				
	80	Antihistamines..................	kg			
	85	Other..................	kg			
	90	Other..................	kg			

32) What is the applicable tariff classification for a heat-and-serve frozen "loaded hot dog" (beef frankfurter with various toppings) in a bun? The ingredients (by weight) of the complete product are wheat flour (37%), cooked beef sausage (34%), water, chopped onions, pickle relish, mustard, crispy bacon topping bits (4%), yeast, dextrose and spices.

A) 1602.50.9040   Other prepared or preserved meat, meat offal or blood>>Of bovine animals>>Other>>Other>>Other

B) 2106.90.9995   Food preparations not elsewhere specified or included>>Other>>Other>>Other>>Other>>Other>>Other>>Other>>Other>>Frozen

C) 1602.90.9080   Other prepared or preserved meat, meat offal or blood>>Other, including preparations of blood of any animal>>Other>>Other

D) 1601.00.6020   Sausages and similar products, of meat, meat offal or blood; food preparations based on these products>>Other>>Other>>Beef

E) 0210.12.0020   Meat and edible meat offal, salted, in brine, dried or smoked; edible flours and meals of meat or meat offal>>Meat of swine>>Bellies (streaky) and cuts thereof>>Bacon

 As per HTSUS Chapter 16, Note 2:

2. Food preparations fall in this chapter provided that they contain more than 20 percent by weight of sausage, meat, meat offal, blood, fish or crustaceans, molluscs or other aquatic invertebrates, or any combination thereof. In cases where the preparation contains two or more of the products mentioned above, it is classified in the heading of chapter 16 corresponding to the component or components which predominate by weight. These provisions do not apply to the stuffed products of heading 1902 or to the preparations of heading 2103 or 2104.

The item in question, your typical hot dog and bun with toppings, is 34% beef sausage. So, as per the above-mentioned Chapter 16 Note, it is to be classified in Chapter 16. Next, we can say that the item is prima facie. Meaning, the article descriptions for both "A" and "D" are correct. However, and as per GRI 3(a), the most specific heading description is preferred. Accordingly, the correct answer is "D".

✓ **JUST A SIDE NOTE:** "Offal" is the internal organs (excluding muscle and bone) of animals.

Heading/ Subheading	Stat. Suf- fix	Article Description	Unit of Quantity	Rates of Duty General	Rates of Duty 1 Special	Rates of Duty 2
1601.00		Sausages and similar products, of meat, meat offal or blood; food preparations based on these products:				
1601.00.20		Pork..		0.8¢/kg	Free (A, AU, BH, CA, CL, CO, E, IL, JO, KR, MA, MX, OM, P, PA, PE, SG)	7.2¢/kg
	10	Canned..	kg			
	90	Other...	kg			
		Other:				
1601.00.40		Beef in airtight containers...		3.4%	Free (A, AU, BH, CA, CL, CO, E*, IL, JO, KR, MA, MX, OM, P, PA, PE, SG)	30%
	10	Canned..	kg			
	90	Other...	kg			
1601.00.60		Other...		3.2%	Free (A, AU, BH, CA, CL, CO, E*, IL, JO, KR, MA, MX, OM, P, PA, PE, SG)	20%
	20	Beef..	kg			
		Other:				
	60	Canned..	kg			
	80	Other...	kg			
1602		Other prepared or preserved meat, meat offal or blood:				
1602.10.00	00	Homogenized preparations...	kg	1.9%	Free (A+, AU, BH, CA, CL, CO, D, E*, IL, JO, KR, MA, MX, OM, P, PA, PE, SG)	30%
1602.20		Of liver of any animal:				
1602.20.20	00	Of goose...	kg	4.9¢/kg	Free (A+, AU, BH, CA, CL, CO, D, E, IL, JO, MA, MX, P, PA, PE, SG) 1.4¢/kg (OM) 2.1¢/kg (KR)	22¢/kg
1602.20.40	00	Other...	kg	3.2%	Free (A, AU, BH, CA, CL, CO, E*, IL, JO, KR, MA, MX, OM, P, PA, PE, SG)	20%

33) What is the tariff classification of a sideguard assembly designed specifically for use in a belt conveyor? The XYZ Company's glass ornament production line includes machines such as a furnace, a casting machine, a drawing machine, a molding machine, a grinding machine and coating/lamination machines. Many of the machines are interconnected by means of a belt conveyor system.

A) 8487.90.0080 — Machinery parts, not containing electrical connectors, insulators, coils, contacts or other electrical features, and not specified or included elsewhere in this chapter>>Other>>Other

B) 8475.90.9000 — Machines for assembling electric or electronic lamps, tubes or flashbulbs, in glass envelopes; machines for manufacturing or hot working glass or glassware; parts thereof>>Parts>>Other

C) 8479.90.9496 — Machines and mechanical appliances having individual functions, not specified or included elsewhere in this chapter; parts thereof>>Parts>>Other>>Other>>Other

D) 8431.39.0010 — Parts suitably for use solely or principally with the machinery of headings 8425 to 8430>>Or machinery of heading 8428>>Other>>Of elevators and conveyors

E) 8466.91.5000 — Parts and accessories suitable for use solely or principally with the machines of headings 8456 to 8465, including work or tool holders, self-opening dieheads, dividing heads and other special attachments for machine tools; tool holders for any type of tool for working in the hand>>Other>>For machines of heading 8464>>Other

As per HTSUS Section XVI (includes Chapters 84 & 85), Note 2(a) & 2(b):

(a) Parts which are goods included in any of the headings of chapter 84 or 85 (other than headings 8409, 8431, 8448, 8466, 8473, 8487, 8503, 8522, 8529, 8538 and 8548) *are in all cases to be classified in their respective headings;*

(b) Other parts, if suitable for use solely or principally with a particular kind of machine, or with a number of machines of the same heading (including a machine of heading 8479 or 8543) are to be classified with the machines of that kind or in heading 8409, **8431**, 8448, 8466, 8473, 8503, 8522, 8529 or 8538 *as appropriate. However, parts which are equally suitable for use principally with the goods of headings 8517 and 8525 to 8528 are to be classified in heading 8517;*

 The item in question, a sideguard assembly, is a part "designed specifically" for use in a belt conveyor machine (heading 8431), so the above-mentioned Section Note 2(a) says to proceed to Note 2(b) (even if there were a heading for "sideguards"). Subsequently, Section Note 2(b) says to classify this part under the heading of the part's parent machine, the machine for which it is principally for use with.

"B" and "E" may be discounted as possible answers as the belt conveyor machine is a machine interconnecting but separately identified from the other glass manufacturing machines. "C" could be considered a correct description. Finally, the more specific HTS heading "D" is preferred to "A". The correct answer is "D".

✓ **NOTE:** Multiple choice "D" references "heading 8428", which is the heading for "Other lifting, handling, loading or unloading machinery (for example, elevators, escalators, conveyors, teleferics)".

Multiple choice "E" references "heading 8464", which is the heading for "Machine tools for working stone, ceramics, concrete, asbestos-cement or like mineral materials or for cold working glass".

Heading/ Subheading	Stat. Suffix	Article Description	Unit of Quantity	Rates of Duty General	Rates of Duty Special	Rates of Duty 2
8431		Parts suitable for use solely or principally with the machinery of headings 8425 to 8430:				
8431.10.00		Of machinery of heading 8425..................		Free		35%
	10	Of machinery of subheading 8425.11 or 8425.19.......	X			
	90	Other......	X			
8431.20.00	00	Of machinery of heading 8427.....................	X	Free		35%
		Of machinery of heading 8428:				
8431.31.00		Of passenger or freight elevators other than continuous action, skip hoists or escalators..................		Free		35%
	20	Of skip hoists................	X			
	40	Of escalators..............	X			
	60	Other........	X			
8431.39.00		Other............		Free		35%
	10	Of elevators and conveyors..................	X			
		Other:				
	50	Of oil and gas field machinery..................	X			
	70	Of the woodland log handling equipment of statistical reporting number 8428.90.0210......	X			
	80	Other.............	X			
		Of machinery of heading 8426, 8429 or 8430:				
8431.41.00		Buckets, shovels, grabs and grips...............		Free		35%
	20	Shovel attachments..................	No.			
	40	Clamshell (grappler) attachments............	No.			
	60	Dragline buckets...............	No.			
	80	Other........	No.			
8431.42.00	00	Bulldozer or angledozer blades..................	No.	Free		35%
8431.43		Parts for boring or sinking machinery of subheading 8430.41 or 8430.49:				
8431.43.40	00	Of offshore oil and natural gas drilling and production platforms..................	X	Free		45%
8431.43.80		Other...............		Free		35%
		Of oil and gas field machinery:				
	20	Tool joints, whether or not forged..............	No.			
	40	Drill pipe fitted with tool joints...................	No.			
	60	Other.............	X			
	90	Of other boring or sinking machinery.............	X			

34) What is the tariff classification of a carbon steel bolt imported together with a corresponding steel nut? The bolt has a hexagonal head and a threaded shank that measures 5.4 mm in diameter and 24 mm in length. It is used exclusively in central heating radiators.

A) 7318.15.2065   Screws, bolts, nuts, coach screws, screw hooks, rivets, cotters, cotter pins, washers (including spring washers) and similar articles, of iron or steel>>Threaded articles>>Other screws and bolts, whether or not with their nuts or washers>>Bolts and bolts and their nuts or washers entered or exported in the same shipment>>Having shanks or threads with a diameter of 6 mm or more>>Other>>With hexagonal heads>>Other

B) 7318.29.0000   Screws, bolts, nuts, coach screws, screw hooks, rivets, cotters, cotter pins, washers (including spring washers) and similar articles, of iron or steel>>Non-threaded articles>>Other

C) 7318.15.2010   Screws, bolts, nuts, coach screws, screw hooks, rivets, cotters, cotter pins, washers (including spring washers) and similar articles, of iron or steel>>Threaded articles>>Other screws and bolts, whether or not with their nuts or washers>>Bolts and bolts and their nuts or washers entered or exported in the same shipment>>Having shanks or threads of a diameter of less than 6 mm

D) 7318.16.0085   Screws, bolts, nuts, coach screws, screw hooks, rivets, cotters, cotter pins, washers (including spring washers) and similar articles, of iron or steel>>Threaded articles>>Nuts>>Other>>Other

E) 7322.19.0000   Radiators for central heating, not electrically heated, and parts thereof, of iron or steel; air heaters and hot air distributors (including distributors which can also distribute fresh or conditioned air), not electrically heated, incorporating a motor-driven fan or blower, and parts thereof, of iron or steel>>Radiators and parts thereof>>Other

As per HTSUS Section XV (includes Chapters 72 thru. & 83), Note 2:

2. Throughout the tariff schedule, the expression "parts of general use" means:

*(a) **Articles of heading** 7307, 7312, 7315, 7317 or **7318** and similar articles of other base metals;*

(b) Springs and leaves for springs, of base metal, other than clock or watch springs (heading 9114); and

(c) Articles of heading 8301, 8302, 8308 or 8310 and frames and mirrors, of base metal, of heading 8306.

In chapters 73** to 76 and 78 to 82 (but not in heading 7315) **references to parts of goods do not include references to parts of general use as defined above.

The above-mentioned Section Note says that in Chapter 73 "references to parts of goods do not include references to parts of general use as defined above" (i.e. heading 7318, etc.). This means that even though the item in question, a steel bolt, is "used exclusively" in central heating radiators, the bolt is not to be classified as a part of a radiator for central heating, and multiple choice "E" is to be disregarded. "A" may be disregarded for bolt diameter reasons, "B" may be disregarded for being "non-threaded", and "D" may be disregarded because this classification is for nuts. The correct answer is "C".

✓ **NOTE:** Nuts imported with their corresponding bolts, etc. are classified with the bolt. They are not classified by themselves in this case.

Heading/ Subheading	Stat. Suffix	Article Description	Unit of Quantity	Rates of Duty General	Rates of Duty 1 Special	Rates of Duty 2
7318 (con.)		Screws, bolts, nuts, coach screws, screw hooks, rivets, cotters, cotter pins, washers (including spring washers) and similar articles, of iron or steel: (con.) Threaded articles: (con.)				
7318.15		Other screws and bolts, whether or not with their nuts or washers:				
7318.15.20		Bolts and bolts and their nuts or washers entered or exported in the same shipment...............		Free		3.5%
	10	Having shanks or threads with a diameter of less than 6 mm............	kg			
		Having shanks or threads with a diameter of 6 mm or more:				
	20	Track bolts............	kg			
	30	Structural bolts............	kg			
		Bent bolts:				
	41	Right-angle anchor bolts............	kg			
	46	Other............	kg			
		Other: With round heads:				
	51	Of stainless steel............	kg			
	55	Other............	kg			
		With hexagonal heads:				
	61	Of stainless steel............	kg			
	65	Other............	kg			
		Other:				
	91	Of stainless steel............	kg			
	95	Other............	kg			
7318.15.40	00	Machine screws 9.5 mm or more in length and 3.2 mm or more in diameter (not including cap screws)............	kg	Free		2.2¢/kg
7318.15.50		Studs............		Free		45%
	30	Of stainless steel............	kg			
		Other: Continuously threaded rod:				
	51	Of alloy steel............	kg			
	56	Other............	kg			
	90	Other............	kg			

35) What is the tariff classification of a chocolate production line that includes a conveyor belt, a mixer, a cooling tunnel and cutters? The entire chocolate production line will be imported unassembled in one shipment.

A) 8208.30.0060   Knives and cutting blades, for machines or for mechanical appliances, and base metal parts thereof>>For kitchen appliances or for machines used by the food industry, and parts thereof>>Other

B) 8479.89.9899   Machines and mechanical appliances having individual functions, not specified or included elsewhere in this chapter; parts thereof>>Other machines and mechanical appliances>>Other>>Other>>Other

C) 8438.20.0000   Machinery, not specified or included elsewhere in this chapter, for the industrial preparation or manufacture of food or drink, other than machinery for the extraction or preparation of animal or fixed vegetable fats or oils; parts thereof>>Machinery for the manufacture of confectionery, cocoa or chocolate

D) 8438.90.9030   Machinery, not specified or included elsewhere in this chapter, for the industrial preparation or manufacture of food or drink, other than machinery for the extraction or preparation of animal or fixed vegetable fats or oils; parts thereof>>Parts>>Other>>Of machinery for the manufacture of confectionery, cocoa or chocolate

E) 8428.20.0010   Other lifting, handling, loading or unloading machinery (for example, elevators, escalators, conveyors, teleferics)>>Pneumatic elevators and conveyors>>Conveyors

 As per HTSUS Section XVI (includes Chapters 84 & 85), Note 3:

*3. Unless the context otherwise requires, **composite machines consisting of two or more machines fitted together to form a whole** and other machines designed for the purpose of performing two or more complementary or alternative functions **are to be classified** as if consisting only of that component or **as being that machine which performs the principal function.***

As per the above-mentioned Section Note, and as per GRI 2(a), unfinished or unassembled items are to be classified as if they were in their finished state. The article description for multiple choice "C" is "machinery (no parts) for the manufacture of confectionery, cocoa or chocolate". "C" is thus the clear correct answer.

✓ **NOTE:** Cooling tunnels are used to cool molded or extruded chocolate to room temperature.

Heading/ Subheading	Stat. Suffix	Article Description	Unit of Quantity	Rates of Duty General	Rates of Duty 1 Special	Rates of Duty 2
8438		Machinery, not specified or included elsewhere in this chapter, for the industrial preparation or manufacture of food or drink, other than machinery for the extraction or preparation of animal or fixed vegetable fats or oils; parts thereof:				
8438.10.00		Bakery machinery and machinery for the manufacture of macaroni, spaghetti or similar products............		Free		35%
	10	Bakery machinery............	No.			
	90	Other............	No.			
8438.20.00	00	Machinery for the manufacture of confectionery, cocoa or chocolate............	No............	Free		35%
8438.30.00	00	Machinery for sugar manufacture............	No............	Free		Free
8438.40.00	00	Brewery machinery............	No............	2.3%	Free (A, AU, BH, CA, CL, CO, E, IL, JO, KR, MA, MX, OM, P, PA, PE, SG)	35%
8438.50.00		Machinery for the preparation of meat or poultry............		2.8%	Free (A, AU, BH, CA, CL, CO, E, IL, JO, KR, MA, MX, OM, P, PA, PE, SG)	35%
	10	Meat- and poultry-packing plant machinery............	No.			
	90	Other............	No.			
8438.60.00	00	Machinery for the preparation of fruits, nuts or vegetables............	No............	Free		35%
8438.80.00	00	Other machinery............	No............	Free		40%
8438.90		Parts:				
8438.90.10	00	Of machinery for sugar manufacture............	X............	Free		Free
8438.90.90		Other............		2.8%	Free (A, AU, BH, CA, CL, CO, E, IL, JO, KR, MA, MX, OM, P, PA, PE, SG)	35%
	15	Of bakery machinery and machinery for the manufacture of macaroni, spaghetti or similar products............	X			
	30	Of machinery for the manufacture of confectionery, cocoa or chocolate............	X			
	60	Of machinery for the preparation of meat or poultry............	X			
	90	Other............	X			

36) A U.S. importer sent electronic cigarettes with broken power switches back to China to the original manufacturer for repair. The cigarettes were repaired and returned to the U.S. What is the duty requirement for entering the cigarettes into the U.S.?

A) The importer does not have to pay any duty because it was already paid on the shipment of electronic cigarettes upon the previous importation.
B) The importer does not have to pay any duty because they had a warranty on all parts and labor.
C) The importer must pay duty on the returned shipping charges.
D) The importer must pay duty on the reasonable value of the repairs.
E) The importer must pay the new duty rate assigned to power switches on the appraised value of electronic cigarettes.

 As per HTSUS Chapter 98, Subchapter II, Note 3:

3. Articles repaired, altered, processed or otherwise changed in condition abroad.--The following provisions apply only to subheadings 9802.00.40 through 9802.00.60, inclusive:

(a) The value of repairs, alterations, processing or other change in condition outside the United States shall be:

(i) The cost to the importer of such change; or
*(ii) If no charge is made, **the value of such change**, as set out in the invoice and entry papers; except that, if the appraiser concludes that the amount so set out does not represent a reasonable cost or value, then the value of the change shall be determined in accordance with section 402 of the Tariff Act of 1930, as amended.*

(b) No appraisement of the imported article in its changed condition shall be required unless necessary to a determination of the rate or rates of duty applicable to such article.

*(c) **The duty, if any, upon the value of the change in condition shall be at the rate which would apply to the article itself**, as an entirety without constructive separation of its components, in its condition as imported if it were not within the purview of this subchapter. If the article, as returned to the United States, is subject to a specific or compound rate of duty, such rate shall be converted to the ad valorem rate which when applied to the full value of such article determined in accordance with said section 402 would provide the same amount of duties as the specific or compound rate. In order to compute the duties due, the ad valorem rate so obtained shall be applied to the value of the change in condition made outside the United States.*

The importer is only required to pay duties on the value of the repairs (regardless of whether under warranty or not), not on the value of the articles, if they enter under the HTS Chapter 98 subheading for "articles exported for repairs or alterations". 9802.00.4040 is the primary HTS number in this case. Since the HTSUS for e-cigarettes is 8543.70.9640 (2.6%), duty would be assessed on the value of the repairs at this secondary HTS rate of 2.6%.

The correct answer is "D".

✓ **NOTE:** As per 19 CFR 10.8, the following declaration in essentially the same form must be completed (by the repairing party) and accompany the entry papers for entries made under the above-mentioned Chapter 98 provision. (see second page following this page)

Heading/ Subheading	Stat. Suffix	Article Description	Unit of Quantity	Rates of Duty General	Rates of Duty 1 Special	Rates of Duty 2
9802.00.20	00	Photographic films and dry plates manufactured in the United States (except motion-picture films to be used for commercial purposes) and exposed abroad, whether developed or not.....	X.............	Free		Free
		Articles returned to the United States after having been exported to be advanced in value or improved in condition by any process of manufacture or other means: Articles exported for repairs or alterations:				
9802.00.40		Repairs or alterations made pursuant to a warranty....	....	A duty upon the value of the repairs or alterations (see U.S. note 3 of this subchapter)	Free (AU, B, BH, C, CA, CL, CO, IL, JO, KR, MA, MX, OM, P, PA, PE, SG)	A duty upon the value of the repairs or alterations (see U.S. note 3 of this subchapter)
	20 1/	Internal combustion engines................................	1/			
	40 1/	Other..	1/			
9802.00.50		Other..	....	A duty upon the value of the repairs or alterations (see U.S. note 3 of this subchapter)	Free (AU, BH, CL, CO, IL, JO, KR, MA, MX, OM, P, PA, PE, SG) A duty upon the value of the repairs or alterations (see U.S. note 3 of this subchapter) (B, C, CA)	A duty upon the value of the repairs oralterations (see U.S. note 3 of this subchapter)
	10 2/	Articles for which duty free treatment is claimed under U.S. note 2(b) to this subchapter................	2/			
		Other:				
	30 1/	Internal combustion engines...........................	1/			
	60 1/	Other...	1/			
9802.00.60	00 1/	Any article of metal (as defined in U.S. note 3(e) of this subchapter) manufactured in the United States or subjected to a process of manufacture in the United States, if exported for further processing, and if the exported article as processed outside the United States, or the article which results from the processing outside the United States, is returned to the United States for further processing..........	1/ 3/	A duty upon the value of such processing outside the United States (see U.S. note 3 of this subchapter)	Free (BH, CL, IL, JO, MA, OM, P, SG) A duty upon the value of such processing outside the United States (see U.S. note 3 of this subchapter) (AU, B, C, CA, CO, KR, MX, PA, PE)	A duty upon the value of such processing outside the United States (see U.S. note 3 of this subchapter)

I,_____, declare that the articles herein specified are the articles which, in the condition in which they were exported from the United States, were received by me (us) on _____, 19__, from_____ (name and address of owner or exporter in the United States); that they were received by me (us) for the sole purpose of being repaired or altered; that only the repairs or alterations described below were performed by me (us); that the full cost or (when no charge is made) value of such repairs or alterations are correctly stated below; and that no substitution whatever has been made to replace any of the articles originally received by me (us) from the owner or exporter thereof mentioned above.

Marks and numbers	Description of articles and of repairs or alterations	Full cost or (when no charge is made) value of repairs or alterations (see subchapter II, chapter 98, HTSUS)	Total value of articles after repairs or alterations

(Date)
(Address)
(Signature)
(Capacity)

(2) A declaration by the owner, importer, consignee, or agent having knowledge of the pertinent facts in substantially the following form:

I, _____,

declare that the (above) (attached) declaration by the person who performed the repairs or alterations abroad is true and correct to the best of my knowledge and belief; that the articles were not manufactured or produced in the United States under subheading 9813.00.05, HTSUS; that such articles were exported from the United States for repairs or alterations and without benefit of drawback from _____ (port) on _____, 19__; and that the articles entered in their repaired or altered condition are the same articles that were exported on the above date and that are identified in the (above) (attached) declaration.

(Date)
(Address)
(Signature)
(Capacity)

(This Page Intentionally Left Blank)

37) A welded square tube is made from alloy (not stainless) steel and measures 3 feet in length with a wall thickness of 4 mm. As a result of the welding process, the square tube has a visible seam. What is the tariff classification of the tube?

A) 7304.90.3000   Tubes, pipes and hollow profiles, seamless, of iron (other than cast iron) or steel>>Other>>Having a wall thickness of 4 mm or more>>Of alloy steel

B) 7306.69.3000   Other tubes, pipes and hollow profiles (for example, open seamed or welded, riveted or similarly closed), of iron or steel>>Other, welded, of noncircular cross section>>Of other noncircular cross section>>Having a wall thickness of 4 mm or more>>Of alloy steel

C) 7304.90.7000   Tubes, pipes and hollow profiles, seamless, of iron (other than cast iron) or steel>>Other>>Having a wall thickness of less than 4 mm>>Of alloy steel

D) 7306.61.3000   Other tubes, pipes and hollow profiles (for example, open seamed or welded, riveted or similarly closed), of iron or steel>>Other, welded, of noncircular cross section>>Of square or rectangular cross section>>Having a wall thickness of 4 mm or more>>Of alloy steel

E) 7306.61.5000   Other tubes, pipes and hollow profiles (for example, open seamed or welded, riveted or similarly closed), of iron or steel>>Other, welded, of noncircular cross section>>Of square or rectangular cross section>>Having a wall thickness of less than 4 mm>>Of iron or nonalloy steel

The item in question has a seam, so we may disregard multiple choices "A" and "C" as these HTS are classifications for "seamless" tubes. The item in question has a wall thickness of "4 mm", so "E" may be disregarded as this classification is for a wall thickness of "less than 4 mm". The item in question is a "square" tube, so "D" is a correct description, and "B" (Of other [than square] noncircular cross section) is not a correct description. The correct answer is "D".

✓ **JUST A SIDE NOTE:** "Alloy Steel" is steel (iron and carbon) that has been mixed with other elements to create different properties such as strength, hardness, etc.

Heading/ Subheading	Stat. Suffix	Article Description	Unit of Quantity	Rates of Duty General	Rates of Duty 1 Special	Rates of Duty 2
7306 (con.)		Other tubes, pipes and hollow profiles (for example, open seamed or welded, riveted or similarly closed), of iron or steel: (con.)				
7306.50		Other, welded, of circular cross section, of other alloy steel:				
7306.50.10	00	Having a wall thickness of less than 1.65 mm.......	kg........	Free		35%
		Having a wall thickness of 1.65 mm or more:				
7306.50.30	00	Tapered pipes and tubes of steel principally used as parts of illuminating articles.................	kg........	Free		45%
7306.50.50		Other..............		Free		10%
	10	Suitable for use in boilers, superheaters, heat exchangers, condensers, refining furnaces and feedwater heaters, whether or not cold-drawn...........	kg			
	30	Other, cold-drawn or cold-rolled (cold-reduced)............	kg			
		Other:				
	50	With an outside diameter not exceeding 114.3 mm.........	kg			
	70	With an outside diameter exceeding 114.3 mm but not exceeding 406.4 mm.....	kg			
		Other, welded, of noncircular cross section:				
7306.61		Of square or rectangular cross section:				
		Having a wall thickness of 4 mm or more:				
7306.61.10	00	Of iron or nonalloy steel.............	kg........	Free		1%
7306.61.30	00	Of alloy steel............	kg........	Free		28%
		Having a wall thickness of less than 4 mm:				
7306.61.50	00	Of iron or nonalloy steel.............	kg........	Free		25%
7306.61.70		Of alloy steel............		Free		35%
	30	Of stainless steel............	kg			
	60	Other............	kg			
7306.69		Of other noncircular cross section:				
		Having a wall thickness of 4 mm or more:				
7306.69.10	00	Of iron or nonalloy steel.............	kg........	Free		1%
7306.69.30	00	Of alloy steel............	kg........	Free		28%
		Having a wall thickness of less than 4 mm:				
7306.69.50	00	Of iron or nonalloy steel.............	kg........	Free		25%
7306.69.70		Of alloy steel............		Free		35%
	30	Of stainless steel............	kg			
	60	Other............	kg			
7306.90		Other:				
7306.90.10	00	Of iron or nonalloy steel.............	kg........	Free		5.5%
7306.90.50	00	Of alloy steel............	kg........	Free		10%

38) What is the tariff classification for the auto upholstery described below, which is comprised of a polyester/cotton fabric laminated with PVC (Polyvinyl Chloride)?

- PVC – 17.82 Ounce/Square Meter
- 75% Polyester/25% Cotton – 4.22 Ounce/Square Meter

A) 5903.10.1000 Textile fabrics impregnated, coated, covered, or laminated with plastics, other than those of 5902>>With Poly(vinyl chloride)>>Of cotton

B) 5903.10.2090 Textile fabrics impregnated, coated, covered, or laminated with plastics, other than those of 5902>>With Poly(vinyl chloride)>>Of man-made fibers>>Other>>Over 70% by weight of rubber or plastics>>Other

C) 5903.10.2500 Textile fabrics impregnated, coated, covered, or laminated with plastics, other than those of 5902>>With Poly(vinyl chloride)>>Of man-made fibers>>Other>>Other

D) 5903.10.3000 Textile fabrics impregnated, coated, covered, or laminated with plastics, other than those of 5902>>With Poly(vinyl chloride)>>Other

E) 5903.20.2000 Textile fabrics impregnated, coated, covered, or laminated with plastics, other than those of 5902>>With Polyurethane>>Of man-made fibers>>Other>>Over 70% by weight of rubber or plastics

To begin with, the item in question is made predominately of Polyester (man-made fiber), so let's eliminated multiple choice "A" (of cotton) and "D" (of other). We may also disregard "E" as this classification is for laminated with "Polyurethane", while the item in question is laminated with "Polyvinyl Chloride".

Next, based on the below percentage of weight calculation, we classify the item in question as having "over 70% by weight of rubber or plastics" instead of the alternative "Other", multiple choice "C". The correct answer is "B".

  17.82 ounce/square meter PVC (plastic)
÷22.04 ounce/square meter total weight (17.82 oz. PVC + 4.22 oz. Polyester/Cotton)
= 80.9% plastic

✓ **JUST A SIDE NOTE:** Heading 5903 references "other than those of 5902". Heading 5902 is for "Tire cord fabric of high tenacity yarn of nylon or other polyamides, polyesters or viscose rayon".

Heading/ Subheading	Stat. Suffix	Article Description	Unit of Quantity	Rates of Duty General	Rates of Duty Special	2
5903		Textile fabrics impregnated, coated, covered or laminated with plastics, other than those of heading 5902:				
5903.10		With poly(vinyl chloride):				
5903.10.10	00	Of cotton.............	m² kg	2.7%	Free (A, AU, BH, CA, CL, CO, E, IL, JO, KR, MA, MX, OM, P, PA, PE, SG)	40%
		Of man-made fibers: Fabrics specified in note 9 to section XI:				
5903.10.15	00	Over 60 percent by weight of plastics............	m² kg	Free		40%
5903.10.18	00	Other (229).............	m² kg	14.1%	Free (AU, BH, CA, CL, CO, IL, JO, KR, MA, MX, OM, P, PA, PE, SG)	83.5%
		Other:				
5903.10.20		Over 70 percent by weight of rubber or plastics............		Free		25%
	10	Fabrics, of yarns sheathed with poly(vinyl chloride), not otherwise impregnated, coated, covered or laminated............	m² kg			
	90	Other............	m² kg			
5903.10.25	00	Other (229).............	m² kg	7.5%	Free (AU, BH, CA, CL, CO, IL, JO, MA, MX, OM, P, PA, PE, SG) 4.5% (KR)	84.5%
5903.10.30	00	Other.............	m² kg	2.7%	Free (AU, BH, CA, CL, CO, E*, IL, JO, KR, MA, MX, OM, P, PA, PE, SG)	40%

39) What is the tariff classification of food grade, stainless steel, 12 gallon (45 liter) tanks used for home beer brewing? These tanks are not fitted with mechanical or thermal equipment.

A) 7311.00.0090 Containers for compressed or liquefied gas, of iron or steel>>Other
B) 7309.00.0030 Reservoirs, tanks, vats and similar containers for any material (other than compressed or liquefied gas), of iron or steel, of a capacity exceeding 300 liters, whether or not lined or heat insulated, but not fitted with mechanical or thermal equipment>>Tanks
C) 7310.29.0025 Tanks, casks, drums, cans, boxes and similar containers, for any material (other than compressed or liquefied gas), of iron or steel, of a capacity not exceeding 300 liters, whether or not lined or heat insulated, but not fitted with mechanical or thermal equipment>>Of a capacity of less than 50 liters>>Other>>Containers, of circular cross section, of a volume capacity between 11.4 liters and 26.6 liters, of a kind used for the conveyance of goods
D) 7310.29.0050 Tanks, casks, drums, cans, boxes and similar containers, for any material (other than compressed or liquefied gas), of iron or steel, of a capacity not exceeding 300 liters, whether or not lined or heat insulated, but not fitted with mechanical or thermal equipment>>Of a capacity of less than 50 liters>>Other>>Other
E) 7310.10.0010 Tanks, casks, drums, cans, boxes and similar containers, for any material (other than compressed or liquefied gas), of iron or steel, of a capacity not exceeding 300 liters, whether or not lined or heat insulated, but not fitted with mechanical or thermal equipment>>Of a capacity of 50 liters or more>>Empty steel drums and barrels

This exam question is relatively straightforward. The item in question is not for gas, so let's disregard multiple choice "A". Second, the item in question is for 45 liters, so due to volumetric capacity reasons we may disregard "B" (exceeding 300 liters), "C", (between 11.4 & 26.6 liters) and "E" (50 liters or more). The correct answer is "D".

✔ **JUST A SIDE NOTE:** Although much of Chapter 73 is dedicated to supplies such as pipes, screws, bolts, etc., the chapter also includes various miscellaneous articles of iron or steel, including garment hangers, barbed wire, ladders, paint roller frames, and burial caskets to name a few.

Heading/ Subheading	Stat. Suffix	Article Description	Unit of Quantity	Rates of Duty General	Rates of Duty Special	Rates of Duty 2
7310		Tanks, casks, drums, cans, boxes and similar containers, for any material (other than compressed or liquefied gas), of iron or steel, of a capacity not exceeding 300 liters, whether or not lined or heat insulated, but not fitted with mechanical or thermal equipment:				
7310.10.00		Of a capacity of 50 liters or more..	....	Free		25%
	10	Empty steel drums and barrels...	No. kg			
	50	Other..	X			
		Of a capacity of less than 50 liters:				
7310.21.00		Cans which are to be closed by soldering or crimping...	....	Free		25%
	25	Containers, of circular cross section, of a volume capacity between 11.4 liters and 26.6 liters, of a kind used for the conveyance of goods.................	No.			
	50	Other...	No.			
7310.29.00		Other...	....	Free		25%
	25	Containers, of circular cross section, of a volume capacity between 11.4 liters and 26.6 liters, of a kind used for the conveyance of goods.................	No.			
	50	Other...	No.			
7311.00.00		Containers for compressed or liquefied gas, of iron or steel.... Certified prior to exportation to have been made in accordance with the safety requirements of sections 178.36 through 178.68 of title 49 CFR or under a specific exemption to those requirements:	....	Free		25%
	30	Seamless steel containers not overwrapped, marked DOT 3A, 3AX, 3AA, 3AAX, 3B, 3E, 3HT, 3T or DOT-E followed by a specific exemption number.....................	No. kg			
	60	Other...	No. kg			
	90	Other...	No. kg			

Category VI: Valuation

40) ABC Inc., purchases 10,000 glass vases from Overseas Trading Company. The wholesale price charged by overseas trading Company is $3 per vase with the following volume discounts. What is the transaction value for the vases?

- 1 - 1,000 vases: full price
- 1,001 - 5,000 vases: 5 % discount
- 5,001 - 15,000 vases: 10% discount
- 15,001 - 25,000 vases: 15% discount

A) $30,000
B) $29,700
C) $27,000
D) $26,730
E) $26,700

 As per 19 CFR 152.103(a):

(a) Price actually paid or payable—(1) General. **In determining transaction value, the price actually paid or payable will be considered without regard to its method of derivation. It may be the result of discounts,** *increases, or negotiations, or may be arrived at by the application of a formula, such as the price in effect on the date of export in the London Commodity Market. The word "payable" refers to a situation in which the price has been agreed upon, but actual payment has not been made at the time of importation. Payment may be made by letters of credit or negotiable instruments and may be made directly or indirectly.*
... ...
(4) Rebate. **Any rebate of, or other decrease in, the price actually paid or payable made or otherwise effected between the buyer and seller after the date of importation of the merchandise will be disregarded in determining the transaction value under** *§152.103(b).*

The transaction value for the vases is the price actually paid or payable. Assuming that the discount was made at the time of the order (i.e. BEFORE the date of importation), we calculate as per below. The correct answer is "C".

10,000 vases x $3 per vase = $30,000

Less 10% ($3,000) discount = $27,000

✓ **NOTE:** Had the discount taken place AFTER the date of importation, the transaction value would be $30,000.

41) A used mold was provided free of charge to a Korean manufacturer by the U.S. importer. The used mold cost the importer $75,000 prior to sending it to Korea. Because of its poor condition, the importer had it repaired for $2,500 before shipping the mold to Korea. The importer paid freight cost of $1,000 and the Korean manufacturer paid $500 import duty for the mold. What is the total value of the assist?

A) $75,000
B) $76,000
C) $77,500
D) $78,500
E) $79,000

 As per 19 CFR 152.103(d):

(d) Assist. If the value of an assist is to be added to the price actually paid or payable, or to be used as a component of computed value, the port director shall determine the value of the assist and apportion that value to the price of the imported merchandise in the following manner:

(1) If the assist consist of materials, components, parts, or similar items incorporated in the imported merchandise, or items consumed in the production of the imported merchandise, acquired by the buyer from an unrelated seller, the value of the assist is the cost of its acquisition. If the assist were produced by the buyer or a person related to the buyer, its value would be the cost of its production. In either case, the value of the assist would include transportation costs to the place of production.

*(2) If the assist consists of tools, dies, molds, or similar items used in the production of the imported merchandise, acquired by the buyer from an unrelated seller, the value of the assist is the cost of its acquisition. If the assist were produced by the buyer or a person related to the buyer, its value would be cost of its production. If the assist has been used previously by the buyer, regardless of whether it had been acquired or produced by him, the original cost of acquisition or production would be adjusted downward to reflect its use before its value could be determined. If the assist were leased by the buyer from an unrelated seller, the value of the assist would be the cost of the lease. In either case, **the value of the assist would include transportation costs to the place of production. Repairs or modifications to an assist may increase its value.***

$75,000 (cost of mold) + $2,500 (repairs to mold) + $1,000 (transportation) = $78,500. In terms of calculating the value of the assist, foreign duties are not included as part of the transportation cost. The correct answer is "D".

✓ **JUST A SIDE NOTE:** In regards to assists in the form of design work:

Example 1. A U.S. importer supplied detailed designs to the foreign producer. These designs were necessary to manufacture the merchandise. The U.S. importer bought the designs from an engineering company in the U.S. for submission to his foreign supplier.

Should the appraised value of the merchandise include the value of the assist?

No, design work undertaken in the U.S. may not be added to the price actually paid or payable.

42) Which of the following describes what elements may be considered for an article produced in a beneficiary country to qualify for preferential tariff treatment under the Generalized System of Preferences?

A) Only the cost or value of the materials produced in the beneficiary country

B) Only the direct costs of processing operations performed in the beneficiary country

C) The cost or value of the materials produced in the beneficiary country plus the direct costs of processing operations performed in the beneficiary country that are greater than or equal to 35% of the appraised value of the article

D) The cost or value of the materials produced in the beneficiary country plus the direct costs of processing operations performed in the beneficiary country that are less than 35% of the appraised value of the article

E) Only the cost or value of the materials produced in the United States

 As per HTSUS General Note 4(c):

*... ... Whenever an eligible article which is the growth, product, or manufacture of a designated beneficiary developing country listed in subdivision (a) of this note is imported into the customs territory of the United States directly from such country or territory, such article shall be eligible for duty-free treatment as set forth in the "Special" subcolumn, unless excluded from such treatment by subdivision (d) of this note; provided that, in accordance with regulations promulgated by the Secretary of the Treasury the sum of **(1) the cost or value of the materials produced in the beneficiary developing country** or any 2 or more countries which are members of the same association of countries which is treated as one country under section 507(2) of the Trade Act of 1974, **plus (2) the direct costs of processing operations performed in such beneficiary developing country or such member countries is not less than 35 percent of the appraised value of such article** at the time of its entry into the customs territory of the United States. No article or material of a beneficiary developing country shall be eligible for such treatment by virtue of having merely undergone simple combining or packing operations, or mere dilution with water or mere dilution with another substance that does not materially alter the characteristics of the article.*

 HTSUS General Note 4 explains the Generalized System of Preferences (GSP). The correct answer is "C".

✓ **JUST A SIDE NOTE:** As referred to in the above-mentioned excerpt from the General Note, "unless excluded from such treatment by subdivision (d) of this note" refers to certain classifications from certain beneficiary countries that are not eligible for GSP treatment. Snapshot of this subdivision (d) shown below FYI.

(d) Articles provided for in a provision for which a rate of duty of "Free" appears in the "Special" subcolumn of rate of duty column 1 followed by the symbol "A*" in parentheses, if imported from a beneficiary developing country set out opposite the provisions enumerated below, are not eligible for the duty-free treatment provided in subdivision (c) of this note:

0302.45.11	Ecuador	1702.90.35	Belize;	3923.21.00	Thailand
0302.46.11	Ecuador		Brazil	4011.10.10	Brazil;
0302.54.11	Ecuador	1702.90.40	Brazil		Indonesia;
0302.55.11	Ecuador	1703.90.30	India		Thailand

43) Which of the following is NOT an addition to the price actually paid or payable?

A) The packing cost incurred by the buyer with respect to the imported merchandise
B) Any selling commission incurred by the buyer
C) The value, apportioned as appropriate, of any assist
D) Any royalty or license fee that the buyer is required to pay as a condition of sale
E) The international freight cost incurred by the buyer

 As per 19 CFR 152.103(b):

*(b) Additions to price actually paid or payable. **(1) The transaction value of imported merchandise is the price actually paid or payable for the merchandise when sold for exportation to the United States, plus amounts equal to:***

*(i) The **packing costs** incurred by the buyer with respect to the imported merchandise;*

*(ii) Any **selling commission** incurred by the buyer with respect to the imported merchandise;*

*(iii) The value, apportioned as appropriate, of any **assist**;*

*(iv) Any **royalty or license fee** related to the imported merchandise that the buyer is required to pay, directly or indirectly, as a condition of the sale of the imported merchandise for exportation to the United States; and*

*(v) The **proceeds of any subsequent resale, disposal, or use** of the imported merchandise that accrue, directly or indirectly, to the seller.*

… ….

 Freight is not included as part of the price actually paid or payable. The correct answer is "E".

✔ **NOTE:** An easy-to-remember tool on what to add to the price actually paid or payable is to remember the acronym **"C.R.A.P.P."** (Commissions, Royalties, Assists, Packaging, Proceeds).

44) A shipment is invoiced at $100,000. The price for the merchandise includes international shipment costs, insurance costs, customs duties, and other federal taxes. The ocean freight paid is $6,000, the insurance paid is $850, the Duty rate is 6.5%, and a Harbour Maintenance Fee and Merchandise Processing Fee are paid at .125% and .3463%, respectively. What is the Transaction Value of the shipment?

A) $93,150.00
B) $87,079.35
C) $93,482.93
D) $100,000.00
E) $92,712.95

 As per 19 CFR 152.103(i):

*(i) Exclusions from transaction value. **The transaction value of imported merchandise does not include any of the following, if identified separately from the price actually paid or payable** and from any cost or other item referred to in paragraph (b) of this section:*

(1) Any reasonable cost or charge that is incurred for—

(i) The construction, erection, assembly, or maintenance of, or the technical assistance provided with respect to, the merchandise after its importation into the United States; or

(ii) The transportation of the merchandise after its importation.

*(2) **The customs duties and other Federal taxes** currently payable on the imported merchandise by reason of its importation, and any Federal excise tax on, or measured by the value of, the merchandise for which vendors in the United States ordinarily are liable.*

This is a commonly asked question on the exam, which is, how to calculate the transaction value of a shipment if the commercial invoice value includes all charges, particularly duty. First off, let's deduct for both the non-dutiable Insurance and Freight from the invoice value.

$100,000 (invoice value)
- $6,000 (freight)
- $850 (insurance)

= $93,150

Now, to back out the duty, MPF, and HMF for this DDP (Delivered Duty Paid) shipment divide this amount by the duty and fees factor of 1.069714 (1 + duty rate of 0.065 + MPF 0.003464 + HMF 0.00125)

$93,150 ÷ 1.069714 = $87,079.35 (rounded up to the nearest cent)

The correct answer is "B".

✔ **NOTE:** Remember that for formal entries, the minimum MPF amount is $25 and the maximum is $485. For the HMF, there is neither a minimum nor a maximum amount.

VII: Free Trade Agreements

45) Under the Korea Free Trade Agreement, who has primary responsibility to insure compliance on a Preferential Tariff Treatment claim?

A) Freight Forwarder
B) Customs House Broker
C) Importer
D) Producer
E) Exporter

 As per 19 CFR 10.1005(a):

*(a) General. **An importer who makes a claim for preferential tariff treatment under §10.1003(b) of this subpart:***

(1) Will be deemed to have certified that the good is eligible for preferential tariff treatment under the UKFTA;

*(2) **Is responsible for the truthfulness of the claim and of all the information and data contained in the certification** provided for in §10.1004 of this subpart; and*

(3) Is responsible for submitting any supporting documents requested by CBP, and for the truthfulness of the information contained in those documents. When a certification prepared by an exporter or producer forms the basis of a claim for preferential tariff treatment, and CBP requests the submission of supporting documents, the importer will provide to CBP, or arrange for the direct submission by the exporter or producer of, all information relied on by the exporter or producer in preparing the certification.

 The correct answer is "C".

✓ **JUST A SIDE NOTE:** 19 CFR Part 10, Subpart R (10.1001 thru. 10.1034) contains regulations for the U.S.-Korea Free Trade Agreement.

46) Which Free Trade Agreements (FTAs) examine whether a good is substantially transformed in order to determine whether it qualifies for preferential tariff treatment?

A) Korea FTA, Singapore FTA, CAFTA-DR
B) Israel, Egypt Qualifying Industrial Zone, Jordan FTA
C) Chile FTA, Panama TPA, Peru TPA
D) Australia FTA, Panama TPA
E) CAFTA-DR, Chile FTA

 As per GN 3(a)(v)(C):

(C) The term "new or different articles of commerce" means that articles must have been substantially transformed in the West Bank, the Gaza Strip or a qualifying industrial zone into articles with a new name, character or use.

 AND as per GN 3(a)(v)(G)(1):

(G) For the purposes of this paragraph, a "qualifying industrial zone" means any area that--

(1) encompasses portions of the territory of Israel and Jordan or Israel and Egypt;

 The correct answer is "B".

✔ **NOTE:** The relatively large amount of exam reference material (i.e. the HTSUS and 19 CFR) that is required to be looked up in order to answer this question makes such a potential exam question a good candidate to "skip for now and return to later".

47) When importing goods into the U.S., and preferential tariff treatment is claimed under the U.S. Morocco Free Trade Agreement (MFTA), which General Note and Authority are applicable to that program?

A) General Note 26 and 19 CFR 10.401-490 (Subpart H)
B) General Note 12 and 19 CFR 181 and Appendix 19 CFR 102
C) General Note 25 and 19 CFR 10.501-570 (Subpart L)
D) General Note 27 and 19 CFR 10.761-781 (Subpart M)
E) General Note 18 and 19 CFR 10.701-712 (Subpart K)

 As per GN 27:

27 United States-Morocco Free Trade Agreement Implementation Act.

(a) Originating goods under the terms of the United States-Morocco Free Trade Agreement (UMFTA) are subject to duty as provided for herein. For the purposes of this note, goods of Morocco, as defined in subdivisions (b) through (h) of this note, that are imported into the customs territory of the United States and entered under a provision for which a rate of duty appears in the "Special" subcolumn of column 1 followed by the symbol "MA" in parentheses are eligible for the tariff treatment and quantitative limitations set forth in the "Special" subcolumn, in accordance with sections 201 through 203, inclusive, of the United States-Morocco Free Trade Agreement Implementation Act (Pub. L. 108-302; 118 Stat. 1103). For the purposes of this note, the term "UMFTA country" refers only to Morocco or to the United States.
... ...

 AND as per 19 CFR, Part 10, Subpart M

Subpart M—United States-Morocco Free Trade Agreement

General Provisions
§10.761 Scope.
§10.762 General definitions.
... ...

Origin Verifications and Determinations
§10.784 Verification and justification of claim for preferential treatment.
§10.785 Issuance of negative origin determinations.

Penalties
§10.786 Violations relating to the MFTA.

Goods Returned After Repair or Alteration
§10.787 Goods re-entered after repair or alteration in Morocco.

 The correct answer is "D".

✓ **NOTE:** Currently, the U.S.-Morocco FTA is covered under 19 CFR parts 10.761-10.**787** (not 10.761-**781**).

48) Where in the HTS can the general "NAFTA Change in Tariff Classification Rules" be located?

A) 19 CFR Part 102
B) Chapter Notes
C) General Note 12
D) General Note 3
E) General Note 5

As per GN 12(t):

12. North American Free Trade Agreement.

(a) Goods originating in the territory of a party to the North American Free Trade Agreement (NAFTA) are subject to duty as provided herein. For the purposes of this note--
... ...

(t) Change in Tariff Classification Rules.

Chapter 1

A change to headings 0101 through 0106 from any other chapter

Chapter 2

A change to headings 0201 through 0210 from any other chapter.
....

The correct answer is "C".

✓ **JUST A SIDE NOTE:** Here's an illustration of the above-mentioned NAFTA Change in Tariff Classification Rules. Using HTSUS Chapter 2 (Meat and Edible Meat Offal) as an example, a change (i.e. transformation) occurring in a NAFTA country to heading 0201 (Meat of bovine animals, fresh or chilled) through heading 0210 (meat and edible meat offal, salted, in brine, dried or smoked; edible flours and meals of meat offal) of non-NAFTA inputs from any other Chapter of the HTSUS would result in the imported item qualifying for NAFTA special treatment.

49) CBP issued a Request for Information to an importer for a valid NAFTA Certificate of Origin for an entry in which a duty free claim under the NAFTA was made. The importer failed to produce the Certificate of Origin. Which of the following is true concerning possible penalty action by CBP?

A) The importer is not subject to a recordkeeping penalty because only the exporter is required to retain the NAFTA Certificate of Origin.

B) The importer is not subject to a recordkeeping penalty because the NAFTA Certificate of Origin is not on the "(a)(1)(A) list".

C) If CBP liquidates the entry without NAFTA duty preference, CBP cannot also issue a penalty.

D) The importer may be subject to a recordkeeping penalty for failure to comply with the lawful demand.

E) CBP may issue a penalty only after serving a Customs summons in addition to the Request for Information.

 As per 19 CFR 163.6(b):

(b) Failure to produce entry records—(1) Monetary penalties applicable. The following penalties may be imposed if a person fails to comply with a lawful demand for the production of an entry record and is not excused from a penalty pursuant to paragraph (b)(3) of this section:
... ...

 The correct answer is "D".

✓ **NOTE:** The NAFTA Certificate of Origin (CBP Form 434) is completed by the Canadian or Mexican exporter, but recordkeeping responsibilities of the certificate are that of the U.S. importer.

50) The Certificate of Origin must be in the importer's possession at the time of entry when making a _____ claim.

A) US-Korean Free Trade Agreement (UKFTA)
B) US-Morocco Free Trade Agreement (UMFTA)
C) US-Chile Free Trade Agreement (CFTA)
D) North American Free Trade Agreement (NAFTA)
E) Dominican Republic-Central America-US Free Trade Agreement (CAFTA)

 As per 19 CFR 181.21(a):

181.21 Filing of claim for preferential tariff treatment upon importation.

(a) Declaration. **In connection with a claim for preferential tariff treatment, or for the exemption from the merchandise processing fee, for a good under the NAFTA, the U.S. importer must make a formal declaration that the good qualifies for such treatment.** *The declaration may be made by including on the entry summary, or equivalent documentation, including electronic submissions, the symbol "CA" for a good of Canada, or the symbol "MX" for a good of Mexico, as a prefix to the subheading of the HTSUS under which each qualifying good is classified. Except as otherwise provided in 19 CFR 181.22 and except in the case of a good to which Appendix 6.B to Annex 300-B of the NAFTA applies (see also 19 CFR 102.25),* **the declaration must be based on a complete and properly executed original Certificate of Origin, or copy thereof, which is in the possession of the importer and which covers the good being imported.**

 The correct answer is "D".

✓ **JUST A SIDE NOTE:** The 19 CFR 181.22(b) paragraph, which immediately follows the above-mentioned paragraph, provides instructions on how to proceed if a NAFTA was incorrectly claimed on an entry.

(b) Corrected declaration. If, after making the declaration required under paragraph (a) of this section or under §181.32(b)(2) of this part, the U.S. importer has reason to believe that a Certificate of Origin on which a declaration was based contains information that is not correct, the importer shall within 30 calendar days after the date of discovery of the error make a corrected declaration and pay any duties that may be due. A corrected declaration shall be effected by submission of a letter or other written statement to the CBP office where the original declaration was filed.

VIII: Drawback

51) Which of the following is NOT a type of drawback entry?

A) Direct identification manufacturing
B) Direct identification unused merchandise
C) Substitution modified merchandise
D) Substitution manufacturing
E) Substitution of finished petroleum derivatives

 As per 19 CFR 191.21:

Subpart B—Manufacturing Drawback

191.21   Direct identification drawback.

 AND as per 19 CFR 191.31:

Subpart C—Unused Merchandise Drawback

191.31   Direct identification.

 AND as per 19 CFR 191.22:

Subpart B—Manufacturing Drawback

191.21   Direct identification drawback.
191.22   Substitution drawback.

 AND as per 19 CFR 191.171:

Subpart Q—Substitution of Finished Petroleum Derivatives

191.171   General; drawback allowance.

 "Substitution Modified Merchandise" is not an actual type of (U.S.) drawback entry. The correct answer is "C".

✔ **JUST A SIDE NOTE:** "Duty Drawback" is the "drawback" of already paid customs duties upon the exportation (or otherwise disposal) of the drawback item.

52) Based on the information below, what is the claimed amount for the merchandise processing fee (MPF) on an Unused Direct Identification 1313(j)(1) drawback claim?

- Imported merchandise:
  - 500 bikes ($200 per unit) $100,000
  - 500 spare parts ($175 per unit) $87,500
  - Invoice value $187,500
  - Less Non-Dutiable Charges (NDC) -$2,500
  - Total Entered Value $185,000
  - Total MPF paid $485.00
  - MPF rate .3464%

- Exported merchandise for drawback purposes: 200 bikes

A) $103.47
B) $102.43
C) $138.56
D) $137.17
E) $480.15

 As per 19 CFR 191.51 (b)(2)(iv)

(b) Drawback due—(1) Claimant required to calculate drawback. Drawback claimants are required to correctly calculate the amount of drawback due. The amount of drawback requested on the drawback entry is generally to be 99 percent of the import duties eligible for drawback. (For example, if $1,000 in import duties are eligible for drawback less 1 percent ($10), the amount claimed on the drawback entry should be for $990.) Claims exceeding 99 percent (or 100% when 100% of the duty is available for drawback) will not be paid until the calculations have been corrected by the claimant. Claims for less than 99 percent (or 100% when 100% of the duty is available for drawback) will be paid as filed, unless the claimant amends the claim in accordance with §191.52(c).

(2) Merchandise processing fee apportionment calculation. Where a drawback claimant seeks unused merchandise drawback pursuant to 19 U.S.C. 1313(j), or drawback for substitution of finished petroleum derivatives pursuant to 19 U.S.C. 1313(p)(2)(A)(iii) or (iv), for a merchandise processing fee paid pursuant to 19 U.S.C. 58c(a)(9)(A), the claimant is required to correctly apportion the fee to that merchandise that provides the basis for drawback when calculating the amount of drawback requested on the drawback entry. This is determined as follows:

(i) Relative value ratio for each line item. The value of each line item of entered merchandise subject to a merchandise processing fee is calculated (to four decimal places) by dividing the value of the line item subject to the fee by the total value of entered merchandise subject to the fee. The resulting value forms the relative value ratio.

(ii) Merchandise processing fee apportioned to each line item. To apportion the merchandise processing fee to each line item, the relative value ratio for each line item is multiplied by the merchandise processing fee paid.

(iii) Amount of merchandise processing fee eligible for drawback per line item. The amount of merchandise processing fee apportioned to each line item is multiplied by 99 percent to calculate that portion of the fee attributable to each line item that is eligible for drawback.

(iv) Amount of merchandise processing fee eligible for drawback per unit of merchandise. To calculate the amount of a merchandise processing fee eligible for drawback per unit of merchandise, the line item amount that is eligible for drawback is divided by the number of units covered by that line item (to two decimal places).

Example 1:

Line item 1—5,000 articles valued at $10 each total $50,000

Line item 2—6,000 articles valued at $15 each total $90,000

Line item 3—10,000 articles valued at $20 each total $200,000

Total units = 21,000

Total value = $340,000

Merchandise processing fee = $485 (for purposes of this example, the fee cap of $485, as per 19 U.S.C. 58c(a)(9)(B)(i), is applicable).

Line item relative value ratios. The relative value ratio for line item 1 is calculated by dividing the value of that line item by the total value ($50,000 ÷ 340,000 = .1470). The relative value ratio for line item 2 is .2647. The relative value ratio for line item 3 is .5882.

Merchandise processing fee apportioned to each line item. The amount of fee attributable to each line item is calculated by multiplying $485 by the applicable relative value ratio. The amount of the $485 fee attributable to line item 1 is $71.295 (.1470 × $485 = $71.295). The amount of the fee attributable to line item 2 is $128.3795 (.2647 × $485 = $128.3795). The amount of the fee attributable to line item 3 is $285.277 (.5882 × $485 = $285.277).

Amount of merchandise processing fee eligible for drawback per line item. The amount of merchandise processing fee eligible for drawback for line item 1 is $70.5821 ÷ (.99 × $71.295). The amount of fee eligible for drawback for line item 2 is $127.0957 (.99 × $128.3795). The amount of fee eligible for drawback for line item 3 is $282.4242 (.99 × $285.277).

Amount of merchandise processing fee eligible for drawback per unit of merchandise. The amount of merchandise processing fee eligible for drawback per unit of merchandise is calculated by dividing the amount of fee eligible for drawback for the line item by the number of units in the line item. For line item 1, the amount of merchandise processing fee eligible for drawback per unit is $.0141 ($70.5821 ÷ 5,000 = $.0141). If 1,000 widgets form the basis of a claim for drawback under 19 U.S.C. 1313(j), the total amount of drawback attributable to the merchandise processing fee is $14.10 (1,000 × .0141 = $14.10). For line item 2, the amount of fee eligible for drawback per unit is $.0212 ($127.0957 ÷ 6,000 = $.0212). For line item 3, the amount of fee eligible for drawback per unit is $.0282 ($282.4242 ÷ 10,000 = $.0282).

Example 2: This example illustrates the treatment of dutiable merchandise that is exempt from the merchandise processing fee and duty-free merchandise that is subject to the merchandise processing fee.

Line item 1—700 meters of printed cloth valued at $10 per meter (total value $7,000) that is exempt from the merchandise processing fee under 19 U.S.C. 58c(b)(8)(B)(iii)

Line item 2—15,000 articles valued at $100 each (total value $1,500,000)

Line item 3—10,000 duty-free articles valued at $50 each (total value $500,000)

The relative value ratios are calculated using line items 2 and 3 only, as there is no merchandise processing fee imposed by reason of importation on line item 1.

Line item 2—1,500,000 ÷ 2,000,000 = .75 (line items 2 and 3 form the total value of the merchandise subject to the merchandise processing fee).

Line item 3—500,000 ÷ 2,000,000 = .25.

If the total merchandise processing fee paid was $485, the amount of the fee attributable to line item 2 is $363.75 (.75 × $485 = $363.75). The amount of the fee attributable to line item 3 is $121.25 (.25 × $485 = $121.25).

The amount of merchandise processing fee eligible for drawback for line item 2 is $360.1125 (.99 × $363.75). The amount of fee eligible for line item 3 is $120.0375 (.99 × $121.25).

The amount of drawback on the merchandise processing fee attributable to each unit of line item 2 is $.0240 ($360.1125 ÷ 15,000 = $.0240). The amount of drawback on the merchandise processing fee attributable to each unit of line item 3 is $.0120 ($120.0375 ÷ 10,000 = $.0120).

If 1,000 units of line item 2 were exported, the drawback attributable to the merchandise processing fee is $24.00 ($.0240 × 1,000 = $24.00).

 Relative value ratio for bikes line item: $100,000 (bikes invoice value) ÷ $187,500 (invoice value) = 0.5333

MPF apportioned to bikes line item: 0.5333 (above relative value ratio) x $485 (MPF paid) = $258.65

MPF eligible for drawback for bikes: $258.65 (above) x 0.99 (drawback %) = 256.06

MPF eligible for drawback per unit: $256.06 (above) ÷ 500 (bikes imported) = $0.5121

Drawback on MPF: $0.5121 (above) x 200 (bikes exported) = $102.42

The fact that Non-Dutiable Charges were deducted from the invoice values at the time of the import entry does not affect the relative value ratio of the line items. The above calculation is 1 cent different from the value given in the exam answer key, but this is close enough to deduce that the correct answer is "B".

✓ **JUST A SIDE NOTE:** "NDC" stands for "Non-Dutiable Charges". They include freight, insurance, etc., which are deducted from the invoice value to calculate entered value. On the other side of the coin, "MMV" stands for "Make Market Value". This includes assists, etc. which are added to the invoice value to calculate entered value.

53) Merchandise processing fees are only subject to drawback for merchandise processing fees for _____.

A) indirect identification of unused merchandise
B) substitution of used merchandise
C) substitution of finished petroleum
D) rejected merchandise
E) substitution of indirect used merchandise

 As per 19 CFR 191.3(b):

(b) Duties and fees not subject to drawback include:

(1) Harbor maintenance fee (see §24.24 of this chapter);

(2) Merchandise processing fees (see §24.23 of this chapter), except where unused merchandise drawback pursuant to 19 U.S.C. 1313(j) or drawback for substitution of finished petroleum derivatives pursuant to 19 U.S.C. 1313(p)(2)(A)(iii) or (iv) is claimed; and

(3) Antidumping and countervailing duties on merchandise entered, or withdrawn from warehouse, for consumption on or after August 23, 1988.

 The correct answer is "C".

✓ **JUST A SIDE NOTE:** "Petroleum Derivatives" are products that are "derived" from petroleum (crude oil), such as gasoline, tar, lubricating oils, etc.

54) Which CBP form is required to request a drawback claim?

A) CBP Form 7551
B) CBP Form 5106
C) CBP Form 301
D) CBP Form 3124
E) CBP Form 19

 As per 19 CFR 191.51(a)(1):

191.51 Completion of drawback claims.

(a) General—(1) Complete claim. **Unless otherwise specified, a complete drawback claim under this part shall consist of the drawback entry on Customs Form 7551**, applicable certificate(s) of manufacture and delivery, applicable Notice(s) of Intent to Export, Destroy, or Return Merchandise for Purposes of Drawback, applicable import entry number(s), coding sheet unless the data is filed electronically, and evidence of exportation or destruction under subpart G of this part.

 The correct answer is "A".

✓ **JUST A SIDE NOTE:** Page 1 of Customs form 7551 looks like this…

IX: Antidumping and Countervailing Duties

55) Company A imported seven ball bearings with integral shafts from Germany, which are classified under subheading 8482.10.10, Harmonized Tariff Schedule of the United States, at a 2.4% ad valorem duty rate and subject to antidumping duties. The ball bearings are shipped by air and formally entered at John F. Kennedy International Airport. The total value of the shipment is $7,598.00. The applicable antidumping duty cash deposit rate is 68.89%. What are the total amount of fees and estimated duties that should be reported on CBP Form 7501?

A) $5,260.58
B) $5,234.26
C) $5,416.61
D) $5,442.93
E) $208.67

 As per 19 CFR 24.23(b):

*(b) Fees—(1) Formal entry or release—(i) Ad valorem fee—(A) General. Except as provided in paragraph (c) of this section, **merchandise that is formally entered or released is subject to the payment to CBP of an ad valorem fee of 0.3464 percent**. The 0.3464 ad valorem fee is due and payable to CBP by the importer of record of the merchandise at the time of presentation of the entry summary and is based on the value of the merchandise as determined under 19 U.S.C. 1401a. In the case of an express consignment carrier facility or centralized hub facility, each shipment covered by an individual air waybill or bill of lading that is formally entered and valued at $2,500 or less is subject to a $1.00 per individual air waybill or bill of lading fee and, if applicable, to the 0.3464 percent ad valorem fee in accordance with paragraph (b)(4) of this section.*

*(B) Maximum and minimum fees. Subject to the provisions of paragraphs (b)(1)(ii) and (d) of this section relating to the surcharge and to aggregation of the ad valorem fee respectively, the ad valorem fee charged under paragraph (b)(1)(i)(A) of this section **must not exceed $485 and must not be less than $25.***
... ...

The question asks for the total amount of FEES (keyword) AND DUTIES (keywords). So, we can simply add up all of the duties and fees (including MPF) percentages and then multiply that total rate by the shipment's value.

0.716364 combined duties and fees rate (0.024 duty rate + 0.6889 antidumping rate + 0.003464 MPF rate)
x $7598.00 entered value
= $5,442.93

The correct answer is "D".

✓ **JUST A SIDE NOTE:** An entered value of $7,217.09 (or less) is charged the minimum MPF of $25. An entered value of more than 7,217.09 is charged at the 0.003464 MPF rate.

Math: $25.00 ÷ 0.003463 = $7,217.09

56) Brown Industries imported a shipment of taper roller bearings manufactured by Beijin Bearings in Shenzhen, China. The taper roller bearings are exported by Seoul Enterprise, a company incorporated in South Korea, and are used in various automotive engine parts. Taper roller bearings are specifically classified under 8482.20.00. The Department of Commerce has instructed CBP to collect antidumping duty cash deposits at a rate of 115% for all shipments of taper roller bearings manufactured by Beijin Bearings. The Department of Commerce has further instructed CBP to apply the "country-wide rate" of 45% for all shipments of taper roller bearings manufactured by Chinese companies with no established individual cash deposit rates. Further, the scope of the order excludes taper roller bearings used in the manufacture of exercise equipment and home appliances. What is the antidumping duty cash deposit rate collected for Brown Industries' shipment of taper roller bearings?

A) Do not collect antidumping duties because these taper roller bearings were exported by a Korean company

B) 45%

C) 115%

D) Do not assess antidumping duties because these bearings are excluded from the scope of the antidumping duty order

E) 160%

 As per 19 CFR 351.107(b):

(b) Cash deposit rates for nonproducing exporters—(1) Use of combination rates—(i) In general. In the case of subject merchandise that is exported to the United States by a company that is not the producer of the merchandise, the Secretary may establish a "combination" cash deposit rate for each combination of the exporter and its supplying producer(s).
... ...

(2) New supplier. In the case of subject merchandise that is exported to the United States by a company that is not the producer of the merchandise, if the Secretary has not established previously a combination cash deposit rate under paragraph (b)(1)(i) of this section for the exporter and producer in question or a noncombination rate for the exporter in question, the Secretary will apply the cash deposit rate established for the producer. If the Secretary has not previously established a cash deposit rate for the producer, the Secretary will apply the "all-others rate" described in section 705(c)(5) or section 735(c)(5) of the Act, as the case may be.

Taper roller bearings made by Beijin Bearings are already specifically assigned an individual cash deposit rate of 115% by the Department of Commerce. Thus, the "all others" country-wide rate of 45% for the same item manufactured by un-named Chinese companies does not additionally or otherwise apply. These bearings are used in automotive engine parts (not exercise equipment and home appliances) and so they are NOT excluded from the scope of the antidumping order. The correct answer is "C".

✓ **JUST A SIDE NOTE:** The above-mentioned Part 351 of Title 19 CFR is in Chapter III of title 19, and regulated by the Department of Commerce. Parts 0 thru 199 of 19 CFR are in Chapter I of title 19, and regulated by the Department of Homeland Security.

57) A (n) _____ is required prior to liquidation of an antidumping/countervailing liquidation order.

A) certificate of manufacturing
B) sales receipt
C) reimbursement certificate
D) meeting with Import Specialists
E) invoice

 As per 19 CFR 351.402(f):

... ...

(2) Certificate. **The importer must file prior to liquidation a certificate in the following form with the appropriate District Director of Customs:**

I hereby certify that I (have) (have not) entered into any agreement or understanding for the payment or for the refunding to me, by the manufacturer, producer, seller, or exporter, of all or any part of the antidumping duties or countervailing duties assessed upon the following importations of (commodity) from (country): (List entry numbers) which have been purchased on or after (date of publication of antidumping notice suspending liquidation in the Federal Register) or purchased before (same date) but exported on or after (date of final determination of sales at less than fair value).

(3) Presumption. **The Secretary may presume from an importer's failure to file the certificate required in paragraph (f)(2) of this section that the exporter or producer paid or reimbursed the antidumping duties or countervailing duties.**

 The correct answer is "C".

✓ **JUST A SIDE NOTE:** The above-mentioned antidumping/countervailing (non-reimbursement declaration) statement is commonly issued as a blanket statement and good for one year.

Category X: Marking

58) Mr. Smith contacts your brokerage from the Customs area at the local international airport. He has just flown in from the UK and was attempting to bring in new Scottish 100% wool sweaters to sell at his new store. The sweaters were examined by CBP, and while an appropriate country of origin label was found, Mr. Smith was told that the sweaters were not properly labeled with the fiber content of the material. Which of the following actions should the local CBP cargo office take?

A) The sweaters should be released to Mr. Smith because no labeling is needed due to the exemption of wool wearing apparel.

B) The sweaters should be released to Mr. Smith because the textiles of the sweaters are not 50% or more manmade materials, and therefore, are exempt from marking.

C) The sweaters must be returned to the UK and cannot be imported in their current condition.

D) The sweaters should be released to Mr. Smith, but he will have to label the sweaters at his own expense under Customs supervision.

E) The sweaters should be released to Mr. Smith, but a 10% marking duty should be assessed against Mr. Smith.

 As per 19 CFR 11.12(b):

(b) If imported wool products are not correctly labeled and the port director is satisfied that the error or omission involved no fraud or willful neglect, the importer shall be afforded a reasonable opportunity to label the merchandise under Customs supervision to conform with the requirements of such act and the rules and regulations of the Federal Trade Commission. The compensation and expenses of Customs officers and employees assigned to supervise the labeling shall be reimbursed to the Government and shall be assessed in the same manner as in the case of marking of country of origin, §134.55 of this chapter.

 The correct answer is "D".

✓ **JUST A SIDE NOTE:** If the above-mentioned labeling nonconformity was fraudulent, rather than inadvertent, then Customs could have seized the merchandise.

59) Which of the following articles are exempted from country of origin marking requirements, according to the General Exceptions to marking requirements under 19 CFR 134.32?

A) Articles that are incapable of being marked; articles that cannot be marked prior to shipment to the United States without injury; articles which are crude substances; and articles imported for use by the importer and not intended for sale

B) All articles have to be marked; no exceptions

C) Articles from the parent company abroad do not require markings; shipments under $1500 do not require marking

D) You may apply for a marking waiver; small businesses are not required to provide markings

E) Household articles; the first importation does not have to be marked

 As per 19 CFR 134.32:

134.32 General exceptions to marking requirements.

The articles described or meeting the specified conditions set forth below are excepted from marking requirements (see subpart C of this part for marking of the containers):

(a) Articles that are incapable of being marked;

(b) Articles that cannot be marked prior to shipment to the United States without injury;

(c) Articles that cannot be marked prior to shipment to the United States except at an expense economically prohibitive of its importation;

(d) Articles for which the marking of the containers will reasonably indicate the origin of the articles;

(e) Articles which are crude substances;

(f) Articles imported for use by the importer and not intended for sale in their imported or any other form;

(g) Articles to be processed in the United States by the importer or for his account otherwise than for the purpose of concealing the origin of such articles and in such manner that any mark contemplated by this part would necessarily be obliterated, destroyed, or permanently concealed;

... ...

 The correct answer is "A".

✔ **JUST A SIDE NOTE:** In addition to CBP product marking requirements, other U.S. agencies (also known as Partner Government Agencies [PGA]) have their own marking requirements, depending on the product. These agencies include the FCC, FDA, among others.

60) Which of the following are NOT exempt from country of origin marking requirements?

A) Cards, playing
B) Bearings, ball, ½ inch in diameter
C) Weights, analytical and precision in sets
D) Flowers, artificial, bunches
E) Shingles (fir wood), bundles of

 As per 19 CFR 134.33:

134.33 J-List exceptions.

Articles of a class or kind listed below are excepted from the requirements of country of origin marking in accordance with the provisions of section 304(a)(3)(J), Tariff Act of 1930, as amended (19 U.S.C. 1304(a)(3)(J)). However, in the case of any article described in this list which is imported in a container, the outermost container in which the article ordinarily reaches the ultimate purchaser is required to be marked to indicate the origin of its contents in accordance with the requirements of subpart C of this part. All articles are listed in Treasury Decisions 49690, 49835, and 49896. A reference different from the foregoing indicates an amendment.

Articles	*References*
Bearings, ball, 5/8-inch or less in diameter.	
Cards, playing.	
*Flowers, artificial, **except bunches**.*	
Shingles (wood), bundles of (except bundles of red-cedar shingles)	
Weights, analytical and precision in sets	*T.D.s 49750; 51802.*

 The correct answer is "D".

✓ **NOTE:** The above J-List Exceptions Table is a truncated version of the origin in the regulations. The actual table includes over 80 items.

61) Which of the following examples constitutes a substantial transformation for purposes of country of origin marking?

A) Copper wire that is sent from Korea and coated in Canada

B) A nail lacquer base of Vietnam origin is further manufactured in Taiwan with colorants and other essential ingredients

C) Bulk body powder from the United States is sent to China, where it is measured and encased inside the powder puff

D) Chinese woven fabrics that are imported into the United States where it will be cut and sewn into women's and girls' pants, jackets, blouses, dresses, and skirts

E) An unfinished hand stamp without its die from Hong Kong; the die will be put on the stamp in Mexico

 As per 19 CFR 134.1(b):

(b) Country of origin. "Country of origin" means the country of manufacture, production, or growth of any article of foreign origin entering the United States. **Further work or material added to an article in another country must effect a substantial transformation in order to render such other country the "country of origin" within the meaning of this part**; *however, for a good of a NAFTA country, the NAFTA Marking Rules will determine the country of origin.*

Although the application of the term "substantial transformation" may be somewhat of a subjective (rather than objective) endeavor, I believe most would agree that of the five multiple choice options, "D" describes a more substantial transformation relative to the others'. The correct answer is "D".

✔ **JUST A SIDE NOTE:** "NAFTA Marking Rules" are rules that determine whether a product is of a NAFTA country of origin.

Category XI: Broker Compliance

62) A broker is permitted to conduct Customs business in the ports of Las Vegas, Nevada and Los Angeles, California. The licensed individual for the Los Angeles district permit leaves the brokerage. How long does the brokerage have to replace that individual before the district permit can be revoked?

A) 60 days
B) 90 days
C) 120 days
D) 150 days
E) 180 days

 As per 19 CFR 111.45(b):

*(b) Permit. **If a broker who has been granted a permit for an additional district fails, for any continuous period of 180 days, to employ within that district** (or region, as defined in §111.1, if an exception has been granted pursuant to §111.19(d)) **at least one person who holds a valid individual broker's license, that failure will, in addition to any other sanction that may be imposed under this part, result in the revocation of the permit** by operation of law.*

 The correct answer is "E".

✓ **JUST A SIDE NOTE:** The above question and answer is in regards to a business' "permit". In terms of a business' "license", the time frame is 120 days.

63) When must Form 3347, Declaration of Owner, be filed?

A) Within 90 days from the time of entry
B) At the time of entry
C) Any time before final liquidation
D) Within 180 days from the time of entry
E) When the entry summary is filed

 As per 19 CFR 141.20(a):

141.20 Actual owner's declaration and superseding bond of actual owner.

*(a) Filing—(1) Declaration of owner. A consignee in whose name an entry summary for consumption, warehouse, or temporary importation under bond is filed, or in whose name a rewarehouse entry or a manufacturing warehouse entry is made, and who desires, under the provisions of section 485(d), Tariff Act of 1930, as amended (19 U.S.C. 1485(d)), to be relieved from statutory liability for the payment of increased and additional duties shall declare at the time of the filing of the entry summary or entry documentation, as provided in §141.19(a), that he is not the actual owner of the merchandise, furnish the name and address of the owner, and **file with the port director within 90 days from the time of entry (see §141.68)** a declaration of the actual owner of the merchandise acknowledging that the actual owner will pay all additional and increased duties. The declaration of owner shall be filed on Customs Form 3347.*

 The correct answer is "A".

✓ **JUST A SIDE NOTE:** Customs Form 3347 snapshot below:

64) A _____ must be presented to CBP to receive a CBP-Assigned Importer identification number.

A) CBP Form 3461
B) CBP Form 6043
C) CBP Form 5106
D) CBP Form 7501
E) CBP Form 3495

 As per 19 CFR 24.5(c):

(c) Assignment of importer identification number. Upon receipt of a Customs Form 5106 without an Internal Revenue Service employer identification number or a Social Security number, an importer identification number shall be assigned and entered on the Customs Form 5106 by the Customs office where the entry or request for services is received. The duplicate copy of the form shall be returned to the filing party. This identification number shall be used in all future Customs transactions when an importer number is required. If an Internal Revenue Service employer identification number, a Social Security number, or both, are obtained after an importer number has been assigned by Customs, a new Customs Form 5106 shall not be filed unless requested by Customs.

 The correct answer is "C".

✓ **JUST A SIDE NOTE:** Snapshot of Custom Form 5106 below:

65) Which part of 19 CFR _____ addresses Inspection, Search and Seizure?

A) 134
B) 133
C) 162
D) 128
E) 112

 As per 19 CFR 162.0:

PART 162—INSPECTION, SEARCH, AND SEIZURE

162.0 Scope.

This part contains provisions for the inspection, examination, and search of persons, vessels, aircraft, vehicles, and merchandise involved in importation, for the seizure of property, and for the forfeiture and sale of seized property. It also contains provisions for Customs enforcement of the controlled substances laws. Additional provisions concerning records maintenance and examination applicable to U.S. importers, exporters and producers under the U.S.-Chile Free Trade Agreement, the U.S.-Singapore Free Trade Agreement, the Dominican Republic-Central America-U.S. Free Trade Agreement, the U.S.-Australia Free Trade Agreement, the U.S.-Morocco Free Trade Agreement, the U.S.-Peru Trade Promotion Agreement, the U.S.-Korea Free Trade Agreement, the U.S.-Panama Trade Promotion Agreement, and the U.S.-Colombia Trade Promotion Agreement are contained in Part 10, Subparts H, I, J, L, M, Q, R, S and T of this chapter, respectively.

 The correct answer is "C".

✓ **JUST A SIDE NOTE:** 19 CFR Part 162 is subdivided into eight subparts:

Subpart A—INSPECTION, EXAMINATION, AND SEARCH
Subpart B—SEARCH WARRANTS
Subpart C—SEIZURES
Subpart D—PROCEDURE WHEN FINE, PENALTY, OR FORFEITURE INCURRED
Subpart E—TREATMENT OF SEIZED MERCHANDISE
Subpart F—CONTROLLED SUBSTANCES, NARCOTICS, AND MARIHUANA
Subpart G—SPECIAL PROCEDURES FOR CERTAIN VIOLATIONS
Subpart H—CIVIL ASSET FORFEITURE REFORM ACT

66) How long does a protestant have to file a summons in the Court of International Trade, once the protestant is denied?

A) 60 days
B) 180 days
C) 314 days
D) 2 years
E) 90 days

 As per 19 CFR 174.31:

Any person whose protest has been denied, in whole or in part, may contest the denial by filing a civil action in the United States Court of International Trade in accordance with 28 U.S.C. 2632 within 180 days after—

(a) The date of mailing of notice of denial, in whole or in part, of a protest,

(b) The date a protest, for which accelerated disposition was requested, is deemed to have been denied in accordance with §174.22(d), or

(c) The date that a protest is deemed denied in accordance with §174.21(b), or §151.16(g) of this chapter.

 The correct answer is "B".

✓ **JUST A SIDE NOTE:** A protest to CBP must be filed within 180 days from the entry liquidation date.

Category XII: Fines and Penalties

67) Disclosure of the circumstances of a violation under 19 USC 1592 means the act of providing to Customs a statement either orally or in writing that:

A) Provides a general overview of a suspected violation of 19 USC 1592 that includes a listing of the ports of entry involved; the class or kind of merchandise involved in the violation; and a request for additional time to provide specific details of the violation

B) Identifies the class or kind of merchandise involved in the violation; identifies the importation or drawback claim included in the disclosure by entry number or by indicating each concerned Customs port of entry and the approximate dates of entry or dates of drawback claim; specifies the material false statements, omissions or acts, including an explanation as to how and when they occurred; sets forth, to the best of the disclosing party's knowledge, the true and accurate information or data that should have been provided in the entry or drawback claim documents and states that the disclosing party will provide any information or data unknown at the time of the disclosure within 30 days of the initial disclosure date

C) Provides a statement that the company is researching a possible violation of 19 USC 1592 and is submitting a letter advising CBP that it intends to file a prior disclosure within 30 days of the letter's submission to CBP

D) Identifies the class or kind of merchandise involved in the violation; identifies the importation or drawback claim included in the disclosure by entry number or by indicating each concerned Customs port of entry and the approximate dates of entry or dates of drawback claim; specifies the material false statements, omissions or acts, including an explanation as to how and when they occurred

E) Provides a listing of entry numbers, ports of entry and dates of the violation, and a request for a 30 day extension to provide remaining details

 As per 19 CFR 162.74(b):

(b) Disclosure of the circumstances of a violation. The term "discloses the circumstances of a violation" means the act of providing to Customs a statement orally or in writing that:

(1) Identifies the class or kind of merchandise involved in the violation;

(2) Identifies the importation or drawback claim included in the disclosure by entry number, drawback claim number, or by indicating each concerned Customs port of entry and the approximate dates of entry or dates of drawback claims;

(3) Specifies the material false statements, omissions or acts including an explanation as to how and when they occurred; and

(4) Sets forth, to the best of the disclosing party's knowledge, the true and accurate information or data that should have been provided in the entry or drawback claim documents, and states that the disclosing party will provide any information or data unknown at the time of disclosure within 30 days of the initial disclosure date. Extensions of the 30-day period may be requested by the disclosing party from the concerned Fines, Penalties, and Forfeitures Officer to enable the party to obtain the information or data.

 The correct answer is "B".

68) A petition for relief from penalties must be filed within ____ days of the mailing of the notice of penalty incurred.

A) 30
B) 60
C) 45
D) 90
E) 15

 As per 19 CFR 171.2(b):

171.2 Filing a petition.

(a) Where filed. A petition for relief must be filed with the Fines, Penalties, and Forfeitures office whose address is given in the notice.

(b) When filed—(1) Seizures. Petitions for relief from seizures must be filed within 30 days from the date of mailing of the notice of seizure.

(2) Penalties. Petitions for relief from penalties must be filed within 60 days of the mailing of the notice of penalty incurred.

 The correct answer is "B".

✓ **JUST A SIDE NOTE:** In general, both Protests AND Petitions are filed on a Customs Form 19.

69) **When submitting an Offer in Compromise on behalf of a client to settle a claim for liquidated damages, or a penalty, the broker must also submit _____.**

A) a petition for relief
B) a copy of the penalty notice
C) a tender of funds
D) a copy of the Power of Attorney
E) an additional copy of the submission

 As per 19 CFR 172.31:

172.31 Form of offers.

Offers in compromise *submitted pursuant to the provisions of section 617 of the Tariff Act of 1930, as amended (19 U.S.C. 1617), must expressly state that they are being submitted in accordance with the provisions of that section.* ***The amount of the offer must be deposited with Customs*** *in accordance with the provisions of §161.5 of this chapter.*

 The correct answer is "C".

✓ **JUST A SIDE NOTE:** An Offer in Compromise (OIC) is most commonly known for its use with the IRS.

70) Supplemental petitions filed in cases involving violations of 19 USC § 1641 will be forwarded to the Chief, Penalties Branch, Border Security and Trade Compliance Division, Regulations and Rulings, Office of International Trade when the amount exceeds:

A) $30,000
B) $10,000
C) $20,000
D) $50,000
E) $25,000

 As per 19 CFR 171.62(a):

171.62 Supplemental petition decision authority.

*(a) Decisions of Fines, Penalties, and Forfeitures Officers. Supplemental petitions filed on cases where the original decision was made by the Fines, Penalties, and Forfeitures Officer, will be initially reviewed by that official. The Fines, Penalties, and Forfeitures Officer may choose to grant more relief and issue a decision indicating that additional relief to the petitioner. If the petitioner is dissatisfied with the further relief granted or if the Fines, Penalties, and Forfeitures Officer decides to grant no further relief, the supplemental petition will be forwarded to a designated Headquarters official assigned to a field location for review and decision, **except that supplemental petitions filed in cases involving violations of 19 U.S.C. 1641 where the amount of the penalty assessed exceeds $10,000 will be forwarded to the Chief, Penalties Branch, Border Security and Trade Compliance Division, Regulations and Rulings, Office of International Trade.***

 The correct answer is "B".

✓ **JUST A SIDE NOTE:** In general, original petitions for relief are to be sent to the Fines, Penalties, and Forfeitures office "whose address is given in the notice".

71) A petition for the cancellation of a claim for liquidated damages should be submitted to_____.

A) The Port Director
B) A Fines, Penalties, and Forfeitures Officer
C) The Assistant Commissioner
D) The port of entry
E) The bonding surety

 As per 19 CFR 172.2(a):

172.2 Petition for relief.

(a) To whom addressed. **Petitions for the cancellation of any claim for liquidated damages or remission or mitigation of a fine or penalty secured by a Customs bond incurred under any law or regulation administered by Customs must be addressed to the Fines, Penalties, and Forfeitures Officer designated in the notice of claim.**

 The correct answer is "B".

✓ **JUST A SIDE NOTE:** The above-mentioned petition does not have to be in any particular form, though it must include the following elements.

(1) The date and place of the violation; and

(2) The facts and circumstances relied upon by the petitioner to justify cancellation, remission or mitigation.

Category XIII: Bonds

72) Entry summary documentation was not filed in a timely manner for a shipment of $100,000 entered with a Single Transaction Bond (STB) in the amount of $110,000. Liquidated damages will be assessed at_____.

A) The entire amount of the STB ($110,000)
B) $100,000 plus duties and fees
C) $100,000 plus duties
D) 10% of the value of the merchandise
E) The cost of the duties and fees

 As per 19 CFR 142.15:

142.15 Failure to file entry summary timely.

If the entry summary documentation is not filed timely, the port director shall make an immediate demand for liquidated damages in the entire amount of the bond in the case of a single entry bond. *When the transaction has been charged against a continuous bond, the demand shall be for the amount that would have been demanded if the merchandise had been released under a single entry bond. Any application to cancel liquidated damages incurred shall be made in accordance with part 172 of this chapter.*

 The correct answer is "A".

✓ **JUST A SIDE NOTE:** The above-mentioned Single Transaction Bond is also commonly known as a Single Entry Bond. A Single Transaction Bond will be in an amount equal to the entered value of the single entry plus all duties and fees. If the shipment is subject to other U.S. government agencies' review, then the amount is to be three times the entered value of the entry.

73) A broker files an informal entry on CBP Form 368 valued at $2,500 and does not utilize statement processing and ACH. Which of the following actions is the broker required to take?

A) Take no further action; CBP Form 368 is all that is required for entry.
B) File an entry summary CBP Form 7501 within 10 calendar days.
C) Obtain a bond prior to entry release.
D) Deposit any estimated duties and taxes at the time of entry.
E) File a CBP Form 7501 within 10 working days of the date of entry.

 As per 19 CFR 143.28:

143.28 Deposit of duties and release of merchandise.

Unless statement processing and ACH are used pursuant to §24.25 of this chapter, the estimated duties and taxes, if any, shall be deposited at the time the entry *is presented and accepted by a Customs Officer, whether at the customhouse or elsewhere. If upon examination of the merchandise further duties or taxes are found due, they shall be deposited before release of the merchandise by Customs. When the entry is presented elsewhere than where the merchandise is to be examined, the permit copy shall be delivered through proper channels to the Customs officer who will examine the merchandise.*

 The correct answer is "D".

✓ **JUST A SIDE NOTE:** Customs Form 368 is not widely used. Instead, Customs Form 7501 (Entry Summary) is almost always the form used for filing both formal and informal entries.

74) Jack files a temporary importation bond entry in March 2012. In February 2013 he calls Customs to find out if the entry has liquidated. Which of the following is correct?

A) Temporary importation bond entries liquidate within 90 days from the date of summary.
B) Temporary importation bond entries liquidate 1 year from the date of release.
C) Temporary importation bond entries don't liquidate.
D) Temporary importation bond entries are valid for 1 year and then may be converted into a consumption entry and therefore liquidate within 2 years.
E) None of the above

 As per 19 CFR 10.31(h):

(h) After the entry and bond have been accepted, the articles may be released to the importer. The entry shall not be liquidated as the transaction does not involve liquidated duties. However, a TIB importer may be required to file an entry for consumption and pay duties, or pay liquidated damages under its bond for a failure to do so, in the case of merchandise imported under subheading 9813.00.05, HTSUS, and subsequently exported to Canada or Mexico (see §181.53 of this chapter).

 The correct answer is "C".

✔ **JUST A SIDE NOTE:** The above-mentioned "subheading 9813.00.05" refers to articles imported temporarily in bond for repairs. Here's a snapshot of the subheading in the HTSUS:

Heading/ Subheading	Stat. Suffix	Article Description	Unit of Quantity	Rates of Duty 1	
				General	Special
9813.00.05		Articles to be repaired, altered or processed (including processes which result in articles manufactured or produced in the United States)...............	....	Free, under bond, as prescribed in U.S. note 1 to this subchapter	Free (AU, BH, CA, CL, IL, JO, KR, MA, MX, OM, P, PA, PE, SG)
	20 1/	Articles to be processed into articles manufactured or produced in the United States..................	1/		
	40	Other..................	X		

75) When merchandise is withdrawn from a bonded warehouse, how long must the records relating to the withdrawal be retained?

A) At least 5 years after the date of entry
B) At least 5 years from the date of withdrawal of the last merchandise withdrawn under the entry
C) Within 30 calendar days, or such longer time as specified by CBP
D) Records must be retained indefinitely
E) At least 5 years after the date of revocation of the Power of Attorney

 As per 19 CFR 111.23(b):

(b) Period of retention. The records described in this section, other than powers of attorney, must be retained for at least 5 years after the date of entry. Powers of attorney must be retained until revoked, and revoked powers of attorney and letters of revocation must be retained for 5 years after the date of revocation or for 5 years after the date the client ceases to be an "active client" as defined in §111.29(b)(2)(ii), whichever period is later. **When merchandise is withdrawn from a bonded warehouse, records relating to the withdrawal must be retained for 5 years from the date of withdrawal of the last merchandise withdrawn under the entry.**

 The correct answer is "B".

✓ **JUST A SIDE NOTE:** Customs records may be kept in paper form or in electronic form (with prior approval from Customs). Whichever medium is used, the records must be maintained within the United States.

Category XIV: Intellectual Property Rights

76) In regard to "prohibited or restricted importations" relative to "articles involved in unfair competition," after the U.S. International Trade Commission (the Commission) issues an exclusion order pursuant to 19 USC § 1337, an importer of record has the following option with respect to the entry of merchandise subject to that exclusion order:

A) The importer may enter merchandise subject to an exclusion order if the importer's basic importation bond contains a provision authorizing such action.

B) The importer may enter merchandise subject to an exclusion order for thirty days after the exclusion order issues, at which point the Commission's exclusion order becomes final and entry is no longer permitted.

C) Until the time the Commission's exclusion order becomes final, the importer may enter merchandise subject to the exclusion order by filing a single entry bond with CBP in an amount determined by the U.S International Trade Commission to be sufficient to protect the complainant from any injury.

D) Until the time the Commission's exclusion order becomes final, the importer may enter merchandise subject to the exclusion order by filing a single entry bond with CBP in an amount set by the port director to ensure compliance with the customs and related laws.

E) None of the above because an exclusion order is effective on the date it is issued and merchandise subject to that exclusion order cannot be entered lawfully after this point.

 As per 19 CFR 12.39(b):

(b) Exclusion from entry; entry under bond; notice of exclusion order. (1) ... ...

(2) During the period the Commission's exclusion order remains in effect, excluded articles may be entered under a single entry bond in an amount determined by the International Trade Commission to be sufficient to protect the complainant from any injury. On or after the date that the Commission's determination of a violation of section 337 becomes final, as set forth in paragraph (a) of this section, articles covered by the determination will be refused entry. If a violation of section 337 is found, the bond may be forfeited to the complainant under terms and conditions prescribed by the Commission. To enter merchandise that is the subject of a Commission exclusion order, importers must:

(i) File with the port director prior to entry a bond in the amount determined by the Commission that contains the conditions identified in the special importation and entry bond set forth in appendix B to part 113 of this chapter; and

(ii) Comply with the terms set forth in 19 CFR 210.50(d) in the event of a forfeiture of this bond.

 The correct answer is "C".

✓ **JUST A SIDE NOTE:** Here, "unfair (foreign) competition" refers to patent, trademark, and copyright infringements.

77) Imported merchandise has been detained for more than 30 days from the date the merchandise was presented for examination because CBP believes the merchandise may constitute "prohibited or restricted importations" relative to "articles involved in unfair competition," and may be subject to an exclusion order issued by the Commission. Given that CBP failed to make a determination with respect to admissibility within 30 days after the merchandise was presented for examination, the importer may take the following action:

A) File a protest with the Commission under 19 CFR 174 because CBP is detaining the merchandise due to the potential violation of an exclusion order
B) File a protest with CBP under 19 CFR 174
C) File a petition with CBP under 19 CFR 171
D) Commence an action in the U.S. Court of International Trade
E) None of the above because CBP has not formally acted on the merchandise and only suspects that the merchandise may be subject to an exclusion order

 As per 19 CFR 151.16(f):

(f) Effect of failure to make a determination. **The failure by Customs to make a final determination with respect to the admissibility of detained merchandise within 30 days after the merchandise has been presented for Customs examination, or such longer period if specifically authorized by law, shall be treated as a decision by Customs to exclude the merchandise** *for purposes of section 514(a)(4) of the Tariff Act of 1930, as amended (19 U.S.C. 1514(a)(4)).* **Such a deemed exclusion may be the subject of a protest.**

 The correct answer is "B".

✓ **JUST A SIDE NOTE:** Protests are submitted on CBP Form 19. Snapshot of form below:

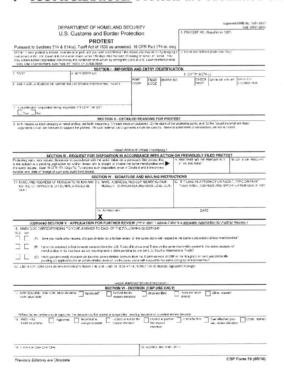

78) If imported merchandise is detained because CBP suspects it bears a counterfeit version of a mark that is registered with the U.S. Patent and Trademark Office and recorded with CBP, and the importer, upon written notification, does not provide information within seven days of such notification that establishes to CBP's satisfaction that the suspect mark is not counterfeit, or provides information that is insufficient to establish that the suspect mark is not counterfeit, CBP may disclose to the right holder:

A) The entry documents and a sample or digital images of the merchandise including serial numbers, dates of manufacture, lot codes, batch numbers, universal product codes or other identifying marks appearing on the merchandise or its retail packaging

B) The names and addresses of the exporter and importer

C) The entry documents and the name and address of the manufacturer

D) A sample or digital images of the merchandise including serial numbers, dates of manufacture, lot codes, batch numbers, universal product codes or other identifying marks appearing on the merchandise or its retail packaging, but no entry documents

E) All of the above

 As per 19 CFR 133.21(b):

... ...

(ii) Failure of importer to respond or insufficient response to notice. Where the importer does not provide information within the seven business day response period, or the information provided is insufficient for CBP to determine that the merchandise does not bear a counterfeit mark, CBP may proceed with the disclosure of information described in paragraph (b)(3) of this section to the owner of the mark and will so notify the importer.

*(3) Disclosure to owner of the mark of information appearing on detained merchandise and/or its retail packaging, including unredacted photographs, images or samples. When making a disclosure to the owner of the mark under paragraph (b)(2)(ii) of this section, CBP may disclose information appearing on the merchandise and/or its retail packaging (including labels), images (including photographs) of the merchandise and/or its retail packaging in its condition as presented for examination (i.e., an unredacted condition), or a sample of the merchandise and/or its retail packaging in its condition as presented for examination. The release of a sample will be in accordance with, and subject to, the bond and return requirements of paragraph (c) of this section. **The disclosure may include any serial numbers, dates of manufacture, lot codes, batch numbers, universal product codes, or other identifying marks appearing on the merchandise or its retail packaging (including labels), in alphanumeric or other formats.***
... ...

 The correct answer is "D".

✓ **JUST A SIDE NOTE:** Customs defines "counterfeit mark" in 19 CFR 133.21(a). (Note: The definition of "spurious" is something that is not what it claims to be, false or fake.)

(a) Counterfeit mark defined. A "counterfeit mark" is a spurious mark that is identical with, or substantially indistinguishable from, a mark registered on the Principal Register of the U.S. Patent and Trademark Office.

79) Gray market articles, bearing a trademark registered with the U.S. Patent and Trademark Office and recorded with CBP, whose importation is restricted by CBP pursuant to regulation on the basis of physical and material differences:

A) Can never be imported

B) Can only be imported with the consent of the U.S. trademark owner

C) Can be imported, after detention, if information appearing on the merchandise or its retail packaging, including, but not limited to, serial numbers, dates of manufacture, lot codes, batch numbers, and universal product codes, is disclosed to the U.S. trademark owner within five days of the date of importation

D) Can be imported notwithstanding any physical and material differences if it bears a conspicuous and legible label designed to remain on the imported articles in order to indicate that they are physically and materially different from the product authorized for sale in the U.S.

E) All of the above

 As per 19 CFR 133.23(b):

(b) Labeling of physically and materially different goods. Goods determined by the Customs Service to be physically and materially different under the procedures of this part, bearing a genuine mark applied under the authority of the U.S. owner, a parent or subsidiary of the U.S. owner, or a party otherwise subject to common ownership or control with the U.S. owner (see §§133.2(d) and 133.12(d) of this part), shall not be detained under the provisions of paragraph (c) of this section where the merchandise or its packaging bears a conspicuous and legible label designed to remain on the product until the first point of sale to a retail consumer in the United States stating that: "This product is not a product authorized by the United States trademark owner for importation and is physically and materially different from the authorized product." The label must be in close proximity to the trademark as it appears in its most prominent location on the article itself or the retail package or container. Other information designed to dispel consumer confusion may also be added.

 The correct answer is "D".

✔ **JUST A SIDE NOTE:** Gray market goods are not counterfeits. For example, it is well known that pharmaceuticals are shipped or carried to the United States from Canada, where they are cheaper to purchase, even though they are from the same drug company.

80) A shipment of imported merchandise valued in excess of $50,000 is detained on suspicion that the merchandise bears a suspect version of a federally registered trademark that is recorded with CBP. The importer is notified of the detention and given seven days in which to provide information that would establish that the merchandise does not bear a counterfeit mark. Because no information is provided in a timely manner, CBP provides the owner of the recorded trademark with digital images of the merchandise and its retail packaging, to include images that feature universal product codes that appear on the merchandise. Following receipt of the images, the trademark owner advises CBP that the suspect marks were not applied to the merchandise with authorization. CBP seizes the merchandise on the basis that it bears a counterfeit trademark. Which of the following actions can the importer take to secure the release of the shipment?

A) Remove or obliterate the counterfeit mark in such a manner as to render the mark illegible or incapable of being reconstituted

B) Establish that the personal use exemption allowed under 19 CFR § 148.55 is applicable in this situation

C) Obtain the trademark owner's written consent to allow entry of the seized merchandise in its condition as imported or its exportation and entry after obliteration of the mark or other appropriate disposition

D) Export the merchandise bearing the counterfeit mark to the country of exportation

E) Remove or obliterate the counterfeit mark in such a manner as to render the mark illegible or incapable of being reconstituted then export it to the country of exportation

 As per 19 CFR 133.21(g):

(g) Consent of the mark owner; failure to make appropriate disposition. **The owner of the mark, within thirty days from notification of seizure, may provide written consent to the importer allowing the importation of the seized merchandise in its condition as imported or its exportation, entry after obliteration of the mark, or other appropriate disposition.** *Otherwise, the merchandise will be disposed of in accordance with §133.52 of this part, subject to the importer's right to petition for relief from forfeiture under the provisions of part 171 of this chapter*

 The correct answer is "C".

✓ **JUST A SIDE NOTE:** "Trademark infringement" as defined by the U.S. Patent and Trademark Office:

Trademark infringement is the unauthorized use of a trademark or service mark on or in connection with goods and/or services in a manner that is likely to cause confusion, deception, or mistake about the source of the goods and/or services

Book 2 Part 1

Book 2 Introduction
How to Start Your Own CHB Business

Most customs brokers have thought to themselves, "what would it be like to run my own customs brokerage business?" Well, once you have a little experience under your belt and have acquired some resources and potential clients, then utilizing this book will end up saving you much wasted time and frustration.

What caused me to write this book is that when I first decided to start my own customs brokerage business, instructions on doing so from US Customs or the customs brokerage community were nowhere to be found. I resolved to methodically log and document all the steps that I actually took in setting up my own customs brokerage business from start to finish. I knew that doing so would prove to be an invaluable service for others following the same path.

$ Money Saving Tip $
Some regional banks offer free checking accounts with relatively high interest that might suit your new small business. ACH services may be extra, so shop around. See also kasasa.com

So, with this book, the reader is able to bypass the trial and error method that I used when setting up my own customs brokerage business. This guide systematically outlines, step-by-step, how to most efficiently open your own customs brokerage business—and how to do it on a budget.

You may have a long list of prospective customers or few such contacts. Either way, your ambition to offer a service, superior to any other in your market, will, by itself, eventually grow your business. Refer to this book for direction, be pro-active, yet patient, and GROW YOUR BUSINESS.

Book 2 Part 2

Necessary Links

Customs website:
cbp.gov

Code of Federal Regulations (CFR) Online:
www.eCFR.gov

Harmonized Tariff Schedule (HTS) Online:
hts.usitc.gov/current

Customs Forms:
cbp.gov/xp/cgov/toolbox/forms/

IRS Small Business:
irs.gov/businesses/small/index.html

$ Money Saving Tip $
Have not yet been able to purchase your own 19 CFR or HTSUS? The online versions of these texts are convenient, easily searchable (e.g., use your computer's "find" function [Ctrl + F] to quickly locate item descriptions and HTS numbers within these PDF files), and they're always up-to-date.

Book 2 Part 3

Start with Customs
Start Here

Customs Broker License

First, let's assume that you do have your customs broker license. If you don't, then let's get that first. Read part one of this book on how to become a licensed customs broker. If you're already studying for the exam, then keep it up and good luck—the international trade community needs more licensed brokers and you're nearly there.

To Operate Under a Trade Name

Some individual customs brokers operate under their own personal names (e.g. John Doe). Others choose to give their small business a name (e.g. John Doe, DBA Perfect Customs Brokerage). Either way will work, but if you choose to operate under an assumed business name or Doing Business As (DBA) trade name, then Customs requires that the individual customs broker first submit a proposal to operate under a trade name in the form of a letter (see sample letter on the following page, and also refer to 19 CFR 111.30(c) to verify all information is up-to-date) to the Customs Broker Compliance Branch before proceeding with district permit application, filer code application, etc.

In your letter to Broker Compliance, refer to and attach evidence of your authority to use the trade name (usually in the form of your State's department of licensing confirmation letter or license). Also be sure to include your customs broker license number with this and all other such correspondence to Customs.

Customs will review your letter and will send back written approval to you within a couple weeks. They may be kind enough to email or fax confirmation back to you if politely asked to do so in your letter.

$ Money Saving Tip $
Need to courier docs overseas? Although no current US domestic service still exists, DHL, or an authorized reseller of DHL, can sometimes offer small businesses international rates at nearly half that of standard UPS and FedEx rates.

Sample: Proposal to operate under a trade name

John Doe
Perfect Customs Brokerage
3000 NE 309th Ave
Port City, WA 98682
Tel: 360-123-4567
(email address)

(Date)

U.S. Customs and Border Protection
1300 Pennsylvania Ave., NW
Attn: 1400 L St., Broker Compliance Branch
Washington, DC 20229

Re: Proposal to operate under a trade name

Dear Sir or Madam,

Per 19 CFR 111.30 (c) I am submitting evidence of my authority to use the trade name (John Doe, DBA) **"Perfect Customs Brokerage"** per attached acknowledgement letter from the Washington State Department of Licensing (unified business identifier number 600000000).

Best Regards,

John Doe
License#12345

District Permit Request

A customs broker can only conduct customs business in the ports that he or she has permits for. The first permit that you will want to apply for is for the district in which you will initially be making customs entries.

Afterwards a national permit can be applied for, yet only subsequently to receipt of the district permit. An individual customs broker may utilize remote location filing (RLF) if he or she has a national permit. RLF will allow you to make entry on regular informal or formal entry at any port even if you don't have an office at that port. At this point, however, RLF is just something to keep in mind and consider down the road. Just go to cbp.gov and search "remote location filing" for more information on the subject, if you would like.

> Include the following information in your **district** permit application (see sample letter on following page)...

1) Broker license number, date of issuance, and delivered through port (attach copy of license)

2) Your office address (attach copy of lease agreement or title)

3) Evidence of right to use assumed business name if applicable (attach approval from state)

4) Name of individual broker to exercise responsible supervision and control (usually your name)

5) List of other districts for which you have a permit (write "none" if none)

6) "Records retained at" address, and recordkeeping contact name

7) All other persons employed by applicant (write "none" if none)

8) Note $100.00 permit fee (attach check, and see 19 CFR 111.96 to verify amount is up-to-date).

9) Note $138.00 annual user fee (attach check, and see 19 CFR 111.96 to verify amount is up-to-date).

Be sure to make your checks out to "Customs and Border Protection". As of 2017, the 19 CFR still oddly instructs payments to be made out to the "United States Customs Service". Also be sure to keep a copies of all such correspondence with Customs for your records.

Sample: District Permit Request

John Doe
DBA Perfect Customs Brokerage
3000 NE 309th Ave
Port City, WA 98682
Tel: 360-123-4567
(email address)

(Date)

Ms. Jane Smith, Port Director, CBP

Re: Application for District Permit for Port of Port City

Dear Ms. Smith,

Please accept this letter as application for a district permit to perform customs business in the port of Port City. Required information per CFR19, 111.19 (b) is as follows:
1) Broker License Number 12345, Date of issuance 4/22/05 (delivered through port of New Orleans, copy of license attached)
2) Office address: 3000 NE 309th Ave, Port City, WA 98682 Tel: 360-123-4567 (copy of lease attached)
3) Copy of document which reserves applicant's business name with the state of Washington (attached)
4) Individual broker to exercise responsible supervision and control: John Doe
5) Other districts for which I have a permit: None
6) Records retained at: 3000 NE 309th Ave, Port City, WA 98682. Recordkeeping contact: John Doe
7) All other persons employed by applicant: None
8) $100.00 permit fee (attached)
9) $138.00 annual user fee (attached)

Best Regards,

John Doe, **License#12345**

Filer Code Request

Each broker conducting business with Customs will be issued a three-character (alpha, numeric, or alpha-numeric) code that will be included with entry numbers for all customs entries. This three-character code is called the "filer code". To obtain a filer code, submit a filer code request letter (separate from the district permit request), and include the following information (see sample letter on following page)…

1) Full legal name of requestor (you)
2) Business contact (probably you)
3) Business address and telephone number
4) Broker license number, date of issuance, and "delivered through" port.

$ Money Saving Tip $

Need inexpensive or free accounting software such as "BS1 Free Accounting Software"? Check out CNET's website for downloads and reviews. Search for business software>>accounting and billing software. download.com

NOTE: The requests for district permit and filer code can be submitted together (verify with the port director or equivalent just in case). They will provide you with a receipt for your checks, and will notify you of approval within about two to three weeks.

Sample: Filer Code Request

John Doe
DBA PERFECT Customs Brokerage
3000 NE 309th Ave
Port City, WA 98682
Tel: 360-123-4567
(Email address)

(Date)

Ms. Jane Smith
Port Director
Customs and Border Protection (Port of Port City)

Re: Filer Code Request

Dear Ms. Smith,

Please accept this letter as application for a filer code. Information required to process this application is as follows:

1) Full legal name of requestor: John Doe
2) Business contact (Individual broker to exercise responsible supervision and control): John Doe
3) Business address: 3000 NE 309th Ave, Port City, WA 98682   Tel: 360-123-4567
4) Broker License Number 12345, Date of issuance 4/22/05 (delivered through port of New Orleans)

Thank you very much for your consideration. Please feel free to contact me should you require further information.

Best Regards,

John Doe
License#12345

Book 2 Part 4

Type of Organization
Keep it simple

Legal Designation

While you're patiently waiting for Customs to get back to you on your district permit and filer code applications, it may be a good time to focus on the structure of the business. Many large freight forwarder and customs brokerage operations are incorporated. For your start-up business, however, it may be best to keep it simple. By that I mean that I mean consider initially registering your new business with your state as a sole proprietorship rather than an LLC or corporation.

I would not suggest a partnership for any type of business. The saying goes "the 'partnership' is the one ship that won't sail"? Hours worked and perceptions of contributions to the partnership will vary, eventually leading to discontent and resentment between the parties involved.

As your business grows you can later decide to expand on your sole proprietorship by easily converting to an S-Corporation. You can also purchase liability and/or errors and omissions insurance from an insurance or surety bond company to help protect your company and your personal interests.

$ Money Saving Tip $
Some companies charge a substantial monthly fee to list your business in their publications. Note, however, that there are many free print directories, online directories, and search engines for you to register with.

Taxes

Taxes on your business will depend on several different factors, including legal designation, estimated income, and local tax code. It will be worth your time to consult with a recommended CPA in your area to try to gain a better understanding of your specific tax considerations. A consultation may cost you some money upfront (maybe about $100.00 for a short visit?), but will, without a doubt, give you peace of mind that is hard to put a price on.

One thing that every business owner must do, however, is to separate personal finances from business finances. This means setting up a separate bank account for your business. All business-related expenses come out of your business' account, and all business-related income goes into this account—no exceptions. Doing so will allow you to accurately compute your taxes, as well as let you know if your business is making a profit.

As a general rule of thumb, set aside about 1/4 of all withdrawn profits into yet another separate bank account (most may prefer a savings type account) for your business so that you will have these funds available for taxes. So, for example, if taking out $1,000.00 from your business' checking account, only $750.00 will go into your personal bank account, and the other $250.00 will go into and remain in your business' savings account in preparation for your quarterly tax payments and annual tax time. Again, consult with a good CPA for details that will be relevant to you own unique situation.

An EIN (employee identification number) is not absolutely necessary to run your sole-proprietor business (as opposed of other forms of business), but some of your vendors may require this ID number when applying for credit with them. You may obtain an EIN from the IRS if you wish by applying online at the following…

irs.gov/smallbiz

The IRS's small business website also provides very informative online tutorials, among other useful tools. You can even sign up for a free newsletter to help keep you up-to-date on IRS-related regulations and tips.

$ Money Saving Tip $
Use the EFTPS (Electronic Federal Tax Payment System) method of paying your IRS taxes. It is the quickest, most accurate, and the cheapest method of all for a small business. Go to irs.gov/smallbiz to learn more regarding EFTPS.

Book 2 Part 5

Marketing Your CHB Business
Get the Word Out

Still waiting for your district permit and filer code? Now is a perfect time to start working on your marketing plan.

You do not have to spend a lot of money to advertise your business. Here are just a few of the best methods of getting your business' name out there. And, they're all free.

Customs Website

Ask your port director (or equivalent) if they can list your new business on CBP's list of brokers as soon as your filer code is created. All active brokers are listed by the port within they operate on the Customs website (cbp.gov), and importers often search and are shepherded here (by Customs, etc.) when looking for someone to clear their shipment. Getting listed may take a little patience and persistence, but the amount of exposure your company gets from this is well worth the wait.

Port Website

Most ports (e.g. The Port of Tacoma, The Port of Norfolk, etc.) have very business-friendly websites. Among the various port-related resources they often provide for the benefit of local commerce, is a directory of local warehouses, trucking companies, freight forwarders, and customs brokers. Contact your port (air, ocean, or both) and ask to be added to the list. This service should also be free, and is another great way to receive a reference from a credible source.

Other Marketing Advice

I also recommend the book *Guerilla Marketing* by Jay Conrad Levinson. This book is just full of creative, yet proven ideas to advertise your on-a-budget business. It is extensive in its description of all different types of effective marketing techniques.

$ Money Saving Tip $
Making multiple trips to Customs, etc.? Deduct about 50¢ per mile as an expense. See irs.gov/smallbiz for the current rate.

Book 2 Part 6

ABI Vendor
Test Drive it for the Right Fit

Selecting an ABI Vendor

Finding "any" ABI provider is easy. However, choosing the "right-fit-for-your-company" ABI provider takes some shopping around.

An initial one-time licensing fee will run anywhere from $10,000.00 to $2,000.00. After that, monthly maintenance fees for ABI providers can be as expensive as $1,000.00 per month or as low as about $200.00 per month. Most offer a full array of ABI capabilities, but some may offer more accounting and other optional features than others. Some require you to buy an on-site server to run their software off of, while others allow you to do everything online thru the use of their server—as if you were creating and sending an email from your Hotmail or Gmail email account.

Feel free to compare the actual functionality of a couple different vendors with actual one-on-one demo's, either in-person or remotely online. Also, get a good feel for a company's culture. Your instincts should tell you whether they will offer excellent or below-average customer service for when you have a question or problem with their system. My best advice to you on the subject is to not only choose your ABI vendor based on their pricing, but also based on their technical and customer support expertise. We chose SmartBorder smartborder.com, after trying two other ABI vendors. They absolutely made ABI Certification a relatively pain-free process. It is easy for me to endorse them because I know their product is one of the best in the industry (note: this is a non-paid endorsement). Their system is accessible from anywhere with an internet connection, and handles necessary Customs transactions such as: Entries (7501,3461), RLF, ISF, truck manifest, ocean manifest, electronic invoice, In-bond 7512, Exports, Reconciliation, Protests, OGA filing, 5106, Statement processing, and PMS.

A current listing of all ABI vendors, certified by US Customs, can be found at cbp.gov/document/guidance/abi-software-vendors-list

Reproducing Customs Forms

The Customs Forms Management Office (located in Washington, DC) requires all ABI providers to submit their versions of US Customs forms (3461, 7501, etc.) to their office for approval before the forms are printed and used by individual brokers (via their laser or inkjet printers). Customs is concerned that their forms be kept uniform, and Customs may request this letter of approval at anytime.

Interestingly enough, not all ABI providers seem to have this important letter of proof, so it is important to request that your prospective ABI provider provide a copy of this letter for your file before you commit to buying their product.

Letter of Intent

Once you have received your district permit and filer code from Customs, you will ask the ABI provider to provide a letter of intent template (see sample letter on following page, and see 19 CFR 143.2 to verify information is up-to-date) that you or your ABI provider can send to the Customs Office of Information and Technology (OIT). The only thing that you will need to add to the template should be your new filer code and a signature. Have the letter of intent mailed to the OIT or call them at (703) 650-3500 to ask if you can fax the letter in order to expedite the process. Make sure that your ABI provider also gets a copy of the submitted letter. Go to www.cbp.gov and type "getting started with ABI" for current instructions in detail or go to the following URL: cbp.gov/document/guidance/letter-intent-instructions

$ Money Saving Tip $
Thinking of printing your own business cards or promotional material? Instead, why not consider outsourcing the task to a local printing company? It's the most convenient and cost effective way.

Sample: ABI Letter of Intent

John Doe
Perfect Customs Brokerage
3000 NE 309th Ave
Port City, WA 98682
Tel: 360-123-4567
(Email address)

(Date)

Office of Information and Technology
Director of Client Representatives Branch
7501 Boston Blvd. 2nd Floor, Room 211
Springfield, VA 22153

RE: Letter of intent to participation in ACS/ABI.

Per 19 CFR 143.2, this letter of intent sets forth our commitment to develop, maintain and adhere to the performance requirements and operational standards of the ABI system in order to ensure the validity, integrity and confidentiality of the data transmitted.

1) The following is a description of the computer hardware, communications and entry processing systems to be used and the estimated completion date of the programming: **(*ABI provider will advise these details*)**.
2) Our offices are located at: 3000 NE 309th Ave
   Port City, WA 98682. Contact: John Doe.
   Estimated Start Date: Feb. 1st 2017.
3) The name of the participant's principal management and contact person regarding the system: John Doe
4) The system is being developed by the following data processing company: PDQ Systems. Contact: Denise Richards
5) Entry filer code: XYZ

Please feel free to contact us should you have any questions.

Best regards,

John Doe, LCB, License#12345

The letter of intent will be processed in about a week. Customs will assign an "ABI representative" (not to be confused with your "ABI vendor") to you. He or she will contact you to introduce themselves, and you can advise your ISA confirmation number (see next paragraph) at that time as well. Once an ABI rep is assigned, you will work closely with him or her and with your ABI provider to test your ABI transmissions. Ask your ABI provider to help you prepare for and walk you through this ABI testing period, which can be completed within a couple days (depending on your provider).

VPN Interconnection Security Agreement

The Trade Virtual Private Network (VPN) Interconnection Security Agreement (ISA) is how Customs informs the ABI applicant of the importance of keeping the connection between your computer and Customs' servers secure. Go to the following online form, read the agreement, and complete and submit the security agreement acceptance form.

apps.cbp.gov/tvpn/tvpn.asp

Once the VPN ISA has submitted you will receive a confirmation number via email. Simply reply to the confirmation email from Customs to complete the ISA acceptance process. Keep this confirmation number and provide it to your ABI representative when they contact you.

Book 2 Part 7

Selecting a Surety Company
That was Easy

The surety company that you choose will be able to issue single transaction bonds and continuous bonds to accompany your customs entries.

Before deciding on a surety company, check with your ABI provider to see if they integrate a specific company's bonds in their system. If they do, and if the surety's rates are reasonable, then use them.

Otherwise, selecting a surety company can still be much easier than selecting an ABI provider as prices seem to be relatively competitive between competing surety companies. Ask for a few quotes to get a better idea of what's out there.

$ Money Saving Tip $
Want shipping industry news for free? Sign up for the Journal of Commerce's free newsletter at joc.com

We recommend choosing a surety company that does not charge a minimum for your single transaction bonds, and one that has an easy-to-use bond application system. Some may let you get your single transaction bonds directly online (web-based), while others will have you download (stand-alone) software that will allow you to issue bonds directly from your desktop.

To get a current listing of Customs approved surety companies that can provide you with a quote go to www.cbp.gov and search for "surety names/codes". Or try typing the following URL cbp.gov/sites/default/files/documents/surety%20codes_1.pdf

Book 2 Part 8

Running Your CHB Business
Do it Differently

The day-to-day operations of your new customs brokerage business is entirely up to you. You can get as creative as you want. That's to your advantage. Most of the customs brokerage businesses out there appear to be doing the same thing. And some may have (just as any corporation is susceptible to) lost their soul.

Power of Attorney

A signed customs power of attorney (POA) from the importer is required in order for a customs broker to conduct customs business on behalf of that importer.

In regards to the POA, an individual customs broker can do one of two things. One option is to purchase a boilerplate-type POA form in bulk from another company. The National Customs Brokers & Forwarders Association of America (NCBFAA), for example, has published several different versions of the power of attorney for the transportation industry. The NCBFAA Power of Attorney can be located and purchased at the NCBFAA website under "Publications and Resources" and then under "Commercial Docs".
ncbfaa.org

One of your other options is to refer to Customs' example of the power of attorney (as written in 19 CFR 141.32) as a benchmark, and customize it to fit your company (see sample POA on following page). For starters, we recommend this method as it is FREE and could be made more user-friendly for customers than the long form published by the NCBFFAA.

As a side note, as you have your customer fill out the power of attorney, ask them to also complete and return what I call the "customers instructions to broker" (see sample following POA). The importer can use this form to describe their imported product, and clarify delivery and billing details. This supplemental form also serves the purpose of letting your new client know that you care about their input, and provides up-front information in writing.

Sample: Customs Power of Attorney

Customs Power of Attorney

KNOW ALL MEN BY THESE PRESENTS, THAT

_____
(Full name of company or individual)

_____
(Legal designation, such as corp., individual, sole prop., LLC, or partnership)

located at

_____
(Business Address)

and doing business under the laws of the State of

_____, using EIN or SSN_____
hereby appoints the grantee, **John Doe, DBA Perfect Customs Brokerage** as a true and lawful agent and attorney of the principal named above with full power and authority to do and perform every lawful act and thing the said agent and attorney may deem requisite and necessary to be done for and on behalf of the said principal without limitation of any kind as fully as said principal could do if present and acting, and hereby ratify and confirm all that said agent and attorney shall lawfully do or cause to be done by virtue of these presents until written notice of revocation is delivered to the grantee. In the case of a partnership, this power of attorney will only be effective two years from the date below.

_____ _____
(Principal's signature)   *(Date)*

Sample: Customer Instructions to Broker

Customer Instructions to Broker

1) The product that I am importing can best be described as...

_____
(What is it? What is it made of?)

_____
(What is it used for? What is it used in conjunction with?)

2) Please deliver to...

_____
(delivery address)

_____
(delivery location contact name and telephone#)

*This location **does / doesn't** have a loading dock. (Please circle one)*

3) Please bill to...

_____
(billing address)

_____
(billing contact name and telephone#)

ACH Payment

Complete Customs Form 401 (ACH Credit Enrollment Application) and fax, email, or mail the completed application to the Customs Revenue Division. Upon receipt, they will send instructions to you on ACH payer procedures as well as show you how to send an ACH pre-note test (necessary test for ACH user approval) through your bank to Customs. Once approved, you can work with your ABI provider and bank to get everything else set up. Until then, Customs will accept checks submitted with the entry or entry summary. Go to cbp.gov and search "signing up for ach" for details and current instructions. Or try going direct via the following URL: https://www.cbp.gov/trade/trade-community/automated/automated-systems/gs-automated-systems/ach/signing

Accounting Software

If you're not a seasoned CPA (like the rest of us), then keeping track of your company's finances may require the acquisition of a bare-bones, easy-to-use accounting software solution. If your ABI provider offers accounting software that is integrated within their ABI software product, then feel free to use that as it may help simplify things.

If they do not offer such integrated accounting software, then stand-along accounting software such as QuickBooks® will work as well. Because of its widespread use, many ABI providers include functions in the ABI software that allow you to easily transfer data to and from QuickBooks.

Pricing

Be aware of your competitors' pricing. You may want to beat their pricing and/or offer importers a much more simplified version of the typical customs brokerage invoice. If you can boast about your great rates then feel free to compare yours to the "typical" customs broker on your website or via other methods of advertising.

Creativity can also enter into your method of pricing of your customs brokerage services. You might not have the cash on hand that a larger business has, so you could offer a substantial discount to an importer if he or she submits payment to you at the time of or before delivery of her shipment. This will help you to cash flow your business, as well as give you a chance to go out and meet your customers.

Truckers

Contact several different truckers and get an account setup with them before your first shipment. Most will require you to complete a credit check application, while others will ask for payment to be made on a COD basis for the first couple of shipments. Either way, it is nice to have a friend in your trucking company.

Necessary Office Equipment

In regards to necessary office equipment, a minimalist would only really need a computer, printer, telephone, and shredder (Customs requires all information-sensitive material to be shredded rather than put in the dumpster). Some ABI vendors may require you to purchase a stand-alone server in order to operate their software.

$ Money Saving Tip $
Cleared a small shipment and have some free time? Deliver using your own car or rent a truck (your car insurance co. may have weight restrictions). This is also a good chance to see your customer.

Recordkeeping

Customs requires brokers to keep records (either in paper or electronic form) of transaction for five years from the entry date. The IRS requires an individual or business to keep tax-related records for three years (though some recommend keeping longer).

However, there is no need to invest in a row of file cabinets if you're on a budget. Just go to Wal-Mart or Target and buy manila file folders, some hanging files to organize them in, and a few banker boxes to hang the hanging files in. Not only is this method more economical, but the banker boxes are easier to move around and store.

Working with Customs

Customs doesn't care whether the customs broker that is submitting an entry to them works for the largest freight forwarder in America, or whether he or she is working off a card table in the corner of their apartment. Just do your best to build a reputation as an honest and straight-forward broker, and Customs will treat you fairly.

Also, be aware that Customs is a government institution and things take time (including their role in processing your fore mentioned applications and request submittals).

In closing, I would simply like to wish you a sincere "keep your head up" on your customs brokerage business.

! Final Tips !
Finally, I recommend that you try to avoid the use debt to finance your business. Instead of "jumping from" your current job/situation, time it right and "jump to" your own business opportunity. Have a "long-term game plan" and grow the business with a patient heart.

References

United States Customs and Border Protection Home Page.
http://www.cbp.gov/
Web 2017.

United States Government Printing Office Home Page.
Title 19 Electronic Code of Federal Regulations "Customs Duties"
http://www.ecfr.gov/
Web 2017.

Wikipedia
http://www.wikipedia.org/
Web 2017.

United States International Trade Commission Home Page
"Harmonized Tariff Schedule of the United States"
http://www.usitc.gov/
Web 2017.

Made in the USA
Middletown, DE
11 April 2017